*Thomistic
Bibliography,
1940–1978*

Thomistic Bibliography, 1940–1978

Compiled by
Terry L. Miethe
and Vernon J. Bourke

GREENWOOD PRESS
Westport, Connecticut • London, England

Library of Congress Cataloging in Publication Data

Miethe, Terry L 1948–
      Thomistic bibliography, 1940–1978.

      Includes indexes.
      1.   Thomas Aquinas, Saint, 1225?–1274—Bibliography.
2.   Neo-Scholasticism—Bibliography.   I.   Bourke,
Vernon Joseph, 1907–   joint author. II.   Title.
Z8870.M53   [B765.T54]   016.23'02   80-1195
ISBN 0-313-21991-5 (lib. bdg.)

Library of Congress Catalog Card Number: 80-1195
ISBN: 0-313-21991-5

First published in 1980

Greenwood Press
A division of Congressional Information Service, Inc.
88 Post Road West, Westport, Connecticut 06881

Printed in the United States of America

10 9 8 7 6 5 4 3 2 1

Contents

Acknowledgments

It is a pleasant duty to acknowledge the use of facilities in, and the help of the reference staffs of, the following libraries: the Pius XII Library and the Divinity School Library of Saint Louis University; the Robert Pace and Ada Mary Dougherty Library and the Hugh Roy Marshall Collection of the Center for Thomistic Studies, University of Saint Thomas, Houston, Texas; University of California at Los Angeles Library; and Honnold Library of Claremont Graduate School, in Claremont, California.

For help with Polish entries our thanks are due to the Reverend Francis J. Lescoe of Saint Joseph College, West Hartford, Connecticut, the Reverend Andrew N. Woznicki of the University of San Francisco, and Joseph Koterski of the philosophy department at Saint Louis University. Father William A. Wallace and Father James A. Weisheipl have assisted with up-to-date information on the progress of the Leonine Commission. Finally, the editorial advice of Arthur H. Stickney, Editor for Research and Professional Books at Greenwood Press, is gratefully acknowledged.

Introduction

Preparation of this bibliography of Thomistic studies published between 1940 and 1978, inclusive, took place a century after the appearance of the papal encyclical, *Aeterni Patris*, in 1879. This letter initiated the modern renewal of interest in the life and thought of Thomas Aquinas. Prior Thomistic bibliographies were published in 1921, by Mandonnet-Destrez, covering studies issued before 1920, and in 1945, by Bourke, for the twenty years from 1920 to 1940. Such one-volume bibliographies cannot be critical; that is, there is no room in one volume for comments or reviews of the entries. Thus, articles and books listed here may be good or bad as pieces of scholarship; inclusion does not imply either approval or disapproval by the compilers. For those who require guidance as to the worth and content of the entries there are appraisals by reviewers in the periodic bibliographies. Most helpful among them are the *Répertoire Bibliographique de la Philosophie* (Louvain), the *Bulletin Thomiste*, and the *Rassegna di Letteratura Tomistica*, which began publication in 1969, covering the years 1966 onward. Another useful journal, the *Divus Thomas* (Fribourg, Switzerland), changed its name in 1954 to *Freiburger Zeitschrift für Philosophie und Theologie*; the other *Divus Thomas*, published in Piacenza, Italy, has retained its name.

During the past century a large number of studies in all learned languages have focused on Saint Thomas Aquinas. Born in southern Italy at Roccasecca, near Aquino, he studied at the Benedictine monastery at Monte Cassino, then at the University of Naples and, after entering the Order of Preachers in 1244, at the Dominican houses of study in Paris and Cologne. Thomas served as professor of theology for two periods (1256–1259 and 1269–1272) at the University of Paris. The writings, theological and philosophical, he produced in the quarter century ending with his death in 1274 have continued to be the object of much scholarly attention during the past four decades, to which the four thousand entries in this bibliography attest.

USING THE BIBLIOGRAPHY

Consultation of this bibliography will be facilitated by careful inspection of the contents page. The five major divisions (life, writings, philosophy, theology, and doctrinal and historical relations) represent the broad categories of classification established in the Mandonnet-Destrez *Bibliographie* and followed in the *Thomistic Bibliography: 1920–1940*. With some modifications the *Bulletin Thomiste* and its successor the *Rassegna di Letteratura Tomistica* continued these divisions. Within each major division are several subcategories distinguished by specific titles. Thus, if one wishes a listing of books and articles on the life of Thomas Aquinas, he will consult "Biographies" and "Critical Studies of His Life" in chapter 1. If interested in man's psychic make-up and functions, one would see chapter 3, "Psychology and Philosophy of Man." For theological studies of the Incarnation, for instance, the appropriate category is "Christology" in chapter 4. There is some overlapping among these classifications; thus studies of man's natural desire to see God may be found under psychology, ethics, or moral theology—depending on the emphasis of the authors. Some histories of the relation between Islamic thought and Saint Thomas may also include information on the connections with Judaic thought. An effort has been made to avoid duplicate listings but, in some cases, a study has been consciously entered in more than one category to simplify the reader's search.

The section in chapter 5 entitled "Nineteenth and Twentieth Centuries" is quite large, partly because it includes recent problems and schools of interpretation that are difficult to place in the earlier categories. Thus, for example, articles and books on Transcendental Thomism will usually be found in this section. However, some studies by people in this interpretive school that deal directly with epistemology or metaphysics are listed in chapter 3 under "Logic, Grammar, Epistemology" or under "Metaphysics."

In the present century the distinction between philosophical ethics and moral theology has become blurred. Formerly it was clear that ethics as pursued by philosophers made no use of revealed truths or pronouncements by ecclesiastical authorities but that moral theologians do appeal to divine law and even to religious tradition and canon law. With the increased use of the term "Christian Ethics" for what was formerly called moral theology, and with the phrase "natural law" sometimes signifying revealed divine law and sometimes regulations knowable in the unaided light of natural experience and reasoning, the line of demarcation between ethics and moral theology is no longer as evident. As a result, the student of Thomistic teaching on morals will find some material in the ethics section in chapter 3 and still other studies in the moral theology category in chapter 4. Indeed, some references to natural law have been put under a third category, "Socio-Political-Legal Philosophy" in chapter 3.

The Personal Name Index furnishes references to the Thomistic writings of all the authors of entries listed by serial number in the various categories. In the case of some well-known and prolific writers, only their studies that bear directly on Saint Thomas and his thought are included. For people such as Jacques Maritain, Etienne Gilson, Sofia Vanni Rovighi, Cornelio Fabro, Martin Grabmann, Josef Pieper, A. C. Pegis, and so on, there are specialized bibliographies available, some of which are listed in chapter 2, "Reference Tools." Note also that "Symposia and Collections" (alphabetized by title rather than by editor) is a separate section in the chapter immediately following this Introduction. Full titles of periodicals cited can be found in the Appendix. Abbreviations of periodical titles are complete enough to be self-explanatory.

Some unavoidable difficulties occur in compiling a bibliography that includes materials written in more than ten languages. For those that would require a different alphabet the titles have been transliterated. Because Polish titles employ a modified roman type, their spelling has been approximated in some cases. Frequently the German umlaut has been replaced by an 'e' following the main vowel and, in all cases, the umlauted vowels are treated as having the 'e' for purposes of alphabetizing. Names of medieval authors before 1450 are listed by the given (not the family or place) name; where the authors are Christian, this is the baptismal name. Thus Abelard is listed under "Peter" and Ockham under "William" or "Guillelmus." Arabic names are usually given under the standardized forms used in English works, thus Avicenna or Averroes rather than Ibn Sina or Ibn Rushd.

Prefixes such as de, di, van, and von have been placed after the family name. Thus "De Finance" becomes "Finance, de." It has not been possible to secure complete uniformity in this. Where "Van" is not separated from the rest of the name, in Dutch or Belgian names, such as "Vansteenkiste", the listing is under 'V,' but "Van Steenberghen" is alphabetized under 'S.' Some Italian names starting with "Degli" may need to be sought under both types of listing. In the case of anglicized family names that were originally non-English, for example, Van Roo or D'Arcy, the listing has followed standard English practice: "Van Roo" comes under 'V.' Names beginning with 'Mac' or 'Mc' have been placed before all other 'M' entries. Spanish family names that are compound, such as "Gonzalez Rodriguez," have presented insuperable obstacles, for some publications may appear under one family name, while others by the same author are printed under both names. One can only suggest that, if your writer is not located under "Gonzalez," please look under "Rodriguez." There are also cases of writers who change their first names to a different form when publishing in different languages. Thus Kalinowski, Jerzy, becomes Kalinowski, Georges, in French. And still more confusing, Ramirez, Santiago becomes Ramirez, Jacobus M., when he publishes in Latin.

NEW RESEARCH TOOLS

THE LEONINE EDITION

Although it is far from being completed, much progress has been made in recent years on the publication of a critical edition of the *Opera Omnia* of Saint Thomas. Shortly after he issued his encyclical, *Aeterni Patris*, Pope Leo XIII called for a new edition of the Latin works of Aquinas. Previous *Opera Omnia* (such as the Piana, the Vivès, and the Parma editions) were not critically edited. Under the editorship of Italian, Dutch, and English Dominicans, the "Leonine" edition was begun in 1882. By 1886 three volumes containing some of Saint Thomas' commentaries on Aristotle had been printed. These first volumes made little improvement on previous editions since they were not really critical texts. Moreover, Pope Leo was more interested in seeing the theological writings in print and in 1886 he asked for a change in editorial policy. By 1893 control of the work was turned over to the General of the Order of Preachers. (For information on these early years, see Pierre M. de Contenson, "Documents sur les premières années de la Commission Léonine," *St. Thomas Aquinas 1274-1974,* Toronto, 1974, 2:331-88.) Volumes 4 to 12 were devoted to the *Summa Theologiae* with Cajetan's *Commentary* (1888-1906). Such rapid production meant that little work was done on the manuscript sources which were gradually being assembled in Rome. It is generally agreed that these early volumes of the Leonine must be redone. Some revision of the Aristotle commentaries has already started. In the meantime, the Ottawa printing of the *Summa Theologiae*, with annotations by I. Th. Eschmann, is the most useful Latin text.

World War I and other impediments disrupted the work of the Leonine Commission until 1918 but by 1930 the *Summa contra Gentiles* with the *Commentary* by Silvester of Ferrara had been printed in volumes 13 to 15. The Leonine text of this *Summa* is much better than the texts in the earlier volumes. However, except for an index volume (16) issued in 1948, nothing appeared in the Leonine edition during the thirty-five years between 1930 and 1965.

After World War II the commission was reorganized, more thorough studies of the manuscripts were conducted, and between 1965 and 1979 nine excellent volumes were printed. As of the end of 1979, there are five centers at which editorial work is conducted. (See Cullen Murphy, "All the Pope's Men: Putting Aquinas Together Again," *Harper's*, June, 1979, 45–64.) In Washington, D.C., under William A. Wallace, O.P. (now Director General of the Leonine Commission), the commentaries on Boethius' *De heb-domadibus*, Pseudo-Dionysius' *De divinis nominibus,* and Aristotle's *Metaphysics* are being edited. At the Dominican house of studies in Ottawa, Canada, some of the Scripture Commentaries are being prepared for publication. The Dominican Priory at Louvain, Belgium, is concentrating on the exposition of Boethius' *De Trinitate* and on the *Disputed Questions De virtutibus*. Finally, at the sales office in Rome (Editori di San Tommaso, Piazza Pietro d'Illiria, 1) some editorial checking of sources is carried on, while at nearby Grottaferrata, in a monastery occupied jointly by Franciscans and Dominicans, editorial work is in progress on some theological writings and on the commentaries on Aristotle's logical treatises. In spite of this reorganization, not enough trained younger Dominican editors are available to complete the edition promptly. Moreover, with the recent increases in production expenses, funds to print and market the Leonine edition are insufficient. This means that, in spite of the many separately edited works of Saint Thomas, we still lack a complete critical edition of his *Opera Omnia*.

THE INDEX THOMISTICUS

This is a reference tool of such grandiose proportions that it cannot be ignored. Since the mid forties, Roberto Busa, S.J., a professor of philosophy at the Jesuit scholasticate in Gallarate, North Italy, has been planning and directing the work of many associates on this concordance of the writings of Aquinas. With the assistance of IBM technology they have published, by the end of 1979, ten volumes in Section 1, covering "Indices of Distribution," "Summaries of the Dictionary," and "Indices of Frequency." Section 2 is in thirty-one volumes containing a complete concordance for all the works of Saint Thomas. This second section is useful for students of the thought (rather than simply the linguistic usage) of Aquinas. Of its five subsections, two (nouns and verbs in their various inflections, and uninflected adverbs plus other special terms) are of most help for the doctrinal study of Saint Thomas. The other parts of the concordance show word usage in the context of citations of various sorts. Eight volumes in Section 3 (scheduled to appear in 1979/80) are devoted to "terms in other authors.'' These are people who have added to Aquinas' writings in various ways and whose additions are found in the older *Opera Omnia.* It is difficult to understand why such extraneous writings were indexed in this Thomistic concordance, since they represent neither the thought nor the language of Saint Thomas. A seven-volume printing of the Latin works of Aquinas is to be added later, although it is not clear what edition will be used. An introductory volume to the whole *Index Thomisticus* will appear last.

Just how useful for Thomistic research this *Index Thomisticus* may be is difficult to estimate, for it is not completely printed at the end of 1979. One reviewer who has seen but a small part of the *Index* but who has been acquainted with Busa's project since 1946 (R. W. Schmidt, ''An Historic Research Instrument: the *Index Thomisticus*,'' *New Scholasticism* 50, 1976, 237–49) calls it ''of incomparable importance to Thomistic research.'' But the directors of the Humanities Computing Consultants in Cambridge, England, who have experience with similar concordances for the humanities, consider Busa's pioneer work a rather primitive effort. While computer technology has much to offer in the reference field—and Father Busa has helped to establish this value—it is still necessary for human beings to select the terms and usage contexts. Mistakes may abound in such initial compilation, particularly in dealing with an inflected language with many homonyms and polyvalent terms. Schmidt notes (p. 243), for instance, that the *Index* lists among prepositional phrases three cases in which *cum* is used as a conjunction. Without doubt the *Index Thomisticus* has some utility for students of medieval Latin usage but the very size of the *Index* renders it cumbersome for the investigation of Saint Thomas' thought. As an example, the word *civitas* (not one of Aquinas' favorite terms) occupies more than forty pages in the concordance. For the average scholar the smaller concordances by Peter of Bergamo, Ludwig Schütz, and Roy Deferrari and Sister M. Inviolata Berry, are easier to consult. All three have been printed or reprinted in the forty-year period of this bibliography and are listed in the reference section.

RECENT DEVELOPMENTS IN THOMISTIC SCHOLARSHIP

In 1974, the septicentenary of the death of Thomas Aquinas, many meetings of scholars were held throughout the world. This occasioned the publication of a large number of collected studies. The proceedings and symposia issuing from this flurry of academic activity are listed under ''Symposia and Collections.'' Many of the short papers delivered at these meetings in 1974 are not listed in this bibliography, either because they are too brief, or of no apparent importance, or because they were duplicates of studies published elsewhere.

The largest septicentennial meeting was the Congresso Internazionale under the direction of members of the Order of Preachers teaching at the University of Saint Thomas (Angelicum) in Rome. This meeting took place in Rome and Naples from April 17 to 24, 1974. Approximately 1800 people from all over the world attended and participated. The *Proceedings* entitled *Tommaso d'Aquino nel suo VII Centenario* included one preliminary volume and eight later volumes. Many subsequent journal articles (see chapter 5, "Nineteenth and Twentieth Centuries") speculated on the significance of this vast collection. One writer (Dandenault, entry no. 3770) wondered whether it was the first breath of a new spring in Thomistic studies or, perhaps, the end of an era.

In fact, since Vatican Council II, there has been a noticeable decrease of interest in Saint Thomas on the part of Roman Catholic philosophers and theologians. It was not that the voice of Aquinas was stilled at this council, but some people thought it was not sufficiently emphasized. In any case this decline is particularly evident in seminaries, where most students are no longer required to know Latin and, as a consequence, are unable to read the original documents of western Christendom. The much-discussed opening of the windows of Roman Catholic scholarship has not only admitted valuable new concepts, it has also permitted much traditional knowledge (including some of the "golden wisdom" of Saint Thomas) to fly away. Not all recent developments are negative; the establishment of a Center for Thomistic Studies at the University of Saint Thomas, Houston, and of a Jacques Maritain center at Niagara University, are indications that research in this field is not dead in the United States.

The recent decline of Thomistic scholarship at some of the most noted Catholic institutions of learning is obvious in their course offerings and from the contents of journals and books that they have published in the past twenty years. Many studies listed below are the product of older scholars, some now dead. It is in a few European countries and in Canada and the United States that the decrease of interest is most obvious. A chronological study of the *Proceedings* of the American Catholic Philosophical Association, which is the largest such society in the world, will illustrate this trend. Papers on Thomism are very few. Surprisingly, however, the number of studies of Aquinas stemming from non-Roman Catholic writers has grown to impressive proportions. Excellent publications have issued from centers in Scandinavia and England, as well as from the larger secular universities in America. Anglican thinkers (Mascall, Veatch, Sillem, Farrer, Owen, and others) have been particularly influential.

Two countries, Japan and Poland, whose languages are not widely used in western scholarship are the source of many recent Thomistic studies. While a few transliterated Japanese titles are listed below, and some other studies written by Japanese in German, French, and English are entered, it must be admitted that our entries for Thomistic scholarship in Japan are incomplete. Much the same applies to the listings from Poland. Despite an unfavorable political and cultural climate, Catholic thinkers at Krakow and Lublin have written in the past forty years important works on the philosophy and theology of Saint Thomas. They are only beginning to become known in other western countries.

In the 1940s the World Union of Catholic Philosophical Societies was founded by I. M. Bochenski, O.P. One of the compilers of this bibliography, Vernon J. Bourke, served as its president from 1948 to 1958. About thirty-five societies of philosophers from almost as many different countries constitute its membership and take part in periodic world meetings. (Information about this organization is available from its General Secretary, G. F. McLean, O.M.I., Catholic University of America, Washington, D.C.) Though by no means exclusively Thomistic in orientation, the World Union has done much to maintain interest in the thought of Aquinas.

As in earlier centuries our period has witnessed the continuation of traditional schools of interpretation of Thomism and the appearance of new approaches. Some modern Thomists still follow the lead of Renaissance commentators such as Cajetan, Sylvester of Ferrara, John of St. Thomas, Francis Suarez, Dominic Bañez, and others. However this dependence on the "second scholasticism" is growing less popular. There are also many first-rate scholars who use the textual-historical methods associated with the names of Martin Grabmann and Etienne Gilson. At least as many others regard the systematic approach of thinkers such as Reginald Garrigou-Lagrange and Jacques Maritain as most profitable.

Probably the most distinctive new school of interpretation, however, is Transcendental Thomism. Actually this movement has gone well beyond the exploration of what Aquinas thought. It has become a new type of twentieth-century Christian philosophy. Starting with the epistemological and metaphysical writings of Joseph Maréchal, S.J., early in this century, a group of scholars trained as Thomists (mainly German Jesuits) endeavored to combine certain features of Immanuel Kant's theory of knowledge and reality with Thomism. To some extent this movement was a reaction to what was regarded as the excessive emphasis by Saint Thomas on material objects, as known through sense experience, as the proper objects of human understanding. An effort was made to open Thomism to a more direct awareness of the "world of the spirit." One version of this trend is found in Karl Rahner, S.J., *Geist in Welt* (1939). The 1968 English translation by William Dych (*Spirit in the World*) is based on a revision by Johannes Metz. Rahner and Metz admit that Saint Thomas held that all man's terrestrial knowledge arises from sense experience but they insist that man finds in his own self-presence an a priori grasp of the totality of being. One may thus transcend the awareness of extra-mental things and find existent being as "something questionable" within his self. The great Jesuit philosopher of the Renaissance, Francis Suarez, had espoused a similar appeal to introspective knowledge in his theory of intellection.

To more traditional interpreters of Saint Thomas the Kantian apriority latent in Transcendental Thomism seems far removed from the objective realism of Aquinas. The movement has been popularized in America chiefly by younger Jesuits. (See an approbative account in Helen James John, *The Thomist Spectrum*, 1966.) The views of Bernard Lonergan, S.J., in philosophy and theology are close to this transcendental movement but his position is a highly personal and independent approach to Thomism.

Another trend toward subjectivism is evident among interpreters who attempt to associate the thought of Saint Thomas with the phenomenology of Husserl and Heidegger. One version of this is found among the younger philosophers at the University of Louvain in Belgium. It has been brought to America by visiting professors from Holland at Duquesne University in Pittsburgh. Quite different is the approach of Developmental Thomism (see the articles by J. V. Mullaney and William Wallace, O.P.). In this view it is recognized that thirteenth-century Thomism must be updated to satisfy the changed conditions of today. While retaining the basic epistemological and metaphysical positions of Aquinas, Developmental Thomism sees the need to adapt to new facts and discoveries, particularly in the area of natural science.

In the past forty years there has been a growing awareness that Thomism is not merely a baptized Aristotelianism. Starting with the work of L. B. Geiger, O.P., and Arthur Little, S.J., among others, many scholars came to see the strong influence of Platonism on Aquinas. (See R. J. Henle, S.J., *Saint Thomas and Platonism,* 1956.) The Platonic theme of participation has been made central in Thomistic metaphysics by Cornelio Fabro. In particular, studies of Saint Thomas' commentaries on Boethius, Pseudo-Dionysius, and the *Liber de Causis* have demonstrated that some of the roots of Thomism lie in non-Aristotelian ground.

Chronological List of
Thomas Aquinas' Works

1. *De propositionibus Modalibus* (1244–1245?)
2. *De fallaciis ad quosdam nobiles artistas* (1244–1245?)
3. *Principium Fr. Thomae de Aquino, quando incepit Parisius ut Baccelarius Biblicus* (1252)
4. *De ente et essentia* (1254–1256)
5. *De principiis naturae ad fratrem Silvestrum* (1255)
6. *Scriptum super IV libros Sententiarum magistri Petri Lombardi* (1254–1256)
7. *Breve Principium Fr. Thomae de Aq., quando incepit Parisius ut magister in theologia* (1256)
8. *Contra impugnantes Dei cultum et religionem* (1256–1257)
9. *Expositio in Evangelium Matthaei* (1256–1259 Unfinished, possibly a *reportatio* made by Leodegarius Bissuntinus, or by Fr. Petrus de Andria.)
10. *Quaestiones disputatae De Veritate* (1256–1259)
11. *Quaestiones Quodlibetales* (1256–1272 Detailed chronology of the individual *Questions* is difficult to establish. For attempts see Mandonnet, Pelster, Synave, Destrez, and Grabmann.)
12. *Expositio super Boetium De Trinitate* (1257–1258 Incomplete)
13. *Expositio in librum Boetii De Hebdomadibus* (1257–1258)
14. *Summa contra Gentiles, seu De Veritate Catholicae Fidei* (1258–1264 There is no MS sanction for the title, Summa Philosophica.)
15. *Expositio in S. Pauli Apostoli epistolas, a capitulo xi primae ad Corinthios usque ad finem Pauli* (1259–1265 The text of the editions is corrupt and the question of authenticity is difficult. Saint Thomas did lecture on the *Epistles* of Saint Paul possibly twice. The present section of this exposition is probably a *reportatio* made by Reginald of Piperno.)
16. *Expositio in Isaiam prophetam* (1259–1261)
17. *Expositio primae decretalis ad archidiaconum Tudertinum* (1259–1268)

18. *Expositio super secundum decretalem ad eundem* (i.e. archidiaconum Tudertinum) (1259-1268)
19. *Expositio in Dionysium De divinis nominibus* (1260-1268)
20. *De regimine Judaeorum ad ducissam Brabantiae* (1261?)
21. *Expositio in Job* (1261-1264)
22. *De articulis fidei et ecclesiae sacramentis ad archiepiscopum Panormitanum* (1261-1268)
23. *De emptione et venditione ad tempus* (1262-1263)
24. *Contra Errores Graecorum ad Urbanum Pontificem Maximum* (1263)
25. *Officium de festo Corporis Christi ad mandatum Urbani Papae IV* (1264)
26. *De rationibus fidei contra Saracenos, Graecos et Armenos ad cantorem Antiochenum* (1264-1268)
27. *Catena Aurea in Matthaeum* (1261-1264)
28. *Catena Aurea in Marcum* (1265)
29. *Catena Aurea in Lucam* (1266)
30. *Catena Aurea in Joannem* (1267)
31. *Expositio in Cantica Canticorum* (1264-1269 Saint Thomas did comment on the *Canticle of Canticles,* but the two printed versions attributed to him [one beginning, "Salomon inspiratus. . .," the other, "Sonet vox tua . . ."] are not authentic.)
32. *Expositio in Threnos Jeremiae prophetae* (1264-1269)
33. *De rege et regno, sive de regimine principum* (1265-1266 Saint Thomas wrote only to the second or fifth chapter of Book II; it was finished by some other writer, possibly Tolomeus Lucensis.)
34. *Responsio ad Fr. Joannem Vercellensem, Gen. Mag. Ord. Praed., de articulis CVIII sumptis ex opere Petri de Tarantasia* (1265-1266 Doubtful authenticity.)
35. *Quaest. Disp. de Potentia Dei* (1265-1267)
36. *In X libros Ethicorum ad Nicomachum Expositio* (1266-1269)
37. *In III primos libros Politicorum Expositio* (1266-1268 Saint Thomas commented on the first two books and to the end of chapter 7 of Book III, *lectio* 6; Petrus de Alvernia finished the Commentary. See O'Rahilly, "The Comment of the Politics," *Irish Eccl. Record* 63, 1927, 614-22.)
38. *Summa Theologiae* (1266-1273 Incomplete; the *Supplementum tertiae Partis* is taken from the *Script. in Sent.* and was compiled by Reginald of Piperno; Guillelmus Sudre and Petrus Alvernensis also wrote supplements to it.)
39. *Quaest. Disp. de Spiritualibus Creaturis* (1266-1269)
40. *In VIII libros Physicorum Expositio* (1268)
41. *Expositio in Jeremiam prophetam* (1267-1269 Incomplete, stops at chapter 42.)
42. *Quaest. Disp. de Unione Verbi Incarnati* (1268-1272)
43. *Quaest. Disp. de Malo* (1268-1269)
44. *De Secreto* (1269 Record of the findings of a Dominican commission, of which Saint Thomas was a member.)
45. *De perfectione vitae spiritualis, contra magistrum Geraldum* (1269)
46. *In libros perihermeneias Expositio* (1269-1272)
47. *In libros posteriorum analyticorum Expositio* (1268)

48. *In XII libros metaphysicorum Expositio* (1268–1272)
49. *Quaest. Disp. de Anima* (1269–1270)
50. *Contra pestiferam doctrinam retrahentium homines a religionis ingressu* (1270)
51. *Quaest. Disp. de Virtutibus* (1269–1272 Includes *De virtut. in communi*; *De virtut. cardinalibus*; *De caritate*; *De correctione fraterna*; *De spe.*)
52. *De sortibus ad dominum Jacobum* (1269–1272 The MSS and editions give a wide variety of place names for Jacobus: de Burgo, de Tolongo, de Bonoso, de Turoneio, de Borgo, and de Tonengo!)
53. *De forma absolutionis ad Generalem Magistrum Ordinis* (1269–1272 Addressed to John of Vercelli.)
54. *De occultis operationibus naturae ad quemdam militem* (1269–1272)
55. *De judiciis astrorum ad. Fr. Reginaldum socium suum carissimum* (1269–1272)
56. *In librum de Causis Expositio* (1269–1273)
57. *De aeternitate mundi contra murmurantes* (1270)
58. *De unitate intellectus contra Averroistas* (1270)
59. *Expositio in Evangelium S. Joannis* (1269–1272)
60. *In libros de Anima Expositio* (1270–1272 Book I is a *reportatio* by Reginald of Piperno; remainder is written by Saint Thomas.)
61. *In librum de Sensu et Sensato Expositio* (1270–1272)
62. *In librum de Memoria et Reminiscentia Expositio* (1270–1272)
63. *In Psalmos Davidis Expositio* (1270–1272 Incomplete *reportatio* by Reginald of Piperno; goes up to Psalm 54.)
64. *Declaratio XLII quaestionum ad magistrum Ordinis* (1271)
65. *Responsio ad lectorem Bisuntinum de articulis VI* (1271)
66. *Declaratio XXXVI quaestionum ad lectorem Venetum* (1271–1272)
67. *Compendium Theologiae ad Fratrem Reginaldum, sive De fide et spe* (1271–1273 Incomplete.)
68. *In primos libros de Caelo et Mundo Expositio* (1272 Incomplete; Saint Thomas wrote to end of *lectio* 8, Book III; Petrus de Alvernia did the section from *lectio* 9 to the end of Book IV.)
69. *In primos libros Meteorologicorum Expositio* (1272 Incomplete; Saint Thomas did the exposition of Book I and of II up to *lectio* 8; Petrus de Alvernia commented on the remainder of Book II and on III; possibly Jean Quidort did Book IV.)
70. *Expositio in S. Pauli apostoli epistolas, ad Romanos et primam ad Corinthios usque ad finem cap. 10* (1272–1273 Toward the end of his life Saint Thomas undertook this second exposition of the Pauline Epistles [for the first see item 15]. Saint Thomas finished up to *lectio* 2 of the *Epist. ad Corinth.:* the section from I Cor. 7, 14, seems to have been added by Peter of Tarentaise. The text of the printed editions is corrupt.)
71. *De substantiis separatis, sive de natura Angelorum* (1272–1273)
72. *In libros de Generatione et Corruptione Expositio* (1272–1273 Incomplete; Saint Thomas did only Book I to *lectio* 17; Thomas of Sutton finished Book I, *lectio* 18-25, and all of Book II.)
73. *De mixtione elementorum ad magistrum Philippum de Castrocoeli* (1273)

74. *De moto cordis ad magistrum Philippum de Castrocoeli* (1273)
75. *Expositio devotissima orationis dominicae* (1273 Probably a *reportatio.*)
76. *Devotissima Expositio super Symbolum apostolorum, scilicet Credo in Deum* (273 Probably a *reportatio.*)
77. *De duobus praeceptis caritatis et decem legis praeceptis* (1273 A *reportatio,* possibly by Petrus de Andria.)
78. *Devotissima Expositio super salutatione angelica, scilicet Ave Maria* (1273)
79. *Responsio ad Bernardum abbatem Casinensem* (1274 Written in Lent, this letter is one of Saint Thomas' last works.)

The Following Works of Doubtful Authenticity are Undatable

1. *Adoro te devote latens deitas* (Mandonnet holds that it is undoubtedly authentic. See Wilmart, D.A., "La tradition littéraire et textuelle de l'Adoro te devote," *Rech. de Théol. anc. et méd.* 1, 1929, 21–40; 149–76.)
2. *Sermones seu Collationes dominicales, festivae et quadragesimales* (There is no doubt that Saint Thomas left many sermons and sermon notes. The printed *Sermones*, however, are not all authentic and doubtless there are many sermons which have not been printed. For a survey of the tangled question of MSS, See Grabmann, *Die Werke*, 1931, pp. 329–42.)
3. *Epistola de modo studendi*
4. *Piae Preces*

Works Admitted as Authentic by Grabmann but Rejected as Spurious by Mandonnet (They contain Thomistic passages or doctrine but their use and value is questionable.)

1. *De demonstratione*, no. 48, pp. 171–73.
2. *De differentia verbi divini et humani,* no. 61, pp. 365–67.
3. *De instantibus*, no. 56, pp. 284–95.
4. *De quattuor oppositis*, no. 50, pp. 176–92.
5. *De natura accidentis,* no. 54, pp. 265–69.
6. *De natura generis*, no. 53, pp. 221–64.
7. *De natura materiae et dimensionibus interminatis*, no. 52, pp. 197–220.
8. *De natura verbi intellectus*, no. 62, pp. 368–75.
9. *De principio individuationis*, no. 52, pp. 193–96.

      (Number and page references for these nine works are to Mand. Opusc. t. V, *Opuscula Spuria.*)

Thomistic
Bibliography,
1940–1978

Previous Bibliographies, Symposia, and Collections

PREVIOUS BIBLIOGRAPHIES

1. Anonymous. "Bibliografia del VII Centenario della morte di Tommaso d'Aquino." Tommaso d'Aquino 8 (Symp Roma 1975): 307-28.

2. _____. Guide Bibliografiche. Ser. 2: Filosofia. Milano: Vita e Pensiero, 1944.

3. _____. Répertoire bibliographique de la philosophie. Belgium: University of Louvain. Annual Bibliography.

   Supplement to: Revue Néoscolastique de Philosophie. Louvain. Which changed its name in 1946 to: Revue Philosophique de Louvain.

4. Bochenski, I. M. Bibliographische Einführungen in das Studium der Philosophie (BESP) Berne: Franke, 1948-.

   See Paul Wyser, "Thomas von Aquin," BESP 13-14 (1950); "Der Thomismus," ibid. 15-16 (1951).

5. Bourke, Vernon J. Thomistic Bibliography: 1920-1940. St. Louis: The Modern Schoolman, supplement to 21 (1945) 312 pp.

   4856 entries.

6. Brie, G. A. de. Bibliographia philosophica, 1934-1945. I; Bibliographia Historia Philosophica, 2. Bruxelles: Editiones Spectrum, 1950-1954.

7. Byrns, Ruth. "A Bibliography of Jacques Maritain, 1910-1942." The Maritain Volume of The Thomist. New York: Sheed & Ward, 1943. 345-71.

8. Destrez, J. Bulletin Thomiste. Kain, Belgique: Le Saulchoir, et Paris: Editions du Cerf, 1924-1939.

   First printed as supplement to Revue Thomiste. Publication ceased with tome V, 10, avril-juin, 1939, XVI$^{\underline{me}}$ année. See Vansteenkiste, Rassegna.

9. Eschmann, Ignatius T. "A Catalogue of St. Thomas's Works: Bibliographical Notes," in E. Gilson, The Christian Philosophy of St. Thomas Aquinas. New York: Random House, 1956. 381-439.

10. Evans, Joseph W. "A Maritain Bibliography." The New Scholasticism 46 (1972) 118-28.

11. Fabro, Cornelio. "Rassegna di letteratura tomistica." Doctor Communis 30 (1977) 130-35.

12. Gagné, Armand. Bibliographie de Charles De Koninck, dans Mélanges à la Memoire de Ch. De Koninck. Québec: Univ. Laval, 1968, 7-22.

13. Gallagher, Donald and Idella. Jacques Maritain: A Selected Bibliography. Reprinted from the Catholic Library World. Villanova, PA: Villanova University, 1961. 12 pp.

14. _____. The Achievement of Jacques and Raissa Maritain: A Bibliography, 1906-1961. New York: Doubleday, 1962. 256 pp.

15. Garceau, Benoit. "Les etudes thomistes (1966-1974)." Colloque (Ottawa Symp) 275-310.

     537 entires.

16. Giacon, Carlo. Il pensiero cristiano con particolare riquardo alla Scolastica. Guide bibliografiche. Milano: Vita e Pensiero, 1943.

17. Guerry, Herbert. A Bibliography of Philosophical Bibliographies. Westport, CT: Greenwood Press, 1977. xiii-332 pp.

     Lists 24 bibliographies dealing with Aquinas.

18. Guzie, Tad W. "St. Thomas and Learning Theory: A Bibliographical Survey." The New Scholasticism 34 (July 1960) 275-96.

19. Inagaki, Bernard R. Scholastic Bibliography in Japan. Nanzan: Catholic University of Nagoya, 1957. 50 pp.

20. McLean, George F., ed. An Annotated Bibliography of Philosophy in Catholic Thought, 1900-1964. New York: F. Ungar, 1968. xiv-371 pp.

21. _____. A Bibliography of Christian Philosophy and Contemporary Issues. New York: F. Ungar, 1968. viii-312 pp.

22. _____. Philosophy in the Twentieth Century, Catholic and Christian. 2 vols. New York: F. Ungar, 1967.

23. Mandonnet, Pierre et Destrez, J. Bibliographie Thomiste, (Bibliographie Thomiste, I) Le Saulchoir, Kain (Belgique): Revue des Sciences

24 - 35   PREVIOUS BIBLIOGRAPHIES

Philosophiques et Theologiques, 1921.

    2nd ed. revised by M.-D. Chenu. Paris: J. Vrin, 1960. xxii-122 pp.

24. Matczak, Sebastian A. Philosophy: A Select, Classified Bibliography of Ethics, Economics, Law, Politics, Sociology. Louvain, Belgium:
Nauwelaerts, 1969.

25. Miethe, Terry L. "The Cosmological Argument: A Research Bibliography." The New Scholasticism 52 (Spring 1978) 285-305.

    330+ entries.

26. _____. "The Ontological Argument: A Research Bibliography."
The Modern Schoolman 54 (January 1977) 148-66.

    330+ entries.

27. O'Donnell, J. R., ed. Publications of Anton C. Pegis, in Essays
in Honor of A. C. Pegis. Toronto: Pont. Inst. Med. Studies, 1974. 9-16.

28. Ols, Daniel. "VII Centenario di S. Tommaso d'Aquino, Rassegna di
alceene pubbicazione commemorative." Tomismo e antitomismo (Symp) 2,
369-414.

29. Regis, Sister M. The Catholic Bookman's Guide: A Critical Evaluation of Catholic Literature. New York: Hawthorn Books, 1962. 638 pp.

30. Ruello, Francis. "Le VIIe Centenaire de S. Thomas d'Aquin. Bulletin." Recherches de Science Réligeuse (Paris) 64 (1976) 341-58.

31. Sciacca, Michele F., ed. Storia della filosofia Italiana, ed. za.
Milano: Bocca, 1947.

32. Simon, Anthony O. Bibliographie d' Yves René Simon, 1923-1968.
Revue Philosophique de Louvain 67 (1969) 285-305; Complément (1969-
1974); Revue Philosophique de Louvain 73 (1975) 361-66.

33. Vansteenkiste, Clemens. Rassegna di letteratura tomistica. Rome:
Herder: Napoli: Edizioni Domenicane, I (1966).

    Continuing as vol. 13 of Bulletin Thomiste.

34. Wyser, Paul von, ed. "Der Thomismus," in Bibliographische Einfuh-
rungen in das Studium der Philosophie. 13-14, 15-16 Bern: A. Francke
Verlag, 1950-1951.

SYMPOSIA AND COLLECTIONS

35. Acta pontificae Academiae S. Thomae aq. et religionis catholicae.
Nova series I-13, anno 1934-1947. Taurini-Romae: Marietti.

    Superseded by periodical: Doctor Communes.

SYMPOSIA AND COLLECTIONS   36 - 49

36. Actualité de saint Thomas. Préface de Charles Journet. Paris-
Tournai: Desclée, 1972. 152 pp.

37. Année charnière. Mutations et continuités. 3me Partie: Thomas et
Bonaventure. Michel Mollat, ed. Paris-Lyons: Editions du C.N.R.S.,
1977, 1008 pp.

38. L'Anthropologie de Saint Thomas. Conferences...du 7e centenaire...
N. A. Luyten, ed. Fribourg: Editions Universitaires, 1974. 206 pp.

39. Aquinas. A Collection of Critical Essays. Anthony Kenny, ed.
Notre Dame, IN: University Press, 1977. 389 pp.

    Articles by D. Knowles, P. Geach, Patterson Brown, J.N. Deck,
    A. Kenny, P. Sheehan, and A. Donagan.

40. Aquinas and Problems of His Time. G. Verbeke and D. Verhelst, eds.
Leuven: University Press; The Hague: M. Nijhoff, 1976. viii-229 pp.

41. Aquinas Septicentennial Conference, University of Calgary, 1974.
Anthony Parel, ed. Toronto: Pont. Inst. Med. Studies, 1978. 174 pp.

42. Aristote et Saint Thomas d'Aquin. Louvain: Publications Universitaires de Louvain, 1955.

43. Atti del Congresso Internazionale, Tommaso d'Aquino nel suo VII
Centenario. 8 vols. Roma-Napoli: Edizioni Domenicane, 1974ff.

44. Bonaventure & Aquinas: Enduring Philosophers. Robert W. Shahan
and Francis J. Kovach, eds. Norman: University of Oklahoma Press, 1976.
ix-194 pp.

45. Celebrating the Medieval Heritage. A Colloguy on the Thought of
Aquinas and Bonaventure. David Tracy, ed. Supplement to The Journal
of Religion Chicago: University of Chicago Press, 1978.

46. Colloque commémoratif Saint Thomas d'Aquin. 1274-1974. Eglise et
Theologie. Ottawa: Vol. 5, 1974.

47. The Concept of Matter. Ernan McMullin, ed. Notre Dame, IN:
University Press, 1963.

48. Congressus Thomistici Internationalis. Roma: Officium Libri Catholici, Via del Vaccaro, 5.

    IV. Sapientia Aquinatis, 2 vols. Roma, 1955-1956.
    V. Thomistica Morum Principia, 2 vols. Roma, 1960-1961.
    VI. De Deo in Philosophia S. Thomae, 2 vols. Roma, 1965-1966.
    VII. De Homine, 2 vols. Roma 1970-1972.

49. The Dignity of Science. James A. Weisheipl, ed. Washington: The
Thomist Press, 1961.

50 - 62   SYMPOSIA AND COLLECTIONS

50. Dziejow myśli Swietego Tomasza z Akwinu. Stefan Swiezawski and J.
Czerkawski, eds. Lublin: Towarzystwo Naukowe Polskiego Uniwersytetu
Katolickiego, 1978.

Articles by M. Krapiec, L. Kuz, J. Domanski, K. Pomian, J. Korelec,
M. Markowski, B. Dembowski, M. Gogacz, B. Wosiek, T. Adamek, and
S. Swiezawski.

51. Eglise et Théologie. Saint Thomas Aquinas Commemorative Colloquium.
1274-1974. Ottawa, Canada: Université Saint-Paul, 1974. 322 pp.

52. Essays in Honour of Anton Charles Pegis. J. Reginald O'Donnell, ed.
Toronto: Pont. Inst. Med. Studies, 1974.

Pegis Bibliography by O'Donnell, "The De Regno (of Aquinas) and The
Two Powers," by L. E. Boyle.

53. Essays in Modern Scholasticism. Anton C. Pegis, ed. Westminster,
MD: Newman, 1944.

54. Essays in Thomism. Robert E. Brennan, ed. New York: Sheed & Ward,
1942.

Articles by: J. Maritain, R. Allers, V.J. Bourke, J.K. Ryan, H.
Carpenter, J.O. Riede, A.C. Pegis, C.J. O'Neil, M.J. Adler, Y. Simon,
W. Farrell, J.A. Ryan, R.J. Slavin, I. Chapman, H.T. Schwartz.

55. Estetica. Atti del VII convegno di studi filosofici cristiani.
Gallorate 1951. Padova: Ed. Liviana, 1952. 526 pp.

56. An Etienne Gilson Tribute. Charles J. O'Neil, ed. Milwaukee:
Marquette University Press, 1959. x-347 pp.

Articles by J.F. Anderson, V.J. Bourke, M.F. Griesbach, R.J. Henle,
H. Johnston, G.P. Klubertanz, A.C. Pegis, J.H. Robb, R.W. Schmidt,
K. Schmitz, G. Smith, L. Sweeney, L.H. Thro, E. Gilson.

57. L'Existence de Dieu. Cahiers de l'Actualité Religieuse, 16. ed.
Collége Dominician à la Sarte-Huy. Tournai: Casterman, 1961.

58. Existence of God, The. Proceedings of the American Catholic Philosophical Association 46 (1972) 239 pp.

59. Festgabe Joseph Lortz. 2 vols. Baden-Baden: Grimm, 1958. 586,
590 pp.

60. La filosofia della natura nel Medioevo. Milano: Vita e Pensiero,
1966.

61. From an Abundant Spring, The Walter Farrell Memorial Volume of The
Thomist. New York: Kenedy, 1952. xiv-556 pp.

62. Gedenkband zu Ehren des heiligen Thomas von Aquinas. 1274-1974.

SYMPOSIA AND COLLECTIONS   63 - 75

Herausgegeben von Zeno Bucker, Ansgar Paus and Maximilian Roesle.
Salzburger Jahrbuch für Philosophie, 19. Salzburg-München: A. Pustet,
1974. 360 pp.

63. Geschichte und System. Festschrift E. Heintel. Wien: 1972.

64. A Gilson Reader, A. C. Pegis, ed. New York: Doubleday, 1957.
358 pp.

65. God in Contemporary Thought. A Philosophical Perspective.
Sebastian A. Matezak, ed. Jamaica, N.Y.: Learned Publications, Inc.,
Louvain: Nauwelaerts, 1978. 1210 pp.

66. L'Homme et son destin. Actes du Premier Congrès International de
Philosophie Medievale. Louvain-Paris: Nauwelaerts, 1960. 845 pp.

67. In Search of St. Thomas Aquinas. The McAuley Lectures, 1966.
West Hartford, Conn.: St. Joseph's College, 1966. 44 pp.

    This volume consists of two lectures: Anton C. Pegis, "Catholic
    Intellectualism at the Crossroad." And Etienne Gilson: "On the
    Art of Misunderstanding Thomism."

68. Symposium in Honor of St. Thomas and St. Bonaventure. 1274-1974.
International Philosophical Quarterly 14 (December 1974).

    Articles by: E.H. Cousins, W.N. Clarle G.A. McCool, G.A. Kmieck,
    M.L. LaDriere, R.T. Zegers, and F. Wilhelmsen.

69. Jacques Maritain: Oeuvres 1912-1939. Henry Bars, ed. Bruges:
Desclée, 1974.

70. Laval Théologique et Philosophique. Numero commemoratif...saint
Thomas d'Aquin. 30, 3 (1974) Quebec: Université Laval, 1974.

    Cited as Laval Thomas d'Aquin.

71. Maritain Volume of The Thomist. New York: Sheed & Ward, 1943.

    Articles by: W. Gurian, J.C. Osbourn, F.E. McMahon, R.M. Hutchins,
    R.N. Anshen, Y. Simon, R.E. Brennan, E. Chapman, G.B. Phelan, M.J.
    Adler, W.R. Thompson, G. Smith, D. Sargent, A.C. Pegis, Wm. O'Meara.

72. Mélanges a la Memoire de Charles de Koninck. Quebec: Presses de l'
Université Laval, 1968. 521 pp.

73. Mélanges offerts à Etienne Gilson. Paris: Vrin, 1959. 704 pp.

74. Mélanges offerts à M.-D. Chenu, Maitre en théologie. Paris: Vrin,
1967. 480 pp.

75. Mélanges Joseph Maréchal. Museum Lessianum, 31. 2 vols. Bruxelles:
Edition Universelle; Paris: Desclée de Brouwer, 1950.

76 - 86   SYMPOSIA AND COLLECTIONS

76. Mikael. Revista de Seminario de Paraná. S. Tomas 1974. Paraná.
Argentina, 1974.

77. Miscellanea Albert Dondeyne. Godsdienstfilosofie. Philosophie de
la religion. Leuven: University Press. Gembloux, Duculot, 1974.
456 pp.

78. Miscellania Mediaevalia. Paul Wilpert, ed. Berlin: W. de Gruyter,
1964. xii-360 pp.

78A. Modern Catholic Thinkers. R. Caponigri, ed. London: Burns Oates,
1961.

79. The Monist. Los Gatos, CA: Thomas Aquinas 1274-1974. 58, 1 (1974)

     Articles by: A.C. Pegis, J. Owens, L. Velecky, V.J. Bourke, J.
     Donceel, J.F. Ross, J.I. Dienstag, C.J. O'Neil, R.E.A. Shanab,
     R. Duska, and R.W. Clark.

80. Natural Law and International Relations. Proceedings of the American
Catholic Philosophical Association 24 Washington, D.C.: Catholic
University of America, 1950.

81. The Natural Law Reader, Brendan F. Brown, ed. New York: Oceana
Publishers, 1960.

82. Nel VII Centenario della morte di S. Tommaso d'Aquino. Aquinas,
vol. 17-18 (1974). Roma: Pontificia Universita Lateranense, 1974.
413 pp.

83. The New Scholasticism. Aquinas Septicentenary Commemoration.
48, 1 (1974) 1-132.

     Articles by: M.J. Adler, W.N. Clarke, J. Owens, H.B. Veatch,
     J.A. Weisheipl, L.E. Wilshire.

84. The New Scholasticism. Maritain's Ninetieth Birthday. 46, 1 (1972)
1-128.

     Articles by: J.W. Evans, R. Caldera, O. Lacombe, C. Journet,
     R. Speaight, A.A. Lima, J. Wright.

85. Philosophical Studies in Honor of Ignatius Smith. J. K. Ryan, ed.
Westminster, MD: Newman, 1952.

     Articles by: J.M. Marling, G. Benkert, J.A. Baisnée, R. Allers,
     J.B. McAllister, J.T. Noonan, F.X. Meehan, O. Bennett, J. Collins,
     J.A. McWilliams, W.J. McDonald, B.F. Brown, E.A. Maziarz.

86. Philosophy and the Integration of Contemporary Catholic Education.
George F. McLean, ed. Washington: Catholic University of America Press,
1962.

SYMPOSIA AND COLLECTIONS   87 - 98

87. The Philosophy and Theology of Anders Nygren. Carbondale-Edwards-
ville: Southern Illinois University Press; London-Amsterdam: Feffer
& Simons, 1970. xiv-434 pp.

88. Philosophy and Totality. J. McEvoy, ed. Belfast: The Queen's
University, 1977. 147 pp.

89. Philosophy of Biology. Vincent E. Smith, ed. New York: St. John's
University Press, 1962.

90. The Philosophy of Physics. Vincent E. Smith, ed. New York: St.
John's University Press, 1961.

91. Presencsa Filosofica. Homenagem a S. Tomàs. Sao Paulo: Sociedad
Brasileira de Filosofos Catolicos, 1974. 222 pp.

92. Progress in Philosophy. Studies in Honor of Charles A. Hart.
J. A. McWilliams, ed. Milwaukee: Bruce, 1955. vi-216 pp.

    Contributors: J.D. Collins, J.A. McWilliams, J. Maritain, E.G.
    Salmon, N. Clarke, F.X. Meehan, V.E. Smith, L.A. Foley, I. Brady,
    A.C. Pegis, G.B. Phelan, I. Smith.

93. Rivista di Filosofia Neo-Scolastica. Milano. Special Aquinas
Centenary Issue. 46 (1974) fasc. II-IV.

    Articles by: R. McInerny, P. Mazzarella, M. Nèdoncelle,
    E. Bertola, I. Biffi, J. DeFinance, A. Bempf, O.N. Derisi, J.C.
    Doig, G. Baget-Bozzo, C. Fabro, L.B. Geiger, A. Ghisalberti, C.
    Giacon, L. Hödl, B. Mondin, U. Poppi, F. Ruello, M.F. Sciacca,
    M. Seckler, S. Vanni Rovighi, F. Van Steenberghen, F.J. von
    Rintelen, G. Verbeke, R. Bessero, E. Bettoni, G. Bontadini, V.J.
    Bourke, P.O. Kristeller, M. Paolinelli, K. Riesenhuber, G.B. Sala.

94. The Role of the Christian Philosopher. Proceedings of the American
Catholic Philosophical Association 32. Washington, D.C.: Catholic
University of America Press, 1958.

95. Saggi sulla rinascità del Tomismo nel sec. xix. Antonio Piolanti,
ed. Roma: Libreria Ed. Vaticana, 1974. 450 pp.

96. St. Thomas Aquinas 1274-1975: Commemorative Studies, 2 vols.
Armand Maurer, ed. Toronto: Pontifical Institute of Mediaeval Studies,
1974. 488, 526 pp.

97. Saint Thomas d'Aquin Aujourd'hui. Comitè de rèdaction: Regis
Jolivet et alü. Recherches de Philosophie, 6. Paris: Desclèe de
Brouwer, 1963. 264 pp.

98. Saint Thomas d'Aquin pour le septième centenairo de sa mort. Essais
d'actualisation de sa philosophie. Stanislaw Kaminski, Marian Kurdzialek,
Zofia J. Zdybicka, eds. Lublin: Katolickiego Universytetu Lubelskiego,
1976. 352 pp.

99 - 113   SYMPOSIA AND COLLECTIONS

99. Salzburger Jahrbuch fur Philosophie. xix, 1974. Gedenkband zu
Ehren des hl. Thomas von Aquin. Salzburg-München: A. Pustet, 1974.
360 pp.

100. San Tommaso. Fonti e riflessi del suo pensiero. Studi Tomistici,
1. Antonio Piolanti, ed. Roma: Pontificia Accademia Romana di S.
Tommaso, 1974. 438 pp.

101. San Tommaso e L'odierna problematica teologica. Studi Tomistici,
2. Roma: Pontificia Accademia di S. Tommaso, 1974. 346 pp.

102. San Tommeso e il pensiero moderno. Studi Tomistici, 3. Roma:
Pont. Acc. di S. Tom. 1974, 334 pp.

103. San Tommaso e la filosofia del diritto, oggi. Studi Tomistici, 4
Roma: Pont. Acc. di S. Tom. 1974. 299 pp.

104. San Tommaso d'Aquino nella ricorrenza del centenario. Roma:
Accademia nazionale dei Lincei, 1975. 99 pp.

105. Sapientiae Procerum Amore. Mélanges...J.-P. Müller   and Theodor
W. Kohler, eds. Roma: Ed. Anselmiana, 1974. xix-494 pp.

106. Sidic. Reuve du service international de documentation judéo-
chrétienne. vol. 7: Saint Thomas d'Aquin à l'écoute de Maimonide.
Rome, 1974.

107. Studia Mediaevalia in honorem...Raymundi J. Martin. Brieges: De
Tempel, 1948.

108. Studia z Dziejow Mysli Swietego Tomasza z Akwinu. Stefan
Swiezauski and Jan Czerkawski, eds. Lublin: Towarzystwo Naukowe
Katholickiego Uniwersitetu Lubelskiego, 1978. 398 pp.

109. Studies in Maimonides and St. Thomas Aquinas. Jacob I. Dienstag,
ed. New York: KTAV Publishing House, 1975. ix-350 pp.

110. Teaching Thomism Today. George F. McLean, ed. Washington, D.C.:
Catholic University of America Press, 1963. 394 pp.

111. Theology and Evolution. E. C. Messenger, ed. London: Sands, 1949.

112. Thomas and Bonaventure. A Septicentenary Commemoration. Proceedings of the American Catholic Philosophical Association. 48. Washington,
D.C.: Catholic University of America, 1974.

        Articles by C. Fabro, D.H. Salman, H. Veatch, J. Owens, K.L.
        Schmitz, K. Riesenhuber, J.B. Reichmann, D. Tracy, F.J. von
        Ristelen, V.J. Bourke, R. Reilly, K. McDonnell, M.P. Golding,
        J.V. Lewis, E.P. Mahoney, J.P. Reilly, L. Dewart, and R. McInerny.

113. Thomas von Aquin. Interpretation und Rezeption. Studien und Texte.
Willehad Eckert, ed. Mainz: Matthias Grünewald, 1974. xx-980 pp.

SYMPOSIA AND COLLECTIONS   114 - 126

114. Thomas von Aquin 1274-1974. Herausgegeben von Ludger Oeing-
Hanhoff. München: Kösel, 1974. 176 pp.

115. Thomas von Aquin im philosophischen Gespräch. Wolfgang Kluxen,
Freiburg i. Br. München: Alber, 1975. 291 pp.

116. The Thomist. Centenary of St. Thomas Aquinas 1274-1974. 38, 1, 2,
3, and 4 (1974). Washington, D.C.

    Articles by: E.L. Mascall, Y. Congar, M.J. Adler, C.J. Peter,
    J.A. Weisheipl, V.J. Bourke, W.J. Hill, L. Chamberlain, A.J. Kelly,
    L.E. Boyle, C. Williams, R. McInerny, A. Moreno, J.B. Reichmann,
    C. Ernst, J. Farrelly, W.A. Wallace, C. Fabro, L.G. Walsh, O.H.
    Pesch, F.L. Peccorini, T.F. O'Meara, E. Stiegman, C. Journet,
    P. DeLetter, R. Lauer, A. McNicholl, J. Zagar, J.N. Deely.

117. The Thomist Reader. Washington: Thomist Press, 1957.

118. Thomistic Principles in a Catholic School. Theodore Brauer, ed.
St. Louis: B. Herder, 1943.

119. Thomistica morum principia. Romae: Officium Libri Catholici,
1960. 470 pp.

120. Tommaso d'Aquino nel suo VII Centenario. Il pensiero di Tommaso
d'Aquino e i problemi fondamentali del nostro tempo. Preliminary volume of Congreso Internazionale, Roma-Napoli, 1974. Roma: Herder;
Napoli: D'Auria, 1975. 536 pp.

121. Tommaso d'Aquino nel suo VII Centenario. Atti del Congresso Internazionale, Roma-Napoli, 1974. 9 vol. B. D''Amore, ed. Roma: Herder;
Napoli: D'Auria, 1975-1978.

    Contributions by several hunderd scholars on Aquinas in the history
    of thought; on the economy of salvation; moral action; being; man;
    the cosmos and science.

122. Tomismo e neotomismo, Vol. 1; Tomismo e antitomismo, vol. 2.
Centenario di S. Tommaso d'Aquino. Pistora: Memorie Domenicane, 1, 1975;
2, 1976. 428 pp.

123. Universidad de Navarra. Scripta Theologica, 6. Pamplona, 1974.

124. Virtus Politica. Festgabe...Alfons Hufnagel. Joseph Möller and
Helmut Kohlenberger, eds. Stuttgart-Bad Cannstatt: Frommann-Holzboog,
1974. 413 pp.

125. Voce della Coltura, La. S. Tommaso...1274-1974. P. P. Domenicane,
ed. Parabita, 1974. 72 pp.

126. Zbornik v. povodu 700. obljetnice smrti Tome Akvinskoga. 1274-1974.
Zagreb, 1974. 288 pp.

    All contributions in Croatian with short Latin summaries.

1
Life of
Thomas Aquinas

SOURCES

127. Eckert, Willehad Paul, ed. & tr. Das Leben des hl. Thomas von Aquino erzählt von W. von Tocco. Dusseldorf: Patmos, 1965.

128. _____. "Stilisierung und umdeutung der Persoenlichkeit des hl Thomas von Aquino durch die frnehen Biographen." Freiburger Zeitschrift fur Philosophie und Theologie 18 (1971) 7-28.

129. Ferrua, Angelico, ed. S. Thomas Aquinatis Vitae Fontes Praecipuae. Alba: Ed. Domenicane, 1968. 411 pp.

130. Foster, Kenelm, ed. & tr. The Life of Saint Thomas Aquinas. Biographical Documents. London: Longmans, Green, 1959; Baltimore, MD: Helicon, 1959. xii-172.

131. Hinnebusch, W. A. The Early English Friars Preachers. Rome: Institutum historicum FF. Praedicatorum, 1951.

132. Kaeppeli, T. Acta Provincialium Provinciae Romanae. 1243-1344. Romae: Monumenta Ordinis Praedicatorum Historica, 1947.

BIOGRAPHIES

133. Boulogne, Charles D. S. Thomas d'Aquin. Paris: Novuelles editions latines, 1968. 220 pp.

134. Bourke, Vernon J. Aquinas' Search for Wisdom. Milwaukee: Bruce, 1965. x-244 pp.

135. Chesterton, G. K. St. Thomas Aquinas: The "Dumb Ox." With an appreciation by Anton C. Pegis. Garden City, N.Y.: Doubleday, 1956. 198 pp.

136. Coffey, Reginald M. The Man from Rocea Sicca. Milwaukee: Bruce, 1944.

BIOGRAPHIES   137 - 153

137. D'Arcy, Martin C. Thomas Aquinas. Westminster, MD: Newman,
1944. 292 pp.

138. De Wohl, Louis. The Quiet Light. A novel based on the life of
life of St. Thomas. Philadelphia: Lippincott, 1950. 317 pp.

139. Fabro, Cornelio. "Tommaso d'Aquino," in Enciclopedia Cattolica
Citta del Vaticano, 1949-1954. t. xii, col. 251-97.

140. Gutierrez Zuluaga, Maria Isabel. Santo Tomas de Aquino, el maestro.
Valencia: Universidad de Valencia, 1976. 164 pp.

141. Maritain, Jacques. St. Thomas Aquinas: The Angel of the Schools.
J. F. Scanlon, tr. New York: Sheed & Ward, 1946; New York: Meridian
Books, 1958, 1964.

142. Ols, Daniel. "Tommaso d'Aquino," in Enciclopedia delle Religioni.
Firenze: Vallecchi, 1973. V, col. 1809-25.

143. Petitot, Hyacinthe. The Life and Spirit of Thomas Aquinas. Cyprian
Burke, tr. Chicago: Priory Press, 1966. 174 pp.

       Translation of 1923 French work.

144. Pittenger, William N. Saint Thomas Aquinas, The Angelic Doctor.
New York: Watts, 1969. 150 pp.

145. Saffrey, H.D. "Petite biographie de A. Thomas d'Aquin. 1225-1274."
Vie Spirituelle. Paris. 101 (1959) 307-21.

146. Simone, L. De. San Tommaso d'Aquino. La storia, l'opera, la dottrina. Nopoli: L. Loffredo Editore, 1943.

147. Taurisano, J. San Tommaso d'Aquino, Turin: Marietti, 1941. 229 pp.

148. Toso, Agostino. Tommaso d'Aquino e il suo tempo. Roma: Marietti,
1941. 198 pp.

149. Vann, Gerald. Saint Thomas Aquinas. London: J.M. Dent & Sons,
1940. ix-182. New York: Benziger, 1947. 212 pp.

150. Vansteenkiste, C. M. J. "Tommaso d'Aquino." Biblioteca Sanctorum
12 (Rome 1969) 544-63.

151. Walz, Angelus. San Tommaso d'Aquino. Rome: Angelicum, 1945.
248 pp.

152. _____. St. Thomas Aquinas: A Biographical Study. Sebastian
Bullough, tr. Westminster, MD: Newman, 1951. 265 pp.

153. _____. Saint Thomas d'Aquin. adaptation francaise par Paul
Novarina. Louvain: Publications Universitaires, 1962. 210 pp.

154 - 168   CRITICAL STUDIES OF LIFE

154. Walz, Angelus. Thomas von Aquin. Basel: Thomas Morus Verlag,
1953. 154 pp.

155. Weisheipl, James A. Friar Thomas d'Aquino. His Life, Thought,
and Work. Garden City, N.Y.: Doubleday, 1974. 476 pp.

CRITICAL STUDIES OF HIS LIFE

156. Abate, Giuseppe. "Intorno alla cronologia di San Tommaso d'Aquino,"
c. 1220 nascita del santo. Miscellanea Francescana 5 (1950) 97-130.

157. _____. Per la storia e la cronologia di S. Bonaventura, O. Min.
c. 1217-1274. Roma: Editrice 'Miscellanea Francescana.' 1950. 66 pp.

    Originally in Miscellanea Francescana 49 (1949) 534-568; 50 (1950)
    97-130.

158. Anderson, James F. "Was St. Thomas a Philosopher?" The New
Scholasticism 38 (1964) 435-44.

159. Centi, Tito S. "E finita per i manichei!" Revue d'Ascètique et
de Mystique. Toulouse. 25 (1974) 257-73.

160. Chenu, M. D. "S. Thomas innovateur dans la créativité d'un monde
nouveau." Tommaso d'Aquino...problemi fondamentali (Symp 1974) 27-33.

161. Colledge, Edmund. "The Legend of St. Thomas Aquinas." St. Thomas
Aquinas 1274-1974. 1 (Symp) 13-28.

162. Crowe, Michael Bertram. "On Re-Writing the Biography of Aquinas."
Irish Theological Quarterly 41 (1974) 255-73.

163. _____. "Peter of Ireland, Teacher of St. Thomas." Studies.
Dublin. 45 (1956) 443-56.

164. Dettloff, W. "Cur Divus Thomas?" Wissenschaft und Weisheit 18
(1955) 64-71.

165. Dondaine, Antoine. Les Secrètaire de s. Thomas. 2 vols. Rome:
Commissio Leonina, 1956.

166. Eckert. W. P. "Das Selbstverständnis des Thomas von Aquino als
Magister S. Theologiae." Beiträge zum Berufsbewusstsein des mittelalter-
lichen Menschen. Berlin: Miscellanea Mediaevalia, 3, 1964, 105-34 pp.

167. _____. "Stilisierung und Umdeutung der Persönlichkeit des hl.
Thomas von Aquin durch die frühen Biographen." Freiburger Zeitschrift fur
Philosophie und Theologie 18 (1971) 7-28.

168. Fabro, Cornelio. "Tommaso d'Aquino, santo." in Enciclopedia
Cattolica. Firenze: Tipografia 'L' Impronta'. 12 (1954) 252-97.

CRITICAL STUDIES OF LIFE   169 - 185

169. Gagnebet, P.-M.-R. "Thomas d'Aquin. II. Le docteur et le saint." Dictionnaire de Theologie Catholique. 15 (1946) col. 631-635.

170. Galli, Dario. "S. Tommaso, Filosofo della mediazione." Tommaso d'Aquino 2 (Symp) 67-73.

171. Giannini, Giorgio. "San Tommaso d'Aquino, genio dell' ordine." Giornale di Metafisica 29 (1974) 441-60.

172. Grabmann, Martin. Das Seelenleben des hl. Thomas von Aquin. 3 aufl. Freiburg i.S: Paulusverlag, 1949. 124 pp.

173. _____. The Interior Life of St. Thomas Aquinas. Presented from his works and the acts of his canonization process. (of Das Seelenleben...) Nicholas Ashenbrener, tr. Milwaukee: Bruce, 1951. 92 pp.

174. _____. Thomas von Aquin: Personlichkeit und Gedankenwelt. 2 aufl. München: Kösel, 1946.

175. Leccisotti, T. "IL Dottore Angelico a Montecassino." Rivista di Filosofia Neoscolastica 32 (1940) 519-47.

176. Lippini, Pietro. "La santità di Tommaso d'Aquino." Tommaso d'Aquino 2 (Symp) 74-9.

177. Munoz-Alonso, Adolfo. "Tomás de Aquino, Peregrino de Dios." Sapientia 26 (1971) 95-102.

178. O'Meara, Thomas F. "Paris as a Cultural Milieu of Thomas Aquinas' Thought." The Thomist 38 (1974) 689-722.

179. Pocino, Willy. Roccasecca patria di San Tommaso d'Aquino. Documentazione storico-bibliografica. Pref. di A. Walz. Roma: Lazio ieri e oggi, 1974. 136 pp.

180. Ponferrada, Gustavo Eloy. "Tomas de Aquino en la Universidad de Paris." Sapientia 26 (1971) 233-62.

181. Sesnic, Milan. "Sv. Toma propovjednik." (St. Thomas as a preacher) Zbornik (Symp) 143-53.

182. Sullivan, Frank. "The Historical Thomas Aquinas." The Modern Schoolman 18 (1941) 61-3.

183. Vanni Rovighi, Sofia. "Il Convegno sul Conciliv di Lione, S. Bonaventura e San Tommaso." Rivista di Filosofia Neoscholastica 67 (1975) 127-35.

184. Walz, Angelus. "Abt Joachim und der 'neue Geist der Freiheit' in Toccos Thomasleben, c. 20." Angelicum 45 (1968) 314ff.

185. _____. "L'Aquinate a Orvieto." Angelicum 35 (1958).

186 - 200   CRITICAL STUDIES OF LIFE

186. _____. "L'Aquinate a Viterbo." Memorie Domenicane 72 (1955)

187. _____. "Il detenuto di Montesangiovanni." Memorie Domenicane 73 (1956).

188. _____. Luoghi di San Tommaso. Roma: Herder, 1961.

Special study of life, places where Thomas lived and worked.

189. _____. "Papst Johannes XXII und Thomas von Aquin, zur Geschichte der Heiligsprechung des Aquinaten." in St. Thomas Aquinas (Toronto Symp) vol I, 29-47.

190. _____. "La presenza di S. Tommaso a Orvieto e ufficiatura del 'Corpus Domini.'" Studi Eucaristici (Orvieto 1966) 337-45.

191. _____. "Riassunti storiografici sul luogo di nascità di San Tommaso." Angelicum 37 (1960).

192. _____. "S. Tommaso d'Aquino dechiarato dottore della Chiesa nel 1567." Angelicum 44 (1967) 148ff.

193. _____. San Tommaso d'Aquino, Studi biografici. Roma: Herder, 1945. 238 pp.

194. _____. "Thomas d'Aquin: I. Vie." Dictionnaire de Théologie Catholique 16 (1946).

195. _____. "Wege des Aquinaten." Historisches Jahrbuch. München. 78 (1958) 221-28.

AQUINAS IN ART

196. Anonymous. "St. Thomas Aquinas." Los Angeles: Center for Medieval and Renaissance Studies, 1974.

A one-hour television program co-produced by the UCLA Media Center on KCET in 1974 to commemorate the 700th anniversary of the philosopher's death. Can be obtained from the Center, University of California, 90024.

197. Adamek, Tadeusz. "Wybrane problemy ikonografii sw. Tomasza z Akwinu w sztuce polskiej." (Select problems of St. Thomas iconography in Polish art) Studia Sw. Tomasza (Lublin Symp) 367-78.

198. Beebe, Maurice. "Joyce and Aquinas: the Theory of Aesthetics." Philological Quarterly 36 (1957) 20-35.

199. Bianchi, L. Vita D. Thomae Aquinatis Othonis Vaeni ingenio et manu delineata. (Reproduction of a Life, with engravings, dated 1610) Rome: Angelicum, 1940.

200, Bredin, Hugh. "T. S. Eliot and Thomistic Scholasticism." Journal

AQUINAS IN ART   201 - 216

of the History of Ideas 33 (1972) 299-306.

201. Brennan, Rose Emmanuel. "St. Thomas as a Critic." The New Scholasticism 21 (1947) 303-30.

202. Centi, Tito S. "La teologia di S. Tommaso nell'arte del Beato Angelico." Sapienza 8 (1955) 143-57.

203. Chamberlain, Lewis. "Ode to Thomas." The Thomist Centenary of St. Thomas Aquinas 1274-1974. 38 (January 1974) 3-7.

204. D'Onofrio, Tobia. "S. Tommaso nella poesia Dantesca." Tommaso d'Aquino 2 (Symp) 141-48.

205. Gilson, Etienne. Dante et Béatrice. Etudes dantesques. (On Aquinas pp. 9-45, 73, 79-102) Paris: Vrin, 1974. vii-147 pp.

206. Godwin, Frances G. "An Illustration to the De sacramentis of St. Thomas Aquinas." Speculum 26 (1951) 609-14.

207. Iturgaiz, Domingo. "Santo Tomás a través de la iconografia cristiana. (Ensayo parcial)." Ciencia Tomista. Salamanca. 101 (1974) 307-49.

208. Kaftal, G. Iconography of the Saints in Tuscan Painting. Florence, 1952.

209. Koudelka, V. J. "La cappella di S. Tommaso d'Aquino in Monte Savello a Roma." Archivum Fratrum Praedicatorum 32 (1962) 126-44.

210. Lechner, Gregor M. "Iconographia Thomasiana. Thomas von Aquin und seine Darstellungen in der bildenden Kunst." Thomas...Interpretation (Symp) 933-73 pp.

211. Lourié, Arthur. "Motet: De Ordinatione Angelorum." Orchestration for mixed voices and five instruments of selection of texts by Raïssa Maritain from S.T. I, q. 108. Maritain...Thomist (Symp) 319-44 pp.

212. Morin, Edward. "Joyce as Thomist." Renascence 9 (1957) 127-31.

213. Noon, Wm. T. Joyce and Aquinas. New Haven, CT: Yale University Press, 1956. 308 pp.

214. O'Malley, John W. "Some Renaissance Panegyrics of Aquinas." Renasissance Quarterly 27 (1974) 174-92.

215. Peiser, W. "Aristotelianism and Thomism in Romanic Literature." The New Scholasticism 16 (1942) 365-92

216. Poinsenet, M. D. Saint Thomas d'Aquin, histoire avec des images. Tourcoing: Ed. Flandre-Artois, 1951. 26 pp.

        For children.

217. Sargent, Daniel. "Dante and Thomism." Maritain...Thomist (Symp) 256-64 pp.

218. Scaltriti, Giacinto Arturo. "S. Tommaso d'Aquino in Savonarola." Tommaso d'Aquino 2 (Symp) 152-8.

219. Smith, A. "When St. Thomas Sang of God." Dominicana 27 (October-December 1942) 155-60, 252-8.

220. Vanni, M. La rappresentazione di San Tommaso d'Aquino (da una 'legenna de S. Tomasci' del sec. xv). Roma: Ist. B. Angelico di studi per l'arte, 1946. 142 pp.

221.Veen, Ottone Van. Vita illustrata di S. Tommaso d'Aquino. A cura di P. Giuseppe Zaccaria. Subiaco: Ed. Iter, 1974. 72 pp.

2
Writings of
Thomas Aquinas

GENERAL STUDIES OF WORKS AND MSS

222. Anonymous. Nel VII Centenario di Tommaso d'Aquino. Contributo
alla catalogazione dell'opera...di S. Domenico Maggiore e...di Capodimonte.
Napoli: Assessorato per l'istruzione e la cuttura, 1975. 101 pp.

223. _____. San Tommaso e San Bonaventura nella Biblioteca Vaticana.
Mostra in occasione del VII Centenario (1274-1974). Catalogo. Citta
Vaticana: Biblioteca Apostolica Vaticana, 1974. 127 pp.

224. Bataillon, Louis-Jacques. "La Commission Léonine à Grottaferrata
(1973-1977)." Archivam Franciscanum Historicum. Roma. 70 (1977)
569-71.

225. Bernath, Klaus, ed. Thomas von Aquin. I. Chronologie und Werk-
analyse. Darmstadt: Wissenschaftliche Buchgesellschaft, 1978. 469 pp.

226. Chenu, M.-D. Introduction à l'étude de s. Thomas d'Aquin. Montréal
and Paris: Institut d'études médiévales, 1950; 2 me éd. 1954; 3 me éd.
1974. 305 pp.

227. _____. Toward Understanding St. Thomas. A.-M. Landry and D.
Hughes, tr. Chicago: Regnery, 1964. 386 pp.

228. _____. Das Werk des hl. Thomas von Aquin. Heidelberg: Kerle,
1960.

229. Contenson, Pierre M. de. "Documents sur les origines et les
premières années de la Commission Léonine." St. Thomas Aquinas 1274-
1974 2 (Symp) 331-88.

230. Contenson, P. M. De. "L'Edition critique des oeuvres de s. Thomas
d'Aquin." Bulletin de Philosophie Médiévale 10-12 (1968-1970) 175-86.

231. Contenson, Pierre M. De. "Principles, Methods and Problems of the
Critical Edition of the Works of St. Thomas as Presented in the 'Leonine

GENERAL STUDIES OF WORKS AND MSS 232 - 245

Edition'." Tÿdschrift voor Philosophie. Leuven. 36 (1974) 342-64.

232. Dondaine, H.-F. and Hugues V. Shooner. Codices manuscripti operum Thomae de Aquino. 3 vols. Roma: Editori di San Tommaso, 1967ff.

    I. Autographa et Bibl. Admont--Fulda, 1967.
   II. Bibl. Gdańsk--Münster, 1973;
 III. Bibl. Montserrat--Zwettl (not yet printed)

233. Engelbert, Pius. "Schreiber und Intellektuelle im Umkreis des Thomas von Aquin. Textkritische Bemerbungen zu eiser neuen Edition." Scriptorium. Bruxelles. 27 (1973) 49-60.

234. Frank, J. "Thomistische Handschriften in Klosterneuberg." Jahrbuch des Stiftes Klosterneuburg 3 (1963) 27-47.

235. Grabmann, Martin. Die Werke des hl. Thomas von Aquin. Eine literarhistorische Untersuchung und Einführung. 3 Aufl. Münster Westf: Aschendorff, 1949. xx-479 pp.

236. Kaeppeli, Th. Scriptores Ordinis Praedicatorum Medii Aevi. Romae: Commissio Leonina, 1970.

237. Knowles, David. The Historical Context of the Philosophical Works of St. Thomas Aquinas. London: Blackfriars, 1958. 14 pp.

238. Pattin, Adriaan. "Bÿdrage tot de kronologie van St. Thomas Werken." Tÿdschrift voor Philosophie 19 (1957) 477-502, resumé 502-504.

239. Pieper, Josef. Hinführung zu Thomas von Aquin. Zwölf Vorlesungen. München: Kösel, 1958. 246 pp.

240. Ramirez, Santiago M. (Jacobus) Introducción a Thomás de Aquino. Biografía. Obras, Autoridad doctrinal. Act. por V. Rodriguez. Madrid: Editoria Católica, 1975. 341 pp.

241. Reilly, James P. "The Leonine Commission and the Seventh Centenary of Saint Thomas Aquinas." Proceedings of the American Catholic Philosophical Association 48 (1974) 286-294.

242. Steenberghen, Fernand van. "L'Edition Léonine des oeuvres de saint Thomas." Revue Philosophique de Louvain 72 (1974) 5-10.

243. Suermondt, Clemens S. "Il contributo dell'Edizione Leonina per la conoscenza di S. Tommaso." Scholastica. Rome. (1951) 233-82.

244. Vansteenkiste, C. M. Joris. "'Versus' dans les oeuvres de s. Thomas." St. Thomas Quinas 1274-1974 (Symp) 77-86.

245. Walz, Angelus. "Thomas d'Aquin: III. Ecrits." Dictionnaire de Théologie Catholique. Paris, 1943.

RECENT EDITIONS OF LATIN WORKS

246. S. Thomae Aquinatis. Opera Omnia. Parma: Fiaccadori, 1852-1873, 25 vols. (The Parma Edition)

> Reprinted with English Introduction by V. J. Bourke. New York: Musurgia, 1948-1950, 25 vols.

247. S. Thomae de Aquino. Opera Omnia. Iussu Leonis XIII P.M. edita. (The Leonine Edition) Romae: Editori di San Tommaso, 1882--.

> Incomplete in 1979: vols. 21, 23-25, 27, 29-39, 43-46, 49 & 50 not yet published; vols. 1 through 10 out of print.

248. S. Thomae Aquinatis. Opuscula Omnia necnon Opera Minora. J. Perrier, ed. Paris: Lethielleux, Tome I, 1949.

> Somewhat critical editions of several short works, see Chenu, Toward Understanding St. Thomas. Regnery, 1964, 325-30 pp. for list of "opuscules" printed in Perrier.

249. D. Thomae Aquinatis. Opuscula Philosophica. R. M. Spiazzi, ed. Turino-Roma: Casa Marietti, 1954.

> Many other individual works of St. Thomas have been printed by the Marietti Co. of Turin, Italy, at various times since the 1920's. These are usually the same non-critical texts found in Parma and Vives.

250. S. Thomae de Aquino. Opuscula Philosophica. in Opera Omnia iussu Leonis XIII edita. Tomus XLiii. Roma: Editori di San Tommaso, 1976.

> De principiis naturae, De aeternitate mundi, De motus cordis, De mixtione elementorum, De operationibus occultis naturae, De indiciis astrorum, De sortibus, De unitate intellectus, De ente et essentia, De fallaciis, De propositionibus modalibus. 458 pp.

251. D. Thomae Aquinatis. Opuscula Theologica. R. A. Varardo, et al, ed. 2 vols. Torino-Roma: Casa Marietti, 1954.

252. _____. Aeternitate mundi contra murmurantes, De. (A.D. 1270)

> Leonine, vol 43.
> Parma, vol 16; Vives, vol. 27.
> Marietti (1954) Op. Philos.

253. Crit. ed. by W. J. Dwyer. Louvian: Inst. de Philos, Sup. 1937.

254. St. Thomas Aquinas, Siger of Brabant, and St. Bonaventure. On the Eternity of the World. Cyril Vollert, Lottie A. Kendzierski and Paul M. Byrne, trs. Milwaukee: Marquette University Press, 1964. xii-117 pp.

Angelorum natura, De. See De substantiis separatis.

RECENT EDITIONS OF LATIN WORKS 255 - 261

Anima, Q.D. de. see Quaest. Disp.

255. _____. Anima Aristotelis, Sententia super De. A.D. 1269-1271.

    Leonine, vol. 45 (Not yet published).
    Parma, vol. 20; Vivès, vol. 24.
    Marietti, 1948.

255A. _____. Aristotle's de anima with the Commentary of St. Thomas
Aquinas. K. Foster and S. Humphries, trs. New Haven: Yale; London:
Routledge, 1951-1954. 504 pp.

256. _____. Articulis fidei et sacramentis ecclesiae, De. A.D. 1261-
1265.

    Leonine, Vol. 42.
    Parma, vol. 16; Vivès, vol. 27.
    Marietti (1954) Op. Theol. I, 141-51.

257. _____. Catechetical Instructions of St. Thomas. J. B. Collins,
tr. New York: Wagner, 1939, 1953.

    Treatise II, On the Sacraments, only.

258. _____. Articulis VI, ad lectorem Bisuntinum, De. Date uncertain.

    Leonine, 42.
    Parma, vol. 16; Vivès, vol. 27.
    Marietti (1954) Op. Theol. I, 243-44. No English version.

259. _____. Articulis XXXVI ad lectorem Venetum, De. A.D. 1271.

    Leonine, vol. 42.
    Parma, vol. 16; Vivès, vol. 27 et 32, 832-33.
    Marietti (1954) Op. Theol. I, 193-97 and 199-207.
    Also J. Destrez, ed. in Milanges Mandonnet. Paris, 1930. 156-72.
    No English version.

260. _____. Articulis XLII ad magistrum Ordinis (Joannem Vercellensem) De. A.D. April 2, 1271.

    Leonine, vol. 42.
    Parma, vol. 16; Vivès, vol. 27.
    Marietti (1954) Op. Theol. I, 211-18. No English version.

261. _____. Articulis CVIII ad fratrem Joannem Vercellensem, De.
A.D. 1265-1266.

    Leonine, Vol. 42
    Parma, vol. 16; Vivès, vol. 27.
    Marietti (1954) Op. Theol. I, 223-40.
    Some textual correction in: R. J. Martin. "Notes critiques au

262 - 272   RECENT EDITIONS OF LATIN WORKS

sujet de l'opuscule IX." Mélanges A. Pelzer. Louvain, 1947.
303-23 pp. No English version.

262. _____. Ave Maria, Collationes super. A.D. 1273.

Leonine, vol. 44 (Not yet published).
Parma, vol. 16; Vivès, vol. 27.

263. _____. S. Thomae Aq. Expositio Salutationis Angelicae. J. F.
Rossi, ed. Crit. ed, in Divus Thomas. Piacenza. 34 (1931) 465-76;
also offprinted: Piacenza: Collegio di Piacenza, 1931; and Marietti
(1954) II, 239-41.

264. _____. The Three Greatest Prayers. L. Shapcote, trs. London:
1937.

265. _____. Also trans. in J. B. Collins, Catechetical Instructions
of St. Thomas. New York: Wagner, 1953.

266. _____. Also by L. Every, Explanation of the Hail Mary in
Dominicana. Washington. 39 (1954) 31-8.

267. _____. Bernardum abbatem Cassinensem, Responsio ad. A.D. 1274.

Leonine, vol. 42.
Parma, Musurgia reprint, New York: 1948, I, xxvi; Vivès, vol. 32.
Marietti (1954) Op. Theol. I, 249-50.
Partial English version in V.J. Bourke. Aquinas' Search for Wisdom.
(1965) 209-210 pp.

268. _____. "La lettre de S. Thomas a l'ablé de Mont-Cassin." A.
Dondaine, ed., Crit. Ed, in St. Thomas Aquinas, 1274-1974. Toronto:
PIMS, 1974. I, 102-108 pp.

269. _____. Boethii de Hebdomadibus, Expositio. A.D. 1256-1259.

Leonine, vol. 50 (Not yet published)
Parma, vol. 17; Vivès, vol. 28.
Marietti (1954). No English version.

270. _____. Expositio super librum Boetii 'de Hebdomadibus', an
edition and a study. Peter O'Reilly, ed. Tronto: University of Toronto
Dissertation, 1960. 136 pp.

271. _____. Boethu de Trinitate, Expositio. A.D. 1258-1259.

Leonine, vol. 50 (Not yet published).
Parma, vol. 17; Vivès, vol. 28.
Marietti (1954) also ed. P. Wyser. Fribourg: 1948, Q. 5 and 6.

272. _____. Bruno Decker, ed. Leiden: Brill, 1955. xv-243 pp.

Best Latin text.

RECENT EDITIONS OF LATIN WORKS 273 - 284

273. _____. The Trinity and the Unicity of the Intellect. R. E. Brenna, tr. St. Louis: Herder, 1946.

274. _____. On Searching Into God. Q. 2. V. White, tr. Oxford: Blackfriars, 1947.

275. _____. Divisions and Methods of the Sciences. A. Maurer, tr. Toronto: PIMS, 1953. qq. v-vi.

276. _____. Caelo et mundo Aristotelis, Sententia de. A.D. 1272-1273.
    Leonine, vol. 3 (1886).
    Parma, vol. 19
    Marietti, (1952).

277. _____. On the Heavens. P. Conway and R. F. Larcher, trs. Columbus, Ohio: Alum Creek Press.

278. _____. Canticum Cantiorum, In.

    There is no printed text or known MS of this Commentary on the Songs of Songs. The texts printed in Parma, vol. 14; and Vivès, vol. 18 are spurious; See I. T. Eschmann, Catalogue, no. 19.

Caritate, Q. D. de, see Quaest. Disp.

Catena Aurea, see Glossa continua.

279. _____. Causis, Expositio super liberum de. A.D. 1271-1272.

    Leonine, vol. 49 (Not yet published).
    Parma, vol. 21.
    Marietti, (1955).

280. _____. H. D. Saffrey, ed. Fribourg: Société Philosophique; Louvian: Nauwelaerts, 1954. 223 pp. No English version.

281. _____. Liber de Causis et Sancti Thomae de Aquino Super Librum De Causis Expositio. Textus Philosophici -2. Vincentius Maria Pouliot, ed. Nagoya: Institutum Sancti Thomae de Aquino, 1967. 145 pp.

282. _____. Compendium theologiae ad fratrem Reginaldum. Date uncertain, A.D. 1265 or 1273.

    Leonine, vol. 42.
    Parma, vol. 16; Vivès, vol. 27.
    Marietti (1954) I, 13-138.

283. _____. Compendium of Theology. Cyril Vollert, tr. St. Louis: B. Herder, 1952.

284. _____. Also Lawrence Lynch, tr. New York: McMullen, 1947.

285 - 295 RECENT EDITIONS OF LATIN WORKS

285. _____. Compendium Theologiae, Grundriss der Glaubenslehre.
deutsch - lateinisch. Uebersetzt von Hans Louis Fäh. Hsg. von Rudolf
Tannhof. Heidelberg: Kerle, 1963.

286. _____. Compendio de theologia. Buenos Aires: Editiora
Cultural, 1943.

287. _____. Credo in Deum, Collationes super. A.D. 1273.

      Leonine, vol. 44 (Not yet published).
      Parma, vol. 16; Vivès, vol. 27.
      Marietti (1954) Op. Theol. II, 193-217.

288. _____. The Three Greatest Prayers. L. Shapcote, tr. London:
Burns, Oates, 1939; Westminster, MD: Newman, 1956.

289. _____. Decem praeceptis, Collationes de. A.D. 1273. De
duobus praeceptis caritatis. etc.

      Leonine, vol. 44 (Not yet published).
      Parma, vol. 16; Vivès, vol. 27.
      Marietti (1954) Op. Theol. 2, 245-71.

290. _____. The Commandments of God. L. Shapcote, tr. London:
Burns, Oates, 1937;

291. Also in J.B. Collins, Catechetical Instructions. 1953. 69-116
      pp.

Correctione fraterna, Q.D.de, see Quaest. Disp.

292. _____. Decretalem, Expositio super primam et secundam. A.D.
1260-1269.

      Leonine, vol. 40E (Rome 1968).
      Parma, vol. 16; Vivès, vol. 27.
      Marietti (1954) Op. Theol. I, 417-26. No English version.

293. _____. Divinis nominibus, Espositio Dionysii de. A.D. 1265-
1267.
      Leonine, vol. 49 (Not yet published).
      Parma, vol. 15; Vivès, vol. 29.
      Marietti (1950). No English version.

294. _____. Emptione et venditione ad tempus, De. seu Responsio
super materia venditionis. A.D. 1262.

      Leonine, vol. 43.
      Parma, vol. 17; Vivès, vol. 28.

295. _____. "Notes on St. Thomas, on Credit." Alfred O'Rahilly,
Crit. ed. Irish Ecclesiastical Record 64 (1928) 159-68.

RECENT EDITIONS OF LATIN WORKS   296 - 309

English version by O'Rahilly, ibid. 164-54. Reprinted in V.J.
Bourke, The Pocket Aquinas. 1973. 223-5.

296. _____. Ente et Essentia, De. A.D. 1252-1256.

Leonine, vol. 43.
Parma, vol. 16; Vivès, vol. 27.
Perrier (1949) 24-50.
Marietti (1954) Op. Philos. Corrected text by C. Boyer.

297. _____. Ludwig Baur, ed. Münster, 1926.

298. _____. M.D. Roland Gosselin, ed. Paris, 1948.

299. _____. Jos. Bobik, ed. Notre Dame University Press, 1965.

300. _____. On Being and Essence. A. A. Maurer, tr. Toronto:
PIMS, 1949.

301. _____. Also trans. A. H. Bachhuber. St. Louis: The Modern
Schoolman, 1957.

In sense lines.

302. _____. Also trans. G. Leckie. New York: Appleton. C. 1957

303. _____. Also trans. J. Bobik. Notre Dame University Press,
1965.

304. _____. Yu to Honshitsu ni tsuite (De ente et essentia).
Japanese version by V. M. Pouliot and A. Kusaka. Nagoya: Cath. Univ.
Press, 1955.

305. _____. Toma Akvinski. O biću i sustihi. Preveo i predgovor
napisao Dr. Vladimir Premec. Beograd: Beogradski izdavacko-grafichi
zavod, 1973. viii-36 pp.

The De ento et essentia in Croatian.

306. _____. Epistolas Pauli Apostoli, Expositio et lectura super.
A.D. 1270-1272.

Leonine, vols. 32-35 (Not yet published).
Parma, vol. 13; Vivès, vol. 20-21.
Marietti (1953).

307. _____. On St. Paul's Epistle to the Ephesians. M. L. Lamb, tr.
New York: Magi, 1966.

308. _____. On St. Paul's Epistle to the Galatians. R. F. Larcher,
tr. New York: Magi, 1966.

309. _____. On St. Paul's Epistle to the Philippians and First

310 - 317 RECENT EDITIONS OF LATIN WORKS

Thessalonians. R. F. Larcher, tr. New York: Magi, 1969.

310. _____. Errores Graecorum ad Urbanum, Contra IV P. M. A.D. 1263.

      Leonine, vol. 40A (Rome 1967).
      Parma, vol. 15; Vivès, vol. 29.
      Marietti (1954) Op. Theol. I, 315-46; plus the Libellus which
      Thomas reviewed in this work, I, 347-412 pp.

311. _____. Also P. Glorieux, ed. Monumenta Christiana Selecta,
Paris 1957.

      No English version.

312. _____. Ethicorum Aristotelis, Sententia libri. A.D. 1271.

      Leonine, vol. 47 (1969). This critical edition by R.A. Gauthier
      is by far the best text. vol. I Praefatio-Libri I-III; vol. II.
      Libri IV-X, Indices.
      Parma, vol. 21; Vivès, vol. 25-26.
      Marietti (1949, 1964).

313. _____. Commentary on the Nicomachean Ethics. C. I. Litzinger,
tr. 2 Vols. Chicago: Regnery, 1964.

      Based on the old vulgarized text.

314. _____. Fallaciis ad quosdam nobiles artistas, De. A.D. 1244-
1245.

      Leonine, vol. 43.
      Parma, vol. 16; Vivès, vol. 27.
      Perrier (1949) 430-61.
      Marietti (1954) Op. Philos. 225-40. No English version.
      Authenticity probable.

315. _____. Forma absolutionis sacramentalis ad generalem magistrum
Ordinis, De. A.D. 1269.

      Leonine, vol. 40C (Rome 1969).
      Parma, vol. 16; Vivès, vol. 27.

316. _____. "L'Opuscolo 'De forma absolutionis' di San Tommaso d
'Aquino. Introduzione e testo critico." P. Castagnoli, Crit. ed. Divus
Thomas. Piacenza.

      Reprinted, Marietti (1954) Op. Theol, I. No English version.

317. _____. Generatione at corruptione Aristotelis, Sententia De.
A.D. 1272-1273.

      Leonine, vol. 3 (1886)
      Parma, vol. 19; Marietti (1952)

RECENT EDITIONS OF LATIN WORKS   318 - 327

Marietti (1952).

318. _____. F. E. Kelley, ed. Beck, 1977.

319. _____. On Generation and Corruption. P. Conway and W. H. Kane, trs. Columbus, Ohio: Alum Creek Press.

320. _____. Glossa continua super Evangelia. Catena Aurea. A.D. 1262-1267.

Leonine, vols. 36-39 (Not yet published).
Parma, vols. 11-12.
Marietti, 2 vols. (1953).

321. _____. English: Catena Aurea. 4 Vols. J. H. Newman, et al, trs. Oxford: Parker, 1841-1845.

322. _____. The Golden Chain. By a Religious of C.S.M.V. London: Mowbray, 1956. 90 pp. Partial translation.

Hebdomadibus, Expositio in librum Boethii De, see Boethii.

Immortalitate animae, Q.D. de. see Quaest. Disp.

323. _____. Impugnastes Dei cultum et religionem, Contra. A.D. 1256.

Leonine, vol. 41A (Rome 1970).
Parma, vol. 15; Vivès, vol. 29.
Marietti (1954) Op. Theol. II, 5-110.

324. _____. An Apology for the Religious Orders. J. Procter, tr. London: Sands, 1902.

Reprint: Westminster, MD: Newman, 1950.

325. _____. Isaiam, Postilla super. Date uncertain.

Leonine, vol. 28 (1974) 85 + 293 pp.
Parma, vol. 14, 427-576; Vivès, vol. 18, 688-821; vol. 19, 1-65.
No English version.

326. _____. Jeremaiam et super Threnos, Postilla super. Date uncertain.

Leonine, vol. 29 (Not yet published).
Parma, vol. 14; Vivès, vol. 19, 66-198. No English version.

327. _____. Job, Expositio in. A.D. 1261-1264.

Leonine, vol. 26 (1965).
Parma, vol. 14; Vivès, vol. 18. No English version.

328 - 335   RECENT EDITIONS OF LATIN WORKS

328. _____. Johannem, Lectura super. A.D. 1269-1272.

Leonine, vol. 31 (Not yet published).
Parma, vol. 10; Vivès, vol. 19.
Marietti (1952). On the Gospel of St. John, R.F. Larcher, tr.
Albany, New York: Magi Books, 1970.

329. _____. Judiciis astrorum De. Date uncertain.

Leonine, vol. 43.
Parma, vol. 16; Vivès, vol. 27.
Marietti (1954) Op. Theol. I, 159-67.   No English version.

Malo, Q.D. de, see Quaest. Disp.

330. _____. Matthaeum, Lectura super. A.D. 1256-1259.

Leonine, vol. 30 (Not yet published).
Parma, vol. 10; Vivès, vol. 19.
Marietti (1951). No English version.

331. _____. Memoria et reminiscentia Aristotelis, Sententia De.
A.D. 1270.

Leonine, vol. 45 (Not yet published).
Parma, vol. 20; Vivès, vol. 24.
Marietti (1949). No English version.

332. _____. Metaphysicam Aristotelis, Sententia super.   A.D. 1269-
1272.

Leonine, vol. 46 (Not yet published).
Parma, vol. 20; Vivès, vols. 24-25.
Marietti (1950, 1964).

333. _____. Commentary on the Metaphysics of Aristotle.   J. P. Rowan,
tr. 2 Vols. Chicago: Regnery, 1961.

334. _____. Meteora Aristotelis, Sententia super.   A.D. 1269-1273.

Leonine, vol. 3 (1886).
Parma, vol. 19.
Marietti (1952). No complete English but for a version of Bk I,
lectiones 8-10, see Lynn Thorndike, Latin Treatises on Comets,
Chicago: University of Chicago Press, 1950. 77-86 pp.

335. _____. Mixtione elementorum, De. A.D. 1270-1271.

Leonine, vol. 43.
Parma, vol. 16; Vivès, vol. 27.
Marietti (1954) Op. Philos.
Perrier I, 19-22 pp.

RECENT EDITIONS OF LATIN WORKS   336 - 346

336. _____ . "On the Combining of the Elements." V. R. Larkin, tr.
Isis 51 (1960) 67-72.

337. _____ . Modo studendi ad fratrem Joannem, Epistola de.   Date
uncertain.

      Parma, vol. 17; Vivès, vol. 28.
      Marietti (1954) Op. Theol. I, 451.

338. _____ . "The Letter of Thomas Aquinas to Brother John De modo
studenti." V. White, tr. Life of the Spirit. Oxford: Blackfriars,
1944. Supplement 161-80.

339. _____ . How to Study, being the letter of St. Thomas Aquinas to
Brother John, De modo studendi. Trans. and exposition by Victor White.
4th ed. London: Blackgriars, 1953. 44 pp.

340. _____ . Motu cordis, De. A.D. 1270-1271.

      Leonine, vol. 43.
      Parma, vol. 16; Vivès, vol. 27.
      Marietti (1954) Op. Philos.
      Perrier, vol. 1, 63-9.

341. _____ . On the Movement of the Heart. V. R. Larkin, tr.
"Thomas Aquinas on the Heart." Journal of the History of Medicine
15 (1960) 22-30.

342. _____ . Occultis operationibus naturae, De. A.D. 1269-1272.

      Leonine, vol. 43.
      Parma, vol. 16; Vivès, vol. 27.
      Marietti (1954) Op. Philos.
      Perrier (1949) 202-10.

343. _____ . The Letter of St. Thomas De occultis... J. B. McAllister,
tr. Washington, D.C.: Catholic University of America Press, 1939.

344. _____ . Officium de festo Corporis Christi. A.D. 1264.

      Parma, vol. 15; Vivès, vol. 29.
      Marietti (1954) Op. Theol. II, 275-81.   No English version.
      The text in the modern Breviary is from the vulgarized printing,
      edited by A. Pizzamano in 1497. Revision by Aquinas of an earlier
      liturgy.
345. _____ . Pater Noster, Collationes super. A.D. 1273.

      Leonine, vol. 44 (not yet published).
      Parma, vol. 16; Vivès, vol. 27.
      Marietti (1954) Op. Theol. II, 221-35.

346. _____ . Trans in: The Three Greatest Prayers. L. Shapcote, tr.
London: Barns, Oates, 1937; Westminster, MD: Newman 1956.

347.   _____. Perfectione vitae spiritualis, De. A.D. 1269-1270.

Leonine, vol. 41B (Rome 1969).
Parma, vol. 15; Vivès, vol. 29.
Marietti (1954) Op. Theol. II, 115-53.

348.   _____. The Religious State, the Episcopate, the Priestly
Office. J. Procter, tr. London: Sands, 1902.

Reprinted by: Westminister, MD: Newman, 1950.

349.   _____. Also trans. by G. J. Guenther, C. G. Kloster, and J. X.
Schmitt, in Three Master's Theses. St. Louis University, 1942-1944.

350.   _____. Perihermenias Aristotelis, Sententia super. A.D.
1270-1271.

Leonine, vol. I (1882).
Parma, vol. 18, 1-83.
Marietti (1955).

351.   _____. Aristotle on Interpretation: Commentary by St. Thomas
and Cajetan. Jean t. Oesterle, tr. Milwaukee: Marquette, 1962.

Pestiferam doctrinam, Contra, see Retrahentes Contra.

352.   _____. Physicam Aristotelis, Sententia super. A.D. 1269-1270.

Leonine, vol. 2 (1884).
Parma, vol. 18.

353.   _____. A. M. Pirotta, ed. Meapoli: D'Auria, 1953.

354.   _____. M. Maggiolo, ed. Marietti: 1954.

355.   _____. Commentary on Aristotle's Physics. R. J. Blackwell, et
al, trs. New Haven: Yale: London: Routledge, 1963. xxxii-599 pp.

356.   _____. Piae Preces. Dates uncertain.

Parma, vol. 24. Vivès, vol. 32.
Marietti (1954) Op. Theol. I, 285-89.
Authenticity doubtful. Just what prayers Thomas composed is un-
certain; there is no point, then, in listing English versions.

357.   _____. Politicorum Aristotelis, Sententia libri. A.D. 1269-
1272. Authentic only to BK III, 6, 1280 ab.

Leonine, vol. 48 (1971) Also contains Tabula Libri Ethicorum.
Parma, vol. 21.
Marietti (1951). No English version. Authentic only to BK #, 6,
1280ab. Quebec: Tremblay et Dion, 1940. Photo-lith. reprint.

RECENT EDITIONS OF LATIN WORKS   358 - 369

358. _____ . Posterior Analytica Aristotelis, Sententia super. A.D.
1269-1272,

   Leonine, vol. I (1882),
   Parma, vol. 18, 226-538.
   Marietti (1955).

359. _____ . Commentary on the Posterior Analytics of Aristotle.
P. H. Conway, and W. H. Kane, tr. Albany, New York: Magi, 1969.

360. _____ . Commentary of the Posterior Analytics of Aristotle.
F. R. Larcher, tr. Albany, New York: Magi Books, 1970. 252 pp.

361. _____ . Principiis naturae, De. A.D. 1252-1256.

   Leonine, vol. 43.
   Perrier (1949) 2-17.
   Marietti (1954) Op. Philos.

362. _____ . Crit. ed.: J. J. Pauson, ed. Fribourg - Louvain:
Textus Philosophici Friburgesses, II, 1950.

363. _____ . Also See: Basil Mattingly. University of Notre Dame
Press, 1957. 355 pp.

364. _____ . On the Principles of Nature. Complete trans. in V. J.
Bourke, The Pocket Aquinas. New York: Pocket Books, 1973. 61-77 pp.

365. _____ . Also R. A. Kocourek, tr. Introduction to the Philosophy
of Nature. St. Paul, Minn: North Central, 1948.

366. _____ . Les principes de la réalité naturelle. Trad par Jean
Madiran. Paris: Nouvelles Editions Latines, 1963.

367. _____ . Propositionibus modalibus, De. A.D. 1244-1245.

   Leonine, vol. 43.
   Parma, vol. 16; Vivès, vol. 27.
   Perrier (1949) 461-4.
   Marietti (1954) Op. Philos. Authenticity probable.

368. _____ . "De modalibus opusculum et doctrina. M. Bochenski, ed.
Angelicum 17 (1940) 180-218. No English version.

369. _____ . Psalmos, Postilla super. A.D. 1272-1273.

   Leonine, vol. 27 (Not yet published).
   Parma, vol. 14.
   Expositio Ps. 52-54, P.A. Uccelli, ed. Roma: 1880.
   No English version. Commentary goes only to Ps. 54.

Potentia Dei, Q.D. de. see Quaest. Disp.

370 - 378   RECENT EDITIONS OF LATIN WORKS

370.   _____.   Quaestiones Disputatae de anima.   A.D. 1269.

Leonine, vol. 24 (Not yet published).
Parma, vol. 8; Vivès, vol. 13.
Marietti (1953) vol. 2.

371.   _____.   Quaestiones, etc.   James H. Robb, ed.   Toronto: Pont.
Inst. Med. Studies, 1968.   282 pp.

372.   _____.   The Soul.   J. P. Rowan, tr.   St. Louis: Herder, 1949.

Translation of St. Thomas Aquinas' Work.

372A.   _____.   Quaestio disputata utrum anima conjuncta cognoscat
seipsam per essentiam.   Unedited, text in Oxford, Bodlerian, Cod. Laud.
Misc. 480.

Attributed to St. Thomas by Dondaine and Pelster; see Eschmann,
Catalogue, no. 4.

373.   _____.   Quaestis Disputata de caritate.   A.D. 1269-1272.

Leonine, vol. 24 (Not yet published).
Parma, vol. 8.
Marietti (1953) vol, 2.

374.   _____.   On Charity.   Lottie H. Kendzierski, tr.   Milwaukee:
Marquette, 1960.   115 pp.

375.   _____.   Quaestiones disputatae de correctione farterna, de spe,
de virtutibut cardinalibus.   A.D. 1269-1272.

Leonine, vol. 24 (Not yet published)
Parma, vol. 8.
Marietti (1953) vol. 2.   No English versions.

376.   _____.   Quaestio disputata de immortalitate animae.   Date uncertain.

Leonine, vol. 24.   (Not yet published).
Text in: Ms Vat. lat. 781, fol. 47^r-48^r considered authentic by
Dondaine & Eschmann.   Microfilm obtainable from Vatican Microfilms,
Saint Louis University Library, St. Louis, MO. 63103.   No English
version.

377.   _____.   Quaestiones disputatae de malo.   A.D. 1266-1267.

Leonine, vol. 23 (Not yet published).
Parma, vol. 8.
Marietti (1953) vol. 2.   No English version.

378.   _____.   Quaestiones disputatae de potentia.   A.D. 1265-1266.

RECENT EDITIONS OF LATIN WORKS   379 - 388

Leonine, vol. 21 (Not yet published).
Parma, vol. 8.
Marietti (1953) Turin.

379. _____. On the Power of God. L. Shapcote, tr. 3 vols. London:
Burns, Oates; New York: Benziger 1932-1934.

Reprinted in one vol. Westminster, MD: Newman, 1952.

380. _____. Quaestiones disputatae de spiritualibus creaturis. A.D.
1267-1268.

Leonine, vol. 24 (Not yet published).
Parma, vol. 8.
Marietti (1953) vol. 2.

381. _____. De Spiritualibus creaturis. L. W. Keeler, ed. Rome:
Gregorianum, 1946.

382. _____. On Spiritual Creatures. M. C. Fitzpatrick and J. J.
Wellmuth, trs. Milwaukee: Marquette University, 1951. 135 pp.

383. _____. Quaestio disputata de unione verbi increati. A.D. 1272.

Leonine, vol. 24. (Not yet published).
Parma, vol. 8; Vivès, vol. 13.
Marietti (1953) vol. 2. No English version.

384. _____. Quaestiones disputatae de veritate. A.D. 1256-1259.

Leonine, vol. 22 (Three parts, Rome 1970-1976).
Marietti (1953, 1961, and other dates; Turin.
Parma, vol. 9.

385. _____. On Truth. R. W. Mulligan, J.V. McGlynn, and R.W. Schmidt,
trs. Chicago: Regnery, 1952-1954. 3 vols.

386. _____. Quaestiones quodlibetales. A.D. 1256-1259 & 1269-1272.

Leonine, vol. 25 (Not yet published).
Parma, vol. 9; Vivès, vol. 18. P. Mandonnet, ed. Paris: Lethielleux, 1926. Marietti (1949). No English version.

387. _____. Quaestis Disputata De virtutibus in communi. A.D. 1269-
1272.

Leonine, vol. 24 (Not yet Published).
Parma, vol. 8.
Marietti (1953) vol. 2.

388. _____. On the Virtues in General. J. P. Reid, tr. Providence,
R.I.: Providence College, 1951.

389 - 400   RECENT EDITIONS OF LATIN WORKS

389.   . Rationibus fidei contra Saracenos, Graecos et Armenos
ad Cantorem Antiochiae, De.   A.D. 1264.

    Leonine, vol. 40B (Rome 1969).
    Parma, vol. 16; Vivès, vol. 27.
    Marietti (1954) Op. Theol. I, 417-426. No complete English version,
    but chap. v: "Why did God the Son become Man?" H. Nash, tr. Life
    of the Spirit. London: Blackfriars, 1952. 245-47 pp.

390.   . Regimine Judaeorum, De.   A.D. 1270-1271.

    Leonine, vol. 42.
    Parma, vol. 16; Vivès, vol. 27.
    Marietti (1954) Op. Philos.

391.   . "De regimine subditorum." I, 213-19. Perrier, ed.

392.   . Also Joseph Mathis, ed. Turin: Marietti, 1948.

    No English version.

393.   . Regno, De. seu De regimine principum. A.D. 1265-1267.

    Leonine, vol. 44 (Not yet published).
    Parma, vol. 16; Vivès, vol. 27.
    Marietti (1954) Op. Philos.
    Perrier (1947) 223-67. Authentic only to II, cap. 4.

394.   . Jos. Mathis, ed. 2d ed. Taurini: Marietti, 1948.

395.   . On Kingship. G. B. Phelan and I. Th. Eschmann, trs.
Toronto: PIMS, 1949. 149 pp.

396.   . El regimen politico. Victorino Rodriguez, tr.   Madrid:
Fuerza Nueva, 1978. 184 pp.

397.   . Retrahentes, contra, seu, Contra Doctrinam retrahentium
a religione. A.D. 1271.

    Leonine, vol. 41C (Rome 1969).
    Parma, vol. 15; Vivès, vol. 29.
    Marietti (1954) Op. Theol. II, 159-90.

398.   . An Apology for the Religious Orders. J. Procter, tr.
London: Sands, 1902; Westminster, MD: Newman, 1950.

399.   . Contro la dottrina pestilenziale di coloro che distlgono
gli uomini dall'abbraeciare la vita religiosa. Traddel Bonifacio Borghini
Siena: Cantagalli, 1975.

400.   . Sacrae Scripturae, Principia I et II, Commendatio. A.D.
1256.

RECENT EDITIONS OF LATIN WORKS   401 - 407

Leonine, vol. 44 (Not yet published).
Parma (1948) vol. i, xxvi-xxx.
Marietti, Opuscula Theologica (1954) I, 435-43.
Mandonnet, P. Opuscula Omnia (Paris 1927) IV, 481-90.
No complete English version of these inaugural lectures: See
V. J. Bourke, Aquinas' Search for Wisdom (1964) 61-62 pp. for
partial version.

401.   . Secreto, De. A.D. 1269.

Leonine, vol. 42.
Parma, vol. 24; Vivès, vol. 32.
Marietti (1954) Op. Theol. I, 447-8; ed. Mandonnet, Opuscula, IV
497-501. No complete English version of this committee report
in which Thomas participated. For an English summary see V.J.
Bourke, Aquinas' Search for Wisdom, 143-6.

402.   . Sensu et sensato Aristotelis, Sententia de. A.D. 1270.

Leonine, vol. 45 (not yet published).
Parma, vol. 20; Vivès, vol. 24.
Marietti (1949). No English version.

403.   . Sententiarum, Scriptum super IV libros,   A.D. 1252-1256.

Parma, vols, 6-8; Mandonnet-Moos ed. Paris: Lethielleux, 1933-47,
4 vols. finishing at Book IV, dist. 22.
Lonine, vols. 17-20 (Not yet published). No English version.

404.   . Sermo de festo corporis Christi. A.D. 1264.

Leonine, vol. 44 (Not yet published).
Parma, vol. 24, 230-1; Vivès, vol. 32, 680-2. No English version.

405.   . Sermones. Dates uncertain.

Leonine, vol. 44 (Not yet published). Bertrand Guyot is editing
the few sermons now known. Almost all sermones printed in the
Opera Omnia, e.g. the Piana ed. vol. 16, are spurious.
Vivès, vol. 32, 663-815, prints nine possibly authentic sermons.
No English version.

406.   . Sortibus ad Dominum Jacobum de Burgo, De. A.D. 1271.

Leonine, vol. 43 (1976).
Parma, vol. 16; Vivès, vol. 27.
Marietti (1954) Op. Theol. I, 159-67. No English version.

Spe, Q.D. de, see Quaest. Disp.

Spiritualibus creaturis, Q.D. de, see Quaest. Disp.

407.   . Substantiis separatis, De seu de angelorum natura.

408 - 418   RECENT EDITIONS OF LATIN WORKS

A.D. 1271-1273.

      Leonine, vol. 40D (Rome 1967-1968).
      Parma, vol. 16; Vivès, vol. 27.
      Marietti (1954) 21-58, Op. Philos.

408. _____. Crit. ed. by F. J. Lescoe, ed. West Hartford, CT: St.
Joseph's College 1962, 207 pp.

409. _____. Treatise on Separate Substances. F. J. Lescoe, tr.
West Hartfort, CT: St. Joseph's College, 1959.

410. _____. Summa theologiae. A.D. 1266-1272.

      Five vols. with notes by I.T. Eschmann. Ottawa: Studium Generalis,
      1941. Best Latin text available.
      Leonine, vols. 4-12 (Rome 1888-1906). Reprinted without apparatus,
      Turin: Mariette, 1948 (4 vols); and Madrid: Biblioteca de Autores
      Cristianos, 1952 (5 vols.)

411. _____. Latin and English: T. Gilby, ed. London - New York:
Eyre and Spottiswoode - McGraw Hill, 1964-1974. 60 vols.

412. _____. Summa Theologica. Trans. by the English Dominicans.
22 vols. London: Burns, Oates & Washbourne 1912-36; reprinted in 3
vols. New York: Benziger 1947-1948.

413. _____. Basic Writings of St. Thomas. 2 vols. A. C. Pegis, ed.
New York: Random House, 1944.

      Contains about half of S.T. in English.

414. _____. Summa theologica. Die deutsche Thomas Ausgabe.
Heidelberg - München: Kerle; Leipzig - Salzburg: Pustet, 1940ff. Bd.
3 (1940) ff.

415. _____. Somme théologique. A.D. Sertillanges et alu. Paris:
Revue des Jeunes, 1925-1967.

      About 60 vols.

416. _____. Thoma Akuinatou: Soumma Theologike. (The Summa
theologiae in Greek), 15 vols. now published. Demetriou Kydone, tr.

      Athenai: Ekdosis Idrymatos Ereynes kai Ekdoseon Neohellenikes
      Philosophias; Athens: Foundation for Research in Neo-Hellenic
      Philosophy, 1976.

417. _____. Theologische Summa van den H. Thomas van Aquino.
Latynische en Nederlandsche tekst uitgegeven door een groep Dominicanen.
Antwerpen: Geloofsverdediging. 1940ff. In many volumes.

418. _____. S. Tomaz de Aquino, Suma Teológica. Trad. portugueza...

RECENT EDITIONS OF LATIN WORKS   419 - 427A

por Alexandro Correia.   Sao Paolo: Faculdade de Filosofia.   1945 ff.

In Many volumes.

419. _____ . Summa de veritate Catholicae fidei contra Gentiles.
A.D. 1259-1264.

Leonine, vols. 13-15 (1918-1930); Turin: Marietti, 1961-1967,
3 vols.

420. _____ . On the Truth of the Catholic Faith. Pegis, Anderson,
Bourke, O'Neil, trs. New York: Doubleday, 1955-1957. 5 vols.

Reprint: Notre Dame University Press, 1975, 5 vols.

421. _____ . Summa contra Gentiles, Exposition of the Truth
of the Catholic Faith. Trans. into Chinese by Matthias Lu. 4 vols.
Hong Kong: Shang Wu Press, 1970-1972.

422. _____ . Of God and His Creatures... trans. of Summa contra
Gentiles of St. Thomas Aquinas by Joseph Rickaby. Westminster, MD:
Carroll Press, 1950. xxi-428 pp.

Reprinted from the incomplete version of 1905.

423. _____ . Contra Gentiles. Texts latine. (et)...trad. francaise
par R. Bernier et alü. 4 vols. Paris: Lethielleux, 1951-1961.

424. _____ . Somma contro i Gentili. T. S. Centi, ed. Torino:
UTET, 1975. 1368 pp.

425. _____ . Suma contra los gentiles. Ed. bilingue con el texto
critico de la leonina. 2 vols. B.A.C. Madrid: Editorial Catolica,
1952-1953.

426. _____ . Summa contra Gentiles oder Die Verteidigung der höchsten
Wahrheiten...übersetzt...von Helmut Fahsel. Zurich: Fraumünster-Verlag,
1942.

Trinitate, In Boethium De, see Boethii

Unione verbi increati, Q.D. de, see Quaest. Disp.

427. _____ . De unitate intellectus contra Averroistas. A.D. 1270.

Leonine, vol. 43.
Parma, vol. 16; Vivès, vol. 27.
Marietti (1954) Op. Philos. 63-90.

427A. _____ . Crit. ed. L. W. Keeler, ed. Roma: Gregorianiem, 1936.

Trattato sull'unità dell'intelletto contro gli averroisti, versione
italiana di Bruno Nardi. Firenze, 1947.

427B. _____ . The Trinity and the Unicity of the Intellect. Rose
E. Brennan, tr. St. Louis: Herder, 1946.

427C. _____ . On the Unity of the Intellect. B. Zedler, trd.
Milwaukee: Marquette University Press, 1968. 96 pp.

Veritate, Q.D. de, see Quaest. Disp.

Virtutibus, Q.D. de, see Quaest. Disp.

428. Pseudo - Thomas Aquinas. Aurora consurgens: A Document attributed
to Thomas Aquinas on the Problem of Opposites in Alchemy. Marie-Louise
von Franz, ed. New York: Pantheon Books, 1966.

    Spurious.

429. _____ . De natura materiae, Attributed to St. Thomas Aquinas.
Introd. and text...by J. M. Wyss. Fribourg (Suisse): Societé Philos.:
Louvain: Nauwelaerts, 1953. 135 pp.

    Spurious. No English version.

SELECTIONS IN TRANSLATION

430. Anonymous. Textes Philosophiques, en usage à la faculté de philosophie, University Laval (Québec). Mimeographiés.

    Latin opuscula of St. Thomas and separate books from his Comment-
    aries on Aristotle, plus sections from the Latin Commentaries by
    John of St. Thomas and Cajetan. Sold in about 100 separate
    fascicles at various prices for class use. Some French and English
    versions also available. Québec: Librairie Philosophique M. Doyon,
    mimeographed at various times in the post 1940 period.

431. Aquinas Scripture Series. Albany: New York: Magi Books, 1966.

    Vol. I, Commentary on St. Paul's Epistle to the Galatians, F.R.
    Larcher, 1966. Vol. 2, Commentary on St. Paul's Epistle to the
    Ephesians. M.L. Lamb, tr., 1966. Vol. 3, On St. Paul's Epistle
    to the Philippians and First Thessalonians. F.R. Larcher, tr.,
    1969.

432. Anderson, James F. ed. An Introduction to the Metaphysics of St.
Thomas Aquinas. Chicago: Regnery, 1953.

433. _____ . St. Thomas Aquinas: Teatise on God. Texts selected and
translated by J.F.A. Englewood Cliffs, N.J.: Prentice-Hall, 1963. 180pp.

434. Beuchot, Mauricio, tr. "Del Maestro (De Veritate) Introduccion y
Traduccion de Mauricio Beuchot." Revista Filosofica. Mexico. 9 (1976)
365-85.

SELECTIONS IN TRANSLATION   435 - 449

435. Bigongiari, Dino, ed. The Political Ideas of St. Thomas Aquinas.
New York: Hafner, 1953. 254 pp.

436. Bourke, V. J., ed. The Pocket Aquinas. New York: Washington
Square Press, 1960, 1973. xxvi-372 pp.

437. Callan, C. J. Sermon Matter from St. Thomas Aquinas on the Epistles
and Gospels. St. Louis: B. Herder, 1950.

438. Cantor, N. F. and P. L. Klein, eds. Medieval Thought: Augustine
and Thomas Aquinas. Monuments of Western Thought. Waltham, Mass:
Blaisdell Pub. Co., 1969. 199 pp.

439. Tomas de Aquino, Santo. Sobre la eternidad del mundo. Suma contra
los Gentiles. Suma teológica. seleción. Trad...por Angel J. Cappelletti.
Buenos Aires: Edición Aquilar, 1975. 136 pp.

440. Ciampini, Raffaele, ed. I. Santi Evangeli col commento che da
scelti passi de' Padri ne fa Tommaso d'Aquino. Firenze: Sansoni, 1973.
LXIV-951 pp.

441. Clark, Mary T., ed. An Aquinas Reader. Selections from the
Writings of Thomas Aquinas. Garden City, N.Y.: Doubleday Image, 1972.
597 pp.

442. Conway, P., tr. St. Thomas Aquinas on Aristotle's Love and
Friendship. Providence: Providence College Press, 1951. 148 pp.

443. D'Entreves, A. P., ed. and J. G. Dawson, tr. Aquinas, Selected
Political Writings. Oxford: Blackwell, 1948; New York: Barnes and
Noble, 1959.

444. Farrell, Walter and M. J. Healey, eds. My Way of Life. Pocket
Edition of St. Thomas. The Summa Simplified. Brooklyn: Confraternity
of the Precious Blood, 1952.

445. Freeman, Eugene and Joseph Owens, eds. Wisdom and Ideas of St.
Thomas Aquinas. New York: Fawcett World, 1970.

446. Gilby, Thomas, tr. St. Thomas Aquinas Philosophical Texts. New
York: Oxford University Press, 1951, 1960. 427 pp.

447. _____. St. Thomas Aquinas Theological Texts. New York: Oxford
University Press, 1955. 441 pp.

448. Goodwin, Robert P., ed. Selected Writings of Thomas Aquinas.
Indianapolis: Bobbs Merrill, 1965. 183 pp.

449. Inagaki, Yoshinori, tr. Ho ni tsuite. On Law. Nagoya: Catholic
University Press, 1958.

       Japanese version of S.T., 1-11,qq. 90-7.

450 - 462   SELECTIONS IN TRANSLATION

450. Keraly, Hugues, tr. Préface à la politique. Proemium, In libros Politicorum. Traduction et explication. Paris: Nouvelles Editions Latines, 1974.

451. _____. Prefacio a la politica. Proemio e explicacion por Hugues Keraly. Mexico: Editorial Tradicion, 1976. 143 pp.

452. Kokubu, K., tr. Ningen-Ron. Treatise on Man. Nagoya: Catholic University Press, 1949.

   Japanese version of S.T., I,qq. 75-89.

453. Lopes, Jesus Carcia, tr. Doctrina de Santo Tomás sobre la verdad. Commentarios a la Cuestion I. De Veritate y trad. castellana. Pamplona: Ed. University de Navarra, 1967.

454. McEniry, E. C., tr. St. Thomas Aquinas, Meditations for Every Day. Translated and illustrated. Columbus, Ohio: Long's College Book Co. 1951. xiv-536 pp.

455. Mamiani, Maurizio, tr. S. Tommaso la Verità. Quaestio I de Veri-tate. "Studium Sapientiae," 13. Padova: Liviana Editrice, 1970. 209 pp.

456. Maritain, Raissa, ed. The Divine Ways; a little work of St. Thomas Aquinas. Margaret Sumner, tr. Detroit, Mich: Basilian Press, 1946. 45 pp.

457. Mennesier, A. I., tr. L'Homme chrétien. Textes choisis, traduits et présentes par A. I. Mennessier. Paris: Editions du Cerf. 1965.

457A. _____. Pattern for a Christian According to St. Thomas Aquinas. N. Halligan, tr. New York: Alba House, 1975.

458. Oesterle, John A., tr. Thomas Aquinas, Treatise on the Virtues. Englewood Cliffs, N.J.: Prentice-Hall, 1966.

459. O'Neill, F., tr. St. Thomas, The Blessed Sacrament and the Mass. Westminster, MD: Newman, 1955.

   With notes by the translator.

460. Papadopoulos, Stylianos G. Hellēnikai metaphraseis Thōmistikōn ergōn. Athens: Bibliothēkē tēs en Athanais Philekpaideutikes Hetaiīeias, 1967. 200 pp.

461. Pegis, A. C., ed. Basic Writings of St. Thomas Aquinas. 2 vols. New York: Random House, 1945. 1097 and 1179 pp.

   Extensive selections from S.T. and S.C.G.

462. _____. Introduction to Saint Thomas Aquinas. New York: Random House, 1948. xxx-690 pp.

STUDIES OF CERTAIN WRITINGS   463 - 478

463. Pieper, Josef, ed. The Human Wisdom of St. Thomas: A Breviary of Philosophy from the Works of Thomas Aquinas. Drostan MacLaren, tr. New York: Sheed and Ward, 1948.

464. Religious of C.S.M.V., trs. The Golden Chain: Selections from the 'Catena Aurea' of St. Thomas. London: Mowbray, 1956. 90 pp.

465. Rolfes, Eugen, tr. Thomas von Aquin, Fünf Fragen über die intellektuelle Erkenntnis. S.T. I, 84-88. Übers. und erkl. von Eugen Rolfes. 2 Aufl. Hamburg: Meiner, 1977. xiv-126.

466. Saranyana, José I., ed. Tomas de Aquino, Santo. Escritos de Catequesis. Edición dirigida por José I. Saranyana. Madrid: Rialp, 1974. 350 pp.

467. Siewerth, Gustav, ed. Die menschliche Willensfreiheit. Text... von Gustav Siewerth. Düsseldorf: Schwann, 1954.

468. Tommaso d'Aquino, San. Opuscoli teologico-spirituali. Roma: Paoline, 1976. 297 pp.

469. Vries, J. De. De cognitione veritatis. Textus selecti S. Thomae Aquinae. Ed altera, Munster: Aschendorff, 1953. 62 pp.

STUDIES OF CERTAIN WRITINGS

470. Allard, Guy-H. "Le 'Contra Gentiles' et le modèle rhétorique," in Laval Thomas d'Aquin (Symp) 237-50.

471. Banez, Domingo. Commentarios ineditos a la Prima secundae de santo Tomás. Ed. V. Beltran de Heredia, 3 vols. Madrid: Instituto Francisco Suarez, 1942-1948.

472. Bataillon, Louis-Jacques. "Les Sermons de s. Thomas et la Catena Aurea," in St. Thomas Aquinas 1274-1974. I, 61-75.

473. Bernard, A. Présentation de la Somme Théologique. Avignon: Maison Aubanel Père, 1954. 172 pp.

474. Bertamini, T. "La Bolla 'Transiturus" di papa Urbano IV e l' Ufficio del 'Corpus Domini' secondo il codice di s. Lorenzo di Bognanco." Aevum 42 (1968) 29-58.

475. Bird, Otto. "How to Read an Article of the Summa." The New Scholasticism 27 (1953) 129-59.

476. Bobik, Joseph. The Commentary of Conrad of Prussia on the De Ente et Essentia of St. Thomas Aquinas. The Hague: Nijhoff, 1974. 203 pp.

477. Bourke, Vernon J. "Faith and Reason: Summa Theologiae by St. Thomas Aquinas." Commonweal 101 (November, 1974) 166-8.

478. _____. "The Pseudo-Thomistic De potentiis animae." St. Louis Univ. Studies I (1945) 39-51.

479 - 492 STUDIES OF CERTAIN WRITINGS

479. _____. "The Unauthenticity of the De intellectu et intelligibili Attributed to St. Thomas Aquinas." The New Scholasticism 14 (1940) 325-45.

480. Boyer, Charles. "Introduction à la Somme Théologique de s. Thomas d'Aquin." Doctor Communis 27 (1974) 13-29.

481. Brady, Ignatius. "John Peckham and the Background of Aquinas' De aeternitate mundi," in St. Thomas Aquinas 1274-1974. (Symp) II, 141-78.

482. Bukowski, Thomas P. "An Early Dating for Aquinas' 'De Aeternitate Mundi.'" Gregorianum 51 (1970) 277-304.

483. Busa, Roberto. "L'attualità dell'impostazione linguistica che san Tommaso dà alla filosofia." Presenca Filosofica. Sao Paulo 1-3 (1974) 186-94.

484. Caparello, Adriana. "Presenza della lingua greca in due commentari tomistici." Doctor Communis 30 (1977) 250-69.

485. _____. "La terminologia greca nel Commentario al De caelo, Tommaso d'Aquino e lingua greca." Angelicum 55 (1978) 415-57.

486. Casciaro, Josè M. "Santo Tomàs ante sus fuentes. Estudio sobra la II-II, q. 173, art. 3. Universidad de Navarra: Scripta Theologica 6 (1974) 11-65.

487. Charette, Lèon. Commentaire de Saint Thomas d'Aquin sur la Politique d'Aristote. Ottawa: University of Ottawa Dissertation, 1967.

488. Chenu, M.-D. "La date du commentaire de s. Thomas sur le De Trinitate de Boèce." Les Sciences philosophiques et théologiques. 2 (1941-1942) 432-34.

489. Congar, Yves. "Le moment 'économique' et le moment 'ontologique' dans la Sacra doctrina (Rèvèlation, Thèologie Somme thèologique)," in Mèlanges...Chenu (Symp) Paris: Bibliothèque Thomiste, 1967. 135-87.

490. Conrad of Prussia, 14th Century. Commentary on the De Ente et Essentia of St. Thomas Aquinas. Intro. and comments by Joseph Bobik. Transcription of the MS by James A. Corbett and J. Bobik. The Hague: Nijhoff, 1974. x-203.

491. Contenson, P. De. "Principles, Methods, and Problems of the Critical Edition of the Works of Saint Thomas as Presented in the Leonine Edition." Tijdschrift voor Philosophie (1974) 342-64.

492. Cranz, F. Edward. "The Publishing History of the Aristotle Commentaries of Thomas Aquinas." Traditio 34 (1978) 157-92.

STUDIES OF CERTAIN WRITINGS   493 - 508

493. Crowe, Michael B. "The Date of St. Thomas's Commentary on the Sentences." Irish Theological Quarterly 24 (1957) 310-9.

494. _____. "St. Thomas against the Gentiles." Irish Theological Quarterly 29 (1962) 93-120.

495. Decloux, Simon. Temps, Dieu, liberté dans les commentaires aristotéliciens de s. Thomas d'Aquin. Bruges: Desclée, 1967. 262 pp.

496. Delaisse, L. M. J. "A la recherche des origines de l'Office du Corpus Christi dans les manuscrits liturgiques." Scriptorium 4 (1950) 220-39.

497. Dondaine, Antoine. "Un commentaire scripturaire de Roland de Crémone sur le livre de Job." Archivum Fratrum Praedicatorum 11 (1941) 107-37.

498. _____. "La lettre de s. Thomas à l'ablé du Montcassin." in St. Thomas Aquinas 1274-1974. Vol. I, 87-108.

499. _____. "Nicolas de cotrone et les sources du Contra errores Graecorum de s. Thomas d'Aquin." Divus Thomas. Fribourg. 28 (1950) 313-40.

500. _____. "Les, 'opuscula fratris Thomae chez Ptolomée de Lucques." Archivum Fratrum Praedicatorum 31 (1961) 152ff.

501. Dondaine, H. F. "Le Contra errores Graecorum de s. Thomas et le IVe liore du Contra Gentiles." Les Sciences philosophiques et théologiques I (1941) 156-62.

502. Doyle, A. I. "A Prayer Attributed to St. Thomas Aquinas." Dominican Studies I (1948) 229-38.

503. Doyle, John J. "The Summa in Symbols: A Reply." The Thomist 32 (1968) 238-44.

504. Duin, J. J. "Nouvelles précisions sur la chronologie du Commentum in Metaphysicam de s. Thomas." Revue Philosophique de Louvain 53 (1955) 511-24.

505. Duska, R. "Aquinas' Definition of Good: Ethical-Theoretical Notes on De Veritate, Q. 21." The Monist 58 (1974) 151-62.

506. Elders, Leo. "Le commentaire sur le quatrième livre de la Méta-physique," in Tommaso d'Aquino (Symp) I, 203-14.

507. _____. Faith and Science, An Introduction to St. Thomas' Expositio in Boethii De Trinitate. Roma: Herder, 1974. 146 pp.

508. _____. "Structure et fonction de l'argument 'sed contra' dans la Somme théologique de s. Thomas." Divus Thomas. Piacenza. 80(1977)245-60.

509 - 524   STUDIES OF CERTAIN WRITINGS

509. Erni, R. Die Theologische Summe des Thomas von Aquin in ihrem Grundbau. 3 vols. Luzern: Räber, 1947-1950. 206, 316, 173 pp.

510. Farrell, Walter. A Companion to the Summa Theologiae. 4 vols. New York: Sheed and Ward, 1938-1942. 457, 720, 266, 474 pp.

Reissued in 1976 with 1918 pp.

511. Fiorentino, Fernando. "Osservazioni sul commento di San Tommaso al 'De Caelo' di Aristotele." Sapienza 27 (1974) 429-40.

512. Fries, Albert. "Thomas und die Quaestio de immoralitate animae." Diuvs Thomas. Fribourg. 31 (1953) 18-52.

513. Garrigou-Lagrange, Réginald. The One God, a Commentary on the First Part of St. Thomas' Theological Summa. Bede Rose, tr. St. Louis: Herder, 1943. viii-736 pp.

514. _____. The Trinity and God the Creator: Comm. on S.T. I, qq. 27-119. Frederic C. Eckhoff, tr. St. Louis: B. Herder, 1952. vi-675 pp.

515. _____. Commentarium in Summan theologicam S. Thomae. De Deo uno. Torino: Berruti, 1950. 582 pp.

516. _____. De beatitudine, de actibus humanis et habitibus. Torino: Berruti, 1951. 485 pp.

517. _____. De gratia. Torino: Berruti, 1947. 431 pp.

518. _____. De virtutibus theologicis. Torino: Berruti, 1949. xi-584 pp.

519. _____. De Eucharistia. Torino: Berruti, 1948. 438 pp.

520. _____. De Deo Trino et Creatore: Comm. in S.T. i, qq. 27-99. Taurini: Marietti; Paris: Desclée, 1944. 466 pp.

521. _____. Beatitude: a Commentary on St. Thomas' Theological Summa, I-II, qq. 1-54. Patrick Cummins, tr. St. Louis: Herder, 1956. vi-397 pp.

522. _____. Grace: a Comm. on S.T. I-II, qq. 109-114. Trans. Dominican Nuns, Corpus Christi Monastery, California. St. Louis: B. Herder, 1952. 535 pp.

523. _____. Christ the Savior: A Commentary on the Third Part of St. Thomas's Theological Summa. B. Rose, tr. St. Louis: Herder, 1950. iv-748 pp.

524. Gatto, Edo Peter. The Doctrine in the Opusculum, De Natura Generis Attributed to St. Thomas. Canada: University of Toronto Dissertation, 1963. 144 pp.

STUDIES OF CERTAIN WRITINGS   525 - 540

525. Gauthier, R. A. "La Date du commentaire de s. Thomas sur l'
Ethique à Nicomaque." Recherches de théologie ancienne et médiévale
18 (1951) 66-105.

526. _____. "Praefatio," in S. Thomae, Sententia Libri Ethicorum.
Roma: Commissio Leonina, 1969. vol. 47, 1-275 pp.

527. Geiger, Louis B. "Les rédactions successives de Contra Gentiles
I, 53 d'après l'autographe," in S. Thomas Aujourd'hui (Symp) 221-40.

528. Glorieux, Palémon. "Autour des opuscules. Thomas d'Aquin on
Thomas de Sutton." Melanges de Science Religieuse 31 (1974) 113-20.

529. _____. "Autour du Contra errores Graecorum." in Autour d'
Aristote: Recueil d'études offert à Mgr. A. Monsion. Louvain: 1955.
497-512.

530. _____. "Essai sur les Commentaires scripturaires de s. Thomas
et leur chronologie." Recherches de théologie ancienne et médiévale
17 (1950) 237-66.

531. _____. La littérature quodlibetique de 1225 à 1320. Paris:
Vrin. 1965.

532. _____. "Le plus beau Quodlibet de s. Thomas est-il de lui?"
Mélanges de sciences religieuse 3 (1946) 235-68.

533. _____. "Pour la chronologie de la Somme." Mélanges de science
religieuse   2 (1945) 59-98.

534. _____. "Les Quodlibets VII à XI de s. Thomas d'Aquin."
Recherches de théologie ancienne et médiévale 13 (1946) 282-303.

535. Grabmann, Martin. "Die Autographe von Werken des hl. Thomas von
Aquin." Historisches Jahrbuch   60 (1940) 514-37.

536. _____. "Die Schrift De rationibus fidei contra Saracenos
Graecos et Armenos...des hl. Thomas von Aquin." Scholastik 17 (1942)
187-216.

537. _____. Die theologische Erkenntnis - und Einleitungslehre und
die philosophische Wissenschaftstheorie des hl. Thomas von Aquin auf
Grund seiner Schrift In Boethium de trinitate. Freiburg/Sch: Paulusverlag, 1947.

538. Guindon, Roger. "A propos de la chronologie du Compendium theologiae
de s. Thomas d'Aquin." Revue de l'Université d'Ottawa 26 (1956) 193-214.

539. Höhn, Erich. "Koln als der Ort der ersten Kommentare zur S.T. des
Thomas von Aquin." in Thomas...Interpretation (Symp) 641-55.

540. Isaac, Jean. "Le Quodlibet IX est bien de s. Thomas." Archives
d'histoire doctrinale et littéraire du Moyen Age 22-23 (1948) 145-85.

541. Jaffa, Harry V. Thomism and Aristotelianism: A Study of the
Commentary by St. Thomas Aquinas on the Nichomachean Ethics of Aristotle.
New York: New School for Social Research Dissertation, 1951. 354 pp.

542. _____. Thomism and Aristoteliansim. A Study of the Commentary
by Thomas Aquinas on the Nicomachean Ethics. Chicago: University of
Chicago Press, 1952. 230 pp.

543. Joannis de s. Thoma. Cursus theologicus in Primam Secundae. De
donis Spiritus Sancti. Ed. Armand Mathieu et Hervé Gagné. Québec:
Université Laval, 1948. xv-383 pp.

544. _____. Cursus theologicus in Primam Secundae. De Habitibus
Ed. Armand Mathieu et Hervé Gagné. Québec: Université Laval, 1949.
xv-357 pp.

545. _____. Cursus theologicus in Secundam Secundae. Ed. Armand
Mathieu et Hervé Gagné. De caritate, 1953. xxxvii-225 pp.

546. _____. De spe. 1953 xxvi-243.

547. _____. De virtutibus, 1952. xxxiv-576.

548. Kaeppeli, Thomas. "Fr. Baxianus von Lodi, Adressat der Responsio
ad lectorem Venetum des hl. Thomas." Archivum Fratrum Praedicatorum
13 (1943) 181-2.

549. _____. "Una raccolta di prediche attribuite a san Tommaso d'
Aquino." Archivum Fratrum Praedicatorum 13 (1943) 59-94.

550. Kuerzinger, J. "Eine Handschrift zum Klagelieder-Kommentar des hl.
Thomas von Aquin." Biblica 23 (1942) 306-317.

551. Lafont, Ghislain. "Simbolo degli apostoli e metodo teologico: il
'Compendium Theologiae' di San Tommaso." Scuola Cattolica. Milano.
102 (1974) 557-68.

552. _____. Structures et méthodes dans la Somme Théologique de s.
Thomas d'Aquin. Bruges/Paris: Desclée, 1961. 494 pp.

553. Lambot, C. "L'Office de la Fête-Dieu, Apercus nouveaux sur ses
origines." Revue Bénédictine 54 (1942) 61-123.

554. Leclercq, Jean. "Un sermon inédit de s. Thomas sur la royauté du
Christ." Revue Thomiste 54 (1946) 158-60.

555. Lescoe, Francis J. "De Substantus Separatus: Title and Date," in
St. Thomas Aquinas 1274-1974 (Symp) I, 51-66.

556. Lorite, Jose. "Preliminares al estadio del estatuto cientifico de
la Suma Teológica." Pensamiento 30 (1974) 289-305.

STUDIES OF CERTAIN WRITINGS   557 - 575

557. Lumbreras P. Praelectiones scholasticae in S.T. D. Thomae. Romae: Angelicum. 12 vols.

558. _____. Vol. 2. De actibus humanis. 1950. xi-298 pp.

559. _____. Vol. 3. De habitibus et virt. in comm. 1950. 282 pp.

560. _____. Vol. 4. De vitiis et peccatis. 1935.

561. _____. Vol. 6. De gratia. 1947. xi-191 pp.

562. _____. Vol. 7. De fide, 1937.

563. _____. Vol. 9. De prudentia. 1952. xi-120 pp.

564. _____. Vol. 10. De justitia. 1938.

565. _____. Vol. 11. De fortitudine et temperantia. 1939.

566. McWilliams, James A. Physics and Philosophy, A Study of St. Thomas' Commentary on the Eight Books of Aristotle's Physics. Washington: American Catholic Philosophical Association, 1945.

567. Mansion, Auguste. "Autour de la date du commentaire de s. Thomas sur l'Ethique a Nicomaque." Revue Philosophique de Louvain 50 (1952) 460-71.

568. Mansion, Suzanne. "L'intelligibilité métaphysique d àprès le 'Prooemium' du commentaire de saint Thomas a la 'Métaphysique' d'Aristote." Rivista Filosofia Neoscholastica 70 (1978) 49-62.

569. Martin, C. "The Vulgate Text of Aquinas' Commentary on Aristotle's Politics." Dominican Studies 5 (1952) 35-64.

570. Martin, R. "Notes critiques au sujet de l'Opuscule IX de s. Thomas." Melanges Auguste Pelzer. Louvain. (1947) 303-23.

571. Mathews, Paul Luke. A Study of the Literary Background and the Methodology of St. Thomas' Commentary on the Posterior Analytics of Aristotle. St. Louis: Saint Louis University Dissertation, 1958.

572. Mendoza, Celina A. L. "Los Comentarios de Santo Tomas y de Robert Grosseteste a la 'Fisica' de Aristoteles." Sapientia 25 (1970) 257-94.

573. Minio-Paluello, L. "L'ignota versione Moerbekiana del Secondi Analitici da san Tommaso." Rivista de filosofia neoscolastica 44 (1952) 389-97.

574. _____. "Les 'trois redactions' de la traduction médiévale grécolatine du De generatione et corruptione d'Aristote." Revue philosophique de Louvain 48 (1950) 247-59.

575. Mohr, Walter. "Bemerkungen zur Verfasserschaft von De regimine

576 - 590   STUDIES OF CERTAIN WRITINGS

principum," in Virtus Politica (Symp. Stuttgart) 127-45.

576. Mondin, Battista. "La dottrina della Imago Dei nel Commento alle Sentenze," in Studi Tomistici (Symp) II, 230-47.

577. _____. "La dottrina tomistica della conoscenza nel Commento alle Sentenze. Doctor Communis 30 (1977) 206-18.

578. _____. "Il fine naturale della vita umana quale fondamento ultimo della morale nel commento alle Sentenze di San Tommaso d'Aquino. Sapienza 28 (1975) 383-92.

579. _____. St. Thomas Aquinas' Philosophy in the Commentary to the Sentences. The Hague: Nijhoff, 1975. 130 pp.

580. Murphy, T. "The Date and Purpose of the Contra Gentiles." Heythrop Journal (1969) 405-15.

581. Oberti Sobrero, Margherita. L'etica sociale in Ambrogio di Milano. Ricostruzione delle fonti ambrosiane nel 'De iustitia' di S. Tommaso. II-II, qq. 57-122. Torino: Asteria, 1970. xi-367.

582. O'Connell, David A. Notes From the Summa On God and His Creatures. Providence, R.I.: Providence College Press, 1956.

583. Ong, Walter J. The Barbarian Within. New York: Macmillan, 1962. 292 pp.

    Discusses Aquinas' poetry.

584. Otto, John. The Commentary of St. Thomas on Book I of the Ethics. Quebec: Laval University Dissertation, 1952. 222 pp.

585. Oudenrijn, M. A. Van den. Eine alte armenische Uebersetzung der Tertia pars der theologischen Summa des hl. Thomas. Bern: Franche, 1955. 240 pp.

586. Owens, Joseph. "An Aquinas Commentary in English." Review of Metaphysics 16 (1963) 503-12.

587. Paris, Gerardus M. Synopsis totius Summae theologicae S. Thomae. Neapoli: M. d'Auria, 1950.

588. Patfoort, A. "L'unité de la Prima pars et le mouvement interne de la Somme theologique de s. Thomas d'Aquin." Revue des Sciences Philosophiques et Théologiques 47 (1963) 513-544.

589. Pauson, J. J. "Postscripts and Addenda to De principiis naturae." The Modern Schoolman 29 (1951-1952) 307-11; 30 (1952-1953) 54-9, and 141-44.

590. Pegis, Anton C. "Qu'est-ce que la Summa contra Gentiles?" in L'Homme devant Dieu: Mélanges offerto au Père Henri de Lubac. Paris:

STUDIES OF CERTAIN WRITINGS   591 - 606

Aubier, 1964. II, 169-82.

591. Pègues, Thomas. Catechism of the 'Summa Theologica' of St. Thomas
Westminster, MD: Newman, 1950. xvi-314.

592. Pelster, Franz. "Literar-historische Probleme der Quodlibeta des
hl. Thomas von Aquin. II" Gregorianum 29 (1948) 63-9.

593. _____. "Die Thomas von Aquin zugeschriebenen Opuscula De instan
tibus...und ihr Verfasser." Gregorianum 36 (1955) 21-49.

594. _____. "Eine ungedruckte Quaestio des hl. Thomas von Aquin
über die Erkenntnis der Wesenheit der Seele." Gregorianum 36 (1955)
618-25.

595. _____. "Literarhistorische Probeme der Quodlibeta des hl.
Thomas, I et II." Gregorianum 28-29 (1947-1948) 78-100, 62-87.

596. Pelzer, Auguste. Le cours inédit d'Albert le Grand sur la Morale
à Nicomaque, recueilli et rédige par s. Thomas d'Aquin. 2 me éd. in
Etudes d'histoire littéraire...Louvain: Publications Universitaires,
1964. 272-335 pp.

597. Perini, Giuseppe. "Il commento di S. Tommaso alla Metafisica di
Aristotele. Osservazioni critiche su una recente monografia." Re J.C.
Doig. Divus Thomas. Piacenza. 77 (1974) 106-45.

598. Ponton, Lionel. "M. Rudolf Boehm et Thomas d'Aquin: a propos de
l'interprétation de Métaphysique z, 3." Laval Théologique et Philosophique 30 (1974) 267-77.

599. Raby, F. J. E. "The Date and Authorship of the Poem Adoro te
devote." Speculum 20 (1945) 236-38.

600. Ramirez, Jacobus (Santiago) M. In S.T. Thomas Aq. Expositiones.
Obras completas, tomos 3-7.

601. _____. De hominis beatitudine. In I-II, qq. 1-5. Tomo 3, 1972.

602. _____. De actibus humanis. In I-II, qq. 6-21, Tomo 4, 1972.

603. _____. De passionibus animae. In I-II, qq. 22-48, Tomo 5, 1973.

604. _____. De habitibus in communi. In I-II, qq. 49-54, Tomo 6,
1973.

605. _____. De donis Spir. Sancti. In I-II, qq. 67-70; In II-II,
qq. 8, 9, 15, 45, 46, 52, 179, 183, Tomo 7, Madrid: C.S.I.C., 1972-1974.

606. _____. Introducción general a la Suma teólogica de S. Tomás de
Aquino. Con un apéndice sobre la premoción física...por Francisco Muniz.
Madrid: Editorial Catolica, 1947. 237, 63, 979-1055 pp.

607 - 621   STUDIES OF CERTAIN WRITINGS

607. Robb, James H. The Nature of the Human Soul in the Quaestiones De Anima, Q. 1-3, of St. Thomas Aquinas. Text and Study. Toronto: University of Toronto Dissertation, 1953.

608. Robinson, T. M. "Averroes, Moerbeke, Aquinas and a Crux in the De anima." Mediaeval Studies 32 (1970) 340-44.

609. Robles, Laureano. "Un opúsculo ignorado de Tomas de Aquino, El 'de mixtione elementorum'." Estudios Franciscanos. Barcelona. 23 (1974) 239-59.

610. _____. "Notas históricas al 'De modalibus' de Sto Tomás." Teorema 4 (1974) 419-38.

611. Rossi, Giovanni F. Antiche e nuove edizioni degli opuscoli di S. Tommaso d'Aquino e il problema della loro autenticità. Piacenza: Collegio Alberoni, 1955. 75 pp.

612. Rossi, Giovanni Felice. Antiche e nuove edizioni degli opuscoli di San Tommaso d'Aquino e il problema della lorro authenticita. Piacenza: Collegio Alberoni, 1955. 74 pp.

613. _____. "L'Autenticità dei testi di s. Tommaso d'Aquino: 'Beata Virgo a peccato originali et actuali immunis fuit," et 'B.V. nec originale peccatum incurrit'." Divus Thomas. Piacenza. 57 (1954) 442-66.

614. _____. "Gli Opuscoli di san Tommaso d'Aquino." Divus Thomas. Piacenza. 56 (1953) 211-36; 362-90.

615. _____. "Il Codice latino 14546 della Bibl. Naz, di Parigi con gli Opuscoli di san Tommaso." Divus Thomas. Piacenza. 54 (1951) 149-88.

616. _____. Il Codice Latino 14546 della Bibliogeca Nazionale di Parigi con gli Opuscoli di San Tommaso. Divus Thomas. Piacenza. (1952) 127 pp.

617. Ruello, Francis. "La doctrine de l'illumination dans le traité 'Super librum Boethii de Trinitate' de Thomas d'Aquin." Recherches de Science Réligieuse 64 (1976) 341-58.

618. Ryan, John K. "The Authenticity of a Homily Attributed to St. Thomas Aquinas." Studies in Philosophy and the History of Philosophy 1 (1961) 216-20.

619. _____. "Philosophy and Theology in a Discourse of St. Thomas Aquinas on the Incarnation and the Kingship of Christ." Studies in Philosophy and the History of Philosophy I (1961).

620. Schmidt, Robert W. "An Emendation of a Reply of St. Thomas Aquinas's De Potentia 9, 7 ad 6." The Modern Schoolman 28 (1950) 58-62.

621. Schoder, Raymond V. "A Section Correlation: Thomas In Ethica

STUDIES OF CERTAIN WRITINGS   622 - 635

Aristotelis with Bekker-Pages of the Greek Text." The Modern Schoolman 21 (1943) 47-8.

622.   Smeraldo, B.   Intorno all'opuscolo IX di san Tommaso d'Aquino. Pietro da Tarentasia ha errato in teologia. Rome: Angelicum, 1945.

623.   Smith, Elwood F. and Louis A. Ryan.   A Guidebook to the Summa. New York: Benzinger, 1950.

624.   Steenberghen, Fernand van. "La lecture et l'étude de s. Thomas. Réflexions et conscels." Revue philosophique de Louvain 53 (1955) 301- 20.

625.   Suermondt, Clemens S. Tabulae schematicae cum introductione de principiis et compositone comparatis Summae Theologiae et Summae contra Gentiles S. Thomas Aquinatis. Roma: Santa Sabina, 1943.

626.   Swierzawski, Waclaw. "Faith and Worship in the Pauline Comment- aries of St. Thomas Aquinas." Divus Thomas. Piacenza. 75 (1972) 389-412.

627.   Synave, Paul and Perre Benoit. Prophecy and Inspiration: A Comm. on S.T., II-II, qq. 171-78. Trans. by Avery R. Dulles and Thomas L. Sheridan. New York: Desclée, 1961. 185 pp.

628.   Thomas de Sutton. (14th century) Expositionis D. Thomae Aquinatis in libros Aristotelis De generatione et corruptione continuatio. Ed. crit. F. E. Kelley. München: Bayerischen Akademie der Wissenschaften, 1976. vi-211 pp.

629.   Turiel, Quintin. "La intención de Santo Tomás en la 'Summa contra Gentiles'." Studium 14 (1974) 371-401.

630.   Twohill, M. Dominic. The Background and St. Thomas Aquinas' Read- ing of the De Divinis Nominibus. New York: Fordham University Dissert- ation, 1960. 135 pp.

631.   Vansteenkiste, C. "Il 'Liber de Causis' negli scritti di San Tommaso." Angelicum 35 (1958) 325-74.

632.   Verbeke, Girard. "La date du commentaire de s. Thomas sur l' Ethique à Nicomaque." Revue philosophique de Louvain 48 (1949) 207-20.

633.   _____. "Les sources et la chronologie du commentaire de s. Thomas au De anima d'Aristote." Revue philosophique de Louvain 45 (1947) 314-38.

634.   _____. "Themistius et le 'De unitate intellectus' de s. Thomas." Revue philosophique de Louvain 53 (1955) 141-64.

635.   Verno, Matthias. "Thomas von Aquinas De regimine Principum im Zusammenhang der geistigen und gesellschaftlichen zituation seiner Zeit." in Gedenkband...Thomas von Aquin, (symp) 321-29.

636. Vitoria, Francisco de (1480-1546). Commentario al tratado de la ley. Beltran de Heredia, ed. Madrid: Studium, 1952.

637. Vostė, Iacobus-M. Commentarius in Summam Theologicam S. Thomae, III, Q. 27-59. Editio altera, Roma: Scuola Tipografica Missionaria Domenicana, 1940. vi-554 pp.

638. _____. "S. Thomas Aquinas epistularum s. Pauli interpres." Angelicum 19 (1942) 257-76.

639. Weisheipl, James. A. "The Commentary of St. Thomas on the De caelo of Aristotle." Sapienza. Napoli. 29 (1974) 11-34.

640. Wippel, John F. "Thomas Aquinas and Avicenna on the Relationship between First Philosophy and the other Theoretical Sciences: A Note on Thomas's Commentary on Boethius's De Trinitate, Q 5, art. 1, and 9. The Thomist 37 (1973) 133-54.

REFERENCE TOOLS

641. Anonymous. Bulletin Thomiste. Tables des tomes IV à VII (Années XI-XXIII) 1934-1946. Le Saulchoir, Etiolles: Rédaction Bulletin Thomiste, 1953. 118 pp.

642. Bachhuber, Andrew W. "Sense Lines: A Techinque for Teaching the Text of St. Thomas." The Modern Schoolman 35 (1957) 62ff.

643. Bergomo, F. Petri de. In Opera Sancti Thomas Aquinatis, Index. Roma: Editiones Paulinae, 1960. 1261 pp. Reprint of Tabula Aurea.

644. Biffi, Imos. "Il Computer a servizio di San Tommaso: L'(Index Thomisticus)." Rivista di Filosofia Neoscolastica 67 (1975) 777-82.

645. Bogliolo, Liugi. Guida alla ricerca scientifica e allo studio de S. Tommaso. Roma: Pont. Università Lateranesse, 1967. 199 pp.

    Introduction, Bibliography, and General Index.

646. Bourke, V. J. "Introduction to the Works of St. Thomas," in Opera Omnia. Parma edition. New York: Musurgia, 1948. I, iii-xxx.

647. Bréhier, Emile. The History of Philosophy: The Middle Ages and the Renaissance. W. Baskin, tr. Chicago: University of Chicago Press, 1965.

648. Brugger, Walter. "Index Thomisticus," (Re Busa). Theologie und Philosophie. 52 (1977) 435-44.

649. Busa, Roberto. "L'Automation appliquée à l'analyse linguistique des ouvrages de s. Thomas d'Aquin: programme, état actuel," in L'Homme et son destin (Symp) 619-25.

650. _____. Index Thomisticus. S. Thomae Aquinatis Operum omnium Indices et Concordantiae...cura Roberti Busa. Introduction - 1 Band

REFERENCE TOOLS   651 - 664

(erscheint als letzter); Sectio I, Indices, 10 Bände; Sectio II, Concordantiae S. Thomae, 31 Bände; Sectio III, Concordantiae aliorum auctorum, 8 Bände. Stuttgart: F. Fromman Verlag, 1979-1980.

651. _____. "L'Index Thomisticus e L'Informatica Filosofica." Revue Internatonale de Philosophie 27 (1973) 31-6.

652. _____. "L'Index Thomisticus e le metodologie delle ricerche tomistiche," in Tommaso d'Aquino (Symp) II, 432-7.

653. Chenu, M.-D. Introduction à l'étude de s. Thomas d'Aquin. Paris: Vrin, 1970.

654. _____. Toward Understanding St. Thomas. A. M. Landry and D. Hughes, trs. Chicago: Regnery, 1964. viii-388.

655. _____. Introduzione allo studio di S. Tommaso d''Aquino. Trad. di R. Poggi e M. Tarchi. Firenze, 1953.

656. Copleston, Frederick. A History of Philosophy. London/Westminster, MD: Newman, 1950ff. Vol. II. From Augustine to Scotus, 1950; Vol. III. From Ockham to Suarez, 1953.

      Reprinted: New York: Doubleday Image, 1962.

657. Deferrari, Roy and M Inviolata Berry, Sister A Complete Index of the Summa Theologica of St. Thomas Aquinas. Washington: Catholic University of America Press, 1956. 2 vols. 395 pp.

658. Deferrari, Roy J. A Latin-English Dictionary of St. Thomas Aquinas. Boston: St. Paul Editions, 1960.

659. DuCange, C. Glossarium mediae et infimae latinitatis   Editio nova...a L. Favre, 5 vols. Niort, 1883-1886.

      Revised as: Glossarium novum mediae latinitatis. F. Blatt, et al., eds. Turin: Bottega d'Erasmo, 1957ff.

660. Eschmann, I. T. "A Catalogue of St. Thomas's Works," in E. Gilson The Christian Philosophy of St. Thomas. New York: 1956. 381-439.

661. Fabro, Cornelio. Breve introduzione al tomismo. Roma: Desclée, 1960.

662. _____. "Tommas d'Aquino." Enciclopedia Catolica. Firenze: Tipografia "L'impornta". xii (1954).

663. Gilson, Etienne. History of Christian Philosophy in the Middle Ages. New York: Random House, 1955. xvii-829 pp.

664. Glenn, Paul J. A Tour of the Summa. St. Louis: B. Herder, 1960. 477 pp.

665 - 677   REFERENCE TOOLS

665. Hubert, Martin. "D'Une actuelle introduction à saint Thomas," in <u>Tommaso d'Aquino</u> (Symp) II, 520-8.

666. Hyman, Arthur and James J. Walsh. <u>Philosophy in the Middle Ages.</u> <u>The Christian, Islamic and Jewish Traditions.</u> New York: Harper and Row, 1967.

    Readings, reprinted: Indianapolis: Hackett, 1973.

<u>Index Thomisticus</u>, see Busa.

667. Judy, Albert G. "The Index Thomisticus, St. Thomas and IBM." <u>Listening</u> 9 (1974) 105-118.

    Cf. Busa.

668. <u>Lexicon of St. Thomas Aquinas</u>: Based on the <u>Summa Theologica</u> and Selected Pasaages of His Other Works. Ed. Roy J. Deferrari and M. Inviolate Barry. 5 Fascicles, in 2 volumes. Washington, D.C.: Catholic University of America Press, 1948-1953.

669. Maurer, Armand. <u>Medieval Philosophy</u>. New York: Random House, 1962. xxvi-435 pp.

670. Michaud-Quantin, Pierre. <u>Etudes sur le vacabulaire philosophique</u> <u>du moyen age</u>. Avec la collaboration de Michel Lemoine. Rome: Ateneo, 1970. 253 pp.

671. _____. <u>Glossaire du latin philosophique médiéval</u>. Paris: Centre National de la Recherche Scientifique, 1972ff.

672. Migoya, Francisco. "Automación del analisis linguistico de las obras de Santo Tomas." <u>Revista Filosofica</u>. Mexico 6 (1974) 237-47.

673. Pieper, Josef. <u>Guide to St. Thomas Aquinas</u>. R. and C. Winston, trs. New York: Pantheon, 1962. 187 pp; New York: Mentor-Omega, 1964. 160 pp.

674. Schmidt, Robert W. "An Historic Research Instrument: the <u>Index</u> <u>Thomisticus</u>." <u>The New Scholasticism</u> 50 (1976) 237-49.

Schutz, Ludwig, see <u>Thomas-Lexikon</u>.

675. Sprokel, Nico. "The 'Index Thomisticus'," <u>Gregorianum</u> 59 (1978) 739-50.

676. Stockhammer, Morris, ed. <u>Thomas Aquinas Dictionary</u>. New York: Philosophical Library, 1965. 232 pp.

677. Suermondt, Clement. <u>Indices auctoritatum omniumque rerum notabilium</u> <u>occurrentium in Summa Theologiae et in Summa Contra Gentiles S. Thomae de</u> <u>Aquino</u>. Vol. XVI, <u>Opera Omnia</u>. Editionis Leoninae. Romae: Apud Sedem Commissionis Leoninae, 1948. 680 pp. Editio Manualis, <u>ibid</u>. 1948. 728pp.

REFERENCE TOOLS   678 - 685

678. Suermondt, Clement. Indices omnium auctoritatum et rerum nota-
bibium occurrentium in commentariis in Summam Theologiae Thomae de Vio
Card. Caietani et...Francisci de Sylvestris Ferrariessis. Vol. XVI,
Opera Omnia editionis Leoninae. Romae: Apud Sedem Commissionis Leoninae,
1948. 680 pp. Editio Manualis, ibid. 1948. 288 pp.

679. Tabula Aurea Fr. Petri a Bergoma, O.P., in omnia opera S. Thomae
Aquinatis. New York: Musurgia Publishers, 1949. 707 pp.

     Reprinted from the Parma ed. Opera Omnia S. Thomae, Vol. XXV,
     1873.

680. Thomas-Lexikon. Sammlung, Übersetzung und Erklarung der in
sämtlichen Werken des h. Thomas von Aquin vorkommenden Kunstausdruckeund
wissenschaftlichen aussprüche, von Dr. Ludwig Schütz-Photolithographis-
cher Nachdruck. New York: Musurgia Publishers, 1949.

     Reprint Stuttgart: Frommann, 1975. x-889 pp.

681. Ueberweg, Friedrich und Bernhard Geyer. Grundriss der Geschichte
der Philosophie. Vol. II: Die Patristische und Scholastische Philosophie, II Aufl. Berlin: Mittler, 1929;

     Reprinted: Graz, 1951.

682. Wallace, W. A. and J. A. Weisheipl. "Thomas Aquinas, saint." The
New Catholic Encyclopedia 14 (1966) 102-15.

683. Weisheipl, James A. "A Brief Catalogue of Authentic Works," in
Friar Thomas D'Aquino. New York: 1974. 355-405.

684. Wippel, John F. and Allan B. Wolter. Medieval Philosophy From St.
Augustine to Nicholas of Cusa. Readings in the History of Philosophy.
New York: Free Press, 1969.

685. Wuellner, Bernard. Dictionary of Scholastic Philosophy. Milwaukee:
Bruce, 1956.

3

Philosophical Teachings

GENERAL AND INTRODUCTORY

686. Andres, T. De. "El horizonte de Santo Tomás de Aquino." Razon y Fé (1974) 75-87.

687. Armstrong, A. Hilary. "The Search for Understanding: Philosophy and Theology." Proceedings of the American Catholic Philosophical Assoication 47 (1973) 43-8.

688. Ashley, Benedict M. "The Thomistic Synthesis," in Teaching Thomism Today (Symp) 39-63.

689. Bernard, A. Introduction à la philosophie thomiste. Avignon: Maison Aubanel Père, 1954. 136 pp.

690. Brasa Diez, Mariano. "El metodo filosoficode S. Tomás." Studium 15 (1975) 81-101.

691. Broad, Charlie D. "Some Basic Notions in the Philosophy of St. Thomas." Philosophy Today 3 (1959) 199-211.

692. Chenu, M.-D. "Szent Tamás az újitó egy új világ kretivitásoban." Mérleg 10 (1974) 311-26.

    Thomas as innovator in the Creativity of a new world.

693. Collins, James D. "Toward a Philosophically Ordered Thomism." The New Scholasticism 32 (1958) 301-26.

694. Copleston, Frederick C. Aquinas. Baltimore: Penguin Books, 1955. 263 pp.

695. _____. Thomas Aquinas. London: Search Press, 1976. 271 pp.

    Reprint of Aquinas, 1955 Penguin.

GENERAL AND INTRODUCTORY   696 - 710

696. _____. A History of Philosophy. Baltimore: Newman Press,
1950; Garden City, New York: Doubleday Image, 1962.

    Vol. 2, II (1962) "St. Thomas," Chaps 31-41, 20-155 pp.

697. _____. Religion and Philosophy. New York: Barnes & Noble,
1974. x-195.

698. Corbin, Michel. "Le Système et le chemin: de Hegel a Thomas d'
Aquin." Archives de Philosophie 39 (1976) 529-566.

699. Cresson, A. S. Thomas d'Aquin, Sa vie, Son oeuvre. Sa philosophie.
Paris: Presses Universitaires, 1942. 133 pp.

700. Crouse, R. D. "St. Thomas, St. Albert, Aristotle: Philosophia
ancèlla theologiae," in Tommaso d'Aquino (Symp) I, 181-6.

701. Dalcourt, Gerald J. The Philosophy of St. Thomas Aquinas. New
York: Monarch Press, Inc., 1965. 126 pp.

702. Dominica, M. "The Methodology of Saint Thomas." Proceedings of
the American Catholic Philosophical Association 19 (1943) 114-8.

703. Duquesne, M. "Philosophie thomiste et libre Aecherche." Mélanges
de Science Religieuse. Lille. 31 (1974) 177-202.

704. Ehrle, Franz. Zur Enzyklika "Aeterni Patris;" Text und Kommentar.
Neu hrsg. von Franz Pelster. Roma: Edizioni di Storia e letteratura,
1954. 202 pp.

705. Fernandez, Aniceto. "Actualité de la philosophie de saint Thomas."
Revue Thomiste 49 (1966) 166-85.

706. Gardeil, Henri D. Initiation à la Philosophie de S. Thomas d'
Aquin. Paris: Editions du Cerf, 1952-1953.

    Vol. I, Introduction, Logique, 253 pp.
    Vol. II, Cosmoloque, 162 pp.
    Vol. III, Psychologie, 248 pp.
    Vol. IV, Métaphysique, 237 pp.

707. _____. Introduction to the Philosophy of St. Thomas Aquinas.
4 vols. J. A. Otto, tr. St. Louis: B. Herder, 1956.

708. Genuyt, F. M. Vérité de l'être et affirmation de Dieu. Essai sur
la philosophie de s. Thomas. Paris: Vrin: 1974. 224 pp.

709. Gerrity, Benignus. Nature, Knowledge and God: And Introduction to
Thomistic Philosophy. Milwaukee: Bruce, 1947. xii-662.

710. Giacon, Carlo. Le grandi tesi del tomismo. Bologna: Patron,
1967. 355 pp.

711. _____. "Tommaso d'Aquino filosofo." Cultura e Scuola 49-50
(1974) 168-76.

712. Gilson, Etienne. The Elements of Christian Philosophy. New York:
Mentor-Omega, 1963; New York: Doubleday, 1960.

713. _____. Introduction à la philosophie Chrétienne. Paris: Vrin,
1960.

714. _____. The Philosopher and Theology. Trans from the French by
Cécile Gilson. New York: Random, 1962. 236 pp.

715. _____. The Spirit of Thomism. New York: P.J. Kenedy, 1964.
127 pp.

716. _____. Le Thomisme: Introduction à la philosophie de s. Thomas
d' Aquin. éd. 5me. Paris: Vrin, 1948; éd. 6me, 1972.

717. _____. The Christian Philosophy of St. Thomas Aquinas. L.
Shook, tr. New York: Random House, 1956. x-502 pp.

718. _____. The Unity of Philosophical Experience. New York: Sheed
and Ward, 1950, 1955.

719. _____, and Anton Pegis. St. Thomas Aquinas and Philosophy.
West Hartford, CT: St. Joseph College, 1961. 29 pp.

720. Grenet, Paul B. Les vingt-quatre thèses thomistes. 2me éd. Paris:
Téqui, 1962. 381 pp.

721. _____. Le Thomisme. Paris: Presses Universitaires, 1953.
128 pp.

722. _____. Thomism. Jas. F. Ross, tr. New York: Harper and Row,
1976.

723. Grenier, H. Thomistic Philosophy. 4 vols. Charlottetown: St.
Dunstan's University Press.

724. Guzie, Tad W. "The Evolution of Philosophical Method in the
Writings of St. Thomas." The Modern Schoolman 37 (1960) 95-120.

725. Hoelhuber, Ivo. "Tomas de Aquino, filósofo: inculpado de fideismo
absoluto." Espiritu. Barcelona. 26 (1977) 49-61.

726. Holz, Harald. Thomas von Aquin und die Philosophie. Ihr Verältnis
zur thomasischen Theologie in kritischer Sicht. Paderborn: Schoningh,
1975. 87 pp.

727. _____. "Philosophische und Theologische Antinomik Bei Kant und
Thomas Von Aquin." Archiv für Geschichte der Philosophie 52 (1970)
71-90.

GENERAL AND INTRODUCTORY   728 - 744

728. _____. "Philosophische und Theologische Antinomik Bei Kant und Thomas von Aquin." Kant Studien 61 (1970) 66-82.

729. Hugon, Edouard. Les vingt-quartre theses thomistes. 8me éd. Paris: Téqui, 1946. 290 pp.

730. Imbach, Ruedi. "Philosophisches Gespräch mit Thomas von Aquin. Zu einem Sammelband, hrsq. von Wolfgang Kluxen." Freiburger Zeitschrift fur Philosophie und Theologie 25 (1978) 217-23.

731. Kane, William H. Approach to Philosophy: Elements of Thomism. Washington: The Thomist Press, 1963. 179 pp.

732. Keegan, Francis L. The Development of Jacques Maritain's Concept of Christian Philosophy: 1910-1929. Notre Dame: University of Notre Dame Dissertation, 1959.

733. McInerny, Ralph M., ed. New Themes in Christian Philosophy. Notre Dame: Notre Dame University Press, 1968.

734. _____. St. Thomas Aquinas. Boston: G. K. Hale, 1977.

735. Manser, G. M. Das Wesen des Thomismus. Freiburg i.d. Schweiz: Paulus-Verlag, 1949. Thomistische Studien V. 752 pp.

736. _____. La esencia del tomismo. Trad. V. Garcia Yebra. 2a ed. Madrid: Consejo S.I.C., 1953. 836 pp.

737. Maritain, Jacques. De Bergson à Thomas d'Aquin: essais de métaphysique et de morale. Paris: P. Hartmann, 1947. 333 pp.

738. _____. An Essay on Christian Philosophy. E. H. Flannery, tr. New York: Philosophical Library, 1955.

739. _____. Oeuores, 1912-1939. Henri Bars, ed. Bruges: Desclée 1974.

740. _____. The Use of Philosophy. Princeton, N.J.: Princeton University Press, 1961. 71 pp.

741. Mascall, Eric L. "The Gulf in Philosophy: Is Thomism the Bridge?" The Thomist. Centenary of St. Thomas Aquinas 1274-1974. 38 (1974) 8-26.

742. Meyer, Hans. The Philosophy of St. Thomas. Frederic Eckhoff, tr. St. Louis: Herder, 1944. 589 pp.

743. _____. Thomas von Aquin Sein System und seine geistesgeschichtliche Stellung. Aufl. 2. Paderborn: Schöningh, 1961.

744. Moody, Ernest A. "Professor Pegis and Historical Philosophy." Francisican Studies 5 (1945) 301-8.

745. Mullaney, James V. "On Being Thomistic: The Authority of St. Thomas in Philosophy. Proceedings of the American Catholic Philosophical Association 25 (1951) 141-7.

746. Oesterle, John A. "St. Thomas as a Teacher: A Reply to Professor Pegis." The New Scholasticism 39 (1965) 451-66.

747. O'Flaherty, Margaret Mary. "Eleven Theses on Thomas Aquinas." Listening 9 (1974) 153-6.

748. Orlando, Pasquale. "Verso un tomismo esistenziale." Aquinas 14 (1971) 531-69; 15 (1972) 338-81; 16 (1973) 227-54; 17 (1974) 576-97.

749. Pegis, Anton C. Christian Philsosophy and Intellectual Freedom. Milwaukee: Bruce, 1960. 89 pp.

     Gabriel Richard Lecture, 1955.

750. _____. St. Thomas and Philosophy. Milwaukee: Marquette University Press, 1964. 89 pp.

751. _____. "Sub Ratione Dei: A Reply to Professor Anderson." The New Scholasticism 39 (1965) 141-57.

752. _____. "Thomism as a Philosophy." West Hartford, CT: St. Joseph College, 1960. 15-30.

     The McAuley Lectures, 1960.

753. Perini, Giuseppe. "Il carattere profetico del tomismo e la filosofia scolastica trascendentale." Aquinas 13 (1970) 215-61.

754. Phelan, Gerald B. Selected Papers. Arthur G. Kirn, ed. Toronto: PIMS, 1967. 248 pp.

755. Pizzuti, Giuseppe M. "Per una interpretazione storicizzata di Tommaso d'Aquino." Sapienza 29 (1976) 429-64.

756. Prenter, R. Thomismen. Bidrag til filosofiens historie, udgivet af det teologiske fakültet ved aarhus universitet. Koebenhavn: G.E.C. Gads Forlag, 1953. 87 pp.

757. Proten, Didier E. Thomas d'Aquin. Paris: Editions Universitaires, 1969. 126 pp.

758. Ramirez, Jacobus (Santiago) M. De ipsa philosophia in universum. Obras completas, tomo 1. Madrid: C.S.I.C. 1970.

759. Reding, Marcel. Die Struktur des Thomismus. Freiburg i. Br: Rombach Verlag, 1974. 140 pp.

760. Rosanas, Juan. Tomistas y tomistas. Buenos Aires-Mexico: Espasa-Calpe argentina, 1942. 102 pp.

GENERAL AND INTRODUCTORY   761 - 777

761. Salmon, Elizabeth, G. "Theological Order and the Philosophy of
St. Thomas." Thought 21 (1946) 667-78.

762. Sciacca, Michele Federico. "Il concetto di 'laicità' del sapere
in S. Tommaso." Rivista de Filosofia Neoscolastica 66 (1974) 626-35.

763. Serrano, Jorge A. "Reflexiones acerca de un texto 'tomista."
Revista Filosofica. Mexico. 6 (1974) 61-74.

764. Sertillanges, A.-D. La philosophie de s. Thomas d'Aquin. Nouv.
éd., 2 vols. Paris: Aubier, 1940. 301, 282 pp.

765. _____. Der heilige Thomas von Aquin. Uebers und Nachw von R.
Grosche. 2 Aufl. Köln: Hegner, 1954. 720 pp.

766. Sillem, Edward A. "Perspectives on Christian Philosophy."
Philosophy Today 5 (1961) 3-13.

767. Spiazzi, Raimondo M. San Tommaso d'Aquino. Firenze: Nardini-
Centro Internazionale del Libro, 1975. 300 pp.

768. Steenberghen, Fernand Van. "The Reading and Study of St. Thomas."
Theology Digest 4 (1956) 166-9.

769. Steiner, Rudolf. Die Philosophie des Thomas von Aquino. Dornach:
Rudolf-Steiner Verlag, 1972. 124 pp.

770. Tranøy, K. E. "Thomas Aquinas," in A Critical History of Western
Philosophy. D. J. O'Connor, ed. New York: St. Martins Press, 1964.

771. Vanni Rovighi, Sofia. Introduzione a Tommaso d'Aquino. Bari:
Laterza, 1973. 212 pp.

772. Verbeke, Gérard. "Certitude et incertitude de la recherche
philosophique selon Saint Thomas d'Aquin." Rivista de Filosofia Neoscolastica 66 (1974) 740-57.

773. Wallace, William A. "The Case for Developmental Thomism." Proceedings of the American Catholic Philosophical Association 44 (1970)
1-16.

774. _____. The Elements of Philosophy: A Compendium for Philosophers
and Theologians. New York: Alba House, 1977. 352 pp.

775. Weinberg, Julius R. A Short History of Mediaevel Philosophy.
Princeton, N.J.: Princeton University Press, 1964.

776. Wheeler, M. Cecelia. Philosophy and the Summa Theologica of St.
Thomas Aquinas. Washington: Catholic University of America Press, 1956.

777. Wulf, Maurice De. Initiation à la philosophie thomiste. 2me éd.
Louvain: Institut Supérieur de Philosophie, 1949.

777A.   . Introduction to Scholastic Philosophy. P. Coffey, tr.
New York: Dover, 1956. 151 pp.

778.   . System of Saint Thomas Aquinas. Ernest Messenger, tr.
New York: Dover, 1960. 151 pp.

LOGIC, GRAMMAR, EPISTEMOLOGY

779. Acri, Francesco. Della cognizione secondo S. Tommaso e Aristotle.
Rome: Libreria Editrice Salesiana, 1965. 64 pp.

779A. Adamczyk, S. "De valore obiecti in epistemologia thomistica."
Gregorianum 38 (1957) 630-57.

779B.   . "Przedmiot formalny w epistemologii tomistycznej."
Roczniki Filosoficzne 1 (1948) 98-122.

780. Alcorta, Jose Ignacio. "La spontanéité de la connaissancei théorique
et pratique selon s. Thomas," in L'Homme et son destin (Symp) 555-60.

781. Allers, Rudolf. "The Intellectual Cognition of Particulars."
The Thomist 3 (1941) 95-163.

782. Almazán Hernandez, Ramón. "Sentido trascendente de la verdad.
Agustin y Tomás de Aquino." Anuario Filosofico 8 (1975) 21-49.

783. Anderson, James F. "Some Disputed Questions on our Knowledge of
Being." Review of Metaphysics 11 (1958) 550-68.

784. Anderson, Thomas C. "Aristotle and Aquinas on the Freedom of the
Mathematician." The Thomist 36 (1972) 231-55.

785.   . "Intelligible Matter and the Objects of Mathematics in
Aquinas." The New Scholasticism 43 (1969) 555-76.

786.   . The Object and Nature of Mathematical Science in Aristotle
and Thomas Aquinas. Milwaukee: Marquette University Dissertation, 1966.
334 pp.

787. Arbuckle, Gilbert B. A Critique of the Thomistic Doctrine of
Definition. Washington, D.C.: Catholic University of America Dissertation, 1962. 194 pp.

788. Arnou, René. "La critique de la connaissance intellectuelle de
l'homme dans la philosophie de Saint Thomas." Gregorianum 52 (1971)
273-98.

789.   . L'Homme a-t-il le pouvoir de connaitre la vérité?
Réponse de saint Thomas: La c onnaissance par habitus. Rome: Presses
de l'Université Gregorienne, 1970. 255 pp.

790. Artola, José Maria. "Dialectica y metafisica en torno a los primer-
os principios según S. Tomás." Revista de Filosofia. Madrid. 1 (1975)47-61.

LOGIC, GRAMMAR, EPISTEMOLOGY   791 - 807

791. Ashmore, Robert B. The Analogical Notion of Judgment in St. Thomas Aquinas. Notre Dame: University of Notre Dame Dissertation, 1966. 239 pp.

792. Bachhuber, Andrew H. Logic. St. Louis: Saint Louis University Bookstore, 1952. viii-278.

793. Barr, Robert, R. "A Relational Analysis of Intentionality." The Modern Schoolman 40 (1963) 225-44.

794. Bartolomei, Maria Cristina. Tomismo e principio di don contraddizione. Padova: CEDAM, 1973. 110 pp.

795. Beach, John D. "Analogous Naming, Extrinsic Denomination, and the Real Order." The Modern Schoolman 42 (1965) 198-213.

796. Bearsley, Patirck J. "Another Look at the First Principles of Knowledge." The Thomist 36 (1972) 566-98.

797. _____. "Aquinas and Wittgenstein on the Grounds of Certainty." The Modern Schoolman 51 (1974) 301-34.

798. Bennett, Owen. The Nature of Demonstrative Proof According to the Principles of Aristotle and St. Thomas Aquinas. Washington, D.C.: Catholic University Press, 1943.

799. _____. "Saint Thomas' Theory of Demonstrative Proof." Proceedings of the American Catholic Philosophical Association 17 (1941) 76-88.

800. Biffi, Inos. "Il giudizio 'per quamdam connaturalitatem' o 'per modum inclinationis' secondo San Tommaso: analisi e prospettive." Rivista di Filosofia Neoscolastica 66 (1974) 356-93.

801. Bochenski, Innocentius M. "On Analogy." The Thomist 11 (1948) 424-47.

802. Bogliolo, L. "Saggio sulla metafisica tomistica del conoscere." Salesianum. Torino. 17 (1955) 3-57.

803. Bolzan, J. E. and Celina A. L. Mendoza. "Santo Tomas y les metodos de las ciencias especulativas." Sapientia 27 (1972) 37-50.

804. Bourke, V. J. "Intellectual Memory in the Thomistic Theory of Knowledge." The Modern Schoolman 18 (1941) 21-4.

805. Bradley, Ritamary. "The Mirror of Truth according to St. Thomas." The Modern Schoolman 31 (1954) 307-17.

806. Breton, Stanislas. "La déduction thomiste des categories." Revue Philosophique de Louvain 15 (1962) 5-32.

807. Burch, George Bosworth. "The Place of Revelation in Philosophical

808 - 823   LOGIC, GRAMMAR, EPISTEMOLOGY

Thought." Review of Metaphysics 15 (1961) 396-408.

808. Burrell, David. "Beyond the Theory of Analogy." Proceedings of
the American Catholic Philosophical Association 46 (1972) 144-21.

809. _____. "Religious Language and the Logic of Analogy." International Philosophical Quarterly 2 (1962) 643-62.

810. Cahalan, John C. "On the Proving of Causal Propositions." The
Modern Schoolman 44 (1967) 129-42.

    Rejoinder: 143-51; reply: 152-60.

811. Cajetan, Thomas de Vio. In Analytica Posteriora E. Babin, et. W.
Baumgaertner, eds. Québec: Université Laval, 1950.

812. Capozzi, Gino. Giudizio, prova e verità l principi della scienza
nell' analitica di Aristotele. Napoli: Edd. Scientifiche Italiane,
1974. 347 pp.

813. Carlo, William E. "Idea and Concept, a Key to Epistemology."
Boston Studies in Philosophy 1 (1966) 47-66.

814. Casado, F. "El apriorismo del conocimiento en S. Tomás de Aquino."
Estudio Agustiniana. Valladolid. 12 (1977) 493-509.

815. Caturelli, Alberto. "La profecia como conocimiento del futuro
historico en S. Tomás." Sapientia 30 (1975) 105-22.

816. Cenacchi, Giuseppe. "Il principio di non-contraddizione fondamento
del discorse filosofico." Aquinas 16 (1973) 255-77.

817. _____. Il problemi intorno al principio del terzo-escluso
secondo Aristotele, Tommaso d'Aquino in relazione al pensiero contemporaneo." Aquinas 18 (1974) 240-63.

818. Chapman, Thomas. "Analogy." The Thomist 39 (1975) 137-41.

819. Clark, Joseph T. Conventional Logic and Modern Logic. Washington:
American Catholic Philosophical Association, 1952. ix-109 pp.

    Preface by W.V. Quine.

820. Clark, Ralph W. "Aquinas on Intentions." The Thomist 40 (1976)
303-10.

821. _____. "Aquinas on the Relationship between Difference in Kind
and Difference in Degree." The Thomist 39 (1975) 116-36.

822. _____. "Per se Judgment in St. Thomas." The Modern Schoolman
51 (1973-1974) 231-6.

823. Coccio, Agostino. "Senso dei limiti della conoscenza umana in

LOGIC, GRAMMAR, EPISTEMOLOGY   824 - 839

San Tommaso d'Aquin," in L'Homme et son destin (Symp) 561-76.

824. Colish, Marcia L. The Mirror of Language: A Study in the Medieval Theory of Knowledge. New Haven-London: Yale University Press, 1968. xxiii-404 pp.

   Chapter 3 on Aquinas.

825. Connell, Desmond. "S . Thomas on Reflection and Judgment." Irish Theological Quarterly. Maynooth. 45 (1978) 234-47.

826. Connolly,F. G. "Abstraction and Modernate Realism." The New Scholasticism 27 (1953) 72-90.

827. Conway, James I. "The Meaning of Moderate Realism." The New Scholasticism 36 (1962) 141-79.

828. Conway, Pierre H. "Induction in Aristotle and St. Thomas." The Thomist 22 (1959) 336-65.

829. Cunningham, Francis A. "Certitudo in St. Thomas Aquinas." The Modern Schoolman 30 (1953) 297-24.

830. _____. "Judgment in St. Thomas." The Modern Schoolman 31 (1954) 185-212.

831. _____. "The Second Operation and the Assent us. Judgment in St. Thomas." The New Scholasticism 31 (1957) 1-34.

832. _____. "A Theory on Abstraction in St. Thomas." The Modern Schoolman 35 (1958) 249-70.

833. Curic, Josip. "'Connaturalitas.' Structuralna srodnost svijesti i stvarnosti prema nauci Tome Akvinskog," in Zbornik (Zagreb Symp. 1974) 39-64.

834. Deck, John N. "St. Thomas Aquinas and the Language of Total Dependence." Dialogue 6 (1967) 74-88.

835. Delehant, M. Dunstan. The Role of Quality in the Philosophy of St. Thomas Aquinas. Washington: Catholic University of America Press, 1950.

836. Derisi, Octavio N. La Doctrina de la Lsteligencia de Aristoteles a Santo Tomàs. Buenos Aires: Cursos de Cultura Católica. 1945.

837. Dhavamony, Mariasusai. Subjectivity and Knowledge in the Philosophy of Saint Thomas Aquinas. Rome: Gregorian University Press, 1965. 168 pp.

838. Dolan, Edmund. "Resolution and Composition." Laval Théologique et Philosophique 6 (1950) 9-62.

839. Dow, Napier Kirkpatrick. The Epistemology of Thomism: An Exposi-

tion and an Evaluation. Madison, N.J.: Drew University Dissertation, 1945. 243 pp.

840. Dufault, Lucien. "The Concept of Being which is the Proper Object of Logic." Proceedings of the American Catholic Philosophical Association 21 (1946) 77-83.

841. Durbin, Paul R. "Unity and Composition in Judgment." The Thomist 31 (1967) 83-120.

842. Farrell, Paul. "The Portals of Doubt." The Thomist 8 (1945) 293-368.

843. Fay, Thomas A. "The Metaphysical Foundation of Axiomatic Mathematics: A Thomistic Inquiry." Aquinas 18 (1974) 293-309.

844. Fernandez Rodriguez, J. Luis. "El concepto en Santo Tomés." Anuario Filosofico 7 (1974) 125-190.

845. _____. "El objeto de la lógica en Santo Tomás." Anuario Filosofico. Pamplona. 8 (1975) 151-204.

846. Finance, Joseph de. Cogito cartésien et réflexion thomiste. Paris: Beauchesne, 1946.

847. Fischl, J. Logik. Ein Lehrbuch mit einem kurzen Abriss über Logistik. Graz-Wien: Styria, 1952. 150 pp.

848. Flippen, Douglas W. Cognitive Species in St. Thomas and Suarez: An Investigation into the Ground of their Differing Views. Toronto: University of Toronto Dissertation, 1977.

849. Garceau, Benoit. "Jugement et vérité chez s. Thomas d'Aquin," in Tommaso d'Aquino (Symp Roma) VI, 189-95.

850. Garcia Lopez, Jesus. "El 'Idealismo' de Santo Tomás de Aquino," in Universidad de Navarra (Symp 1974) 67-92.

851. Gehring, R. B. "The Knowledge of Material Essences According to St. Thomas Aquinas." The Modern Schoolman 33 (1956) 153-81.

852. Giacon, Carlo. "Il principio di non-contraddizione 'scintella rationis'," in Miscellanea...S. Caramella. Palermo: Accademia Scienze, 1974. 209-23.

853. Gilson, Etienne. "Vade Mecum of a Young Realist," Trans. W. J. Quinn, in Philosophy of Knowledge, R. Houde and J. Mullay, eds. Chicago: Lippincott, 1960. 386-94.

854. Gonzalez-Pola, J. G. El idealismo tomista. Valladolid, 1957. xvi-226.

855. Griffin, John J. The Interpretation of the Two Thomistic Definitions

LOGIC, GRAMMAR, EPISTEMOLOGY   856 - 871

of Certitude. Quebec: University Laval Dissertation, 1954.

856. Hachey, Mercedes. An Investigation and Evaluation of Two Interpretations of St. Thomas' Doctrine of the Objectivity of the Concept.
Notre Dame: University of Notre Dame Dissertation, 1957. 156 pp.

857. Hamel, Albert F. "Grandeur et misère de l'intellectualis consider-
atio d'après s. Thomas," in Laval Thomas d'Aquin (Symp) 423-44.

858. Harvanek, Robert F. "The Community of Truth." International
Philosophical Quarterly 7 (1967) 68-85.

859. _____. "The Pursuit of Truth, Thomist and Pragmatist." Thought
30 (1955) 214-30.

860. Hayner, Paul C. "Analogical Predication." Journal of Philosophy
55 (1958) 855-861.

861. Henle, Robert J. Existentialism and the Judgment." Proceedings
of the American Catholic Philosophical Association   21 (1946) 40-53.

862. _____. "St. Thomas and the Definition of Intelligence." The
Modern Schoolman 53 (1976) 335-46.

863. Herx, Frederick C. The Problem of Illumination in St. Bonaventure
And St. Thomas Aquinas: During the Period 1250-1259. Notre Dame: University of Notre Dame Dissertation, 1961. 203 pp.

864. Hoenen, Peter. De noetica geometriae origine theoriae cognitionis.
Romae: Univers. Gregoriana, 1954. 293 pp.

865. _____. "De oordeelstheorie van Thomas van Aquino." Bijdragen...
der Nederlandschen Jezuiten. Nymegen. 2 (1939) 166-97; 3 (1940) 73-110,
265-330; 4 (1941) 28-78, 299-341; 5 (1942) 79-150.

866. _____. La Théorie du jugement d'apres s. Thomas. Rome:
Gregorianim, 1948.

867. _____. Reality and Judgment According to St. Thomas. H. F.
Tiblier. Chicago: Regnery, 1952. 340 pp.

868. Holloway, Maurice R. "Abstraction from Matter in Human Cognition
According to St. Thomas." The Modern Schoolman 23 (1946) 120-30.

869. Houde, Roland and J. J. Fisher. Handbook of Logic. Dubuque:
Brown, 1954. 174 pp.

870. Isaac, Jean. Le Peri Hermeneias en Occident de Boèce à saint Thomas.
Paris: Vrin, 1953. 192 pp.

871. Johannesson, L. Kunskap och Verklighet. En studie i realistik
filosofi med sürskild hänsyn tell Thomismens tolkning av realitets-
problemet. Stockholm: Gleerup, 1945. 79 pp.

872 - 887   LOGIC, GRAMMAR, EPISTEMOLOGY

872. Joseph de Sainte-Marie. "De la psychologie de la connaissance à une philosophie de l'esprit." Doctor Communis. Roma 27 (1974) 3-46.

873. Kadowaki, Johannes K. Cognitio secundum connaturalitatem iuxta S. Thomam. Bern: Herbert Lang, 1974. 107 pp.

874. Kalinowski, Georges (Jerzy). "Norms and Logic." American Journal of Jurisprudence 18 (1973) 165-97.

875. _____. "De la philosophie pratique à la logique déontique. Les racines thomistes de certaines recherches actuelles,' in Saint Thomas (Lublin Symp) 221-39.

876. _____. Teoria poznania praktycznego. Lublin: Tow Nauk. Kul., 1960.

877. Kaminski, Stanislaw. "Racjonalizm w najnowszej metodslogii nauk a intelektualizm w epistemologii Tomasza z Akwinu." Roczniki Filosoficzne Lublin. 22 (1974) 39-53.

878. Kane, William H. "Abstraction and the Distinction of the Sciences." The Thomist 17 (1954) 43-68.

879. _____. "Outline of a Thomistic Critique of Knowledge." The New Scholasticism 30 (1956) 181-97.

880. Keane, Helen V. Knowledge by Connaturality in St. Thomas Aquinas. Milwaukee: Marquette University Dissertation, 1966. 223 pp.

881. Kearney, R. J. "Analogy and Inference." The New Scholasticism 51 (1977) 131-41.

882. Keller, Albert. "Arbeiten zur Sprachphilosophie Thomas von Aquino." Theologie und Philosophie 49 (1974) 464-76.

883. Kelley, Cornelius J. St. Thomas on the Division of Speculative Knowledge. Quebec: Laval University Dissertation, 1964.

884. Kelly, Matthew John. The Interpretation of St. Thomas Aquinas of 191a 7-8: "The Underlying Nature is Known by Analogy?" Notre Dame: University of Notre Dame Dissertation, 1963. 153 pp.

885. Klubertanz, George P. "St. Thomas and the Knowledge of the Singular." The New Scholasticism 26 (1952) 135-66.

886. Kluge, E.-H. W. "Abstraction: a Contemporary Look." The Thomist 40 (1976) 337-65.

887. Kmieck, George A.,   M. La Driere La Verne, and Richard T. Zegers. "The Role of the Sensible Species in St. Thomas' Epistemology: A Comparison with Contemporary Perception Theory." International Philosophy Quarterly 14 (1974) 456-74.

LOGIC, GRAMMAR, EPISTEMOLOGY   888 - 902

888. Köhler, Theodor Wolfram. "Propositiones Verae Ut Frequenter Bei Thomas von Aquin Und Die Haufigkiets - (Wahrscheinlich Keits - title edited.)" Aquinas 18 (1975) 241-53.

889. Koninck, Charles De. "Random Reflections on Science and Calculation." Laval Théologique et Philosophique 12 (1956) 84-119.

889A. Krapiec, M. A. "The Problem of Cognition," in Modern Catholic Thinkers (Symp) 548-62.

890. Lanna, D. La teoria della conoscenza in S. Tommaso d'Aquino. 2a ed. a cura di G. Capasso. Napoli: Conte, 1952. 319 pp.

891. Laso, Jose Alvarez. La Filosofia de las Matematicas en Santo Tomas. Mexico: Editiorial Jus. Mexico, 1952. 200 pp.

892. La Spisa, Mauro. Fenomenologia della conoscenza come atto sinergico Secondo Tommaso d'Aquino. Firenze: GeG, 1970. 72 pp.

893. Lauer, Rosemary Zita. "St. Thomas and Modern Semiotic." The Thomist 19 (1956) 75-99.

894. Lennon, Joseph L. The Nature of Experience and its Role in the Acquisition of Scientific Knowledge According to the Philosophy of St. Thomas Aquinas. Notre Dame: University of Notre Dame Dissertation 1954. 205 pp.

895. Lisska, Anthony J. "Axioms of Intentionality in Aquinas' Theory of Knowledge." International Philosophical Quarterly 16 (1976) 305-22.

896. _____. "Deely and Geach on Abstractionism in Thomistic Epistemology." The Thomist 37 (1973) 548-68.

897. Lobkowicz, Nicholas. "Abstraction and Dialectics." Review of Metaphysics 21 (1968) 468-90.

898. Lofy, Carl A. "The Meaning of 'Potential Whole' in St. Thomas Aquinas." The Modern Schoolman 37 (1959) 39-48.

899. Lonergan, Bernard. Insight. A Study of Human Understanding. New York: Philosophical Library, 1957.

900. _____. La notion de verbe dans les écrits de s. Thomas d'Aquin. Paris: Beauchesne, 1966. x-255 pp.

   Trans. of "Verbum" articles of 1946.

901. _____. Verbum: Word and Idea in Aquinas. D. Burell, ed. Notre Dame: University of Notre Dame Press, 1967. 318 pp.

902. Lopez, Jesus Garcia. "El conocimiento del yo segun Santo Tomas."

903 - 918   LOGIC, GRAMMAR, EPISTEMOLOGY

Anuario Filosofico 4 (1971) 87-117.

903. _____. "Verdad e Inteligibilidad." Anuario Filosofico I (1968) 69-92.

904. McCanles, Michael. "Univocalism in Cajetan's Doctrine of Analogy." The New Scholasticism 42 (1968) 18-47.

905. McInerny, Ralph. "The Analogy of Names is a Logical Doctrine," in Tommaso d'Aquino (Symp Roma) VI, 647-53.

906. _____. "The Logic of Analogy." The New Scholasticism 31 (1957) 149-71.

907. _____. The Logic of Analogy: An Interpretation of St. Thomas Hague: Nijhoff, 1961. 190 pp.

908. _____. Studies in Analogy. Hague: Nijhoff, 1968. 147 pp.

909. _____. "Some Notes on Being and Predication." The Thomist 22 (1959) 315-35.

910. McKian, John D. The Limits of Natural Knowledge According to St. Thomas Aquinas. Chicago: Loyola University of Chicago Dissertation, 1940. 284 pp.

911. McNicholl, Ambrose J. "Epistemology and Metaphysics." Angelicum 38 (1961) 200-12.

912. _____. "On Judging." The Thomist 38 (1974) 768-825.

913. McWilliams, James A. "The Metaphysics of Knowledge." Proceedings of the American Catholic Philosophical Association 35 (1961) 14-20.

914. Malatesta, Michele. "La problematica tomistica delle relazioni alla luce della logica matematica..." in Tommaso d'Aquino (Symp Roma) IX, 140-67.

915. _____. "La problematica tomistica delle relazioni alla luce della logica matematica e dei moderni indirizzi di pensiero." Rassegna di Scienze Filosofiche 27 (1974) 227-57.

916. Marimón Battlo, Ricardo. "El concepto del ser, primer principio del entendimento en S. Tomás de Aquino." Estudios Filosoficos 27 (1978) 127-35.

917. _____. "El conocimiento humano en S. Tomás de Aquino." Sapientia 32 (1977) 25-50.

918. Maritain, Jacques. Distinguish to Unite: The Degrees of Knowledge. G. B. Phelan, ed. New York: Scribner's, 1959.

LOGIC, GRAMMAR, EPISTEMOLOGY   919 - 936

919. _____. Science and Wisdom. New York: Scribner's, 1940.

920. Martin, R. M. "Some Thomistic Properties of Primordiality." Notre Dame Journal of Formal Logic 18 (1977) 567-82.

921. Martins, Diamantino. "O conhecimento da mente humana segundo S. Tomás." Revista Portuguesa de Filosofia 30 (1974) 29-38.

922. Mas Herrera, Oscar E. "Algunos aspectos de la teoria del conocimiento en S. Tomás de Aquino...la doctrina de iluminacion..." Revista de Filosofia de la Universidad de Costa Rica. San José. 13 (1975) 57-71.

923. Maurer, Armand A. "A Neglected Thomistic Text on the Foundation of Mathematics." Mediaeval Studies 21 (1959).

924. _____. "St. Thomas and Changing Truths," in Tommaso d'Aquino (Symp Roma) VI, 267-75

925. _____. "The Unity of a Science: St. Thomas and the Nominalists," in St. Thomas Aquinas 1274-1974 (Toronto Symp) II, 269-91.

926. May, Willian E. "Knowledge of Causality in Hume and Aquinas." The Thomist 34 (1970) 254-88.

927. Meagher, Robert E. "Thomas Aquinas and Analogy: A Textual Analysis." The Thomist 34 (1970) 230-53.

928. Meissner, Willian W. "Some Aspects of the Verbum in the Texts of St. Thomas." The Modern Schoolman 36 (1958) 1-30.

929. Melsen, A. G. M. Van. "St. Thomas' Solution of the Problem of Faith and Reason." Sapienza 29 (1974) 125-34.

930. Miller, Barry. The Range of Intellect. London: Geoffrey Chapman, 1961. 251 pp.

931. Molinaro, Aniceto. "Linguaggio Logica Metafisica. Il problema dell'analogia in S. Tommaso d'Aquino." Aquinas 17 (1974) 41-96.

932. Mondin, Battista. The Principle of Analogy in Protestant and Catholic Theology. Hague: Nijhoff, 1963. 157 pp.

933. Moreau, Joseph. De la connaissance selon S. Thomas d'Aquin. Paris: Beauchesne, 1976. 132 pp.

934. Murnion, William E. "St. Thomas Aquinas's Theory of the Act of Understanding." The Thomist 37 (1973) 88-118.

935. Nemetz, Anthony A. "Logic and the Division of the Science in Aristotle and St. Thomas Aquinas. The Modern Schoolman 33 (1956) 91-109.

936. _____. "The Meaning of Analogy." Franciscan Studies 15

937 - 954   LOGIC, GRAMMAR, EPISTEMOLOGY

(1955) 209-23.

937. Neumann, Siegfried. Gegenstand und Methode: der theoretischen Wissenschaften nach Thomas von Aquin aufgrund der Expositio super librum Boethii De Trinitate. (BGPM 41, 2) Münster: Aschendorff, 1965. 178 pp.

938. O'Brien, Astrid Marie. The Meaning of Resolution as a Reflective Method in the Philosophy of Thomas Aquinas. New York: Fordham University Dissertation, 1975. 229 pp.

939. O'Connell, Matthew J. "St. Thomas and the Verbum: An Interpretation." The Modern Schoolman 24 (1947) 224-34.

940. Oesterle, John A. Two Essays on the Problem of Meaning. Baltimore: MD: Thomist Press, 1945.

941. Owens, Joseph. "Aquinas on Knowing Existence." Review of Metaphysics 29 (1975-1976) 670-90.

942. _____. "Concept and Thing in St. Thomas." The New Scholasticism. 37 (1963) 220-24.

943. _____. "Judgment and Truth in Aquinas." Mediaeval Studies 32 (1970) 138-58.

945. _____. "The Primacy of the External in Thomistic Noetics," in Colloque (Symp Ottawa) 1974. 189-205.

946. _____. "St. Thomas and Elucidation." The New Scholasticism 35 (1961) 421-44.

947. Pallares, Fernando Sodir. "El conocimiento segun Santo Tomás de Aquino." Revista Filosofica. Mexico. 6 (1973) 269-73.

948. Parker, Francis H. Reason and Faith Revisited. Milwaukee: University Press, 1971. 56 pp.

949. Payzs, Kato Kiszely. "The Realism of Saint Thomas." Proceedings of the American Catholic Philosophical Association 21 (1946) 92-102.

950. Peccorini, Francisco L. "Knowledge of the Singular: Aquinas, Suarez and Recent Interpreters." The Thomist 38 (1974) 606-55.

951. Pegoraro, Olinto. "A verdade em S. Tomás e M. Heidegger." A Ordem I (1974) 68-90.

952. _____. "Note sur la verité chez saint Thomas et M. Heidegger." Revue Philosophique de Louvain 74 (1976) 45-55.

953. Peifer, John F. The Concept in Thomism. New York: Bookman Associates, 1952. 225 pp.

954. Phelan, Gerald B. "Being, Order and Knowledge." Proceedings of

LOGIC, GRAMMAR, EPISTEMOLOGY   955 - 971

the American Catholic Philosophical Association 33 (1959) 12-20.

955. Pichette, Henri. "Considérations sur quelques principes fondament-
aux de la doctrine du spéculatif et du pratique." Laval Théologique et
Philosophique I (1945) 52-70.

956. Pieper, Josef. Wahrheit der Dinge. München: Kösel, 1947.

957. Preston, Robert A. Causality and the Thomistic Theory of Knowledge. Washington, D.C.: Catholic University of America Dissertation,
1960. 135 pp.

958. Quinn, J. F. "Certitude of Reason and Faith in St. Bonaventure
and St. Thomas," in St. Thomas Aquinas 1274-1974 (Symp) II, 105-40.

959. Rabade, Sergio. "La gnoseologia tomista a la luz del pensamiento
actual." Estudios Filosoficos. Las Caldas de Besaya. 23 (1974) 203-17.

960. Rahner, Karl. "Aquinas: The Nature of Truth." Andrew Tallon, tr.
Continuum 2 (1964) 60-72.

961. Regis, Louis M. "Analyse et synthese dans s. Thomas," in Studia
Medievalia...R.J. Martin. Brieges: De Tempel, 1948. 303-30.

962. _____. Epistemology. New York: Macmillan, 1959. xiv-550 pp.

963. _____. St. Thomas and Epistemology. Milwaukee: Marquette
University Press, 1946. 96 pp.

964. Reilly, George C. "St. Thomas and the Problem of Knowledge." The
Thomist 17 (1954) 510-24.

965. Reiser, William E. "A Note on Lonergan's Notion of Truth." The
Modern Schoolman 46 (1969) 142-7.

966. Riet, Georges Van. L'Epistémologie thomiste. Louvain: Editions
Universitaires, 1946.

967. _____. Thomistic Epistemology: Studies Concerning the Problem
of Cognition in the Contemporary Thomistic School. Gabriel Franks, tr.
St. Louis: B. Herder, 1963. 352 pp.

968. _____. Problèmes d'Epistemologie. Louvain: Nauwelaerts, 1960.

969. Rivera, Jorge. Konnaturales Erkennen und vorstellendes Denken:
eine phänomenologische Deutung der Erkenntnislehre des Thomas von Aquin.
Freiburg: K. Alber, 1967. 165 pp.

970. Rocha, Filipe. "Modelacao cibernetica e analogia Tomista." Revista
Portuguesa de Filosofia 30 (1974) 163-84.

971. Rodriquez, Victorino. "Analogia del metado en la filosofia tomista."
Estudios Filosoficos 20 (1971) 357-62.

972 -986   LOGIC, GRAMMAR, EPISTEMOLOGY

972. Roig Gironella, Juan. "Un capitulo de filosofia del lenguage:
la metafisica de Santo Tomás y la transcendencia del pensamiento, plant-
eda por la fenomenologia." Espiritu 70 (1974) 131-47.

973. _____ . "Filosofia del lenguaje y la folosofia aristotelica de
Tomás de Aquino." Pensamiento 28 (1972) 29-79.

974. Ross, James F. "Aquinas and Philosophical Methodology." Metaphilosophy 1 (1970) 300-17.

975. _____ . A Critical Analysis of the Theory of Analogy of St.
Thomas Aquinas. Providence, R.I.: Brown University Dissertation, 1958.
236 pp.

976. Rousseau, Mary F. Toward a Thomistic Philosophy of Death: The
Natural Cognition of the Separated Soul. Milwaukee: Marquette University dissertation, 1977. 146 pp.

977. Ruello, Francis. La notion de vérité chez s. Albert le Grand et s.
Thomas d'Aquin de 1243-1254. Louvain: Nauwelaerts, 1969. 328 pp.

978. Rüppel, Ernesto. "Os primeiros principios sugundo a filosofia de
S. Tomas de Aquino." Revista Portuguesa de Filosofia 30 (1974) 135-62.

979. _____ . Unbekanntes Erkennen: Das Erfassen der Wirklichkeit
nach dem hl. Thomas von Aquin. Würzburg: Konrad Triltsch, 1971. ix-
79 pp.

980. Ryan, Bernard. An Aristotelian and Thomistic Interpretation of
Certain Aspects of the Logic of Sociology. New York: New York University Dissertation, 1948.

981. Ryan, Michael. The Notion and Uses of Dialectic in St. Thomas
Aquinas. Notre Dame: University of Notre Dame Dissertation, 1963.
225 pp.

982. Sacheri, Carlos A. "Aspectos lógicos del discurso deliberativo
(Santo Tomás)." Ethos . Buenos Aires. 1 (1973) 175-90.

983. Sala, Giovanni B. "Die Introspektion als Schlüssel zur Erkenntnislehre des hl. Thomas von Aquin." Theologie und Philosophie 49 (1974)
477-82.

984. _____ . "L'Origine del concetto: un problema kantiano e una
risposta tomista." Rivista di Filosofia Neo-Scolastica. Milano. 66
(1974) 975-1017.

985. Salamucha, Jan. "The Proof 'Ex Motu' for the Existence of God:
Logical Analysis of St. Thomas' Arguments." The New Scholasticism 32
(1958) 334-72.

986. Scheu, Marina. The Categories of Being in Aristotle and St. Thomas.
Washington, D.C.: Catholic University of America Dissertation, 1944.

LOGIC, GRAMMAR, EPISTEMOLOGY   987 - 1003

987. Schmidt, Robert W. The Domain of Logic According to St. Thomas Aquinas. Toronto: University of Toronto Dissertation, 1947.

988. _____. The Domain of Logic According to St. Thomas Aquinas. Hague: Nijhoff, 1966. 368 pp.

989. Schmitz, Kenneth L. "Another Look at Objectivity," in Thomas and Bonaventure, Proceedings of the American Catholic Philosophical Association 48 (1974) 86-98.

990. _____. "Enriching the Copula." Review of Metaphysics (Symp St. Thomas) 27 (1974) 492-512.

991. Schwartz, Herbert T. "Analogy in St. Thomas and Cajetan." The New Scholasiticism 28 (1954) 127-44.

992. _____. Plato, Aristotle, St. Thomas, and Univocity." The New Scholasticism 27 (1953) 373-403.

993. Serrano Vilafane, Emilio. "El realismo filosofico en Santo Tomás." Revista de Estudios Politicos 197 (1974) 47-96.

994. Sherry, Patrick. "The Contemporary Significance of Analogy." Philosophy 51 (1976).

995. Siewerth, G. Wort und Bild. Eine ontologische Interpretation. Düsseldorf: Schwann, 1952. 51 pp.

996. Sikora, Joseph J. "The Art and Science of Formal Logic in Thomistic Philosophy." The Thomist 22 (1959) 533-41.

997. _____. "Some Thomistic Reflections on the Foundations of Formal Logic." Notre Dame Journal of Formal Logic 6 (1965) 1-38.

998. Simmons, Edward D. "In Defense of Total and Formal Abstraction." The New Scholasticism 29 (1955) 427-40.

999. _____. "Demonstration and Self-Evidence." The Thomist 24 (1961) 137-62.

1000. _____. "The Nature and Limits of Logic." The Thomist 24 (1961) 47-71.

1001. _____. The Thomsitic Doctrine of Intellectual Abstraction for the Three Levels of Science: Exposition and Defense. Notre Dame: University of Notre Dame Dissertation, 1952. 199 pp.

1002. _____. "The Thomistic Doctrine of the Three Degrees of Formal Abstraction." The Thomist 22 (1959) 37-67.

1003. Smith, Gerard. "A Date in the History of Epistemology," in Maritain...Thomist (Symp) 246-55.

1004 - 1019 LOGIC, GRAMMAR, EPISTEMOLOGY

1004. Smith, Vincent E. "Abstraction and the Empirological Method
(with comments by Mark Heath)." Proceedings of the American Catholic
Philosophical Association 26 (1952) 35-53.

1005. _____. St. Thomas and the Object of Geometry. Milwaukee:
Marquette University Press, 1953. 99 pp.

1006. Snyder, John Julius. The Mode of Science and the Modes of
Demonstration Proper to the Metaphysics of St. Thomas Aquinas. Toronto:
University of Toronto Dissertation, 1969.

1007. Sousa Alves, Vitorino De. "S. Tomás de Aquino e a categoria de
Quantidade." Revista Portuguesa de Filosofia 30 (1974) 3-28.

1008. Spinnenweber, Andrew. Practical Knowledge in the Thought of St.
Thomas Aquinas. Pittsburgh: Duquesne University Dissertation, 1972.

1009. Squire, Aelred. "The Doctrine of the Image in the De veritate of
St. Thomas." Dominican Studies 4 (1961) 164-77.

1010. Steenberghen, Fernand van. Epistemologie. Louvain: Inst. Sup.
de Philos., 1945. 255 pp.

1011. _____. Epistemology. Martin J. Flynn, tr. New York: Wagner,
1949. xiv-324 pp.

1012. _____. Epistemology. Lawrence Moonan, tr. New York: Wagner,
1970. 285 pp.

1013. Steger, Evelyn E. The Verbum Cordis According to St. Thomas
Aquinas. Washington, D.C.: Catholic University of America Dissertation,
1967. 213 p.

1014. Strozewski, Wladyslaw. "Les trois dimensions de la verité. En
marge De veritate, I, 2," in Saint Thomas (Lublin Symp) 155-67.

1015. Takahashi, Wataru. "Self-knowledge According to Augustine and
Thomas Aquinas: Japanese with English summary." Studies in Medieval
Thought. Kyoto. 19 (1977) 1-17, 190-1.

1016. Tallon, Hugh J. "Does Thomism Neglect Multitude?" The New
Scholasticism 37 (1963) 267-92.

1017. Thro, Linus J. "Is there a Distinctively Thomistic Realism? or
the Confusion over Realism," in L'Homme et son destin (Symp) 571-6.

1018. Toccafondi, E. T. La ricerca critica della realtà. Roma: Arnodo,
1941. viii-312 pp.

1019. Trouillard, Jean. "La commaissance selon s. Thomas." Revue Philosophique de la France et de l'Etranger. Paris. 103 (1978) 73-7.

LOGIC, GRAMMAR, EPISTEMOLOGY   1020 - 1036

1020. Tyrrell, Francis M. "Concerning the Nature and Function of the
Act of Judgment." The New Scholasticism 26 (1952).

1021. _____. The Role of Assent in Judgment. Washington: Catholic
University of America Press, 1948.

1022. Van Roo, William A. "A Study of Genus in the Philosophy of St.
Thomas Aquinas." The Modern Schoolman 20 (1943) 89-104, 165-81, 230-44.

1023. Veatch, Henry B. Intentional Logic. A Logic Based on Philosophical
Realism. New Haven: Yale University Press, 1952. xxi-440 pp.

1024. _____. Realism and Nominalism Revisited. (Aquinas Lecture)
Milwaukee: Marquette University Press, 1954.

1025. _____. "St. Thomas and the Question: How are Synthetic
Judgments A Priori Possible?" The Modern Schoolman 42 (1965) 239-64.

1026. _____. "St. Thomas' Doctrine of Subject and Predicate. A
Possible Starting Point for Logical Reform and Renewal," in St. Thomas
Aquinas (Symp Toronto) II, 401-22.

1027. Verneaux, R. "Le principe d'identité chez s. Thomas." Sapienza
29 (1974) 83-106.

1028. Veuthey, Léon. La Commaissance humaine. Rome: Antonianum, 1948.

1029. Walton, William M. "The Second Mode of Necessary or Per Se
Propositions According to St. Thomas Aquinas." The Modern Schoolman 29
(1952) 293-306.

1030. Whittaker, John F. "The Position of Mathematics in the Hierarchy
of Speculative Science." The Thomist 3 (1941) 467-506.

1031. Wilhelmsen, Frederick D. Man's Knowledge of Reality. New York:
Prentice-Hall, 1956.

1032. Zarco Neri, Miguel Angel. "La naturaleza del conocimiento en la
filosofia de Santo Tomás de Aquino." Revista Filosofica. Mexico. 6
(1974) 227-36.

1033. Zdybicka, Zofia J. "Le réalisme de la connaissance et la participation de l'être," in Tommaso d'Aquino (Symp Roma) 6, 440-65.

PHILOSOPHY OF NATURE AND SCIENCE

1034. Abrams, J. W. "The Canons of Scientific Acceptability," in
Tommaso d'Aquino..problemi fondamentali (Symp) 493-501.

1035. Anderson, James F. "Time and the Possibility of an Eternal World."
The Thomist 15 (1952) 136-61.

1036. Anrich, E. Gross göttlich Ordnung. Thomas von Aquin, Paracelsus,

1037 - 1050   PHILOSOPHY OF NATURE & SCIENCE

Novalis und die Astrologie. Tübingen: Matthiesen, 1951. 111 pp.

1037. Ardley, Gavin. Aquinas and Kant. The Foundations of Modern Science. London: Longmans, 1950.

1038. Argerami, M. O. "La cuestión 'de aeternitate mundi': Posiciones doctrinales." Sapientia 27 (1972) 313-34; 28 (1973) 99-124, 179-208.

1039. _____. "El infinito actual en santo Tomás." Sapientia 26 (1971) 217-32.

1040. Ariotti, Piero. "Celestial Reductionism of Time: On the Scholastic Concept of Time from Albert the Great and Thomas Aquinas to the End of the 16th Century." Studi Internazionale di Filosofia. Torino. 4 (1972) 91-120.

1041. Bailleux, E. "Thomisme et evolution." Revue Thomiste 68 (1968) 583-607.

1042. Barath, Desiré. Thomas Aquinas' Physics and the New Sciences. Toronto: University of Toronto Dissertation, 1941. 82 pp.

1043. Belic, Miljenko. "Hylemorphismi locus ejusque mementum in systemate Aristotelis et in systemate S. Thomae," in Tommaso d'Aquino (Symp Roma) 9, 276-82.

1044. Bertola, Ermenegildo. "Tommaso d'Aquino e il problema dell'eternità del mondo." Rivista di Filosofia Neo-Scolastica. Milano. 66 (1974) 312-55.

1045. Blanchette, Oliva. The Perfection of the Universe in the Philosophy of Saint Thomas Aquinas. Quebec: Laval University Dissertation, 1965. 162 pp.

1046. Blic, J. de. "A propos de l'éternité du monde." Bulletin de littérature ecclésiastique 47 (1946) 162-70.

1047. Braun, H. "Der hl Thomas und der gestirnte Himmel..." Angelicum 17 (1940) 32-76.

1048. Bucher, Zeno. "Die Natur als Ordnung bei Thomas von Aquin." Salzburger Jahrbuch für Philosophie. Gedenkband...Thomas v Aquin. 19 (1974) 219-38.

1049. Burns, John V. "The Problem of Specific Natures." The New Scholasticism 30 (1956) 286-309.

1050. Cadden, Joan. The Medieval Philosophy and Biology of Growth in Albertus Magnus, Thomas Aquinas, Albert of Saxony and Masilius of Inghen on Book I, Chapter V of Aristotle's 'De Generatione et Corruptione,' with Translated Texts of Albertus Magnus and Thomas Aquinas. Bloomington: Indiana University Dissertation, 1971. 275 pp.

PHILOSOPHY OF NATURE AND SCIENCE   1051 - 1065

1051. Caldin, E. F. "Modern Physics and Thomist Philosophy." The Thomist 2 (1940) 208-25.

1052. Callus, Daniel A. "The Problem of the Plurality of Forms in the Thirteenth Century. The Thomist Innovation," in L'Homme et son destin (Symp) 577-85.

1053. Casaubon, Juan Alfredo. "La hipótesis del evolucionismo generalizado y el Tomismo." Sapientia. Argentina. 30 (1975) 123-38.

1054. Catalano, Joseph S. The Education of Substantial Forms According to St. Thomas Aquinas. Brooklyn, N.Y.: St. John's University Dissertation, 1962. 162 pp.

1055. Chrisman, John M. A Study of Two Major Thomistic Attempts to Reconcile Stable Intelligibility with Evolutionary Change. Toronto: University of Toronto Dissertation, 1971.

1056. Collingwood, Francis. Philosophy of Nature. Englewood Cliffs, N.J.: Prentice-Hall, 1961.

1057. Dempf, Alois. "Geistesgeschichtliche Bemerkungen zur Naturphilosophie des Aquinaten." Rivista de Filosofia Neoscolastica 66 (1974) 409-14.

1058. Do Carmo Silva, C. H. "Analise da delimitacao metodologica do problema da eternidade do mundo em S. Tomás de Aquino." Didaskalia 4 (1974) 321-56.

1059. Dougherty, Kenneth. Cosmology. An Introduction to the Thomistic Philosophy of Nature. Peekskill: Graymoor Press, 1952. 186.

1060. Dougherty, Kenneth F. The Subject, Object and Method of the Philosophy of Nature According to St. Thomas Aquinas. Washington, D.C. Catholic University of America Press, 1951.

1061. Dubarle, Dominique. "Causalidad y finalidad en S. Tomás y al nivel de las ciencias modernas de la naturaleza." Estudios Filosoficos 23 (1974) 219-38.

1062. _____. "Causalité et finalité chez s. Thomas et au niveau des sciences modernes de la nature," in Tommaso d'Aquino (Roma-Napoli) I, 423-45; 9, 9-25.

1063. _____. "Cosmologie Thomiste et philosophie naturelle contemporaine," in S. Thomas Aujourd 'hui (Symp) 137-69.

1064. Fuente, A. "Carácter cosmologico de la noción de tiempo en S. Tomás." Estudios Filosoficos 3 (1954) 171-210.

1065. Galli, G. M. "San Tommaso d'Aquino e la scienza. S. Tommaso precursore di Copernico?" in Tomismo e Antitomismo (Symp) II, 322-38.

1066 - 1081   PHILOSOPHY OF NATURE & SCIENCE

1066. Ghisalberti, Alessandro. "La concezione della natura nel commento di Tommaso d'Aquino alla 'Metafisica' di Aristotele." Rivista di Filosofia Neoscolastica 66 (1974) 533-40.

1067. Glutz, Melvin. The Manner of Demonstrating in Natural Philosophy. River Forest, Ill: Aquinas Institute, 1956.

1068. _____. "Ordering in the Philosophy of Nature." The Thomist 24 (1961) 402-18.

1069. Goheen, John. The Problem of Matter and Form in the "De Ente et Essentia" of Thomas Aquinas. Cambridge, Mass.: Harvard University Press, 1940. 137 pp.

1070. Hetzler, Florence M. An Introduction to the Philosophy of Nature: The Commentary of St. Thomas Aquinas on Book One of the Physics of Aristotle. New York: Fordham University Dissertation, 1959. 123 pp.

1071. Hoenen, Peter. The Philosophical Nature of Physical Bodies. West Baden, IN: West Baden College, 1955.

1072. Holveck, John E. Aquinas' Interpretation and use of Aristotle's Theory of Matter. Pittsburgh: Duquesne University Dissertation, 1973.

1073. Hughes, M. Cosmas. The Intelligibility of the Universe in the Philosophy of St. Thomas Aquinas. Washington, D.C.: Catholic University of America Dissertation, 1945.

1074. Junkersfeld, M. Julienne. The Aristotelian-Thomistic Concept of Chance. Notre Dame, IN: University of Notre Dame, 1945. 86 pp.

1075. Kiley, John F. Einstein and Aquinas. A Rapprochement. Hague: Nijhoff, 1969.

1076. Kilzer, Ernest R. "Efficient Causality in the Philosophy of Nature." Proceedings of the American Catholic Philosophical Association 17 (1941) 142-50.

1077. Klubertanz, George P. "Causality and Evolution. The Modern Schoolman 19 (1941) 11-4.

1078. _____. "Causality in the Philosophy of Nature." The Modern Schoolman 19 (1942) 29-31.

1079. Kocourek, Roman A. An Introduction to the Philosophy of Nature. St. Paul, Minn: North Central, 1948.

1080. Koninck, Charles de. "Abstraction from Matter: Notes on St. Thomas's Prologue to the Physics." Laval théologique et philosophique 13 (1957) 133-96; 16 (1960) 53-69, 169-88.

1081. _____. The Hollow Universe. London: Oxford University Press, 1960; Québec: Université Laval, 1964. xii-127 pp.

PHILOSOPHY OF NATURE AND SCIENCE   1082 - 1096

1082. Kovach, Francis J. "The Question of the Eternity of the World in St. Bonaventure and St. Thomas--A Critical Analysis." Southwestern Journal of Philosophy 5 (1974) 141-72.

1083. Kurdzialek, Marian. "Mozliwość obrotowego ruchu ziemi w ujeciu sw. Tomasza z Akwinu." Roczniki Filosoficzne. Lublin. 22 (1974) 55-72.

    Thomas on the Possibility of Rotation of the Earth.

1084. _____. "Über die Moglichkeit der Erdrotation in der Auffassung Thomas von Aquin," in Saint Thomas (Lublin Symp) 289-307.

1085. Laer, H. Van. Philosophico-scientific Problems. H. J. Koren, tr. Pittsburgh: Duquesne University Press, 1953. xi-168 pp.

1086. Lertora Mendoza, Celina Ana. "La teoria de la ciencia según S. Tomás y en la actualidad," in Conferenciss Cifina 1976, I. Buenos Aires: Pontificia Universidad Catolica Argentena, 1977. 33-61.

1087. Listfeldt, Hans-Guenther. "Some Concepts of Matter of Avicenna, Averroes, St. Thomas and Heisenberg." Aquinas. Roma. 17 (1974) 310-21.

1088. Litt, Thomas. Les Corps celestes dans l'univers de s. Thomas d'Aquin. Louvain-Paris: Beatrice-Nauwelaerts, 1963. 408 pp.

1089. Lobkowicz, Nikolaus and James A. Weisheipl. "Quidquid movetur ab alio movetur." The New Scholasticism 42 (1968) 401-31.

    Discussion article I and II.

1090. Luyten, Norbert A. "Anthropologie philosophique et philosophie de la nature," in Tommaso d'Aquino (Symp Roma-Napoli) I, 339-53.

1091. McDonald, Joseph B. The Art of Agriculture According to the Teaching of St. Thomas Quebec: Universite Laval Dissertation, 1959. 123 pp.

1092. MacKinnon, Edward J. "Analysis and the Philosophy of Science." International Philosophical Quarterly 7 (1967) 213-50.

1093. _____. "Thomism and Atomism." The Modern Schoolman 38 (1961) 121-41.

1094. McLaughlin, Robert J. Abstraction as Constitutive of Science According to Aristotle and St. Thomas Aquinas. Toronto: University of Toronto Dissertation, 1965.

1095. McMahon, George J. The Order of Procedure in the Philosophy of Nature. Québec: Librairie Doyon, 1958.

1096. McNicholl, Ambrose J. "Contemporary Challenge to the Traditional Ideal of Science," in The Dignity of Science (Symp) 447-68.

1097 - 1111 PHILOSOPHY OF NATURE & SCIENCE

1097. McWilliams, James A. "The Bond Between the Physics and the
Metaphysics of St. Thomas." The Modern Schoolman 22 (1944) 16-23.

1098. _____. "The Interrelationship of Nature and the Final Cause."
Proceedings of the American Catholic Philosophical Association 25 (1951)
108-15.

1099. Maier, Annaliese. Die Impetustheorie der Scholastik. Wien:
Schroll, 1940. 178 pp.

1100. _____. Das Problem der intensiven Grösse in der Scholastik.
Leipzig: Keller, 1940. 78 pp.

1101. Maritain, Jacques. "Hacia una idea tomista de la evolution."
Revista Filosofica. Mexico. 6 (1973) 49-83.

1102. _____. Philosophy of Nature. New York: Philosophical Library,
1951.

1103. Maurer, Armand A. "St. Thomas and Henry of Harclay on Created
Nature," in La Filosofia della Natura nel Medioeoo. Milano: Vita e
Pensiero, 1966.

        Terzo Congresso Internazionale di Filosofia Medivevale.

1104. Mazierski, Stanislaw. Prolegomena do filozofii przyrody inspiracji
arystotelesocosko-tomistycznej. Lublin: Univers. Lubelskiego, 1969.
239 pp.

1105. Meissner, W. W. "Some Notes on a Figure in St. Thomas." The New
Scholasticism 31 (1957) 68-84.

1106. Melsen, Andrew G. van. The Philosophy of Nature. Pittsburgh:
Duquesne University Press, 1953. xii-253 pp.

1107. Meurers, Joseph. "Tamás és a természettudomány ma." Mérleg 10
(1974) 365-78.

        Thomas and Today's Philosophy of Nature.

1108. _____. "Thomas und die Naturwissenschaft heute," in Tommaso
d'Aquino (Roma-Napoli Symp) I, 476-91; 9, 41-59.

1109. Moran, Lawrence. "On Uncaused Events." Proceedings of the
American Catholic Philosophical Association 40 (1966) 86-93.

1110. Moreno, Antonio. "The Law of Inertia and the Principle Quidquid
Movetur ab Alio Movetur." The Thomist. Centenary Edition. 38 (1974)
306-31.

1111. _____. "Some Philosophical Considerations on Biological
Evolution." The Thomist 37 (1973) 417-54.

PHILOSOPHY OF NATURE AND SCIENCE   1112 - 1126

1112. Mullahy, Bernard I. Thomism and Mathematical Physics. 2 vols.
Quebec: Laval University Dissertation, 1946. 977 pp.

1113. Munier, André. A Manual of Philosophy, Vol. I: Cosmology and
Philosophical Psychology. Thomas W. Connolly, tr. New York: Desclée
Co., 1964. 580 pp.

1114. Nicolas, Marie-Joseph. Evolution et Christianisme. De Teilhard de
Chardin à s. Thomas d'Aquin. Paris: Fayard, 1973. xix-243 pp.

        Préface de Jacques Maritain.

1115. _____ . "L'idée de nature dans là pensée de s. Thomas diAquin."
Revue Thomiste 74 (1974) 533-90.

1116. Oudin, J.-M. "St. Thomas d'Aquin et la science moderne. II:
Hylé-morphisme et crise de la croissance." Bulletin du Cercle Thomiste
68 (1974) 38-43.

1117. Owens, Joseph. "Our Knowledge of Nature." Proceedings of the
American Catholic Philosophical Association 29 (1955) 63-86.

1118. Quinn, John Michael. The Doctrine of Time in St. Thomas Aquinas.
Some Aspects and Applications. Washington, D.C.   Catholic University
of America Dissertation, 1961. 141 pp.

1119. Redpath, Peter. The Ontological Status of Time in the Commentary
on the Sentences, the Commentary on the Physics, and the Summa Theologiae
of Thomas Aquinas. Buffalo: State University of New York Dissertation,
1974.

1120. Rehrl, Stefan. "Materie und Form bei Aristoteles und Thomas von
Aquin," in Salzburger...Gedenkband 1974 (Symp) 11-33.

1121. Ruello, Francis. "La signification du mot 'nature' dans le De
principiis naturae de s. Thomas d'Aquin." Rivista di Filosofia Neoscolestica 66 (1974) 613-25.

1122. Russell, John F. "St. Thomas and the Heavenly Bodies." Heythrop
Journal 8 (1967) 27-39.

1123. Saintonqe, Frederick. Summa Cosmologiae seu Philosophia Naturalis
Generalis. Montreal: Imprimerie du Messager, 1941.

1124. Salman, D. H. "De la méthode en philosophie naturelle." Revue
Philosophique de Louvain 50 (1952) 205-29.

1125. Sanguineti, Juan J. La filosofia de la ciencia segùn Santo Tomàs.
Pamplona: Ediciones Universidad de Navarra, 1977. 371 pp.

1126. Saranyana, José I. "Santo Tomàs 'De aeternitate mundi contra
murmurantes'." Anuario Filosofico 9 (1976) 399-424.

1127.   Savagnone, Giuseppe. "La conoscibilità del mondo della natura secondo S. Tommaso." Aquinas   21 (1978) 63-93.

1128.   Selvaggi, Philippus. Cosmologia. Romae: Gregorianum, 1959.

1129.   _____. Filosofia della scienze. Roma: Ed. Civiltà Cattolica, 1953. 348 pp.

1130.   Sikora, Joseph J. "The Philosophy of Nature and Natural Science from a Thomist Viewpoint." The Thomist   20 (1957) 330-48.

1131.   _____. The Scientific Knowledge of Physical Nature. Bruges-Paris: Desclée de Brouwer, 1966. 165 pp.

1132.   Simon, Yves. "Maritain's Philosophy of the Sciences," in Maritain Thomist (Symp) 85-102.

1133.   Siwek, Paul. "Y a-t-il place pour le transformisme dans la philosophie de s. Thomas d'Aquin?" Aquinas   17 (1974) 264-82.

1134.   Slaga, Szczepan W. "Proba úsciślenia tomaszowego okreslenia istoty zycia." Studia Philosophiae Christianae   19 (1974) 67-99.

1135.   Smith, Vincent E. Philosophical Physics. New York: Harpers, 1950.

1136.   _____. The Philosophical Frontiers of Physics. Washington, D.C.: Catholic University of America Press, 1947.

1137.   Steenberghen, Fernand Van. "Le mythe d'un monde 'eternel.'" Revue Philosophique de Louvain   76 (1978) 157-79.

1138.   Taylor, Frank S. The Attitude of St. Thomas to Natural Science. Oxford: Blackfriars, 1944. 24 pp.

         Aquinas papers, 3.

1139.   Thompson, W. R. "Providence," in Maritain...Thomist (Symp) 229-45.

1140.   Tollenaere, M. De. Een Philosophie von de Tyd. De functie van het subject in de tydstructuur volgens het hedendaags thomisme. Louvain: Nauwelaerts, 1952. xxii-218 pp.

1141.   Tonquédec, Jean De. Questions de cosmologie et de physique chez Aristote et Saint Thomas. Paris: Vrin, 1950. 127 pp.

1142.   Torre, D. "S. Tommaso d'Aquino nella storia della medicina." Rivista di Storia della Medicina   18 (1974) 248-68.

1143.   Turner, Walter H. The Concept of 'Casus' in the Philosophy of St. Thomas Aquinas. Toronto: University of Toronto Dissertation, 1941. 82 pp.

PHILOSOPHY OF NATURE AND SCIENCE   1144 - 1160

1144. Ushida, Noriko. "The Problem of Matter as a Principle of Individuation and Unity of Substantial Form in St. Thomas: Japanese Text and
English Summary." Studies in Medieval Thought 17 (1975) 28-45, 147-8.

1145. Veres, Tomo. "Sveti Toma - preteca Kopernika?" Crkva u svijtu
(Split) 3 (1973) 237-45.

1146. Vignon, Paul. Au souffle de l'esprit créateur: science et métaphysique thomistes de la vie. Paris: Beauchesne, 1946. 202 pp.

1147. Vries, F. de. "Das Problem der Naturgesetzlichkeit bei Thomas
von Aquin." Scholastik 49 (1949) 503-17.

1148. Wall, Joseph B. "The Mind of St. Thomas on the Principle of
Individuation." The Modern Schoolman 18 (1941) 41-3.

1149. Wallace, William A. "Aquinas on the Temporal Relation Between
Cause and Effect." Review of Metaphysics. Aquinas Commem. 27 (1974)
569-84.

1150. _____. "Buridan, Ockham, Aquinas: Science in the Middle Ages."
The Thomist 40 (1976) 475-83.

1151. _____. "Causality, Analogy, and the Growth of Scientific
Knowledge," in Tommaso d'Aquino (Roma-Napoli Symp) I, 447-66.

1152. _____. Causality and Scientific Explanation. II. Classical
and Contemporary Science. Ann Arbor: University of Michigan Press,
1974. 422 pp.

1153. _____. "The Measurement and Definition of Sensible Qualities."
The New Scholasticism 39 (1965) 1-25.

1154. _____. Saint Thomas and the Pull of Gravity. West Hartford,
CT: St. Joseph College, 1965.

1155. _____. "St. Thomas Aquinas, Galileo, and Einstein." The
Thomist 24 (1961) 1-22.

1156. _____. "The Thomistic Order of Development in Natural Philosophy," in Teaching Thomism Today (Symp) 247-70.

1157. Weisheipl, James A. "The Concept of Nature." The New Scholasticism
28 (1954) 377-408.

1158. _____. The Dignity of Science. Washington: Thomist Press,
1961.

1159. _____. "Motion in a Void: Aquinas and Averroes," in St.
Thomas Aquinas (Toronto Symp) I, 467-88.

1160. _____. "The Relationship of Medieval Natural Philosophy to
Modern Science: The Contribution of Thomas Aquinas." Manuscripta.

St. Louis. 20 (1976) 181-96.

1161. Wolf, Theodore John. The Function of Qualities in Substantial Change According to St. Thomas Aquinas. St. Louis: Saint Louis University Dissertation, 1945. 144 pp.

1162. Zimmermann, A. "'Mundus est aeternus?-Zur Auslegung dieser these bei Bonaventura und Thomas von Aquin," in Die Auseinandersetzungen an der Pariser Universität in XIII Jahrhundert. Berlin: Miscellanea Mediaevalia, 10, 1976. 317-30.

PSYCHOLOGY AND PHILOSOPHY OF MAN

1163. Adler, Mortimer J. "Sense Cognition: Aristotle vs. Aquinas." The New Scholasticism 42 (1968) 578-91.

1164. Alciatore, Pegge L. and Robert. "Thomism and a Theory of Motivation." Journal of Thought 7 (1972) 84-90.

1165. Allers, Rudolf. "Functions, Factors, and Faculties." The Thomist 7 (1944) 323-62.

1166. _____. "On Intellectual Operations." The New Scholasticism 26 (1952) 1-36.

1167. Aloysius, M. "Toward a Thomistic Theory of Sensation." The Thomist 20 (1957) 143-57.

1168. Anderson, M. Evangeline. The Human Body in the Philosophy of St. Thomas Aquinas. Washington, D.C.: Catholic University of America Press, 1953.

1169. Arnold, M. B. and J. A. Gasson. The Human Person. An Approach to an Integral Theory of Personality. New York: Ronald Press, 1954. x-593 pp.

1170. Aspell, Patrick J. A Thomistic Critique of Trans-subjectivity in Recent American Realism. Washington, D.C.: Catholic University of America Dissertation, 1959. 122 pp.

1171. Baars, Conrad W. "Christian Anthropology of Thomas Aquiaas." The Priest 30 (1974) 29-33.

1172. Baker, Richard R. The Thomistic Theory of the Passions and Their Influence Upon the Will. Notre Dame: University of Notre Dame Press, 1941. 153 pp.

1173. _____. The Thomistic Theory of the Passions and Their Influence Upon the Will. Notre Dame: University of Notre Dame Dissertation, 1941. 147 pp.

1174. Balmori, H. tr. "S. Tomás de Aquino. Reflexio, Antologia de textos sobre el conocimiento del yo." Humanitas. Tucumán. 3 (1954) 367-429.

PSYCHOLOGY AND PHILOSOPHY OF MAN   1175 - 1190

1175. Barrata-Moura, J. "Da pessoa como categoria ontica à pessoa como categoria ética. A proposito do tema da 'pessoa' em s. Tomas de Aquino." Didaskalia 4 (1974) 357-98.

1176. Bastable, P. K. Desire for God. Does Man Aspire Naturally to the Beatific Vision? London-Dublin: Burns Oates & Washbourne, 1947. 177 pp.

1177. Bernath, Klaus. Anima forma corporis. Eine Untersuchung über die ontologischen Grundlagen der Anthropologie des Thomas von Aquin. Bonn: Bouvier, 1969. 246 pp.

1178. Bertola, Ermanegildo. "La dottrina dello 'spirito' in S. Tommaso." Sophia. Padova. 21 (1953) 29-35.

1179. _____. "Il problema dell' immortalità dell'anima umana nelle opere di Tommaso d'Aquino." Rivista Filosofia Neo-Scolastica 65 (1973) 248-302.

1180. Bledsoe, James P. "Aquinas on the Soul." Laval Théologique et Philosophique 29 (1973) 273-89.

1181. Blumberg, Harry. "The Problem of Immortality in Avicenna, Maimonides and St. Thomas," in Harry Austryn Wolfson Jubilee Volume. Saul Lieberman, ed. Jerusalem: Amer. Acad. for Jewish Research, 1965. 165-85.

1182. Bourke, V. J. "Human Tendencies, Will and Freedom," in L'Homme et son destin   (Symp) 71-84.

1183. _____. "The Operations Involved in Intellectual Conception." The Modern Schoolman 21 (1944) 83-89.

1184. _____. "St. Thomas and the Transfer of Intellectual Skills." The Modern Schoolman 18 (1941) 69-73.

1185. _____. Will in Western Thought. New York: Sheed & Ward, 1964. x-247 pp.

1186. Brasa Diez, Mariano. "La historicidad de hombre según S. Tomás." Studium 14 (1974) 309-18.

1187. Brennan, Mary Alethea. The Origin of the Rational Soul According to St. Thomas Aquinas. Washington, D.C.: Catholic University of America Press, 1950.

1188. Brennan, Robert E. General Psychology. A Study of Man Based on St. Thomas Aquinas. New York: Macmillan, 1952. 555 pp.

1189. _____. History of Psychology from the Standpoint of a Thomist. New York: Macmillan, 1945. xvi-277 pp.

1190. _____. "The Thomistic Concept of Imagination." The New Scholasticism 15 (1941) 149-61.

1192 - 1206   PSYCHOLOGY & PHILOSOPHY OF MAN

1192. Brennan, Rose E. The Intellectual Virtues According to the Philosophy of St. Thomas Washington, D.C.: Catholic University of America
Press, 1941; Palo Alto, CA: Pacific Books, 1957.

1193. Breton, Stanislas. "L'unité de l'intellect. Réflexions sur le
sens et la portée d'uve controverse." Revue des Sciences Philosophiques
et Théologiques   62 (1978) 225-33.

1194. Campbell, Bertrand J. A Controversy of One or Plural Forms in
Man as Found in the Works of St. Thomas Aquinas and John Duns Scotus.
Philadelphia: University of Pennsylvania Dissertation, 1936.

1195. Cangemi, Dominic. The Thomistic Concept of the Vis Cogitativa.
Washington: Catholic University of America Press, 1951.

1196. Cantin, Stanislas. Précis de psychologie thomiste. Québec:
Universeté Laval, 1948.

1197. Caparello, Adriana. "Il termine 'tunical' e la sua portata
scientifico-storica nella dottrina aristotelico-tomista della visione."
Divus Thomas. Piacenza. 79 (1976) 369-98.

1198. Carney, William J. Agent Intellect and Phantasm Their Relationship
in the Teaching of St. Thomas and his Commentators. Washington, D.C.:
Ceorgetown University Dissertation, 1950. 176 pp.

1199. Carrascosa, José Maria. "Influencia del entendimiento en el acto
voluntario en la obra de S. Tomás." Revista de Filosofia. Maracaibo.
2 (1976) 33-62.

1200. Caturelli, Alberto. "La antropologia y sus problemas en santo
Tomás de Aquino," in Tommaso d'Aquino (Roma-Napoli Symp) I, 355-77.

1201. Centore, F. F. "Aquinas on inner space." Canadian Journal of
Philosophy 4 (1974) 351-63.

1202. Chenu, M.-D. "Les passions vertueuses. L'anthropologie de s.
Thomas." Revue Philosophique de Louvain 72 (1974) 11-8.

1203. _____. "Ratio superior et inferior. Un cas de philosophie
chrétienne." Revue des Sciences philosophique et théologique 29 (1940)
84-9.

1204. Chorus, A. Thomistische Psychologie en psycho-analyse. Amsterdam:
Streven, 1950.

1205. Combès, André. "Le problème de la liberté d'après s. Thomas."
Divinitas. Roma. 18 (1974) 106-14.

1206. Composta, Dario. "De vi et natura inclinationum naturalium
hominis cum instinctu comparatarum." Doctor Communis 24 (1971) 124-32.

PSYCHOLOGY AND PHILOSOPHY OF MAN   1207 - 1222

1207.   Congar, Yves. "L'Historicité de l'homme selon Thomas d'Aquin."
Doctor Communis 22 (1969) 297-304.

1208.   Connell, Richard J. "The 'Intus Appareus' and the Immateriality
of the Intellect." The New Scholasticism 32 (1958) 151-86.

1209.   Corea, Peter V. Freedom in Plato, Aristotle, Aquinas, and Kant.
Boston: Boston University Dissertation, 1961.

1210.   Crem, Theresa M. "A Thomistic Explanation of the Neurosis."
Laval Théologique et Philosophique 24 (1968) 294-300.

1211.   Crosson, Frederick J. "Psyche and Persona, The Problem of Personal Immortality." International Philosophical Quarterly 8 (1968)
161-79.

1212.   Crowe, Michael B. "Human Nature - Immutable or Mutable."
Irish Theological Quarterly 30 (1963).

1213.   Dalle Nogare, Pedro. "A pessoa em santo Tomás." Presence
Filosofica (Symp) 100-13.

1214.   Daly, Jeanne Joseph. The Metaphysical Foundations of Free Will
as a Transcendental Aspect of the Act of Existence in the Philosophy
of St. Thomas Aquinas. Washington, D.C.: Catholic University of
America, 1958. 110 pp.

1215.   Daros, William R. "La interpretacion rosminiana del intelecto
agente tomista." Pensamiento 34 (1978) 47-72.

1216.   _____. "El lumen naturale en santo Tomás y el essere ideale
en Rosmini." Sapientia 31 (1976) 251-8.

1217.   Deely, John N. "Animal Intelligence and Concept-Formation."
The Thomist 35 (1971) 43-93.

1218.   Del Cura, Alejandro. "La esencia de Rombre en la antropologia
de S. Tomás de Aquino." Estudios Filosoficos 23 (1974) 419-25.

1219.   De Smet, Richard. "The Aristotelian - Thomist Concept of Man."
Indian Philosophical Quarterly 2 (1975) 307-18.

1220.   Doig, James C. "Toward Understanding Aquinas' Commentary in De
Anima. A Comparative Study of Aquinas and Averroes on the Definition of
Soul." Rivista di Filosofia Neoscolestica 66 (1974) 436-74.

1221.   Dubay, Thomas. "An Investigation into the Thomistic Concept of
Pleasure." The New Scholasticism 36 (1962) 76-99.

1222.   Duggan, George. "The Teaching of St. Thomas regarding the Formal
Constitutive of Human Personality." The New Scholasticism 15 (1941)
318-49.

1223 - 1237 PSYCHOLOGY & PHILOSOPHY OF MAN

1223. Elbert, Edmund J. A Thomistic Study of the Psychology of Human Character. Washington, D.C.: Catholic University of America Dissertation, 1956.

1224. Endres, Josef. "Thomasischer Personbegriff und neuzeitlicher Personalismus," in Thomas...Interpretation (Symp) 117-43.

1225. Ermatinger, Charles Joseph. The Coalescent Intellective Soul in Post-Thomistic Debate. St. Louis: Saint Louis University Dissertation, 1963.

1226. Fabro, Cornelio. "L'anima nell'età patristica e medievale," in L'Anima. Brescia: Morcelliana, 1954. 71-105.

1227. Facchi, Giorgio. "L'unità dell'intelletto," in Tommaso d'Aquino (Symp) II, 59-66.

1228. Farrelly, John. "Developmential Psychology and Man's Knowledge of Being." The Thomist 39 (1975) 668-95.

1229. Figurski, Leszek. Final Cause & Its Relation to Intelligence in St. Thomas Aquinas." New York: Fordham University Dissertation, 1977.

1230. Finance, Joseph de. "Le cercle de la connaissance et du vouloir. A propos d'un texte de s. Thomas, De verit. i, 2." Rivista di Filosofia Neoscolastica 66 (1974) 394-408.

    Also Sapientia 29 (1974) 43-56.

1231. Fisher, Alden L. "Psychology or Psychologies - A Study in Methodology." Proceedings of the American Catholic Philosophical Association 31 (1957) 144-57.

1232. Flippen, Douglas W. "A Problem Concerning Relation in Sensation," in Tommaso d'Aquino (Symp Roma) 9, 307-14.

1233. Flynn, Thomas V. "The Cogitative Power." The Thomist 16 (1953) 542-63.

1234. Foley, Thomas Aquin. Authority and Personality Development According to St. Thomas Aquinas. Washington, D.C.: Catholic University of America Dissertation, 1956.

1235. Franz, Edward Q. The Thomistic Doctrine on the Possible Intellect. Washington, D.C.: Catholic University of America Press, 1950.

1236. Garceau, Denoit. Judicium, Vocabulaire, Sources, Doctrine de s. Thomas d'Aquin. Montréal-Paris: Vrin, 1968. 286 pp.

1237. Giglio, Charles J. Freedom of Self-Determination in Saint Thomas Aquinas and Contemporary Western Thought. Washington, D.C.: Catholic University of America Dissertation, 1964.

PSYCHOLOGY AND PHILOSOPHY OF MAN   1238 - 1253

1238. Gilby, Thomas. "Thought, Volition and the Organism." The Thomist
2 (1940) 1-13.

1239. _____. "Vienne and Vienna." Thought 21 (1946) 63-82.

       Definition of soul as "form."

1240. Gumppenberg, Rudolf. "Reflexionen zum Begriff der Person bei
Thomas von Aquin." Doctor Communis. Roma. 27 (1974) 47-60.

1241. Gustafson, Gustaf J. The Theory of Natural Appetency in the
Philosophy of St. Thomas. Washington, D.C." Catholic University of
America Press, 1944.

1242. Hammer, Felix. "Personale Lieblichkeit," in Gedenkband...Thomas
von Aquin (Symp) 199-218.

1243. Hayes, Mary Dolores. Various Group Mind Theories Viewed in the
Light of Thomistic Principles. Washington, D.C.: Catholic University
of America Dissertation, 1942.

1244. Hazard, Paul A. The Passion of Shame in the Teachings of Freud
and Aquinas. Quebec: Universite Laval Dissertation, 1970. 254 pp.

1245. Henle, Robert J. "St. Thomas and the Definition of Intelligence."
The Modern Schoolman 53 (1976) 335-46.

1246. Hess, M. Whitcomb. "Language and Sense Perception." The Thomist
10 (1947) 56-74.

1247. Hislop, Ian. The Anthropology of St. Thomas. London: Blackfriars,
1950. 10 pp.

       Aquinas papers, 13.

1248. Horvath, A. "Das objektive Erkenntnis-licht." Divus Thomas.
Freibourg. 29 (1951) 284-306, 429-56; 30 (1952) 201-32.

1249. Hudeczek, M. M. "De tempore animationis foetus humani secundum
embryologiam hodiernam." Angelicum 29 (1952) 162-81.

1250. Hufnagel, Alfons. "Der Instuitionsbegriff des Thomas von Aquin."
Theologische Quartalschrift. Stuttgart. 133 (1953) 427-36.

1251. Izzalini, Luigi d'. Il principio intellettivo della ragione
umana nelle opere di s. Tommaso d'Aquino. Romae: Gregorianum, 1943.

1252. Jolif, Jean-Yves. "Affirmation rationelle de l'immortalité de
l'ame chez s. Thomas." Lumière et Vie 4 (1955) 59-78.

1253. Jolivet, Régis et Maxence, J.-P. Manuel de Philosophie. I.
Psychologie. Lyon: Vitte, 1953. 481 pp.

1254 - 1268 PSYCHOLOGY & PHILOSOPHY OF MAN

1254. Kahn, Journet David. A Thomistic Theory of Emotion. Notre Dame: University of Notre Dame Dissertation, 1956. 203 pp.

1255. Kasai, T. "The Mind-Body Problem in the Thought of Dōgen and Thomas Aquinas." Journal of Indian and Buddhist Studies 22 (1974) 1109-12.

1256. Kelley, James P. The Continuation Between the Human Sense Powers and the Human Speculative Intellect According to St. Thomas Aquinas. Brooklyn, N.Y.: St. John's University Dissertation, 1963. 143 pp.

1257. Kelly, Matthew J. "Aquinas and the Subsistence of the Soul, Notes on a Difficulty." Franciscan Studies 27 (1967) 213-19.

1258. Kelly, Pascal. An Analysis of the Proper Senses in the Philosophy of St. Thomas Aquinas. New York: Fordham University Dissertation, 1952. 222 pp.

1259. Kennedy, Leonard A. "The Soul's Knowledge of Itself. An Unpublished Work Attributed to St. Thomas Aquinas." Vivarium 15 (1977) 31-45.

1260. Kenny, Anthony. The Anatomy of the Soul. New York: Harper and Row, 1973. vii-147 pp.

    See Essay 4: "Intellect and Imagination in Aquinas."

1261. Kinsella, Noel A. "The Epigenesis of Personality Development: Saint Thomas and Erik H. Erikson." The Thomist 31 (1967) 245-54.

1262. Klubertanz, George P. "De Potentia 5, 8: Note on the Thomistic Theory of Sensation." The Modern Schoolman 26 (1949) 323-31.

1263. _____. The Discursive Power: Sources and Doctrine of the Vis Cogitativa According to St. Thomas. St. Louis: The Modern Schoolman, 1952.

1264. _____. "The Internal Senses in the Process of Cognition." The Modern Schoolman 18 (1941) 27-30.

1265. _____. The Philosophy of Human Nature. New York: Appleton-Century-Crofts, 1953. 444 pp.

1266. _____. "The Psychologists and the Nature of Man." Proceedings of the American Catholic Philosophical Association 25 (1951) 66-87.

1267. _____. "The Unity of Human Activity." The Modern Schoolman 27 (1950) 75-103.

1268. _____. The Vis Cogitativa According to St. Thomas Aquinas, Sources and Doctrine. Toronto: University of Toronto, 1947.

PSYCHOLOGY AND PHILOSOPHY OF MAN   1269 - 1284

1269. Kluxen, Wolfgang. "Anima separata und Personsein bei Thomas von Aquin," in Thomas..Interpretation (Symp) 95-116.

1270. Koenen, Jane. Human Operations and Their Finalities in Saint Thomas Aquinas. St. Louis: Saint Louis University Dissertation, 1959. 202 pp.

1271. Krapf, E. Eduardo. Tomás de Aquino y la Psicopatologia. Index de Neurologia y Psiquiatria, 2. Buenos Aires: R. Orlando, 1943 43 pp.

1272. Krapiec, Mieczyslaw A. Ja-czlowiek. Zarys antropologii filozoficznej. Lublin, Towarzystwo Naukowe K.U.L., 1974 455 pp.

1273. Kreyche, Gerald F. "The Soul-Body Problem in St. Thomas." The New Scholasticism 46 (1972) 466-84.

1274. Lambert, Richard Thomas. Man's Knowledge of His Soul in St. Thomas Aquinas. Notre Dame: University of Notre Dame Dissertation, 1971. 190 pp.

1275. Lanigan, Joseph. "Knowledge of Person Implied in the Thomistic Doctrine of Love, with Comment by Bernard A. Gendreau." Proceedings of the American Catholic Philosophical Association 31 (1957) 179-92.

1276. Laporta, Jorge. "Pour trouver le sens exact des termes Appetitus naturalis, desiderium naturale, amor naturalis, etc. chez Thomas d'Aquin." Archives d'Historie Doctrinale et Littéraire du Moyen Age. Paris. 48 (1973) 37-95.

1277. La Spisa, Mauro. Metaecologia e omni-dimensionalità della via hominis. Secondo Tommaso d'Aquin. Firenze: G. e G., 1970. 110 pp.

1278. Lauer, Rosemary Z. "St. Thomas' Theory of Intellectual Causality in Election." The New Scholasticism 28 (1954) 297-319.

1279. Leahy, Louis. Dynamisme volontaire et jugement libre chez quelques commentateurs Thomistes de la Renaissance. Bruges: Besclée 1963. 171 pp.

1280. Lebacqz, Joseph. Libre arbitre et jugement. Brussels: Desclée, 1960. 164 pp.

1281. Lefevre, Charles. "La relation personelle chez s. Thomas d'Aquin." Mélanges de Science Peligieuse. Lille. 31 (1974) 121-44.

1282. Legrand, J. L'univers et l'homme dans la philosophie de s. Thomas. 2 vols. Bruxelles: Desclée, 1946.

1283. Lennon, Joseph L. "The Notion of Experience." The Thomist 23 (1960) 315-44.

1284. Lisska, Anthony J. "Aquinas' Use of 'Phantasia'." The Thomist 40 (1976) 294-302.

1285 - 1301   PSYCHOLOGY & PHILOSOPHY OF MAN

1285. _____. The Role of Phantasms in Aquinian Perceptual Theory.
Columbus: Ohio State University Dissertation, 1971. 263 pp.

1286. Lobkowicz, Nikolaus. "Deduction of Sensibility: The Ontological
Status of Sense-Knowledge in St. Thomas." International Philosophical
Quarterly 3 (1963) 201-26.

1287. Luyten, Norbert A. "Anthropologie philosophique et philosophie
de la nature," in Tommaso d'Aquino...problemi fondamentali (Symp) 1974
339-53.

1288. _____. "L'Homme dans la conception de s. Thomas," in L'
Anthropologie (Fribourg Symp) 1974. 35-53.

1289. McGinnis, R. R. The Wisdom of Love, A Study in the Psycho-
Metaphysics of Love According to the Principles of St. Thomas. Rome:
Ag. del Libro Catholica, 1951. xvi-148 pp.

1290. McKian, J. D. "The Metaphysics of Introspection According to St.
Thomas Aquinas." The New Scholasticism 15 (1941) 89-117.

1291. McMullin, Ernan. "Who are We." Proceedings of the American
Catholic Philosophical Association 41 (1967) 1-16.

1292. Macken, Raymond. "La doctrine de s. Thomas concernant la volonté
et les critiques d'Henri de Gand," in Tommaso d'Aquino (Symp) II, 84-91.

1293. Mailloux, Noel. "The Problem of Perception." The Thomist 4
(1942) 266-85.

1294. Manzanedo, Marcos F. "Existencia y naturaleza de la memoria
segùn S. Tomas." Studium 13 (1973) 281-99.

1295. _____. "La inteligencia y las manos segun Santo Tomàs."
Studium 14 (1974) 241-63.

1296. _____. "La memoria en sus relaciones con otras facultades
animicas." Studium 14 (1974) 65-95.

1297. Marc, André. Psychologie Réflexive: I. La connaissance; II. La
volonté et l'esprit. Bruxelles-Paris: Beauchesne, 1948-1949.

1298. Martin, Oliver. "The Philosophy of Human Nature." Review of
Metaphysics 7 (1954) 452-65.

1299. Martz, F. La Perfection de l'homme selon s. Thomas d'Aquin.
Rome: U. Grégorienne, 1962. 349 pp.

1300. Massara, Luigi. "La 'Delectatio' dans la psychologie de Saint
Thomas d'Aquin." Archives de Philosophie 32 (1969) 639-63.

1301. Mattos, G. de. "L'intellect agent personnel dans les premiers
écrits d'Albert le Grand et de Thomas d'Aquin." Revue Néoscolastique

PSYCHOLOGY AND PHILOSOPHY OF MAN   1302 - 1317

<u>de Philosophie</u> 43 (1940) 145-61.

1302. Mauro, Letterio. "Umanita" della passione in S. Tommaso.
Firenze: Le Monnier, 1974. 146 pp.

1303. Merks, Karl-Wilhelm. "Anthropologische Perspektiven bei Thomas
von Aquin." <u>Angelicum</u> 54 (1977) 347-76.

1304. Mertens, Joseph. "Functie en wezen van de intellectus agens
volgens S. Thomas." <u>Tijdshrift voor Philosophie</u>. Leuven. 36 (1974)
267-322.

1305. Metz, Johannes B. <u>Christliche Anthropocentrik. Über die Denkform
des Thomas von Aquin</u>. München: Kösel, 1962. 138 pp.

1306. _____. <u>Antropocentrisme cristians. Sobre la forma de
pensiamento de Tomás de Aquino</u>. Salamanca: Ed. Sigueme, 1972.

1307. _____. <u>Antropocentrismo cristiano. Studio sulla mentalità di
Tommaso d'Aquino</u>. Trad. di Aldo Audisio Torino: Borla, 1969. 148 pp.

1308. _____. "Zur Metaphysik der menschlicken Leiblichkeit."
<u>Arzt und Christ</u> 4 (1968) 78 ff.

1309. Mondin, Battista. "La persona umana e il suo destino in S.
Tommaso e nel pensiero moderno." <u>Aquinas</u> 17 (1974) 366-402.

1310. Montague, Michael. <u>Secondary Causality in the Act of Will-to-End
in the Writings of Saint Thomas Aquinas</u>. St. Louis: Saint Louis
University Dissertation, 1953.

1311. Moreau, Joseph. "L'Homme et son ame, selon saint Thomas d'Aquin."
<u>Revue Philosophique de Louvain</u> 74 (1976) 5-29.

1312. Muller-Thym, Bernard J. "The Common Sense, Perfection of the
Order of Pure Sensibility." <u>The Thomist</u> 2 (1940) 315-43.

1313. Mulligan, Robert W. "Ratio Superior and Ratio Inferior: the
Historical Background." <u>The New Scholasticism</u> 29 (1955) 1-32.

1314. _____. "<u>Ratio Inferior</u> and <u>Ratio Superior</u> in St. Albert and
St. Thomas." <u>The Thomist</u> 19 (1956) 339-67.

1315. Munos, Jesus. "Optimismo o pessimismo en la concepción del hombre,
segun Sto. Tomás?" in <u>L'Homme et son destin</u> (Symp) 587-94.

1316. Murphy, Richard T. "Concept and Object." <u>The New Scholasticism</u>
42 (1968) 254-69.

1317. Murray, Michael V. "The Man of St. Augustine and St. Thomas."
<u>Proceedings of the American Catholic Philosophical Association</u> 24 (1950)
90-6.

1318. Naus, John. The Nature of the Practical Intellect According to St. Thomas Aquinas. Rome: Gregorian University, 1959. 220 pp.

1319. Nolan, Paul. Saint Thomas and the Unconscious Mind. Washington, D.C.: Catholic University of America Dissertation, 1953.

1320. O'Callaghan, Louis T. The Function of Reflection in the Psychology of Saint Thomas Aquinas. New York: Fordham University Dissertation, 1948. 278 pp.

1321. O'Connor, William R. The Eternal Quest. The Teaching of St. Thomas Aquinas on the Natural Desire for God. New York: Longmans, 1947 290 pp.

1322. _____ . St. Thomas Aquinas and the Natural Desire for God. New York: Fordham University Dissertation, 1943. 335 pp.

1323. _____ . "Natural Appetite." The Thomist 16 (1953) 361-409.

1324. Oeing-Hanhoff, Ludger. "Zur thomistischen Freiheitslehre." Scholastik 31 (1956) 172 ff.

1325. O'Neil, Charles J. "St. Thomas and the Nature of Man." Proceedings of the American Catholic Philosophical Association 25 (1951) 41-65.

1326. Orlando, Pasquale. "L'esperienza intellettiva Tomista." Aquinas 18 (1974) 204-39.

1327. Osika, Kazumasa. "Thomas Aquinas on the Agent Intellect: Japanese Text and English Summary." Studies in Medieval Thought. 17 (1975) 1-27, 147.

1328. Owens, Joseph. "Soul as Agent in Aquinas." The New Scholasticism (1974) 40-72.

1329. _____ . "The Unity in a Thomistic Philosophy of Man." Mediaeval Studies 25 (1963) 55-82.

1330. Paul, David L. Intentional Identity: An Analysis of the Metaphysics of Perception in Contemporary Thomistic Thought. Los Angeles: University of Southern California Dissertation.

1331. Peccorini, Francisco L. "Dazzling Messages of Personal Immortality in Sciacca's and Aquinas' Akin Conceptions of Spirit." Rivista Rosminiana Domodossola/Milano. 70 (1976) 405-27.

1332. Péghaire, Julien. "Forgotten Sense, the Cogitative According to St. Thomas Aquinas." The Modern Schoolman 20 (1943) 123-40; 20 (1943) 210-29.

1333. _____ . "Peut-on encore parler des facultés de l'ame?" Revue de l'Université a 'Ottawa 2 (1941) 111-43.

PSYCHOLOGY AND PHILOSOPHY OF MAN   1334 - 1349

1334. Pegis, Anton C. At the Origins of the Thomistic Notion of Man.
New York: Macmillan, 1963. 82 pp.

        St. Augustine Lecture, Villanova, 1962.

1335. _____. "Between Immortality and Death: Some Further Reflections on the Summa Contra Gentiles. The Monist 58 (1974) 1-15.

1336. _____. "In Umbra Intelligentiae." The New Scholasticism 14
(1940) 146-80.

1337. _____. "The Knowledge of the Separated Soul: SCG II, c. 81,"
in St. Thomas Aquinas 1274-1974 (Symp) I, 131-58.

1338. _____. "Man as Nature and Spirit." Doctor Communis 4 (1951)
52-63.

1339. _____. "Necessity and Liberty: An Historical Note on St.
Thomas Aquinas." The New Scholasticism 15 (1941) 18-45.

1340. _____. "Principale Volitum. Some Notes on a Supposed Thomistic
Contradiction." Philosophy and Phenomenological Research 9 (1948) 51-70.

1341. _____. St. Thomas and the Problem of the Soul in the Thirteenth
Century. Revised ed. Toronto: Pont. Inst. Med. Studies, 1976. 213 pp.

1342. _____. "St. Thomas and the Unity of Man," in Progress in
Philosophy (Symp) 153-73.

1343. _____. "The Separated Soul and Its Nature in St. Thomas,"
in St. Thomas Aquinas 1274-1974 (Symp) I, 131-58.

1344. _____. "Some Reflections on Summa contra Gentiles II, 56.
Etienne Gilson Tribute (Symp) 169-88.

1345. _____. "Toward the Rediscovery of Man." Proceedings of the
American Catholic Philosophical Association 19 (1943) 8-16.

1346. Perini, Giuseppe. "Il confronto tra l'uomo e gli animali nell'
antropologia sensuale di S. Tommaso e dei moderni," in Studi Tomistici
(Symp) 1974. 3, 185-221.

1347. Pero-Sanz, Jose M. "La Individuacion operativa del hombre, segun
los principios filosoficos de Santo Tomas." Anuario Filosofico 1 (1968)
137-84.

1348. Peter, Carl J. The Doctrine of Thomas Aquinas Regarding Eviternity
in the Rational Soul and Separated Substances. Rome: Gregorian University Press, 1964. 131 pp.

1349. Petraroja, Sergio. Karen Horney's Theory of Neurosis. An Aristotelian-Thomistic Critique with an Introduction to the School of Interperson-
al Relations. Ottawa: University of Ottawa Dissertation, 1962.

1350 - 1364   PSYCHOLOGY & PHILOSOPHY OF MAN

1350. Philippe, M.-D. "Personne et interpersonalité. Etre et esprit."
in L'Anthropologie (Symp) 1974. 124-60.

1351. Pinon, Manuel. "The Nature and Causes of psychological freedom...
of the will over its acts in the writings of St. Thomas." Philippiniana
Sacra. Manila. 9 (1974) 78-111, 231-66, 449-92.

1352. Plé, Albert. "Saint Thomas et la pscyologie contemporaine."
Angelicum 51 (1974) 558-70.

1353. _____. "St. Thomas and the Psychology of Freud." Dominican
Studies. Oxford. 5 (1952) 1-34.

1354. Reiter, Josef. "Zur Problematik der Identität und Differenz von
Anima und Intellectus bei Thomas von Aquin," in Salzburger...Gedenkband
(Symp) 1974. 177-97.

1355. Renard, Henri. "The Functions of Intellect and Will in the Act
of Free Will." The Modern Schoolman 24 (1947) 85-92.

1356. Reutemann, Charles. The Thomistic Concept of Pleasure as Compared
with Hedonistic and Rigoristic Philosophies. Washington: Catholic
Univeristy of America Press, 1953.

1357. Reyna, Ruth. "On the Soul: A Philosophical Exploration of the
Active Intellect in Averroes, Aristotle, and Aquinas." The Thomist
36 (1972) 131-49.

1358. Richard, Jean. Le processus psychologique de la revelation pro-
phetique selon saint Thomas d'Aquin." Laval Théologique et Philosophique
23 (1967) 42-75.

1359. Riesenhuber, Klaus. "The Bases and Meaning of Freedom in Thomas
Aquinas," in Thomas and Bonaventure (Symp) Proceedings of the American
Catholic Philosophical Association. 99-111.

1360. _____. "A pluridimensionalidade do conceito scolastico de
liberdade." Revista Portuguesa de Filosofia 30 (1974) 79-106.

1361. _____. Die Tranzendenz der Freiheit zum Guten., Der Wille in
der Anthropologie und Metaphysik des Thomes von Aquin. Munchen: Verlag
Berchmanskolleg, 1971. 411 pp.

1362. _____. "Der Wandel Des Freiheitsverstandnisses Thomas von
Aquin zur fruben Neuzeit." Rivista di Filosofia Neo-Scolastica 66
(1974) 946-74.

1363. Riet, G. Van. "La théorie thomiste de la sensation externe."
Revue Philosophique de Louvain 51 (1953) 374-408.

1364. Righi, Giulio. "Filosofia dell'uomo in S. Tommaso e formule della
psico-filosofia." Rivista Rosminiana. Domodosola. 68 (1974) 283-311.

PSYCHOLOGY AND PHILOSOPHY OF MAN   1365 - 1380

1365. Robb, James H. Man as Infinite Spirit. Milwaukee: Marquette University Press, 1974. 64 pp.

1366. Rock, Martin. "Aggression einmal anders. zum Stellenwert der 'aggressio' bei Thomas von Aquin." Triere Theologische Zeitschrift 82 (1973) 367-73.

1367. Rodriquez, Victorino. "Antropologia tomista y antropologia actual." Sapentia 30 (1975) 37-66.

1368. Rossner, William L. "An Inclination to an Intellectually Known God: The Question of the Existence of Intellectual Love." The Modern Schoolman 52 (1974) 65-92.

1369. _____. "The Process of Human Intellectual Love, or Spirating a Pondus." The Thomist 36 (1972) 39-74.

1370. _____. The Theory of Love in the Philosophy of St. Thomas Aquinas. Princeton, N.J.: Princeton University Dissertation, 1953. 377 pp.

1371. Roth, Gottfried. "Psychose-Somatose. Thomanische Gedenkengänge und thomistische Überlegungen in der gegenwärtigen Psychiatrie," in Virtus Politica (Symp) 1974. 69-80.

1372. Rovasenda, Enrico Di. "L'infinità del pensiero nella dottrina di S. Tommaso." Fuoco 22 (1974) 23-35.

1373. Royce, James E. "Life and Living Being." The Modern Schoolman 37 (1960) 213-34.

1374. Ruane, John P. "Self-Knowledge and the Spirituality of the Soul in St. Thomas." The New Scholasticism 32 (1958) 425-442.

1375. Rufner, V. "Innere Zusammenhange in den Denkmotiven bei Thomas v. A., Kant und Heidegger." Kant Studien 57 (1966) 90-9.

1376. Ryan, Edmund J. The Role of the Sensus Communis in the Psychology of Saint Thomas Aquinas. St. Louis: Saint Louis University Dissertation, 1951.

1377. _____. The Role of the 'Sensus Communis' in the Psychology of St. Thomas Aquinas. Carthagena: Messenger Press, 1951. 208 pp.

1378. Rzadkiewicz, A. L. Philosophical Bases of Human Liberty According to St. Thomas Aquinas. Washington, D.C.: Catholic University of America Press, 1949. 194 pp.

1379. _____. The Philosophical Bases of Human Liberty According to St. Thomas Aquinas: A Study in Social Philosophy. Washington, D.C.: Catholic University of America Dissertation, 1949. 311 pp.

1380. St. Hilaire, George. "Does St. Thomas Really Prove the Soul's

1381 - 1396 PSYCHOLOGY & PHILOSOPHY OF MAN

Immortality?" The New Scholasticism 35 (1960) 340-56.

1381. Sandin, B. T. "'Lo primario' en el habito según S. Tomás."
Studium 14 (1974) 265-77.

1382. Santos, Ferrer, Urbano. "La intencionalidad de la voluntad,
según S. Tomás." Studium 17 (1977) 529-39.

1383. Schlueter, Dietrich. "Der Wille und das Gute bei Thomas von
Aquinas." Freiburger Zeitschrift für Philosophie und Theologie 18
(1971) 88-136.

1384. Schneider, Marius. "The Dependence of St. Thomas' Psychology of
Sensation Upon His Physics." Franciscan Studies 22 (1962) 3-31.

1385. Schneider, Theodor. Die Einheit des Menschen: die anthropologische
Formel anima forma corporis im sogenannten Korrebtorienstreit. Munster:
Aschendorff, 1973 vi-288 pp.

1386. Schulte, Heinz. "Johannes Duns Scotus: Der Mensch. Einheit in
Differenz. Zur Ausein-andersetzung des Duns Scotus mit der Anthropologie
des Thomas von Aquin." Theologie und Philosophie 49 (1974) 554-60.

1387. Seidl, Horst. "Zur Leib-Seele-Einheit des Menschen bei Thomas
von Aquin." Theologie und Philosophie 49 (1974) 548-53.

1388. Siegmund, Georg. "Die Frage nach de 'Natur' des Menschen," in
Studi Tomistici (Symp) 3, 78-89.

1389. Silva-Tarouca, Amadeo. "La notion 'formalis' selon s. Thomas
d'Aquin et la formation de l'homme," in L'Homme et son destin (Symp)
545-53.

1390. Simon, Yves R. Freedom of Choice. Peter Wolff, ed. New York:
Fordham University Press, 1969.

1391. _____. Traité du libre arbitre. Liège: Sciences et Lettres,
1951.

1392. _____, and J. L. Péghaire. "The Philosophical Study of Sensation." The Modern Schoolman 23 (1946) 111-9.

1393. Siwek, Paul. La conscience du libre arbitre dans la philosophie
de s. Thomas d'Aquin," in L'Homme et son destin (Symp) 595-600.

1394. Sleva, Fictor E. The Separated Soul in the Philosophy of St.
Thomas Aquinas. Washington, D.C.: Catholic University of America
Press, 1940.

1395. Smith, Gerard. "Intelligence and Liberty." The New Scholasticism
15 (1941) 1-17.

1396. Steenberghen, Fernand Van. "Introducción a la antropologia de Sto

PSYCHOLOGY AND PHILOSOPHY OF MAN   1397 - 1411

Tomás de Aquino." Revista Filosofica. Mexico. 10 (1977) 233-50.

1397. Stipicic, Ivo. Die Grenzsituation des Menschen und seine Eksistenz.
Freiburg, Schev: Universitätsoerlag, 1967. 130 pp.

1398. Stock, Michael. "Sense Consciousness According to St. Thomas."
The Thomist 21 (1958) 415-86.

1399. _____. "Some Moral Issues in Psychoanalysis." The Thomist
23 (1960) 143-88.

1400. _____. "A Thomistic Analysis of the Concept of Repression."
The Thomist 25 (1962) 463-94.

1401. _____. "Thomistic Psychology and Freud's Psychoanalysis."
The Thomist 21 (1958) 125-45.

1402. Strasser, Stefan. Le problème de l'ame. Etudes sur l'objet
respectif de la psychologie métaphysique et de la psychologie empirique.
J. P. Wurtz, tr. Louvain: Nauwelaerts, Paris: Desclée, 1953. xiv-
258 pp.

1403. Stromberg, James S. "An Essay on Experimentum." Laval Théologique et Philosophique 23 (1967) 76-115.

1404. _____. "An Essay on Experimentum, II." Laval Théologique et
Philosophique 24 (1968) 99-138.

1405. Sullivan, Robert P. "Natural Necessitation of the Human Will."
The Thomist 14 (1951) 351-99; 490-528.

1406. _____. The Thomistic Concept of the Natural Necessitation of
the Human Will. River Forest, IL: Pontifical Faculty of Philosophy,
1952.

1407. Tensing, Robert H. A Comparison of the Aristotelian-Thomistic
Analysis of Thought with the Analysis of a Modern American Philosopher.
River Forest, IL: Studium Generale of St. Thomas Aquinas, 1955. 93 pp.

1408. Tillman, Stanley C. The Principle of Contiguity-its Meaning and
Value as Applied by St. Thomas to the Powers of Man. St. Louis: Saint
Louis University Dissertation, 1954.

1409. Tittley R. La douleur sensible: est-elle une passion corporelle
ou une passion selon saint Thomas d'Aquin? Montreal: Pontificia Studiorum Universitas a S. Thoma Aq. in Urbe, 1967. 157 pp.

1410. Toon, Mark. The Philosophy of Sex According to St. Thomas Aquinas.
Washington, D.C.: Catholic University of America Press, 1954.

1411. Uscatescu, Georges. "L'antropologia e i suoi problemi in S.
Tommaso d'Aquino. Dalla 'Physis' aristotelica alla metafisica dei valori."
Giornale di Metafisica 32 (1977) 197-204.

1412 - 1427   PSYCHOLOGY & PHILOSOPHY OF MAN

1412. Ushida, Noriko. Etude comparative de la psychologie d'Aristotle, d'Avicenne, et de S. Thomas." Tokyo: Keio Institute of Cultural and Linguistic Studies, 1968.

1413. Vann, Gerald. The Heart of Man. New York: Longmans, Green, 1945; Doubleday, 1960.

1414. Vanni Rovighi, Sofia. L'Antropologia filosofica di San Tommaso d'Aquino. Milan: Vita e Pensiero, 1965. 183 pp.

1415. Verbeke, Gérard. "De mens als 'grens' volgens Aquinas," Tijdschrift voor Philosophie. Leuven. 36 (1974) 195-231.

1416. _____. "Man as 'Frontier' According to Aquinas," in Aquinas and Problems (Symp) 195-223.

1417. _____. "L'Unité de l'homme: saint Thomas contra Averroes." Revue Philosophique de Louvain 58 (1960).

1418. Vergote, A. "Liberté et determinisme au regard de la psychanalyse et de l'ontologie," in Tommaso d'Aquino...problemi fondamentali (Symp) 1974. 391-404.

1419. Viola, Coloman. L'Unité de l'homme et l'expérience qui la révèle d'après saint Thomas d'Aquin. Louvain: Universitaire "Cardinal Minds-zenty," 1957. 47 pp.

1420. Walgrave, Jan H. "Het natuurverlangen naar de godsanschouwing bij Thomas von Aquino," Tijdschrift voor Philosophie 36 (1974) 232-66.

1421. _____. "Quelques remargues sur le desir natural chez s. Thomas in Studi Tomistici (Symp) 2, 221-9.

1422. Walton, William M. The Person in the Writings of St. Thomas Aquinas. Toronto: University of Toronto Dissertation, 1947.

1423. Ward, Leo R. "Saint Thomas' Defense of Man." Proceedings of the American Catholic Philosophical Association 20 (1945) 31-7.

1424. Warganz, Joseph F. An Examination of the Thomistic Arguments for Immortality in the Light of Peter Pomponazzi's De Immortalitate Animae. Brooklyn, N.Y.: St. John's University Dissertation, 1968. 194 pp.

1425. Wilhelmsen, Frederick D. "The 'I' and Aquinas." Proceedings of the American Catholic Philosophical Association 50 (1977) 47-55.

1426. Wilson, Russell. The Modes of Abstraction According to St. Thomas Aquinas. Washington, D.C.: Georgetown University Dissertation, 1950. 176 pp.

1427. Wojtyla, Karol. Osoba i czyn. Cracow: Polskie Towarzystwo Teologiczne, 1969.

METAPHYSICS   1428 - 1444

1428. Wojtyla, Karol (Pope John Paul II). The Acting Person, Edited
by Anna-Terese Tymieniecka, trans by Andrzy Potocki. Hingham, MA: D.
Reidel, 1979. xxiii-367 pp.

1429. _____. "The Personal Structure of Self-Determination," in
Tommaso d'Aquino...VII Centerario (Symp) 1976. 379-90.

1430. Zamoyta, Casimir Stanislaus. The Unity of Man: St. Thomas's
Solution of the Body-Soul Problem. Washington, D.C.: Catholic University of America, 1957. 135 pp.

1431. Zan, Julio De. "Precisiones sobre la doctrina de la abstraction
segun Santo Tomás." Sapientia 27 (1972) 335-50.

1432. Zimmerman, Albert. "Der Begriff der Freiheit nach Thomas von
Aquin," in Thomas von Aquin 1274-1974 (Symp) 125-59.

METAPHYSICS

1433. Adamczyk, Stanislaus. De Existentia substantiali in doctrina S.
Thomae Aquinatis. Roma: Gregorianum, 1962.

1434. Adler, Mortimer J. "The Equivocal Use of the Word 'Analogical'."
The New Scholasticism (1974) 4-18.

1435. _____. "Problems for Thomists: I. The Problem of Species."
The Thomist I (1939) 80-122, 237-70, 381-443; II (1940) 88-155, 237-300.

1436. _____. Problems for Thomists: The Problem of Species. New
York: Sheed and Ward, 1940. xviii-303 pp.

1437. _____. "Solution of the Problem of Species." The Thomist 3
(1941) 279-379.

1438. Albertson, James S. "The Esse of Accidents According to St.
Thomas." The Modern Schoolman 30 (1953) 263-78.

1439. _____, and Francis E. McMahon. "The Esse of Accidents: A
Discussion." The Modern Schoolman 31 (1954) 125-31.

1440. _____. "Instrumental Causality in St. Thomas." The New
Scholasticism 28 (1954) 409-35.

1441. Allers, Rudolf. "The Subjective and the Objective." Review of
Metaphysics 12 (1959) 503-20.

1442. Anderson, James F. "Bergson, Aquinas, and Heidegger on the Notion
of Nothingness." Proceedings of the American Catholic Philosophical
Association 41 (1967) 143-8.

1443. _____. The Bond of Being. St. Louis: B. Herder, 1949.

1444. _____. The Cause of Being. St. Louis: B. Herder, 1953.

1445. _____. "On Demonstration in Thomistic Metaphysics." The New Scholasticism 32 (1958) 476-94.

1446. _____. An Introduction to the Metaphysics of St. Thomas. Chicago: Henry Regnery Co., 1953. 149 pp.

1447. _____. Reflections on the Analogy of Being. Hague: Nijhoff, 1967. 88 pp.

1448. _____. A Study on Thomistic Metaphysics. Toronto: University of Toronto Dissertation, 1940. 122 pp.

1449. _____. "Two Studies in Metaphysics." The Thomist 3 (1941) 564-87.

1450. Anzenbacher, W. "Systematische Bezuge zum thomasischen Substanz-begriff," in Geschichte und System (Symp) 1972.

1451. Arbuckle, Gilbert B. "St. Thomas Aquinas and the Doctrine of Essence." Studies in Philosophy and in the History of Philosophy 2 (1963) 104-36.

1452. Arndt, Elmer J. The Relation of Value and Being in the Philosophy of Saint Thomas Aquinas. New Haven, CT: Yale University Dissertation, 1943.

1453. Banez, Domingo (16th century). The Primacy of Existence in Thomas Aquinas: A Commentary in Thomistic Metaphysics. Benjamin S. Llamzon, tr. Chicago: Regnery, 1966. 122 pp.

1454. Barral, Mary Rose. "The Philosophy of St. Thomas from a Phenomeno-logical Viewpoint," in Tommaso d'Aquino (Symp Roma) 6, 480-6.

1455. Basave, Agustin. "La doctrina metafisica de la participacion en S. Tomás de Aquino." Giornale di Metafisica 30 (1975) 257-66.

1456. _____. "La doctrina metafisica de la participación en santo Tomás de Aquino," in Presenca Filosofica (Symp) 63-9.

1457. Bassler, Wolfgang. "Die Kritik des Thomas von Aquin am ontologisch-en Gottesbeweis." Franziskanische Studien. Werl-Westfalen. 56 (1974) 1-26.

1457. Beck, Heinrich. Der Akt-Charakter des Seins. Eine speculative Weiterführung der Seinslehre Thomas von Aquins aus einer Anregung durch das dialektische Prinzip Hegels. München: Hueber, 1965.

1459. Bedell, Gary. "Theistic Realism and Monistic Idealism." The Thomist. 35 (1971) 661-83.

1460. Bernard, A. Introduction à la philosophie de s. Thomas d'Aquin. Saint-Marimin. Var. 1954. 136 pp.

METAPHYSICS   1461 - 1477

1461. Beuchot, Mauricio. "El problema de los universales en Tomas de Aquino." Revista Filosofica. Mexico. 11 (1978) 389-420.

1462. Bobik, Joseph. "Some Remarks on Fr. Owen' 'St. Thomas and Elucidation'." The New Scholasticism 37 (1963) 59-63.

1463. _____. "Some Remarks on Father Owens' 'St. Thomas and the Future of Metaphysics'." The New Scholasticism 33 (1959) 68-85.

1464. _____. "Some Disputable Points Apropos of St. Thomas and Metaphysics." The New Scholasticism 37 (1963) 411-30.

1465. Bofill, Jaime. "La Notion de 'proximite''dans les cadres de la métaphysique thomsite." Convivium 41 (1974) 97-100.

1466. Boggi, Giulio. "Dai trascendentali al trascendentale in S. Tommaso." Renovatio 6 (1971) 80-6.

1467. Bontadini, Gustavo. "La concezione classica dell'essere e il contributo del tomismo," in Tommaso d'Aquino (Symp Roma) 6, 29-34.

1468. Borgosz, Jozef. "A Presentist Interpretation of the Unity and Plurality of Being According to St. Thomas." Dialectics and Humanism 2 (1975) 171-82.

1469. Bourke, Vernon J. "The Role of Habitus in the Thomistic Metaphysics of Potency and Act," in Essays in Thomism. R. E. Brennan, ed. New York: Sheed and Ward, 1942. 101-9; 370-3.

1470. Bradley, Denis J. M. "Transcendental Critique and Realist Metaphysics." The Thomist 39 (1975) 631-67.

1471. Brady, Marian. The Philosophical Basis of Human Values According to Thomistic Principles. Washington, D.C.: Catholic University of America Dissertation, 1962. 380 pp.

1472. Braun, E. "Le problème de l'esse chez saint Thomas." Archive de Philosophie 36 (1959) 211-26, 529-65; 37 (1960) 252-59.

1473. Breton, Stanislas. "L'Idie de transcendental et la genèse des transcendentaux chez s. Thomas d'Aquin," in S. Thomas Aujourd'hui (Symp) 45-74.

1474. Brown, Barry F. "Accidental Esse: A Confirmation." The New Scholasticism 44 (1970) 133-52.

1475. _____. The Being of Accidents According to St. Thomas Aquinas. Toronto: University of Toronto Dissertation, 1967.

1476. Brown, Patterson. "St. Thomas' Doctrine of Necessary Being." Philosophical Review 73 (1964) 76-90.

1477. Buckley, George M. The Nature and Unity of Metaphysics. Washington,

D.C.: Catholic University of America Press, 1946.

1478. Buckley, Joseph A. The Dimensions of the Real According to Jacques Maritian. Notre Dame: University of Notre Dame Dissertation, 1966.

1479. Burrell, David B. Analogy and Philosophical Language. New Haven, CT: Yale University Press, 1973. xi-278.

1480. _____. "Classification, Mathematics, and Metaphysics." The Modern Schoolman 44 (1966) 13-34.

1481. _____. "A Note on Analogy." The New Scholasticism 36 (1962) 225-31.

1482. Busa, Roberto. La terminologia tomistica dell'interiorità: saggi di metodo per un'interpretzione della metafisica della presenza. Milano: Fratelli Bocca, 1949. 279 pp.

1483. Byles, W. Esdaile. "The Analogy of Being." The New Scholasticism 16 (1942) 331-64.

1484. Cahill, Mary C. The Absolute and the Relative in St. Thomas and in Modern Philosophy. Washington, D.C.: Catholic University of America Dissertation, 1939.

1485. Cajetan, Thomas de Vio. The Analogy of Names and The Concept of Being. Trans and annotated by E. A. Bushinski, in collaboration with H. J. Koren. Pittsburgh: Duquesne University Press, 1953. 103 pp.

1486. Callus, Daniel A. "The Origins of the Problem of the Unity of Form." The Thomist 24 (1961) 257-85.

1487. Carlo, William E. The Ultimate Reducibility of Essence to Existence in Existential Metaphysics. Hague: Nijhoff, 1966.

1488. Carré, Meyrick H. Realists and Nominalists: Augustine, Abelard, Aquinas, Ockham. London-New York: Oxford University Press, 1946. vi-128 pp.

1489. Chapman, Emmanuel. "To Be--That is the Answer," in Maritain... Thomist (Symp) 137-52.

1490. Chisholm, Roderick M. "Individuation: Some Thomistic Questions and Answers." Grazer Philosophische Studien. Amsterdam. 1 (1975) 25-41.

1491. Ciliberto, Vicente O. "El ser en S. Tomás y en la fenomenologia." Sapientia 32 (1977) 93-110.

1492. Clark, Ralph W. "Saint Thomas Aquinas's Theory of Universals." The Monist 58 (1974) 163-72.

METAPHYSICS   1493 - 1508

1493. _____. The Universal in the Philosophy of Saint Thomas Aquinas. Boulder: University of Colorado Dissertation, 1972. 338 pp.

1494. Clarke, Francis P. "St. Thomas on 'Universals'." Journal of Philosophy 59 (1962) 720-4.

1495. Clarke, W. Norris. "The Limitation of Act by Potency: Aristotelianism or Neoplationism." The New Scholasticism 36 (1952) 167-94.

1496. _____. "The Meaning of Participation in St. Thomas (with comment by John J. Pauson)." Proceedings of the American Catholic Philosophical Association 26 (1952) 147-59.

1497. _____. "The Role of Essence Within St. Thomas' Essence-Existence Doctrine: Positive or Negative Principle?" in Tommaso d'Aquino (Symp Roma) 6, 109-15.

1498. _____. "What Cannot Be Said in St. Thomas' Essence-Existence Doctrine." New Scholasticism Aquinas Septicent. 1974. 19-39.

1499. _____. "What Is Most and least Relevant in the Metaphysics of St. Thomas Today?" International Philosophical Quarterly 14 (1974) 411-34.

1500. _____. "What Is Really Real?" in Progress in Philosophy (Symp) J. A. McWilliams, ed. Milwaukee: Bruce, 1955. 61-90.

1501. Coffey, Brian. "The Notion of Order According to St. Thomas Aquinas." The Modern Schoolman 27 (1949) 1-18; 331-6.

1502. Collins, James D. The Lure of Wisdom. Milwaukee: Marquette University Press, 1962.

1503. _____. The Thomistic Philosophy of the Angels. Washington, D.C.: Catholic University of America Press, 1944. xv-383 pp.

1504. Conway, David A. "Possibility and Infinite Time: A Logical Paradox in St. Thomas' Third Way." International Philosophical Quarterly 14 (1974) 201-8.

1505. Conway, James I. "The Reality of the Possibles." The New Scholasticism 33 (1959) 139-61, 331-53.

1506. Coreth, Emerich. Metaphysik Eine methodischsystematische Grundlegung. Innsbruck: Tyrolia, 1961. Zueite Aufl., 1964. 672 pp.

1507. _____. Metaphysics. Translated and condensed by Joseph Donceel. New York: Herder and Herder, 1968. 200 pp.

1508. Counahan, James. The Quest for Metaphysics: A Study of the Subject of Metaphysics in the Texts of St. Thomas Aquinas. River Forest, IL: Aquinas Institute of Philosophy Dissertation, 1967. 151 pp.

1509. Counahan, James. "The Quest for Metaphysics." The Thomist 33 (1969) 519-72.

1510. Courtes, Pierre-Ceslas. "Coherence de l'etre et premier principe selon saint Thomas d'Aquin." Revue Thomiste 70 (1970) 387-423.

1511. _____. "L'Etre et le non-etre selon saint Thomas d'Aquin." Revue Thomiste 67 (1967) 387-438.

1512. _____. "Participation et contingence selon saint Thomas d' Aquin." Revue Thomiste 69 (1969) 201-35.

1513. _____. "L'Un selon saint Thomas." Revue Thomiste 68 (1968) 198-240.

1514. Cunningham, Francis A. "La compositio in re de Santo Tomás." E. Martino, tr. Pensamiento 33 (1977) 123-54.

1515. Cunningham, J. A. "Distinciton According to St. Thomas." The New Scholasticism 36 (1962) 279-312.

1516. Dalledone, Andrea. "L'autentico 'esse' tomistico e l'equivoco neoscolastico sulla 'esistenza come atto' in Carlo Giacon." Divus Thomas. Piacenza. 81 (1978) 68-82.

1517. D'Amore, Benedetto. "Il problema del fondamento nello metafisica di S. Tommaso." Sapienza 26 (1973) 463-9.

1518. DeCoursey, Mary Edwin. The Theory of Evil in the Metaphysics of St. Thomas. Washington, D.C.: Catholic University of America Press, 1948.

1519. Degl'Innocenti, Umberto. "La struttura ontologica della persona secondo S. Tommaso d'Aquino," in L'Homme et son destin (Symp) 523-33.

1520. Dennehy, Raymond L. The Subject as the Metaphysical Ground of Maritain's Personalism. Toronto: University of Toronto Dissertation, 1974.

1521. Derisi, Octavio N. "El esse y el intelligere divino, fundamento universal e immediate de todo ser...en S. Tomás." Sapienza 29 (1974) 163-76.

1522. _____. "Participación, acto y potencia y analogia en Santo Tomás." Rivista di Filosofia Neo-Scolastica 66 (1974) 415-35.

1523. _____. "El Principio de individuacion en la escuela Tomista." Sapienza 28 (1973) 56-8.

1524. Dewan, Lawrence. "St. Thomas, Capreolus, and Esntitative Composition." Divus Thomas. Piacenza. 80 (1977) 355-75.

1525. _____. "St. Thomas and the Possibles." The New Scholasticism

METAPHYSICS   1526 - 1540

53 (1979).

1526. Diggs, Bernard J. Love and Being. An Investigation into the
Metaphysics of St. Thomas Aquinas. New York: Columbia University
Dissertation, 1947. 180 pp.

1527. Dillon, Thomas E. The Real Distinction Between Essence and
Existence in the Thought of St. Thomas Aquinas. Notre Dame, IN:
University of Notre Dame Dissertation, 1977. 276 pp.

1528. Doig, James C. Aquinas on Metaphysics. A Historico-Doctrinal
Study of the Commentary on the Metaphysics. Hague: Nijhoff, 1972. 451
pp.

1529. Dondeyne, A. "Pensée métaphysique et foi en Dieu," in Tommaso
d'Aquino (Symp) I, 137-47.

1530. Ducharme, Léonard. "L'idée de la métaphysique dans les écrits du
premier enseignement parisien de s. Thomas d'Aquin,' in Colloque...S.
Thomas (Ottawa Symp) 1974. 155-69.

1531. Echauri, Raúl. "Heidegger y el esse tomista." Cuadernos de
Filosofia 11 (1971) 207-14.

1532. Edwards, Sandra. "Some Medieval Views on Identity." The New
Scholasticism 51 (1977) 62-74.

1533. Elders, Leo. "'Contineri' as a Fundamental Structure of St.
Thomas' Ontology." Aquinas. Roma. 17 (1974) 97-106.

1534. Emmett, Dorothy M. The Nature of Metaphysical Thinking.
London, 1946. 169-88 pp.

        Critique of St. Thomas on analogy.

1535. Eslick, L. "The Negative Judgment of Separation: A Reply to
Father Burrell." The Modern Schoolman 44 (1966) 35-46.

        Rejoinder to Dr. Eslick, 47-8.

1536. _____. "The Real Distinction: Reply to Professor Reese."
The Modern Schoolman 38 (1961) 149-60.

1537. _____. "What Is the Starting Point of Metaphysics?" The
Modern Schoolman 34 (1957) 247-63.

1538. Esser, Gerard. Metaphysica Generalis. Ed. altera. Techny, IL:
Domus Missionum ad S. Mariam, 1952. xvi-368 pp.

1539. Evans, Donald. "Preller's Analogy of 'Being'." The New
Scholasticism 45 (1971) 1-37.

1540. Fabro, Cornelio. "Actualité et originalité de l'esse thomiste."

1541. _____. "Attualità della metafisica tomistica della part-
icipazione," in Presenca Filosofica (Symp) 70-80.

1542. _____. "Dall'essere di Aristotele all'esse di S. Tommaso,"
in Mélanges offerts à E. Gilson. Paris: Vrin, 1959. 227-47.

1543. _____. E segesi tomistica. Cathedra Sancti Thomae, II. Roma:
1969. Libreria Editrice della Pontificia Università Lateranense. 478 pp.

1544. _____. "The Intensive Hermeneutics of Thomistic Philosophy:
The Notion of Participation." Review of Metaphysics. Commemorative
Issue 1224-1274. 27 (1974) 449-91.

1545. _____. "L'interpretazione dell'atto in S. Tommaso e Heidegger,"
In Tommaso d'Aquino...problemi fondamentali (Symp) 1974. 505-17.

        Also in Tommaso d'Aquino (Symp) I, 119-28.

1546. _____. La nozione metafisica di partecipazione. Torino:
Società Editrice Internazionale. ed. 2a, 1950, ed. 3a, 1963.

1547. _____. "L'Obscurcissement de l''Esse' dans l'Ecole Thomiste."
Revue Thomiste 58 (1958) 446ff.

1548. _____. Partecipazione e causalità, Torino: Societa Ed.
Internazionale, 1961.

1549. _____. Participation et causalité selon s. Thomas d'Aquin.
Louvain: Publications Universitaires, 1961. 650 pp.

1550. _____. Le retour au fondement de l'etre," in S. Thomas Aujourd'
hui (Symp) 177-96.

1551. _____. "Il ritorno al fondamento. Contributo per un confronto
tra l'ontologia di Heidegger e la metafisica di S. Tommaso d'Aquino."
Sapienza 26 (1973) 265-78.

1552. _____. "Il ritorno al fondamento. Contributo per un confronto
fra l'ontologia di Heidegger e la metafisica di S. Tommaso d'Aquino,"
in Universidad de Navarra (Symp) 93-109.

1553. _____. "The Transcendentality of Ens-Esse and the Ground of
Metaphysics." International Philosophical Quarterly 6 (1966) 389-427.

1554. Fackenheim, Emil L. Metaphysics and Historicity. Milwaukee:
Marquette University Press, 1961.

        Aquinas Lecture.

1555. Farley, Elizabeth H. The Efficacy of Secondary Causes in the
Doctrine of Saint Thomas Aquinas. New York: Fordham University Dissertation, 1955.

METAPHYSICS   1556 - 1571

1556. Farrelly, M. John. "Existenc, the Intellect, and the Will."
The New Scholasticism 29 (1955) 145-74.

1557. _____. "Man's Transcendence and Thomistic Resources."
The Thomist 38 (1974) 426-84.

1558. Farrer, Austin. Finite and Infinite. London: Dacre Press, 1943.

1559. Fay, Charles. St. Thomas' Modification of Boethius' Doctrine on
Being, Goodness, and Participation. St. Louis: Saint Louis University
Dissertation, 1956.

1560. Fay, Thomas A. "The Problem of Intellectual Instuition in the
Metaphysics of Thomas Aquinas." Sapienza. Napoli. 27 (1974) 352-9.

1561. Ferrari, Leo. "Abstractio Totius and Abstractio Totalis." The
Thomist 24 (1961) 72-89.

1562. Ferrer, Gabriel. "Hacia una metafisica tomista de la existencia."
Escritos del Vedat 4 (1974) 375-401.

1563. Fetz, Reto Luzius. Ontologie der Innerlichkeit. Reditio completa
und processio interior bei Thomas von Aquin. Freiburg i. Br., Basel,
Wien: Herder, 1975. 199 pp.

1564. Finance, Joseph de. Etre et agir dans la philosophie de s. Thomas.
Paris: Besuchesne, 1943. 2 me éd., 1966.

1565. Flanigan, Thomas Marquerite. "Secondary Causality in the Summa
Contra Gentiles." The Modern Schoolman 36 (1958) 31-9.

1566. _____. "The Use of Analogy in the Summa Contra Gentiles."
The Modern Schoolman 35 (1957) 21-37.

1567. Fontaine, Raymond G. The Doctrine of Separable Accident in the
Philosophy of St. Thomas. Washington, D.C.: Catholic University of
America Press, 1950.

1568. Forest, Aimé. La Structure métaphysique du concret delon s.
Thomas d'Aquin. 2 me éd. Paris: Vrin, 1956.

1569. French, Mary Anne. Creation in Saint Thomas: A Metaphysical
Study. St. Louis: Saint Louis University Dissertation, 1962.

1570. Gallagher, Thomas A. The Contemporary Status of the Notion of
Existence and its Limitation in Thomistic Metaphysics. Washington, D.C.:
Catholic University of America Dissertation, 1958. 110 pp.

1571. Gardeil, Henri D. Metaphysics, Vol. IV of Introduction to the
Philosophy of St. Thomas Aquinas. John A. Otto, tr. St. Louis:
Herder, 1967.

1572. Gardet, Louis, et Alǔ. Sagesse. Bruges: Desclée, 1951.

1573. Garrigou-Lagrange, Reginald. Dieu, son existence et sa nature.
6 me éd. Paris: Beauchesne, 1946.

1574. _____. "The Fecundity of Goodness." The Thomist 2 (1940)
226-36.

1575. Geiger, Louis B. "Abstraction et séparation d'après S. Thomas."
Revue des Sciences Philosophiques et Théologiques 31 (1947) 3-40.

1576. _____. "Existentialisme, essentialisme et ontologie exist-
entielle," in Etienne Gilson, Philosophe de la Chrétienté. Paris: Ed.
du Cerf, 1949. 227-74.

1577. _____. La participation dans la philosophie de s. Thomas
d'Aquin. Paris: Vrin, 1942; 2 me éd. 1952. 496 pp.

1578. Gelinas, Elmer T. The Relation Between Life and Existence a
Study of Vivere Viventibus Est Esse as Found in Thomas Aquinas. Toronto:
University of Toronto Dissertation, 1955.

1579. Giacon, C. "Il Binomio Causa-Effetto secondo il Tomismo."
Rivista di Filosofia Neo-Scolastica 66 (1974) 541-51.

1580. _____. "Il contributo originale di S. Tommaso all'ontologia
classica," in Tommaso d'Aquino (Roma Symp. Napoli Congr) 1974. I, 281-
94.

        Also in VI, 61-71.

1581. _____. I primi concetti metafiscici: Platone, Aristotele,
Plotino, Avicenna, Tommaso. Bologna: Il Mulino, 1968.

1582. _____. "S. Tommaso e l'esistenza come atto: Maritain, Gilson,
Fabro." Medioevo. Rivista di storia della filosofia medievale. Padua.

1583. Gilson, Etienne. Being and Some Philosophers. Toronto: PIMS,
1949; 2nd ed. 1952. xi-235 pp.

1584. _____. "Eléments d'une métaphysique thomiste de l'etre."
Archived d'Histoire Doctrinale et Litteraire du Moyen Age 48 (1973)
7-36.

1585. _____. "Notes sur le Vocabulaire de l'Etre." Mediaeval Studies
8 (1946) 150-8.

1586. _____. "Propos sur l'etre et sa notion," in Studi Tomistici
(Symp) 3, 7-17.

1587. _____. "Quasi definitio substantiae," in St. Thomas Aquinas
(Symp) 1974. I, 111-29.

METAPHYSICS   1588 - 1602

1588. _____. Wisdom and Love in St. Thomas Aquinas. Milwaukee: Marquette University Press, 1951.

1589. Ginsburg, Norbert D. "Metaphysical Relations and St. Thomas Aquinas." The New Scholasticism 15 (1941) 238-54.

1590. Glutz, Melvin A. "Being and Metaphysics." The Modern Schoolman 35 (1958) 271-85.

1591. _____. "The Formal Subject of Metaphysics." The Thomist 19 (1956) 59-74.

1592. Gogacz, M. and B. Rucinski, et alu. Studia wokól problematzki esse (Tomasz z Akwinu i Boecjusz). Warsaw: Akademia Teologu Katholickiej, 1976. 375 pp.

        Problem of esse: Thomas and Boethius.

1593. Gogolewski, Thaddaeus. De Connexionibus Entium per Ipsorum Causarum Operationem Unitivam in Metaphysica S. Thomae. Rome: Catholic Book Agency, 1963. 132 pp.

1594. Graham, Joseph M. Secondary Causal Influx According to Saint Thomas Aquinas. Notre Dame: University of Notre Dame Dissertation, 1962. 309 pp.

1595. Greif, Gary F. St. Thomas' Method of Establishing the Subject of Metaphysics: A Modern Reconstruction. Toronto: University of Toronto Dissertation, 1965.

1596. Gumppenberg, Rudoff. "Zur Seinslehre in 'De ente et essentia' des Thomas von Aquin." Freiburger Zeitschrift für Philosophie und Theologie 21 (1974) 420-38.

1597. Gurr, John E. The Principle of Sufficient Reason in Some Scholastic Systems, 1970-1900. Milwaukee: Marquette University Press, 1959. 207 pp.

1598. Hallen, Patricia Ann. The Philosophical Problem of Relation in the Philosophies of Aristotle, Aquinas and Hegel. Boston: Boston University Dissertation, 1970. 376 pp.

1599. Hanley, Katharine Rose and J. Donald Monan. A Prelude to Metaphysics. Englewood Cliffs, N.J.: Prentice-Hall, 1967.

1600. Harris, Errol E. The Problem of Evil. Milwaukee: Marquette University Press, 1977.

1601. Hart, Charles A. Thomistic Metaphysics. Englewood Cliffs, N.J.: Prentice-Hall, 1959. 431 pp.

1602. Hawkins, Denis J. B. Being and Becoming. London-New York: Sheed and Ward, 1954.

1603. Hayen, André. La Communication de L'etre a'après Saint Thomas
d'Aquin: I. la Métaphysique d'un Théologien. Bruges: Desclée de
Brouwer, 1957. 191 pp.

1604. _____. La Communication de L'etre d'après Saint Thomas d'Aquin:
II L'Ordre philosophique de Saint Thomas. Bruges: Desclée de Brouwer,
1959. 353 pp.

1605. _____. L'Intentionel dans la philosophie de s. Thomas.
Bruxelles-Paris: Desclée, 1942; 2 me éd. 1954. 317 pp.

1606. Hegyi, Johannes. Die Bedeutung des Seins bei den klassischen
Kommentatoren des heiligen Thomas von Aquin: Capreolus, Silvester,
Von Ferrara, Cajetan. Pullacher philosophische forschungen, Band IV.
Pullach bei München: Verlag Berchmanskolleg, 1959. 183 pp.

1607. Henle, Robert J. Method in Metaphysics. Milwaukee: Marquette
University Press, 1950.

1608. Ho, Joseph Chiu Yuen. "La doctrine de la participation dans le
commentaire de s. Thomas d'Aquin sur le Liber de causis." Revue Philosophique de Louvain 70 (1972) 360-83.

1609. Hollenbach, J. M. Sein und Gewissen...Eine Begegnung zwischen M.
Heidegger und thomistischer Philosophie. Baden-Baden: Kunst und Wissenschaft Verlag, 1954. 347 pp.

1610. Holz, Harald. "Thomistischer Transzendentalismus Moglichkeiten
und Grenzen." Kant Studien 3 (1967) 376-86.

1611. Honings, Bonifacius. "Animazione ritardata e incarnazione immedi-
ata. La spiegazione metafisica di San Tommaso."
Ephemerides Carmelitical. Roma. 25 (1974) 244-66.

1612. Houlihan, Elizabeth M. Metaphysical Necessity in St. Thomas and
Its Historical Foundations. New York: Fordham University Dissertation,
1954.

1613. Huetter, Norbert J. The Eidetic Existentialism of St. Thomas.
New York: Fordham University Dissertation, 1952. 222 pp.

1614. Hunt, Ben B. The Nature and Significance of the One that Follows
Being in the Philosophy of St. Thomas Aquinas. Washington, D.C.:
Catholic University of America Press, 1950.

1615. Inagaki, Bernard R. "Thomas Aquinas and the Problem of Universals:
A Re-examination." Studies in Philosophy and the History of Philosophy
4 (1967) 174-90.

1616. Isaye, Gaston. La Théorie de la mesure et l'existence d'un
maximum selon s. Thomas. Paris: Beauchesne, 1940.

METAPHYSICS   1617 - 1633

1617. Jocobi, Klaus. "Kontingente Naturgeschehnisse. Thomas von Aquino." Studia Mediewistyczne. Warszawa. 18 (1977) 3-70.

1618. _____. "Thomas von Aquinas semantische Analyse des Kontin-genzbegriffs." Rassegna di Scienze Filosofische 27 (1974) 195-212.

1619. Jalbert, Guy. Nécessité et contingence chez s. Thomas d'Aquin et chez ses prédécesseurs. Ottawa: Universite d'Ottawa, 1961. 256 pp.

1620. Johann, Robert O. The Meaning of Love: An Essay Towards a Metaphysics of Intersubjectivity. Westminster, MD: Newman Press, 1955.

1621. John, H. "The Emergence of the Act of Existing in Recent Thomism." International Philosophical Quarterly 2 (1962) 595-620.

1622. _____. "Participation Revisited." The Modern Schoolman 39 (1962) 154-65.

1623. Jordan, Mark D. Creation and Intelligibility in Thomas Aquinas: A Reading of the Contra Gentiles. Austin: The University of Texas at Austin Dissertation, 1977. 278 pp.

1624. _____. "Disputed Questions in Seifert's Essence and Existence." Cf. infra 1823. Aletheia 1 (1977) 461-6.

1625. Kainz, Howard P. "Separate Substances Revisited." The New Scholasticism 44 (1970) 550-64.

1626. _____. "The Suarezian Position on Being and the Real Distinc-tion: An Analytical and Comparative Study." The Thomist 34 (1970) 289-305.

1627. Kalinowski, Georges (Jerzy). "Esquisse de l'évolution d'une conception de la métaphysique," in S. Thomas Oujourd'hui (Symp) 97-133.

1628. Kanbembo, Daniel. "Essai d'une ontologie de L'agir." Revue Philosophique de Louvain 65 (1967) 356-87.

1629. Kane, William H. "Existence and Causality." The Thomist 28 (1964) 76-92.

1630. _____. "The Subject of Metaphysics." The Thomist 18 (1955) 503-21.

1631. _____. The Philosophy of Relation in the Metaphysics of St. Thomas. Washington, D.C.: Catholic University of America Press. 62 pp.

1632. Keller, Albert. Sein oder Existenz? Die Auslegung des Seins bei Thomas von Aquin in der heutigen Scholastik. München: Verlag Hueber, 1968. xiii-291 pp.

1633. Kelly, Matthew J. "Action in Aquinas." The New Scholasticism

52 (1978) 261-7.

1634. _____. "Agency in Aquinas." Laval Théologique et Philosophique Québec. 33 (1977) 33-7.

1635. _____. "A Note on 'Subject,' 'Substance,' and 'Accident' in St. Thomas." The New Scholasticism 50 (1976) 232-6.

1635A. _____. "St. Thomas and the Meaning and use of 'Substance' and 'Prime Matter.'" The New Scholasticism 40 (1966) 177-89.

1636. Kilzer, Ernest R. "The Modes of Existence." Proceedings of the American Catholic Philosophical Association 21 (1946) 66-76.

1637. Klubertanz, George P. Introduction to the Philosophy of Being. New York: Appleton-Century-Crofts, 1955. 200 pp.

1638. _____. "Metaphysics and Theistic Convictions," in Teaching Thomism Today (1963) 271-306.

1639. _____. "The Problem of the Analogy of Being." Review of Metaphysics 10 (1957) 553-79.

1640. _____. St. Thomas Aquinas on Analogy: A Textual Analysis and Systematic Synthesis. Chicago: Loyola University Press, 1960.

1641. _____. "St. Thomas on Learning Metaphysics." Gregorianum 35 (1954) 3-17.

1642. _____. "The Teaching of Thomistic Metaphysics. Gregorianum 35 (1954) 187-205.

1643. Kohls, Henry H. Some Factors in Our Knowledge of Existence Compared with Teaching of Aquinas. Washington, D.C.: Georgetown University Dissertation, 1953.

1644. Kondoleon, Theodore J. Exemplary Causality in the Philosophy of St. Thomas Aquinas. Washington, D.C.: Catholic University of America Dissertation, 1967. 280 pp.

1645. _____. "Substance and Accidents, Potency and Act." The New Scholasticism 51 (1977) 234-9.

1646. Koninck, Charles De. "Metaphysics and International Order." Proceedings of the American Catholic Philosophical Association 16 (1942) 52-64.

1647. Koren, Henry J. Introduction to the Science of Metaphysics. St. Louis: B. Herder Book Co., 1965. 300 pp.

1648. Kossel, Clifford G. Principles of St. Thomas' Distinction Between the Esse and Ratio of Relation." The Modern Schoolman 24 (1947) 24-36, 93-107.

METAPHYSICS   1649 - 1661

1649. _____. The Problem of Relation in the Philosophy of Saint
Thomas Aquinas. Toronto: University of Toronto Dissertation, 1945.
144 pp.

1650. _____. "St. Thomas's Theory of the Causes of Relations."
The Modern Schoolman 25 (1948) 153-66.

1651. Krapiec, Mieczyslaw A. "Analysis formationis conceptus entis
existentialiter considerate." Divus Thomas. Piacenza. 59 (1956)
320-50.

1652. _____.   "Coherence of the notion of being in the
key points of St. Thomas' system. (In Polish) Zeszyty Naukowe Kat.
Univ. Lubelskiego. Lublin. 17 (1974) 1-15.

1652A. _____. "Pour une interprétation de la métaphysique thomiste,"
in Miscellanea Medievalia (Symp) 343-7.

1652B. _____. Structura bytu. Charakter-ystyczne elementy systemu
Arystotelesa i Tomasza z Akwinu. Lublin, 1963. 361 pp.

1653. _____. "Teoria analogii bytu." Divus Thomas. Piacenza. 59
(1956) 79-131.

1654. _____. "O Tomaszowe rosumienie bytu jako bytu," in Studia
Sw. Tomasza   (Lublin Symp) 5-30.

     Thomistic Understanding of Being as Being.

1655. Kreyche, Robert J. First Philosophy. An Introductory Text in
Metaphysics. New York: Holt, 1959. 328 pp.

1656. Kremer, Klaus. "Die neuplatonische Seinsphilosophie und ihre
Wirkung auf Thomas von Aquin," in Studien zur Problemgeschichte der
antiken und miltelalterlichen Philosophie. Leiden: Brill, 1966. 508 pp.

1657. Krempel, Antoine. La doctrine de la relation chez s. Thomas:
exposé historique et systématique. Paris: Vrin, 1952. xiv-718 pp.

1658. Küchenhoff, Günther. "Die Natur der Sache in der Lehre von Aquin,"
in Studi Tomistici 4, 141-54.

1659. Lakebrink, Bernhard. "Die thomistische Lehre vom Sein des Seienden
in Gegensatz zu ihrer existenzialen und dialektischen Umdeutung," in
Thomas...Interpretation (Symp) 48-79.

1660. Lakebrink, Bernhard. "Der thomistische Seinsbegriff und seine
existentiale Umdeutung," in Tommaso d'Aquino (Symp Roma) 6, 219-38.

1661. LaMountain, George F. L. "The Concept of the Infinite in the
Philosophy of St. Thomas Aquinas." The Thomist 19 (1956) 312-38.

1662. Langevin, Gilles. "L'Action immanente d'après s. Thomas d'Aquin." Laval Théologique et Philosophique 30 (1944) 251-66.

1663. Laporte, Jean-Marc. "The Evidence for the Negative Judgment of Separation." The Modern Schoolman 41 (1963) 17-44.

1664. La Spisa, Mauro. L'essere come atto. Secondo Tommaso d'Aquino. Firenze: G. e G., 1970. xv-398 pp.

1665. Lauer, J. Quentin. "The Determination of Substance by Accidents in the Philosophy of St. Thomas." The Modern Schoolman 18 (1941) 31-4.

1666. Lauer, Rosemary Z. "The Notion of the Efficient Cause in the Secunda Via." The Thomist. Centenary Edition. 38 (1974) 754-67.

1667. Lazzaro, Pietro. La dialettica della partecipazione nella Summa contra Gentiles di S. Tommaso d'Aquino. Reggio Calabria: Parallelo 38, 1976. 159 pp.

1668. Lindback, George A. "Participation and Existence in the Inter- pretation of St. Thomas." Franciscan Studies 17 (1957) 1-22, 107-25.

1669. Llamzon, Benjamin S. "Supposital and Accidental Esse. A Study in Banez." The New Scholasticism 39 (1965) 170-88.

1670. Lonergan, Bernard. "Metaphysics as Horizon." Gregorianum 44 (1963) 307-18.

1671. _____. "St. Thomas' Theory of Operation." Theological Studies 3 (1942) 378-400.

1672. _____. The Subject. Milwaukee: Marquette University Press, 1968.

        Aquinas Lecture.

1673. Lopez, Jesus Garcia. "Analogia de la nocion de acto segun santo Tomas." Anuario Filosofico. Pamplona. 6 (1973) 142-76.

1674. Lotz, Johannes B. "A diferenca ontologica em Kant, Hegel, Heidegger e Tomás de Aquino, I - II." Revista Portuguesa de Filosofia 33 (1977) 21-36, 210-84.

1675. _____. "Das Sein nach Heidegger und Thomas von Aquin," in Tommaso d'Aquino...problemi fondamentali (Symp) 1974. 303-21.

1676. _____. Le Jugement de l'etre; les fondements de la métaphysique. R. Givord, tr. Paris: Beauchesne, 1965.

1677. Loughran, Thomas J. Efficient Causality and Extrinsic Denomination in the Philosophy of St. Thomas Aquinas. New York: Fordham University Dissertation, 1969. 259 pp.

METAPHYSICS   1678 - 1693

1678. Lyons, Lawrence F. The Material and Formal Cause of Being in the
Philosophy of Aristotle and St. Thomas Aquinas. Washington, D.C.:
Catholic University of America, 1958.

1679. McCall, Robert E. The Reality of Substance. Washington, D.C.:
Catholic University of America Press, 1956.

1680. McGlynn, James V. and Paul Mary Farley. A Metaphysics of Being
and God. Englewood Cliffs, N.J.: Prentice-Hall, 1966. viii-312 pp.

1681. McGrath, W. E. The Formal Concept of Goodness in the Metaphysics
of St. Thomas. Washington, D.C.: Catholic University of America Press,
1943.

1682. McLean, George F. "Thomistic Metaphysics and the Humanization of
Technological Progress," in Presenca Filosofica (Symp) 112-35.

1683. McMahon, Mary Roberta. Separatio in Recent Thomism. St. Louis:
Saint Louis University Dissertation, 1963. 294 pp.

1684. McNicholl, Ambrose J. "Physical Metaphysics." The Thomist 12
(1949) 425-73.

1685. Maceda, Hernando. Theory of Optimism and Plenitude St. Thomas
and Leibniz: An Interpretation. New York: Fordham University Dissertation, 1953.

1686. Marc, Alexander. "Being and Action." The Modern Schoolman 28
(1951) 175-90.

1687. Marc, André. Dialectique de l'affirmation. Essai de métaphysique
réflexive. Bruxelles: L'Ed. Universelle; Paris: Desclée, 1952.
731 pp.

1688. Marchesi, Angelo. "Analogia ed univocità dell'essere in Tommaso
d'Aquino e Duns Scoto," in Tommaso d'Aquino (Roma Symp) II, 268-78.

1689. Marcolongo, Francis J. Aristotle, Aquinas, Ockham: A Comparative
Study of Three Approaches in Metaphysics and Their Philosophical Significance for Understanding the Medieval Contribution to the Scientific
Revolution. San Diego, CA: University of California, San Diego Dissertation, 1971. 292 pp.

1690. Maréchal, Joseph. Le point de départ de la métaphysique. 3 me
éd. 5 vols. Bruxelles: Ed. Universelle; Paris: Desclée, 1944ff.

1691. Maritain, Jacques. Existence and the Existent. New York:
Pantheon, 1948.

1692. _____ . God and the Permission of Evil. Jos. Evans, tr.
Milwaukee: Bruce, 1966.

1693. _____ . "On the Notion of Subsistence," in Progress in Philosophy (Symp) 29-45.

1694. _____. A Preface to Metaphysics: Seven Lectures on Being.
New York: Sheed and Ward, 1940.

1695. _____. "Réflexions sur la nature blessée et sur l'intuition
de l'etre." Revue Thomiste 66 (1968) 5-40.

1696. _____. St. Thomas and the Problem of Evil. Milwaukee:
Marquette University Press, 1942.

    Aquinas Lecture.

1697. Martin, William O. Metaphysics and Ideology. Milwaukee:
Marquette University Press, 1959. 104 pp.

1698. Mascall, Eric L. Existence and Analogy. London: Longmans,
1949.

1699. Masiello, Ralph J. "The Analogy of Proportion According to the
Metaphysics of St. Thomas." The Modern Schoolman 35 (1958) 91-105.

1700. _____. The Intuition of Being According to the Metaphysics
of St. Thomas Aquinas. Washington: Catholic University of America
Press, 1955.

1701. Maurer, Armand A. "Form and Essence in the Philosophy of St.
Thomas." Mediaeval Studies 13 (1951) 165-76.

1702. _____. "St. Thomas and the Analogy of Genus." The New
Scholasticism 29 (1955).

1703. _____. "St. Thomas and Eternal Truths." Mediaeval Studies
32 (1970) 91-107.

1704. Mazierski, Stanislaw. Pojecie Konieczności w Filozofii św.
Tomasza z Akwinu. Lublin: Katolickiego Uniw. Lubelskiego, 1958.
122 pp.

1705. Meehan, Francis X. Efficient Causality in Aristotle and St.
Thomas. Washington, D.C.: Catholic University of America Press, 1940.
446 pp.

1706. Merlan, Philip. "Abstraction and Metaphysics in St. Thomas'
Summa." Journal of the History of Ideas 14 (1953) 284-91.

1707. Miller, Marianne (Childress). "The Problem of Action in the
Commentary of St. Thomas Aquinas on the Physics of Aristotle. The Modern
Schoolman 23 (1946) 135-65; 200-26.

1708. Miller, Robert J. The Problem of Substantial Form in the Early
Writings of St. Thomas Aquinas. Toronto: University of Toronto Dissertation, 1955.

METAPHYSICS   1709 - 1724

1709. Mondin, Battista. "L'ermeneutica metafisica di S. Tommaso e i grandi, problemi filosofici e teologici." Divinitas. Roma. 20 (1976) 318-23.

1710. Montagnes, Bernard. "L'axiome de continuité chez Saint Thomas." Revue des Sciences Philosophiques et Théologiques 52 (1968) 201-21.

1711. _____. La doctrine de l'analogie de l'etre d'après s. Thomas d'Aquin. Louvain: Publications Universitaires, 1963. 211 pp.

1712. Moreno, Antonio. "The Nature of Metaphysics." The Thomist 30 (1966) 109-35.

1713. Morgan, John D. Towards a Metaphysics of Value. A Critical Study of the Axiological Implications of the Metaphysics of Saint Thomas Aquinas. Los Angeles: University of Southern California Dissertation, 1966. 170 pp.

1714. Morón Arroyo, C. "Possibilidad y hecho de un Tomismo existencial." Salmanticensis 4 (1957) 395-430.

1715. Morton, Edmund W. The Doctrine of Ens Commune in St. Thomas. Toronto: University of Tornoto Dissertation, 1954.

1716. _____. "The Nature of the Possible According to St. Thomas Aquinas." Proceedings of the American Catholic Philosophical Association 32 (1958) 184-8.

1717. Mourant, John A, ed. Essays In Philosophy. University Park, Penn: Penn. University Press, 1962.

1718. Muck, Otto. The Transcendental Method. W. Seidensticker, tr. New York: Herder and Herder, 1968.

1719. Mullaney, Thomas . "Created Personality: The Unity of Thomistic Tradition." The New Scholasticism 29 (1955) 369-402.

1720. Mullen, M. Dominica. Essence and Operation in Thomistic and in Modern Philosophy. Washington: Catholic University of America Press, 1941.

1721. Muller-Thym, Bernard J. "St. Thomas and the Recapturing of Natural Wisdom." The Modern Schoolman 18 (1941) 64-8.

1722. _____. "The 'To Be' Which Signifies the Truth of Propositions." Proceedings of the American Catholic Philosophical Association 16 (1940) 324-45.

1723. Nink, Caspar. Ontologie. Versuch einer Grundlegung. Freiburg in Br: Herder, 1952. xii-496.

1724. Noonan, John P. General Metaphysics. Chicago: Loyola University

Press, 1957. 282 pp.

1725. Nugent, Francis. "Immanent Action in St. Thomas and Aristotle."
The New Scholasticism 37 (1963) 164-87.

1726. Oberarzbacher, Franz Peter. "Visión Tomista del ser."   Logos
Mexico, Universidad La Salle. 2 (1974) 9-32.

1727. O'Brien, Thomas. The Principle of Finality in the Philosophy of
St. Thomas Aquinas. New York: Fordham University Dissertation, 1956.
136 pp.

1728. Ocariz, Fernando. "Cuestiones de metafisica Tomista en torno a
la creación." Divus Thomas. Piacenza. 77 (1974) 403-24.

1729. O'Donnell, Robert A. "Individuation: An Example of the Development in the Thought of St. Thomas Aquinas." The New Scholasticism 33
(1959) 49-67.

1730. Oeing-Hanhoff, Ludger. Ens et unum convertuntur: Stellung und
Gehalt des Grundsatzes in der Philosophie des hl. Thomas von Aquin.
Münster: W. Aschendorff, 1953. xv-194 pp.

1731. O'Grady, Donald. "Esse and Metaphysics." The New Scholasticism
39 (1965) 283-94.

1732. O'Neil, Campion. The Notion of Essence in Some Neoplatonic Writings
of St. Thomas Aquinas. Washington, D.C.: Catholic University of America
Dissertation, 1967. 332 pp.

1733. O'Shaugnessy, Thomas. "La théorie Thomiste de la contingence
chez Plotin et les penseurs arabes." Revue philosophique de Louvain
65 (1967) 36-52.

1734. Owens, Joseph. "The Accidental and Essential Character of Being
in the Doctrine of St. Thomas Aquinas." Mediaeval Studies 20 (1958)
1-40.

1735. _____. "Actuality in the Prima Via of St. Thomas." Mediaeval
Studies 29 (1967) 26-46.

1736. _____. "Analogy as a Thomistic Approach to Being." Mediaeval
Studies 24 (1962) 303-22.

1737. _____. "The 'Analytics' and Thomistic Metaphysical Procedure."
Mediaeval Studies 26 (1964) 83-108.

1738. _____. "Aquinas and the Five Ways." The Monist 58 (1974)
16-35.

1739. _____. "Aquinas and the Proof from the Physics." Mediaeval
Studies 28 (1966) 119-50.

METAPHYSICS   1740 - 1756

1740. _____. "Aquinas-Existential Permanence and Flux."
Mediaeval Studies 31 (1969) 71-92.

1741. _____. "Aquinas on Cognition as Existence." Proceedings of
the American Catholic Philosophical Association 48 (1974) 74-85.

1742. _____. "Aquinas on Infinite Regress." Mind 71 (1962) 244-6.

1743. _____. "The Causal Proposition-Principle or Conclusion?"
The Modern Schoolman 32 (1955) 159-71, 257-70, 323-39.

1744. _____. "Common Nature: A Point of Comparison Between Thomistic
and Scotistic Metaphysics." Mediaeval Studies 19 (1957) 1-14.

        Also in Inquiries into Medieval Philosophy:...F.P. Clarke,
        James Ross, ed. Westport, CT: Greenwood Press. (Symp).

1745. _____. "Diversity and Community of Being in St. Thomas Aquinas."
Mediaeval Studies 22 (1960) 257-302.

1746. _____. An Elementary Christian Metaphysics. Milwaukee:
Bruce, 1963. xiv-384 pp.

1747. _____. "Existential Act, Divine Being, and the Subject of
Metaphysics." The New Scholasticism 36 (1962) 359-63.

1748. _____. "'Ignorare' and Existence." The New Scholasticism
46 (1972) 210-9.

1749. _____. "Immobility and Existence for Aquinas." Mediaeval
Studies 30 (1968) 22-46.

1750. _____. "The Intelligibility of Being." Gregorianum 35 (1954)
169-93.

1751. _____. An Interpretation of Existence. Milwaukee: Marquette
University Press, 1968.

1752. _____. "Maritain's Three Concepts of Existence." The New
Scholasticism 49 (1975) 295-309.

1753. _____. "Metaphysical Separation in Aquinas." Mediaeval Studies
34 (1972) 287-306.

1754. _____. "Note on the Approach to Thomistic Metaphysics." The
New Scholasticism 28 (1954) 454-76.

1755. _____. "Quiddity and Real Distinction in St. Thomas Aquinas."
Mediaeval Studies 28 (1965) 1-22.

1756. _____. "The Real Distinction of a Relation from Its Immediate
Basis." Proceedings of the Catholic American Philosophical Association

39 (1965) 134-9.

1757. _____. St. Thomas and the Future of Metaphysics. Milwaukee: Marquette University Press, 1957. 97 pp.

1758. _____. "Thomistic Common Nature and Platonic Idea." Mediaeval Studies 21 (1959) 211-23.

1759. _____. "Unity and Essence in St. Thomas Aquinas." Mediaeval Studies 23 (1961) 240-59.

1760. Pattin, Adriaan. "La relation transcendantale et la synthèse métaphysique thomiste," in Tommaso d'Aquino (Symp Roma) 6, 303-10.

1761. Pegis, Anton C. "The Dilemma of Being and Unity," in Essays in Thomism (Symp) 1942. 149-83.

1762. _____. "A Note on St. Thomas, S.T. I, 44, 1-2." Mediaeval Studies 8 (1946) 159-68.

1763. _____. "St. Thomas and the Coherence of Aristotelian Theology." Mediaeval Studies 35 (1973) 67-117.

1764. Perillat, Robert J. St. Thomas Aquinas on the Principle of Sub-sistence. Notre Dame: University of Notre Dame Dissertation, 1958. 349 pp.

1765. Perreiah, Alan R. "De conceptu entis: A Reconsideration." The Modern Schoolman 46 (1968) 50-6.

1766. Peters, J. A. J. "Matter and Form in Metaphysics." The New Scholasticism 31 (1957) 447-83.

1767. Phelan, Gerald B. "Being and the Metaphysicians," in From an Abundant Spring (Symp) 423-47.

1768. _____. "The Being of Creatures: St. Thomas' Solution of the Dilemma of Parmenides and Heraclitus, with Comments by William Cario and W. Norris Clarke." Proceedings of the American Catholic Philosophical Association 31 (1957) 118-31.

1769. _____. "The Existentialism of St. Thomas." Proceedings of the American Catholic Philosophical Association 21 (1946) 25-39.

1770. _____. St. Thomas and Analogy. Milwaukee: Marquette University Press, 1941. 58 pp.

1771. Philippe, Marie-Dominique. "Analyse de l'etre chez s. Thomas," in Tommaso d'Aquino (Roma-Napoli Symp) 1974. I, 255-79.

        Alson in 6, 9-28.

1772. _____. De l'etre à Dieu. De la philosophie première à la sagesse.

METAPHYSICS   1773 - 1789

Paris: Tégui, 1977. 525 pp.

1773. Pieper, Josef. Philosophia Negativa. München: Kösel, 1953.

1774. Poissant, Leeward J. An Analysis and Evaluation of Bernard Lonergan's Proposed Method for Verification in Metaphysics." Toronto: University of Toronto Dissertation, 1978.

1775. Poppi, Antonino. "Sul problema della sostanzializzazione del ente e dell'uno in S. Tommaso d'Aquino." Rivista de Filosofia Neoscolastica 66 (1974) 590-612.

1776. Pouillon, Henri. "La Beauté, propriété transcendentale chez les Scolastiques." Archives d'Histoire Doctrinale et Littéraire du Moyen Age 21 (1946) 268-71.

1777. Raeymaeker, Louis De. "L'Analogie de L'etre dans la perspective d'une philosophie thomiste." Revue Internationale de Philosophie 23 (1969) 89-106.

1778. _____. "L'Idée inspiratrice de la métaphysique Thomsite." Aquinas 3 (1960) 81ff.

1779. _____. De metaphysiek van het zyn. Antwerpen: Standaard Bockhandel, 1944. 338 pp.

1780. _____. Philosophy of Being. E. H. Ziegelmeyer, tr. St. Louis: Herder, 1954.

1781. Rahner, Jarl. Geist im Welt. Zur Metaphysik der endlicken Erkenntnis bei Thomas von Aquin. 2nd ed. München: Kösel-Pustet, 1957.

1782. _____. Espiritu en el mundo. Barcelona: Herder, 1963.

1783. _____. L'Esprit dans le monde. Paris: Mame, 1968.

1784. _____. Spirit in the World. Wm. Dych, tr. New York: Sheed and Ward, 1968.

1785. Ramirez, Jacobus (Santiago). De analogia. Obras completas, tomo 2. Madrid: C.S.I.C. 1970-1972.

1786. Rassam, Joseph. La Métaphysique de s. Thomas. Paris: Presses Universitaires, 1968. 128 pp.

1787. Rebollo Pena, Ambrosio. Abstracto y concreto en la filosofia de santo Tomas. Burgos: 1955. xxi-231 pp.

1788. Reese, William L. "Concerning the 'Real Distinction' of Essence and Existence." The Modern Schoolman 38 (1961) 142-8.

1789. Regis, Louis M. L'Odysée de la Métaphysique. Montréal-Paris:

1790 - 1804   METAPHYSICS

Vrin, 1949.

1790. Reichmann, James B. "Logic and the Method of Metaphysics."
The Thomist 29 (1965) 341-95.

1791. _____. "St. Thomas, Capreolus, Cajetan and the Created Person."
The New Scholasticism 33 (1959) 1-31, 202-30.

1792. _____. "The Transcendental Method and the Psychogenesis of
Being." The Thomist 32 (1968) 449-508.

1793. Reilly, John P. Cajetan's Notion of Existence. Hague: Mouton,
1971. 131 pp.

     Chapter 1 on Aquinas's notion of existence.

1794. Reith, Herman. The Metaphysics of St. Thomas Aquinas. Milwaukee:
Bruce. 1958. 420 pp.

1795. Renard, Henri. "Being and Essence." The New Scholasticism
23 (1949) 62-70

1796. _____. "Essence and Existence." Proceedings of the American
Catholic Philosophical Association 21 (1946) 53-65.

1797. _____. "The Habits in the System of St. Thomas." Gregorianum
29 (1948) 88-117.

1798. _____. "The Metaphysics of the Existential Judgment." The
New Scholasticism 23 (1949) 387-94.

1799. _____. "What Is St. Thomas' Approach to Metaphysics?" The
New Scholasticism 30 (1956) 64-83.

1800. Rintelen, Fritz-Joachim von. "O Bonum e o Summum Bonum no pensamiento de s. Tomás de Aquino." Revista Portuguesa de Filosofia 33 (1977)
182-95.

1801. _____. "Die Frage nach Sinn und Wert bei Thomas von Aquin,"
in Salzburger...Gedenkband (Symp) 1974. 129-76.

1802. Robert, J.-D. "Le principe: actus non limitature nisi per
potentiam subiectivam realiter distinctam." Revue Philosophique de
Louvain 47 (1949) 59-78.

1803. Gironella, Jan. "Fenomenologia de las formas filosofia de las
matematicas a través del comentario de Tomás de Aquino a la metafisica."
Espiritu 70 (1974) 131-47.

1804. Rosenberg, Jean R. The Principle of Individuation. Washington,
D.C.: Catholic University of America Press, 1950.

METAPHYSICS   1805 - 1820

1805. Ross, James F. "A New Theory of Analogy." Proceedings of the
American Catholic Philosophical Association 44 (1970) 70-85.

1806. Royce, James E. "St. Thomas and the Definition of Active Potency."
The New Scholasticism 34 (1960) 431-7.

1807. Ruben Sanabria, Jose. "El Ser en la filosofia de S. Tomás de
Aquino. Revista Filosofica. Mexico. 6 (1974) 99-147.

1808. Rucinski, Brunon J. "Zagadnienie istnienia w 'De ente et essentia'
Tomasza Akwinii. Studia Mediewist 15 (1974) 187-219.

    The Problem of esse in the De ente.

1809. Ruppel, Ernesto. "Metafisica de Sao Tomas," in Presenca Filosofica (Symp) 1974. 91-9.

1810. _____. "O ser em Sao Tomás de Aquino." Revista Portuguesa de
Filosofia 27 (1971) 125-46.

1811. Sacchi, Mario Enrique. "La continuidad metafisica del ser en S.
Tomas de Aquino." Estudios Teologicos y filosoficos. Buenos Aires.
8 (1977) 47-80.

1812. _____. "La restauración de la metafisica Tomista," in
Thomas...Interpretation (Symp) 1974. 170-95.

1813. Salerno, Luigi. "Relazione, opposizione e dialettica nel pensiero
moderno e in Tommaso d'Aquino," in Studi Tomistici (Symp) 3, 222-39.

1814. Salgado, Cesareo Lopez. "Unidad de ser y analogia en santo Tomas
de Aquino." Sapientia 29 (1974) 107-24.

1815. Salmon, Elizabeth G. The Good in Existential Metaphysics.
Milwaukee: Marquette University Press, 1952.

    Aquinas Lecture.

1816. _____. "What is Being?" Review of Metaphysics 7 (1954)
613-31.

1817. Saranyana, José I. "Sobre la immaterialidad de las sustancias
espirituales. S. Tomás versus Avicebron." Rivista di Filosofia Neo-
Scolastica 70 (1978) 63-97.

1818. Schindler, David L. "Creativity as Ultimate: Reflections on
Actuality in Whitehead, Aristotle, Aquinas." International Philosophical
Quarterly 13 (1973) 161-72.

1819. Schmidt, Robert W. "L'Emploi de la Séparation en métaphysique."
Revue Philosophique de Louvain 58 (1960) 373-93.

1820. Sciacca, Michele F. "Riflessioni sui principi della metafisica tomista: l'esistenza e l 'essenza; la creazione, la partecipazione e l'analogia," in Studi Tomistici (Symp) 3, 18-29.

1821. Seidel, George J. A Contemporary Approach to Classical Metaphysics. New York: Appleton-Century-Crofts, 1969. 136 pp.

1822. Seifert, Josef. "Answer to 'Disputed Questions' Concerning 'Essence and existence.'" Aletheia 1 (1977) 467-80.

1823. _____. "Essence and Existence, Part I." Aletheia I (1977) 17-157; Part II, 371-459.

1824. Serre, Jacques. Thomas d'Aquin et le Concept de totalite. Montréal: Université de Montréal Dissertation, 1966.

1825. Shine, Daniel J. An Interior Metaphysics. The Philosophical Synthesis of Pierre Scheuer. Weston, Mass: Weston College Press, 1966. viii-198 pp.

1826. Siewerth, Gustav. Das Schicksal der Metaphysik von Thomas zu Heidegger. Einsiedeln: Verlag, 1959. 519 pp.

1827. _____. Der Thomismus als Identitäts system. 2 Aufl. Frankfurt: Verlag Schulte-Bulmke, 1961. 277 pp.

1828. Sikora, Joseph J. The Christian Intellect and the Mystery of Being: Reflections of a Maritain Thomist. Hague: Nijhoff, 1966. 203 pp.

1829. Silva-Tarouca, Amadeo. Thomas heute: zehn Vortrage zum Aufbau einer existentiellen Ordnungs-metaphysik nach Thomas von Aquin. Wien: Herder, 1947. 208 pp.

1830. Simon, Yves R. "An Essay on the Classification of Action and the Understanding of Act." Revue de l'Universite d'Ottawa (1971) 525ff.

1831. Smith, Enid. The Goodness of Being in Thomistic Philosophy and Its Contemporary Significance. Washington, D.C.: Catholic University of America Press, 1947. 155 pp.

1832. Smith, Gerard and Lottie H. Kendzierski. Philosophy of Being. New York: Macmillan, 1961. xvii-408 pp.

1833. Solignac, A. "La doctrine de l'esse chez saint Thomas est-elle d' origine neo-platonicienne." Archives de Philosophie 30 (1967) 439-52.

1834. Sorrentino, Sergio. "La dottrina filosofica dell' analogia in Tommaso d'Aquino." Sapienza. Napoli. 27 (1974) 315-51.

1835. Stallmach, Josef. "Der Actus Essendi bei Thomas von Aquin und das Denker der ontologischen Differenz." Archiv für Geschichte der Philosophie 60 (1968) 134-45.

METAPHYSICS   1836 - 1852

1836. Steenberghen, Fernand van. Ontologie. Louvain: Institut
Supérieur, 1946.

1837. _____. Ontology. Martin J. Flynn, tr. New York: Wagner,
1952. 279 pp.

1838. Stokes, Walter E. "Freedom as Perfection: Whitehead, Thomas and
Augustine." Proceedings of the American Catholic Philosophical Association 36 (1962) 134-41.

1839. Stroick, Clemens. "Commentaire: la métaphysique de s. Thomas,"
in Colloque (Ottawa Symp) 171-88.

1840. Sullivan, Emmanuel F. The Analogy of Instrumental Causality in
Thomistic Metaphysics. Washington, D.C.: Catholic University of
America Dissertation, 1965. 284 pp.

1841. Summers, James A. St. Thomas and the Universal. Washington, D.C.:
Catholic University of America Press, 1955.

1842. Sweeney, Leo. "Analogy and Being." The Modern Schoolman 39
(1962) 253-62.

1843. _____. "Aquinas or Philosophers of Subjectivity?" The
Modern Schoolman 47 (1969) 57-70.

1844. _____. "Bonaventure and Aquinas on the Divine Being as Infinite." Southwestern Journal of Philosophy 5 (1974) 71-91.

1845. _____. Divine Infinity in the Writings of Saint Thomas Aquinas.
Toronto: University of Toronto Dissertation, 1955.

1846. _____. "Existence/Essence in Thomas Aquinas Early Writings."
Proceedings of the American Catholic Philosophical Association 37 (1963)
105-9, 129-30.

1847. _____. "Idealis in the Terminology of Thomas Aquinas."
Speculum 33 (1958) 497-507.

1848. _____. Metaphysics of Authentic Existentialism. Englewood
Cliffs, N.J.: Prentice-Hall, 1965.

1849. _____. "The Mystery of Existence." The Modern Schoolman 44
(1966) 57-73.

1850. Swiezawski, Stefan. Rozum i tajemnica. Krakow: Znak, 1960.

1851. Tallon, Andrew. "Spirit, Matter, Becoming: Karl Rahner's Spirit
in the World, Geist im Welt." The Modern Schoolman 48 (1971) 151-65.

1852. Tougas, Miryam. The Relation of Existence to the Subject of
Metaphysics in the Philosophy of St. Thomas. Washington, D.C.: Catholic
University of America Dissertation, 1962.

1853 – 1869   METAPHYSICS

1853. Trépanier, Emmanuel. "De diverses implications du nom 'ens' en s. Thomas," in Laval Thomas d'Aquin (Symp) 417-22.

1854. Tresmontant, Claude. Christian Metaphysics. New York: Sheed and Ward, 1965. 151 pp.

1855. Twomey, John E. The General Notion of the Transcendentals in the Metaphysics of St. Thomas Aquinas. Washington, D.C.: Catholic University of America Dissertation, 1958. 110 pp.

1856. Tyrrell, Bernard. Bernard Lonergan's Philosophy of God. Notre Dame: University of Notre Dame Press, 1974. 202 pp.

1857. Ulrich, Ferdinand. "Sein und Mitmensch," in Gedenkband...Thomas von Aquin (Symp) 1974. 93-128.

1858. Van Roo, William A. "Act and Potency." The Modern Schoolman 18 (1940) 1-4.

1859. _____ . "Matter as a Principle of Being." The Modern Schoolman 19 (1942) 47-50.

1860. Veres, Tomo. "Eine fundamentale ontologische Dichotomie im Denken des Thomas von Aquin." Philosophisches Jahrbuch. Freiburg-Munchen. 77 (1970) 81-98.

1861. Walton, William M. "Being, Essence and Existence for St. Thomas Aquinas." Review of Metaphysics 3 (1950) 339-66; 5 (1951) 83-108.

1862. _____ . "Is Existence a Valid Philosophical Concept." Philosophy and Phenomenological Research 12 (1952) 557-61.

1863. Watson, Scott Y. Esse in the Philosophy of St. Thomas Aquinas. Roma: Università Gregoriana Dissertation, 1972. 68 pp.

1864. Weidemann, H. Metaphysik und Sprache. Eine sprachphilosophische Untersuchung zu Thomas von Aquin Aristoteles. Freiburg-München: Alber, 1975. 200 pp.

1865. Wells, Norman. "Thomistic Existentialism." Listening 9 (1974) 178-81.

1866. Weltes, B. "Zum Seinsbegriff des Thomas von Aquin," in Auf der Spur des Ewigen. Freiburg-Basel-Wien: Herder, 1965.

1867. Wilhelmsen, Frederick D. "The Concept of Existence and the Structure of Judgment." The Thomist 41 (1977) 317-49.

1868. _____ . "Existence and Esse." The New Scholasticism 50 (1976) 20-45.

1869. _____ . "Metaphysics as Creativity." The Thomist 34 (1970) 369-86.

METAPHYSICS   1870 - 1885

1870. _____. The Paradoxical Structure of Existence. Irving, Texas:
University of Dallas Press, 1970.

1871. _____. "The Triplex Via and the Transcendence of Esse."
The New Scholasticism 44 (1970) 223-35.

1872. Wingell, Albert. "Vivere Viventibus est Esse in Aristotle and
St. Thomas." The Modern Schoolman 38 (1961) 85-120.

1873. Winiewicz, David. "A Note on alteritas and Numerical Diversity
in St. Thomas." Dialogue 16 (1977) 693-707.

1874. Wippel, John F. "Aquinas's Route to the Real Distinction: A
Note on De Ente et Essentia." The Thomist 43 (1979) 279-95.

1875. _____. "Metaphysics and separatio according to Thomas Aquinas."
Review of Metaphysics 31 (1977-1978) 431-70.

1876. _____. "The Title First Philosophy According to Thomas Aquinas
and His Different Justifications for the Same." Review of Metaphysics
(Symp) 1974. 585-600.

1877. Woznicki, Andrew N. The Metaphysical Foundation of the Order of
Being in St. Thomas Aquinas. Toronto: University of Toronto Dissertation,
1967.

1878. _____. "The Unity and Plurality of Being According to St.
Thomas." Dialectics and Humanism 2 (1975) 157-69.

1879. Wright. Thomas B. "Necessary and Contingent Being in St. Thomas."
The New Scholasticism 25 (1951) 439-66.

1880. Zeno, Carl. The Meaning of 'Real' According to Bernard Lonergan.
Milwaukee: Marquette University Dissertation, 1977.

PHILOSOPHY OF GOD

1881. Adler, Mortimer J. "The Demonstration of God's Existence." The
Thomist 5 (1943) 188-218.

        The Maritain Volume.

1882. Anderson, James F. Natural Theology: The Metaphysics of God.
Milwaukee: Bruce, 1962. 192 pp.

1883. Annice, M. "Logic and Mystery in the Quarta Via of St. Thomas."
The Thomist 19 (1956) 22-58.

1884. Ayers, Robert H. "A Viable Theodicy for Christian Apologetics."
The Modern Schoolman 52 (1975) 391-403.

1885. Baisnée, J. A. "St. Thomas Aquinas' Proofs of the Existence of
God Presented in Their Chronological Order," in Philos. Studies...

1886 - 1899   PHILOSOPHY OF GOD

Ignatius Smith (Symp) 29-64.

1886. Barale, Paolo and Giuseppe Muzio. Il Divino nella natura e nella
intelligenza: secondo S. Tommaso. Quaderni di Sodalitas Thomistica,
No. 1. Rome: Scuola Tipografica Italo-Orientale, 1960. 55 pp.

1887. Barbedette, D. Teodicea o teologia natural, Conforme al pensamiento
de Aristoteles y Santo Tomás. Traducido por Salvador A bascal. Mexico
City: Tradición, 1974. 307 pp.

1888. Barnds, William P. Man's Knowledge of God as Set Forth in the
Philosophies of St. Thomas Aquinas and F. R. Tennant. Lincoln, Neb.:
University of Nebraska Dissertation, 1949. 108 pp.

1888A. Bejze, Bohdan. "Problemy dyskusyjne w teodycei tomistycznej."
Studia Philosophiae Christianae I (1965) 5-31.

1889. Blair, George A. "Another Look at St. Thomas' First Way."
International Philosophical Quarterly 16 (1976) 301-14.

1890. Bobik, Joseph. "Further Reflections on the First Part of the
Third Way." Philosophical Studies 20 (1972) 166-74.

1891. _____. "A Seventh Way." The New Scholasticism 50 (1976)
345-52.

1892. _____. "The Sixth Way." The Modern Schoolman 51 (1974)
91-116.

1893. _____. "The Sixth Way of St. Thomas Aquinas." The Thomist
42 (1978) 373-99.

1894. Bochenski, I. M. De cognitione existentiae Dei per viam causali-
tatis relate ad fidem catholicam. Posnaniae: Ksiegarnia Sw. Wojciecha,
1946. xvi-229 pp.

1895. Boehm, A. "Autour du mystère des quinque viae de s. Thomas d'
Aquin." Revue des Sciences religieuses 24 (1950) 217-34.

1896. Bonnette, Dennis. Aquinas' Proofs for God's Existence. St. Thomas
Aquinas on 'the per accidens Necessarily Implies the per se.' Hague:
Nijhoff, 1972. viii-203.

1897. _____. St. Thomas Aquinas on: 'The Per Accidens Neccessarily
Implies the Per Se.' Notre Dame: University of Notre Dame Dissertation,
1970. 286 pp.

1898. Brady, Jules M. "Note on the Fourth Way." The New Scholasticism
48 (1974) 219-32.

1899. Brown, Patterson. "Infinite Causal Regression." Philosophical
Review 75 (1966) 510-25.

PHILOSOPHY OF GOD   1900 - 1916

1900. Brugger, Walter. Theologia naturalis. Freiburg i. Br.-New York: Herder and Herder, 1959; ed. 2 a, 1964.

1901. Bryar, William J. St. Thomas and the Existence of God: Three Interpretations. Chicago: University of Chicago Dissertation, 1950.

1902. _____. St. Thomas and the Existence of God: Three Interpretations. Chicago: Regnery, 1951. xxv-252 pp.

1903. Catania, Francis J. "The Logical and Symbolic Functions of the Third Way of Thomas Aquinas." Listening 9 (1974) 89-104.

1904. Caturelli, Alberto. "Metafisica tomista y existencia de Dios." Presenca Filosofica. Sao Paulo. 4-7 (1975) 139-59.

1905. Cauchy, Venant. "Les cinq voies de l'existence de Dieu chez s. Thomas," in Tommaso d'Aquino (Symp Roma-Napoli) 3 (1976) 257-68.

1906. Cenacchi, Giuseppe. "Esame critico e rigorizzazione delle vie tomistiche per l'esistenza di Dio." Divinitas 18 (1974) 40-61.

1907. Charlesworth, Max. "St. Thomas and the Decline of the Kantian-Kierkegaardian Philosophy of Religion," in Tommaso d'Aquino...problemi fondamentali (Symp) 1974. 323-36.

1908. Charlier, L. "Les cinq voies de s. Thomas. Leur structure méta-physiques." in L'Existence de Dieu. Cahiers de l'actualité religieuse, 16. Paris: Casterman, 1953. 179-227.

1909. Chavannes, Henry E. L'Analogie entre Dieu et le monde selon s. Thomas d'Aquin et Karl Barth. Paris: Cerf. 1970. 330 pp.

1910. Clarke, W. Norris. "Analogical Talk of God: Two Views: An Affirmative Rejoinder." The Thomist 40 (1976) 61-96.

1911. _____. "Analogy and the Meaningfulness of Language About God: A Reply to Kai Nielsen." The Thomist 40 (1976).

1912. _____. "Linguistic Analysis and Natural Theology." Proceedings of the American Catholic Philosophical Association 34 (1960) 110-26.

1913. Cloete, S. The Third Way. Boston: Houghton Mifflin, 1947. 456 pp.

1914. Connolly, Thomas Kevin. "The Basis of the Third Proof for the Existence of God." The Thomist 17 (1954) 281-349.

1915. Cooper, Burton Z. The Idea of God: A Whiteheadian Critique of St. Thomas Aquinas' Concept of God. Hague: Nijhoff, 1974. 123 pp.

1916. Corradi, Enrico. "Le 'cinque vie' e la teoria del caso." Rassegna di Scienze Filosofiche 27 (1974) 259-68.

1917 - 1933   PHILOSOPHY OF GOD

1917. Corvez, Maurice. "La preuve de l'existence de Dieu par les degrès des etres." Revue Philosophique de Louvain 72 (1974) 19-52.

1918. _____. "La prova di Dio," in Sacra Doctrina (Symp) 377-90.

1919. Cosgrove, Matthew R. "Thomas Aquinas on Anselm's Argument." Review of Metaphysics. Commemorative Issue. 27 (1974) 513-30.

1920. Curran, Charles E. "The 'Tertia Via': An Existential Reconstruction." Proceedings of the American Catholic Philosophical Association 46 (1972) 84-9.

1921. Daly, Mary F. Natural Knowledge of God in the Philosophy of Jacques Maritain. Rome: Catholic Book Agency, 1966.

1922. Degl'Innocenti, Umbertus. "Cur viae S. Thomas sunt quinque?" in Studi Tomistici (Symp) 1974. 2, 30-42.

1923. _____. "La validità della tertia via." Doctor Communis 1-2 (1954) 371ff.

1924. Dewan, Lawrence. "The Number and Order of St. Thomas's Five Ways." Downside Review. Bath. 92 (1974) 1-18.

1925. Dilley, Frank B. "Misunderstanding the Cosmological Argument of St. Thomas." The New Scholasticism 50 (1976) 96-107.

1926. Donceel, J. F. Natural Theology. New York: Sheed & Ward, 1962. 182 pp.

1927. Donovan, M. Annice. The Henological Argument for the Existence of God in the Works of St. Thomas. Notre Dame: University of Notre Dame Dissertation, 1946.

1928. _____. "Limited Perfection as Requiring Subsistent Perfection." Proceedings of the American Catholic Philosophical Association 20 (1945) 136-45.

1929. Doyle, John P. "Ipsum Esse as God-Surrogate: The Point of Convergence of Faith and Reason for St. Thomas Aquinas." The Modern Schoolman 50 (1973) 293-6.

1930. Duce, Leonard A. The Knowledge of God in Neo-Thomism as Represented by Pere Reginaldo Garrigou Lagrange. New Haven: Yale University Dissertation, 1946.

1931. Dunphy, William. "The Quinque Viae and Some Parisian Professors of Philosophy," in St. Thomas Aquinas 1274-1974 (Symp) 2, 73-104.

1932. Duquesne, M. "De quinta via. Le preuve de Dieu par le gouvernement des choses." Doctor Communis 18 (1965) 71-92.

1933. Edwards, Rem B. "Another Visit to the 'Third Way.'" The New

PHILOSOPHY OF GOD   1934 - 1951

Scholasticism 47 (1973) 100-4.

1934. _____. "The Validity and Soundness of Aquinas' Third Way."
The New Scholasticism 45 (1971) 117-26.

1936. Esser, Gerard. "The Augustinian Proof for God's Existence and
the Thomistic Fourth Way. with Comment by Robert F. Harvanek."
Proceedings of the American Catholic Philosophical Association 28 (1954)
194-211.

1937. Fabro, Cornelio. "Il fondamento metafisico della IV via."
Doctor Communis 18 (1965) 49-70.

1938. Faricy, Robert L. "The Establishment of the Basic Principle of
the Fifth Way." The New Scholasticism 31 (1957) 189-208.

1939. Fay, Thomas A. "Bonaventure and Aquinas on God's Existence:
Points of Convergence." The Thomist 41 (1977) 585-96.

1940. Finili, A. "Is There a Philosophical Approach to God?" Dominican
Studies 4 (1951) 80-91.

1941. Fontana, Vincent V. "Linguistic Analysis and Inference About God."
The Thomist 32 (1968) 201-12.

1942. Fraasen, B. C. "Theoretical Entities: The Five Ways." Philosophia
Israel. 4 (1974) 95-109.

1943. Franchi, A. "Ricerche sulla seconda via di s. Tommaso." Sapienza
25 (1972) 210-21.

1944. Giacon, Carlo. "Alcune observazioni sulla III e IV via di S.
Tommaso." Doctor Communis 18 (1965) 131-45.

1945. _____. "L'interpretazione tomistica del motore immobile," in
Studi Tomistici (Symp) I, 13-29.

1946. Giannini, Giorgio. "La quarta via tomistica in prospettiva
agostiniana," in Studi Tomistici (Symp) I, 109-18.

1947. Gibson, A. Boyce. "The Two Strands in Natural Theology." The
Monist 47 (1963) 335-64.

1948. Gigon, André C. Demonstratur existentia Dei: S.T. Aquin, I, q. 2,
art. 3. ed. 3 me. Fribourg Sv: Typographia Canisiana, 1949. 35 pp.

1949. Gilson, Etienne. "Can the Existence of God Still Be Demonstrated?"
The McAuley Lectures, 1960. West Hartford,CT: St. Joseph College, 1960.

1950. _____. "L'Etre et Dieu." Revue Thomiste 42 (1962) 181-202.

1951. _____. God and Philosophy. New Haven: Yale University Press,
1941.

1952 - 1968   PHILOSOPHY OF GOD

1952.   . "De la notion d'etre divin dans la philosophie de s.
Thomas d'Aquin." Doctor Communis 18 (1965) 113-29.

1953.   . "Prologoménes á la prima via." Archives d'Histoire
Doctrinale et litteraire du moyen age 30 (1963) 53-70.

1954. Giuliani, S. "Perché cinque le 'vie' di S. Tommaso?' Sapienza
I (1948) 153-66.

1955. Genemmi, Angelo. "Conoscenza metafisica e ricerca di dio in J.
Maritain." Rivista di Filosofia Neo-Scolastica. Milano. 64 (1972)
485-517.

1956. Gonzalez, Manuel. El problema de las fuentes de la 'tercera via'
de santo Tomás de Aquino. Madrid: Ed. Catolica, 1961.

1957. Gonzalez y Gonzalez, Manuel. Las cinco vias de santo Tomás de
Aquino. Huesca: Perez, 1943. 137 pp.

1958. Gonzalez Pola, Manuel. "Dios en la problematica del opusculo 'De
ente et essentia' de Santo Tomás. Studium 14 (1974) 279-96.

1959. Gornall, Thomas. A Philosophy of God: The Elements of Thomist
Natural Theology. New York: Sheed and Ward, 1962. 250 pp.

1960. Grisez, Germain. Beyond the New Theism: A Philosophy of Religion.
Notre Dame-London: University of Notre Dame Press, 1975. xiii-418 pp.

1961. Guérard des Lauriers, Michel. La preuve de Dieu et les cinq
voies. Roma: Università Lateranense, 1949. 229 pp.

1962. Gumppenberg, Rudolf. "Immanenz und Transzendenz--Versuch einer
interpretation von Thomas v. Aquin." Freiburger Zeilschrift für Philosophie und Theologie 16 (1969) 222-47.

1963. Harrison, Frank R. "Some Brief Remarks Concerning the Quinque
Viae of Saint Thomas." Franciscan Studies 21 (1961) 80-93.

1964. Hart, Charles A. "Participation and the Thomistic Five Ways."
The New Scholasticism 26 (1952) 267-82.

1965. Hartshorne, Charles E. Aquinas to Whitehead: Seven Centuries of
Metaphysics of Religion. Milwaukee: Marquette University Press, 1976.
68 pp.

1966. Herrlin, O. The Ontological Proof in Thomistic and Kantian
Interpretation. Uppsala: Lundequistska Bokhandeln; Leipzig: Harassowitz,
1950. 116 pp.

1967. Holloway, Maurice R. An Introduction to Natural Theology. New
York: Appleton-Century-Crofts, 1959. 517 pp.

1968. Holstein, H. "L'Origine aristotélicienne de la tertia via de s.

PHILOSOPHY OF GOD   1969 - 1983

Thomas." Revue philosophique de Louvain 48 (1950) 354-70.

1969. Iammarone, Luigi. "La rigorizzazione dell'itinerario tomistico a Dio," in Studi Tomistici (Symp) 1974. II, 15-29.

1970. _____. Il valore metafisico delle cinque vie tomistiche. Roma: Ed. "Miscellanea Francescana," 1970. 292 pp.

1971. Imbach, Ruedi. Deus est intelligere. Das Verhältnis von Sein und Denken in seiner Bedeutreng für das Gottesverständnis bei Thomas von Aquin und...Meister Echhart. Freiburg, Schw: Universtätsverlag, 1976. xiv-321 pp.

1972. Joyce, G. H. The Principles of Natural Theology. London-New York: Longmans, Green, 1951.

1973. Keating, Mary W. The Relation Between the Proofs for the Existence of God and the Real Distinction of Essence and Existence in St. Thomas Aquinas. New York: Fordham University Dissertation, 1962. 197 pp.

1974. Kehew, Donald R. "A Metaphysical Approach to the Existence of God. Franciscan Studies 32 (1972) 88-122.

1975. Kenny, Anthony. The Five Ways: St. Thomas Aquinas's Proofs of God's Existence. New York: Schocken Books, 1969. 131 pp.

1976. King-Farlow, John. "The First Way in Physical and Moral Space." The Thomist 39 (1975) 349-74.

1977. Klubertanz, George P. "Being and God According to Contemporary Scholastics." The Modern Schoolman 32 (1954) 1-17.

1978. _____, and Mauricer Holloway. Being and God: An Introduction to the Philosophy of Being and to Natural Theology. New York: Appleton-Century-Crofts, 1963. 387 pp.

1979. Knasas, John F. X. An Analysis and Interpretation of the Tertia Via of St. Thomas Aquinas." Toronto: University of Toronto Dissertation, 1975.

1980. _____. "'Necessity' in the Tertia Via." The New Scholasticism 52 (1978) 373-94.

1981. Kowalczyk, Stanislaw. "L'argument thomiste de causalité éfficiente." Divus Thomas. Piacenza. 81 (1978) 109-40.

1982. _____. "Argument from Contingency for the Existence of God, According to Aquinas: Polish Text." Roczniki Filozoficzne. Lublin.21 (1973) 29-46.

1983. _____. "The Argument from Finality in the Thomistic Philosophy of God: Polish Text with French Resume." Studia Philosophiae Christianae

1983A - 1997   PHILOSOPHY OF GOD

11 (1975) 75-112.

1983A. Krapiec, M. A. "O poprawne rozumienie kinetyczego dowodu na istnienie Boga u sw. Tomasza." Polonia Sacra 6 (1953) 97-113.

1984. Kuntz, Paul G. "Omnipotence, Tradition and Revolt in Philosophical Theology." The New Scholasticism 42 (1968) 270-9.

1985. Kusic, Ante. "Tomini psiholoski putevi u spoznaji Boga." in Zbornik (Symp Zagreb) 1974. 25-38.

St. Thomas' Psychological Ways of Knowing God.

1986. Lavatori, Renzo. "La quarta via di S. Tommaso d'Aquino secondo il principio dell'ordine." Divinitas 18 (1974) 62-87.

1987. La Via, Vincenzo. "Necessità o amore. Introduzione al concetto della filosofia come 'via a Dio' ad mentem divi Thomae." Teoresi 29 (1974) 3-18.

1988. Leroy, Marie-Vincent. "La 'troisième voie' de s. Thomas et ses sources," in Recherches d'Islamologie. Offerts à G. C. Anawati et Louis Gardet. Préface de Olivier Lacombe. Louvain: Editions de l'Inst. Sup. de Philosophie, 1977. 171-200.

1989. Lotz, Johannes B. "De secunda via S. Thomas." Doctor Communis 18 (1965) 39-40.

1990. Lyttkens, Hampus. The Analogy Between God and the World. An Investigation of Its Background and Interpretation of Its use by Thomas of Aquino. Uppsala: Almqvist and Wicksells, 1952. 493 pp.

1991. Mabey, Rendell N. "Confusion and the Cosmological Argument." Mind 80 (1971) 124-6.

1992. Mackey, Louis. "Entreatments of God. Reflections on Aquinas' Five Ways." Franciscan Studies 37 (1977) 103-19.

1993. Manding, Benito O. An Analysis of the "Quinque Viae": A Descriptive Analysis of Aquinas' Proofs of God's Existence in the Context of Current Interpretations. New York: Syracuse University Dissertation, 1977. 246 pp.

1994. Maritain, Jacques. Approaches to God. New York: Harper, 1954.

1995. Masi, R. "De prima via S. Thomae." Doctor Communis 18 (1965) 3-37.

1996. Matthews, Gareth B. "Aquinas on Saying that God Doesn't Exist." The Monist 47 (1963) 472-7.

1997. Mautner, Thomas. "Aquinas's Third Way." American Philosophical Quarterly 6 (1969).

PHILOSOPHY OF GOD   1998 - 2013

1998. Meulen, H. Van der. Adaguim 'appetitus naturalis non potest esse frustra' in doctrina S. Thomae. Gernert (Nederl.) Schol. Congreg. Sancti Spiritus, 1953. 55 pp.

1999. Miethe, Terry L. "The Ontological Argument: A Research Bibliography." The Modern Schoolman 54 (1977) 148-66.

2000. Miller, Clyde L. "Maimonides and Aquinas on Naming God." The Journal of Jewish Studies. London. 28 (1977) 65-71.

2001. Miyakawa, Toshiyuki. "The Value and Meaning of the Tertia Via of St. Thomas Aquinas." Aquinas 6 (1963) 239-95.

2002. Muniz, P. "La quarta via di Santo Tomas." Revista de Philosophia 3 (1944) 385-433; 4 (1945) 49-101.

2003. Nash, Peter W. "Ordinary Knowledge and Philosophical Demonstration of God's Existence." Proceedings of the American Catholic Philosophical Association 28 (1954) 55-77.

2004. Nielsen, Kai. "Analogical Talk of God-Two Views: A Negative Critique." The Thomist 40 (1976) 32-60.

2005. Nugent, James B. The Fundamental Theistic Argument in the Metaphysical Doctrine of St. Thomas Aquinas. Washington, D.C.: Catholic University of America Dissertation, 1961. 141 pp.

2006. O'Brien, Thomas C. Metaphysics and the Existence of God. Washington: Thomist Press, 1960. 272 pp.

2007. _____. "Reflexion on the Question of God's Existence in Contemporary Thomistic Metaphysics." The Thomist 23 (1960) 1-89, 211-85, 362-447.

2008. O'Donoghue, Noel D. "In Defense of the Third Way." Philosophical Studies. Ireland. 18 (1969) 172-7.

2009. O'Neil, Martin S. "Some Remarks on the Analogy of God and Creatures in St. Thomas Aquinas." Mediaeval Studies 23 (1961) 206-15.

2010. Osorio, Alberto. "La critique thomiste de l'argument ontologique," in Tommaso d'Aquino (Symp Roma) 3, 408-36.

2011. Owens, Joseph. "Aquinas-'Darkness of Ignorance' in the Most Refined Notion of God." Southwestern Journal of Philosophy 5 (1974) 93-110.

2012. _____. "'Cause of Necessity' in Aquinas' Tertia Via." Mediaeval Studies 33 (1971) 21-45.

2013. _____. "The Conclusion of the Prima Via." The Modern Schoolman 30 (1953) 33-53, 109-21, 203-15.

2014. _____. "The Starting Point of the Prima Via." Franciscan
Studies 27 (1967) 249-84.

2015. Paolinelli, Marco. "San Tommaso e Ch. Wolff sull'argomento
ontologico." Rivista di Filosofia Neo-Soclastica 66 (1974) 897-945.

2016. Pater, Thomas G. "The Question of the Validity of the Tertia
Via." Studies in Philosophy and in the History of Philosophy 2 (1963)
137-77.

2017. Pegis, Anton C. "Four Medieval Ways to God." The Monist 54
(1970) 317-58.

2018. Philippe, Marie Dominique. "La Troisième voie de s. Thomas."
Doctor Communis 18 (1965) 41-8.

2019. Philippe de la Trinité. "Les cinq voies de s. Thomas d'Aquin.
Réflexions méthodologiques." Divinitas 2 (1958) 268-338.

2020. Pieper, Josef. "The Meaning of 'God Speaks'." The New Scholasticism 43 (1969) 205-28.

2021. Pontifex, Mark. The Existence of God: A Thomist Essay.   London-
New York: Longmans, Green, 1947. xv-181 pp.

2022. Prado, C. G. "The Third Way Revisited." The New Scholasticism
45 (1971) 495-501.

2023. Quinn, John M. "The Third Way to God. A New Approach.
The Thomist 42 (1978) 50-68.

2024. Reichenbach, Bruce. The Cosmological Argument: A Reassessment.
Springfield, Illinois: Charles C. Thomas Publisher, 1972. 150 pp.

2025. Reichmann, James B. "Aquinas, God and Historical Process," in
Tommaso d'Aquino (Symp Roma) 9, 427-436.

2026. _____. "From Immanently Transcendent to Subsistent Esse:
Aquinas and the God-Problem. Proceedings of the American Catholic
Philosophical Association 48 (1974) 112-20.

2027. _____. "Immanently Transcendent and Subsistent Esse: A
Comparison." The Thomist 38 (1974) 332-69.

2028. Richard, Jean. "Analogie et symbolesem chez s. Thomas," in
Laval Thomas d'Aquin (Symp) 379-406.

2029. Ridall, Robert. Quinque Viae. The Five Ways to St. Thomas
Aquinas. St. Louis: Concordia Seminary Dissertation, 1963. 176 pp.

2030. Riet, Georges Van. "Le problème du mal dans la philosophie de
la religion de Saint Thomas." Revue Philosophique de Louvain 71 (1973)
5-45.

PHILOSOPHY OF GOD   2031 - 2045

2031.   Rogers, Vera.   St. Thomas's Argument from Motion and Its Critics.
Milwaukee: Marquette University Dissertation, 1943.

2032.   Roig Gironella, Juan.   "Todas las leyes del ser radican en Dois.
La demostracion por la Verdad, en Santo Tomás." Doctor Communis 18
(1965) 265-71

2033.   Ross, James F.   "Analogy as a Rule of Meaning for Religious
Language." International Philosophical Quarterly 1 (1961) 468-502.

2034.   _____.   "Did God Create the Only Possible World?" Review
of Metaphysics 16 (1962) 14-25.

2035.   _____.   Philosophical Theology.   Indianapolis-New York:
Bobbs-Merrill, 1969. 326 pp.

2036.   Rowe, William L.   "Cosmological Argument." Nous 5 (1971)
49-62.

2037.   _____.   The Cosmological Argument.   Princeton, N.J.: Princeton University Press, 1975. 273 pp.

2038.   Russell, Bertrand and Frederick C. Copleston.   "The Existence of
God-A Debate." A British Broadcasting Program, 1948.

        Reprinted in A Modern Introduction to Philosophy. Paul Edwards
        and Edward Pap, eds. New York: Free Press, 1965. 473-502.

2039. Saint-Jaques, Alphonse.   "Saint Thomas d'Aquin et le premier
fondement de notre connaissance de Dieu." Laval Théologique et
Philosophique 30 (1974) 349-78.

2040.   Schmitt, Friedrich.   Die Lehre des hl. Thomas von Aquin vom
göttlicken Wissen des zukünftig Kontingenten bei seinen grossen
Kommentaren. NYmegen: Centrale Drukkerij, 1950. 202 pp.

2041.   Schwartz, Herbert Thomas.   "A Reply: The Demonstration of God's
Existence." The Thomist 6 (1943) 19-48.

2042.   Sheen, Fulton J.   God and Intelligence in Modern Philosophy: a
Critical Study in the Light of the Philosophy of St. Thomas.   Garden
City, New York: Image Books, 1958.

2043.   Sillem, Edward A.   Ways of Thinking About God: Thomas Aquinas
and the Modern Mind. London: Darton, Longman and Todd, 1961; New
York: Sheed and Ward, 1961.

2044.   Smith, Gerard.   Natural Theology: Metaphysics II. New York:
Macmillan, 1951.

2045.   Smith, Vincent E.   "The Prime Mover: Physical and Metaphysical
Considerations." Proceedings of the American Catholic Philosophical
Association 28 (1954) 78-94.

2046. Solon, Thomas P. M. "The Logic of Aquinas' 'Tertia Via.'" Mind 82 (1973) 598-9.

2047. _____. "Some Logical Issues in Aquinas' Third Way." Proceedings of the American Catholic Philosophical Association 46 (1972) 78-83.

2048. Steenberghen, Fernand van. Dieu caché Louvain-Paris: Nauwelaerts, 1961. 371 pp.

2049. _____. Hidden God: How Do We Know that God Exists? Theodore Crowley, tr. St. Louis: B. Herder, 1967. 316 pp.

2050. _____. "Le problème philosophique de l'existence de Dieu." Revue Philosophique de Louvain 45 (1947) 5-20, 141-68, 301-13.

2051. _____. "The Problem of the Existence of God in St. Thomas' Commentary on the Metaphysics of Aristotle." Review of Metaphysics 27 (1974) 554-68.

2052. _____. "Le Problème de l'existence de Dieu dans le Commentaire de Saint Thomas sur la 'Physique' d'Aristote." Sapientia 26 (1971) 163-72.

2053. _____. "Le Problème de L'Existence de Dieu dans les Questions Disputées 'De Potentia Dei.'" Pensamiento 25 (1969) 249-57.

2054. _____. "Le 'Processus in Infinitum' dans les trois premières 'voies' de saint Thomas." Revista Portuguesa de Filosofia 30 (1974) 127-34.

2055. _____. "Le 'processus in infinitum' dans les trois premières 'voices' de s. Thomas." Rassegna di Scienze Filosofiche 30 (1974) 127-34.

2056. _____. "Prolégomènes à la quarta via." Rivista di Filosofia Neo-Scolastica 70 (1978) 99-112.

2057. _____. "Saint Thomas contre l'agnosticisme." Sapienza 29 (1974) 177-84.

2058. _____. "Saint Thomas d'Aquin contre l'evidence de l'existence de Dieu." Rivista di Filosofia Neo-Scolastica 66 (1974) 671-81.

2059. Thum, Beda. "Der unendliche Regress und die Gottesbeweise des hl. Thomas von Aquin," in Salzburger Jahrb....Gedenkband (Symp) 71-82.

2060. Velecky, Lubor. "'The Five Ways' - Proofs of God's Existence?" The Monist 58 (1974) 35-51.

2061. Versfeld, Martin. "St. Thomas, Newman and the Existence of God." The New Scholasticism 41 (1967) 3-30.

PHILOSOPHY OF GOD   2062 - 2077

2062. Walgrave, Jan H. "Spreken over God en analogie bij Thomas von Aquino," in Miscellanea A. Dondeyne (Symp) 1974. 393-414.

2063. Wallace, William A. "The First Way: A Rejoinder." The Thomist 39 (1975) 375-82.

2064. _____. "Newtonian Antinomies Against the Prima Via." The Thomist 19 (1956) 151-92.

2065. _____. "Metaphysics and the Existence of God." The New Scholasticism 36 (1962) 529ff.

2066. Watts, G. S. "The Thomist Proofs of Theism." Australian Journal of Philosophy 35 (1957) 30-46.

2066A. Wilczek-Tuszynaska, Franciszka. Ontologicze podstawy dowodów na istnienie Boga wedlug sw. Tomasza z Akwinu i Dunsa Szkota. Warszawa, 1957. 331 pp.

2067. Williams, C. J. E. "Believing in God and Knowing that God Exists." Nous 8 (1974).

2068. Yardar, John L. "Some Remarks on Metaphysics and the Existence of God." The New Scholasticism 37 (1963) 213-9.

ETHICS

2069. Adler, Mortimer J. A Dialectic of Morals. New York: F. A. Ungar, 1941.

2070. _____. The Time of Our Lives. The Ethics of Common Sense. New York: Holt, Rinehart and Winston, 1970. xiii-361 pp.

2071. Alcocer, Antonio Perez. "El acto moral según Santo Tamás y las corrientes en e Tica." Revista Filosofica. Mexico. 10 (1977) 223-32.

2072. Alcorta, Jose Ignacio. "La moral existencialista y la regulación racional tomista." Sapientia 18 (1963) 31-47.

2073. Allers, Rudolf. "Ethics and Anthropology." The New Scholasticism 24 (1950) 237-62.

2074. Alvira, Rafael. "'Caxus et fortuna' en S. Tomás de Aquino. Anuario Filosofico 10 (1977) 27-69.

2075. Ambrosetti, Giovanni. "Introduzione al trattato sulla giustizia," in Studi Tomistici (Symp) 6, 1-20.

2076. _____. "The Spirit and Method of Christian Natural Law." American Journal of Jurisprudence 16 (1971) 290-301.

2077. Antonelli, Maria T. "Il concetto di imperatività della norma," in Thomistica Morum (Symp) 15-23.

2078. Ardagh, David William. Aquinas on Happiness. Seattle:
University of Washington Dissertation, 1975. 224 pp.

2079. Armstrong, R. A. Primary and Secondary Precepts in Thomistic
Natural Law Teaching. Hague: Nijhoff, 1966. 193 pp.

2080. Arntz, J. T. C. "Die Entwicklung des naturrechtlichen Denkens
innerhalb des Thomismus," in Naturrecht im Disput. herausg. von F.
Böckle, Düsseldorf: Patmos. 1966. 87-120.

2081. _____. "Prima principia propria," in Thomas...Interpretation
(Symp) 3-15.

2082. Ashmore, Robert B. Jr. "Aquinas and Ethical Naturalism."
The New Scholasticism 49 (1975) 76-86.

2083. _____. "On Confusing Aquinas with Kant." The Modern Schoolman
53 (1976) 277-81.

2084. Azagra, Rafael. "Dinamismo y flexibilidad de la ley natural
según S. Tomás de Aquino." Escritos del Vedat 2 (1972) 87-144.

2085. Barbedette, D. Etica O filosofia moral. Conforme al pensamiento
de Aristoteles y Santo Tomás. Traducido por Salvador Abascal. Mexico
City: Tradición, 1974. 331 pp.

2086. Basso, D. M. "Estructura psicologica y analogia de la recta
razón en la moral de S. Tomás." Estudios teológicos y filosoficos
(1963) 37-71.

2087. _____. "Experiencia, ciencia y conducta. Santo Tomás."
Ethos. Buenos Aires. I (1973) 145-74.

2088. Battaglia, Natale A. The Basis of Morals: A Study of Natural
Law in Thomas Aquinas. Princeton, N.J.: Princeton University
Dissertation, 1972. 175 pp.

2089. Beis, Richard H. Modern Ethical Relativism and the Natural Law
Theory of St. Thomas Aquinas. Notre Dame: University of Notre Dame
Dissertation, 1963. 135 pp.

2090. Berghin-Rosé, G. Elementi di filosofia. VII. Morale. Torino:
Marietti, 1953. 396 pp.

2091. Binyon, Millard P. The Virtues. A Methodological Study in
Thomistic Ethics. Chicago: University of Chicago Dissertation
1947. 66 pp.

2092. Birmingham, William, ed. What Catholics Think About Birth Control.
New York: Signet Books, 1964. 256 pp.

2093. Bittle, Celestine. Man and Morals. Milwaukee: Bruce, 1950.

ETHICS   2094 - 2109

2094. Blackstone, William T. "Thomism and Metaethics." The Thomist
28 (1964), 225-46.

Reprinted in K. Pahel and M. Schiller. Readings in Contemporary
Ethical Theory. Englewood Cliffs, N.J.: Prentice-Hall, 1970.
497-512.

2095. Blic, J. de. "Syndérèse ou conscience?" Revue d'Ascétique et de
Mystique 25 (1949) 146-57.

2096. Böckle, Franz. "Theonome Rationalität als Prinzip der Norm-
begründung bei Thomas von Aquin und Gabriel Vasguez," in Tommaso d'Aquin
(Symp Roma) 5, 213-27.

2097. Bontadini, Gustavo. "Con Tommaso oltre Tommaso." Rivista di
Filosofia Neo-Scolastica 66 (1974) 813-7.

2098. Bourke, Vernon J. "Aquinas and Recent Theories of Right."
Proceedings of the American Catholic Philosophical Association 48 (1974)
187-97.

2099. _____. "Role of a Proposed Practical Intellectual Virute of
Wisdom, with Comment by Lottie H. Kendzierski." Proceedings of the
American Catholic Philosophical Association 26 (1952) 160-78.

2100. _____. "The Ethical Justification of Legal Punishment."
American Journal of Jurisprudence 22 (1977) 1-18.

2101. _____.   Ethics: A Textbook in Moral Philosophy. New York:
Macmillan, 1951, 1966. xii-497 pp.

2102. _____.   Ethics in Crisis. Milwaukee: Bruce, 1966. xxi-222 pp.

2103. _____.   History of Ethics, 2 vols. New York: Doubleday,
1970. 432 pp.

2104. _____.   Histoire de la Morale, Trad. par J. Mignon. Paris:
Cerf, 1970. 518 pp.

2105. _____.   Storia dell'Etica. Trad. a cura di Emanuele Riverso.
Roma: Armando, 1972. 540 pp.

2106. _____.   "Is Thomas Aquinas a Natural Law Ethicist?" The Monist
58 (1974) 52-66.

2107. _____.   "Metaethics and Thomism, " in An Etienne Gilson Tribute
C. J. O'Neil, ed. Milwaukee: Marquette University Press, 1959. 20-32.

2108. _____.   "Moral Philosophy without Revelation?" The Thomist
40 (1976) 555-70.

2109. _____.   "Natural Law, Thomism - and Professor Nielsen."
Natural Law Forum. 5 (1960) 112-9.

2110. _____. "Right Reason as the Basis for Moral Action," in
Tommaso d'Aquino (Symp) 5, 122-7.

2111. _____. "Right Reason in Contemporary Ethics." The Thomist.
Centenary of St. Thomas 1274-1974. 38 (1974) 106-24.

2112. Boyle, Joseph M. Jr. "Praeter Intentionem in Aquinas." The
Thomist 42 (1978) 649-65.

2113. Brennan, Augustine J. Moral Action in Aristotle and Aquinas.
Canberra: Canberra Province of the Redemptorist Fathers, 1972. 122 pp.

2114. Burroughs, Joseph A. Prudence Integrating the Moral Virtues
According to St. Thomas Aquinas. Washington: Catholic University of
America Press, 1955.

2115. Bushman, Rita Marie. Right Reason in Stoicism and in the Christian
Moral Tradition up to Saint Thomas. St. Louis: Saint Louis University
Dissertation, 1947.

2116. Byrne, Edmund F. "Situation et probabilite chez saint Thomas
d'Aquin." Revue Philosophique de Louvain 64 (1966) 525-49.

2117. Cabral, Roque. "Reflexoes sobre a prudência. Aristoteles. S.
Tomàs. Actualidade." Theologica 9 (1974) 483-90.

2118. Cauchy, Venant. Désir naturel et béatitude chez saint Thomas.
Montreal-Paris-Saint Boniface: Fides, 1958. 126 pp.

2119. Chenu, M.-D. L'Eveil de la conscience dans la civilization
médiévale. Montréal: Institut d'Etudes Médiévales, 1969.

     Conference Albert-le-Grand, 1968.

2120. Childress, Marianne Miller. "The Prudential Judgment." Proceedings of the American Catholic Philosophical Association 22 (1947)
141-51.

Coffey, Patrick J. "Personal Moral Reasoning and Impersonal Practical
Wisdom." Proceedings of the American Catholic Philosophical Association
40 (1966) 145-51.

2122. Composta, Dario. "Le'inclinationes naturales' e il diritto
naturale in S. Tommaso d'Aquino," in Studi Tomistici (Symp) 6, 40-53.

2123. Cook, Edward M. The Deficient Causes of Moral Evil According
to St. Thomas. Washington, D.C.: Catholic University of America
Dissertation, 1962.

2124. Costello, Edward B. The Problem of Evil in Plotinus, Aquinas and
Leibniz. Evanston, IL: Northwestern University Dissertation, 1959.
140 pp.

ETHICS   2125 - 2142

2125. Cristaldi, Giuseppe. "La libertà come valore esistenziale,"
in Thomistica Morum (Symp) 279-86.

2126. Cronan, E. P. The Dignity of the Human Person. New York:
Philosophical Library, 1955 xvi-207 pp.

2127. Crowe, Michael B. "The Irreplaceable Natural Law." Studies
51 (1962) 268-85.

2128. _____. "St. Thomas and the Natural Law." Irish Ecclesiastical
Record 76 (1951) 293-305.

2129. Cunningham, Robert L. Situationism and the New Morality. New
York: Appleton-Century-Crofts, 1970. x-281 pp.

2130. D'Amato, Alfonso. "Diritti e doveri della proprietà in S.
Tommaso," in Sacra Doctrina (Symp) 401-28.

2131. D'Amore, Benedetto. "Il problema dell'essere e del dover essere
nel pensiero di S. Tommaso." Sapienza. Napoli. 27 (1974) 360-78.

2132. _____. "Il problema dell'essere e del dover essere," in
Tommaso d'Aquino (Symp Roma) 6, 138-54.

2133. D'Arcy, Eric. Conscience and Its Right to Freedom. New York:
Sheed and Ward, 1961.

2134, _____. La conciencia y su derech a la libertad religiose.
Madrid: Ed. Fax, 1964.

2135. _____. Human Acts. Oxford: Clarendon, 1963.

2136. D'Arcy, Martin. The Mind and Heart of Love. London: Faber and
Faber, 1945.

2137. Davitt, Thomas D. Ethics in the Situation. New York: Appleton-
Century-Crofts, 1970. 253 pp.

2138. Dedek, John F. "Moral Absolutes in the Predecessors of St.
Thomas." Theological Studies 38 (1977) 654-80.

2139. Degl'Innocenti, Umberto. "Il desiderio della felicità, molla
delle azioni uname nel pensiero di S. Tommaso d'Aquino." Divinitas
18 (1974) 303-5.

2140. Del Corte, Marcel. "La plus humaine des vertus. Court traité
de la prudence." Itinéraires 180-182 (1974) 180, 140-68; 181, 154-76;
182, 123-43.

2141. Dennehy, Raymond. "The Ontological Basis of Human Rights."
The Thomist 42 (1978) 434-63.

2142. Derisi, Octavio N. Los Fundamentos Metafisicos del Orden Moral.

2143 - 2157   ETHICS

3 a ed. Madrid: Instituto 'Luis Vives' de Filosofia, 1969.

2143. Dingjan, F. "Het existentiele karakter van de prudentia by S.
Thomas." Bydregen van de Philosophie and Theologie 35 (1963) 210ff.

2143A. Elders, Léon. "La morale de s. Thomas, use éthique philosophique?"
Doctor Communis 30 (1977) 192-205.

2144. Eschmann, I. Th. "Bonum Commune Melius Est Quam Bonum Unius.
Eine Studie über den Wertvorrang des Personalen bei Thomas von Aquin."
Mediaeval Studies 6 (1944) 62-120.

2145. _____. "In Defense of Jacques Maritain." The Modern Schoolman
22 (1945) 183-208.

2146. _____. "St. Thomas's Approach to Moral Philosophy."
Proceedings of the American Catholic Philosophical Association 31 (1957)
25-36.

2147. Esser, Gerard. "Intuition in Thomistic Moral Philosophy, with
Comment by Rose Emmanuella." Proceedings of the American Catholic
Philosophical Association 31 (1957) 156-78.

2148. Estebanez, Emilio G. "Estudio sobre el concepto de norma natural
en S. Tomás." Estudios Filosoficos 23 (1974) 5-46, 309-84.

2149. Fabro, Cornelio. "La dialettica d'intelligenza e volontà nella
costituzione dell'atto libero." Doctor Communis 30 (1977) 163-91.

2150. Fagone, Virgilio. "Il problema dell'inizio della vita dell'uomo;
a proposito dell'aborto." Civiltà Cattolica. Roma. 124 (1973) 531-
46.

2151. Fagothey, Austin. Right and Reason. Ethics in Theory and Practice.
3rd ed. St. Louis: Mosby, 1963; 6th ed., 1976.

2152. _____. Right and Reason-an Anthology. St. Louis: Mosby, 1972.

2153. Fay, Charles. "Human Evolution: A Challenge to Thomistic Ethics."
International Philosophical Quarterly 2 (1962) 50-80.

2154. _____. "Toward a Thomistic-Anthropological View of the
Evolution of Obligation." Natural Law Forum 7 (1962) 38-53.

2155. Finance, Joseph de. Ethica Generalis. Roma: Università
Gregoriana, 1959.

2156. _____. "Sur la notion de loi naturelle." Doctor Communis
22 (1969) 201-23.

2157. Fuchs, Josef. Die Sexualethik des heiligen Thomas von Aquin.
Köln: J. P. Bachem, 1949. 329 pp.

ETHICS   2158 - 2173

2158.   . "Sittliche Normen-Universalien und Generalisierungen."
Münchener Theologische Zeitschrift 25 (1974) 18-33.

2159.   . Situation und Entscheidung. Grundfragen christlicher
Situationsethik. Frankfurt am Main: Knecht, 1963.

2160. Gallagher, Donald A. "St. Thomas and the Desire for the Vision
of God." The Modern Schoolman 26 (1949) 159-73.

2161. Galli, Alberto. "Morale della legge e morale della spontaneita
secondo S. Tommaso," in Studi Tomistici (Symp) 3, 108-51.

2162. Garrigou-Lagrange, Reginald. "De valore reali primi principii
rationis practicae secundum S. Thomam," in Thomistica Morum (Symp)
70-82.

2163. Gillon, L. B. "Morale et science." Angelicum 35 (1958) 249-68.

2164. Gilson, Etienne. S. Thomas d'Aquin. Les moralistes. chrétiens.
2 me éd. augmentée, Paris: Vrin, 1974. 386 pp.

        First published in Paris: Gabalda, 1941.

2165.   . Moral Values and the Moral Life. Leo Ward, tr.
St. Louis: B. Herder, 1941.

        Reprint Hamden, CT: Shoe String Press, 1961.

2166. Girodat, Clair Raymond. The Development of Man According to the
Virtues in the Philosophy of St. Thomas Aquinas. Toronto: University
of Toronto Dissertation, 1977.

2167. Grisez, Germain. Abortion: the Myths, the Realities, and the
Arguments. New York: Corpus Books, 1970.

2168.   . "Against Consequentialism." American Journal of
Jurisprudence 23 (1978) 21-72.

2169   . Contraception and the Natural Law. Milwaukee: Bruce,
1964.

2170.   . "The First Principle of Practical Reason: A Commentary
on S.T. 1-2, q. 94, 2." Natural Law Forum 10 (1965) 168-201.

2171.   . "Kant and Aquinas: Ethical Theory." The Thomist
21 (1958) 44-78.

2172.   . "The Logic of Moral Judgment." Proceedings of the
American Catholic Philosophical Association 36 (1962) 67-76.

2173.   . "Toward a Consistent Natural Law Ethics of Killing."
American Journal of Jurisprudence 15 (1970) 64-96.

2174. Hawkins, Denis J. B. Man and Morals. New York: Sheed and Ward, 1960.

2175. _____. Nature as the Ethical Norm. London: Blackfriars, 1951. 18 pp.

        Aquinas papers, 16.

2176. Inagaki, Bernard Ryosuke. "The Contemporary Significance of Thomistic Ethics," in Tommaso d'Aquino (Symp Roma) 5, 527-31.

2177. _____. "The Notion of Ethical Good in Thomas Aquinas." Studies in Medieval Thought 3 (1960) 32-48.

2178. Jannaccone, C. "Il fondamento della morale e del diritto in S. Tommaso," in Thomistica Morum (Symp) 103-9.

2179. Janssens, Louis. "Ontic Evil and Moral Evil." Louvain Studies 4 (1972) 115-56.

2180. Johnson, D. H. "The Ground for a Scientific Ethics According to St. Thomas." The Modern Schoolman 40 (1963) 347-72.

2181. Johnston, Herbert. Business Ethics. New York: Pitman, 1956.

2182. Jolif, Jean-Yves. "Le su et pratique selon saint Thomas d'Aquin," in S. Thomas Aujourd'hui (Symp) 1963. 13-44.

2183. Jolivet, Régis. Traité de philosophie IV. Morale. Lyon: Vitte, 1955. 541 pp.

2184. Kalinowski, Georges (Jerzy). "Application du droit et preidence." Archiv für Rechts- und Sozialphilosophie 53 (1967) 161-78.

2185. _____. Le Problème de la vérité en morale et en droit. Lyon: Vitte, 1967.

2186. Keady, Richard Emmett. The Implications of Whitehead's Concept of God and Order for a Thomistic Understanding of the Natural Law Ethic in Relation to the Problem of Birth Control. Claremont, CA: Claremont Graduate School Dissertation, 1974. 232 pp.

2187. Kendzierski, Lottie. "Object and Intention in the Moral Act." Proceedings of the American Catholic Philosophical Association 24 (1950) 102-10.

2188. Kennedy, Samuel Joseph. Conscience: Its Nature and Role in Moral Activity According to St. Thomas Aquinas. Notre Dame: University of Notre Dame Dissertation, 1963. 190 pp.

2189. Klubertanz, George P. "The Empiricism of Thomistic Ethics." Proceedings of the American Catholic Philosophical Association 31 (1957) 1-24.

ETHICS   2190 - 2204

2190. _____. "Ethics and Theology." The Modern Schoolman   27
(1949) 29-39.

2191. _____. Habits and Virtues: A Philosophical Analysis.
New York: Appleton-Century-Crofts, 1965.

2192. _____. "The Root of Freedom in St. Thomas' Later Works."
Gregorianum 42 (1961) 709-21.

2193. Kluxen, Wolfgang. "Metaphysik und praktische Vernunft. Über ihre
Zuordnung bei Thomas von Aquin." in Thomas von Aquin 1274-1974 (Symp
München) 73-96.

2194. _____. Philosophische Ethik bei Thomas von Aquin. Mainz:
Matthias Grünewald, 1964. 244 pp.

2195. Koninck, Charles de. "In Defence of Saint Thomas: A Reply to
Father Eschmann's Attack on the Primacy of the Common Good." Laval
théologique et philosophique I (1945) 8-109.

2196. _____. De la primauté du bein commun contre les person-
nalistes. Québec: Université Laval, 1943. xxiii-195 pp.

2197. Kossel, Clifford G. "Aquinas, Moral Views." Encyclopedia of
Morals. V. Ferm, ed. New York: Philosophical Library, 1956. 11-22.

2198. Kreyche, Robert J. "Virtue and Law in Aquinas: Some Modern
Implications." Southwestern Journal of Philosophy 5 (1974) 111-40.

2199. Lawler, Ronald. Philosophical Analysis and Ethics. Milwaukee:
Bruce, 1968. viii-119 pp.

2199A. Leclercq, Jacques. "La dimensión social de la moral." Criterio
28 (1955) 163-9.

2200. _____. La Philosophie morale de s. Thomas devant la pensée
contemporaine. Paris: Spes, 1954.

2201. Lindon, Luke J. The Notion of Human Virtue According to Saint
Thomas Aquinas. Toronto: University of Toronto Dissertation, 1955.

2202. _____. "The Significance of the Term Virtus Naturalis in the
Moral Philosophy of St. Thomas Aquinas, with Comment by Richard J.
Westley." Proceedings of the Catholic American Philosophical Association
31 (1957) 97-105.

2203. Lobo, José A. "El valor de la conciencia según S. Tomás."
Estudios Filosoficos 23 (1974) 385-407.

2204. Losada, C. R. "Realismo etico-juridico en S. Tomás de Aquino
come fundamento del orden normativo." Salmanticessis 10 (1963) 501-
53.

2205. Lucks, Henry. "Saint Thomas and the Moral Sense." Proceedings of the American Catholic Philosophical Association 18 (1942) 117-20.

2206. McDonnell, Kevin. "Aquinas and Hare on Fanaticism." Proceedings of the American Catholic Philosophical Association 48 (1974) 218-27.

2207. McGrath, Patrick. The Nature of Moral Judgment. London: Sheed and Ward, 1967.

2208. McInerny, Ralph M. "Naturalism and Thomistic Ethics." The Thomist 40 (1976) 222-42.

2209. _____. "Prudence and Conscience." The Thomist. Centenary Edition. 38 (1974) 291-305.

2210. _____. "The Teleological Suspension of the Ethical." The Thomist 20 (1957) 295-310.

2211. _____. "Truth in Ethics: Historicity and Natual Law." Proceedings of the American Catholic Philosophical Association 43 (1969) 71-82.

2212. Mackey, Robert R. The Role of Prudence in the Act of Obedience According to St. Thomas. New York: Fordham University Dissertation, 1957. 136 pp.

2213. McLean, George F, ed. New Dynamics in Ethical Thinking. Lancaster, PA: Concorde Publ. 1974.

2214. Maguire, Daniel C. Death by Choice. New York: Doubleday, 1974.

2215. Mann, Jesse A. and Gerald F. Kreyche, eds. Approaches to Morality. Readings in Ethics from Classical Philosophy to Existentialism. New York: Harcourt, Brace and World, 1966. xix-697 pp.

        St. Thomas: 131-61 pp.

2216. Marimón Batllo, Ricardo. "El amor a Dios, fin natural del hombre Una conclusion de filosofia tomista." Naturaleza y Gracia. Salamanca. 23 (1976) 251-68.

2217. Marino, Antonio di. "La trasparenza del fine nella coscienza e l'intenzione del medesimo nella carità come fondamento della morale cristiana," in Thomistica Morum (Symp) 62-9.

2218. Maritain, Jacques. La Philosophie morale, tome I. Paris: Gallimard, 1960.

        Only one vol. published.

2219. _____. Moral Philosophy. A Historical and Critical Survey of

ETHICS   2220 - 2234

the Great Systems. Marshall Suther, et AlU, tr. vol I. New York:
Scribner's, 1964. xii-468 pp.

2220. _____. Filosofia Moral. G. Mainar, tr. Madrid: Ed.
Morata, 1962. 599 pp.

2221. _____. Neuf lecons sur les notions premières de la philosophie
morale. Paris: Téqui. 1951.

2222. _____. The Range of Reason. London: G. Bles, 1953.

2223. Martinez, Marie Louise. "Distributive Justice According to St.
Thomas." The Modern Schoolman 24 (1947) 208-23.

2224. _____. Recta Ratio According to Saint Thomas. St. Louis:
Saint Louis University Dissertation, 1950. 176 pp.

2225. Maynard, M. Francis. The Structure of the Human Act According
to Saint Thomas Aquinas. Milwaukee: Marquette University Dissertation,
1941. 172 pp.

2226. Melsen, Andrew G. van. Physical Science and Ethics. H. J.
Koren, tr. Pittsburgh: Duquesne University Press.

2227. Mercken, Paul. "Transformations of the Ethics of Aristotle in
the Moral Philosophy of Thomas Aquinas," in Tommaso d'Aquino (Symp) 5,
151-62.

2228. Messner, Johannes. Ethics and Facts. St. Louis: B. Herder,
1952.

2229. _____. "Modernes und Zeitbedingtes in der Rechtslehre des
hl. Thomas," in Studi Tomistici (Symp) 4, 169-90.

2230. _____. Das Naturrecht Handbuch der Gesellschaftsethik,
Staatsethik und Wirtschaftsethik. 5 Aufl. Innsbruck-Wien-München:
Tyrolia, 1966. 1372 pp.

2231. _____. Social Ethics: Natural Law in the Modern World.
St. Louis: B. Herder, 1949.

        Revised edition in 1965.

2232. Milhaven, John Giles. "Thomas Aquinas on Sexual Pleasure."
Journal of Religious Ethics 5 (1977) 157-81.

2233. Monagle, John Francis. Friendship in Aristotle and St. Thomas
Aquinas: Its Relation to the Common Good. St. Louis: Saint Louis
University Dissertation, 1973.

2234. Morisset, Bernard. "Prudence et fin selon s. Thomas." Sciences
Ecclésiastiques 15 (1963) 73-98.

2235. Morisset, Bernard. "Le syllogisme prudentiel." Laval Théologique
et Philosophique 19 (1963) 62-92.

2236. Morkovsky, Theresa Clare. "Morality and Real Relations." The
Thomist 29 (1965) 396-419.

2237. Mullaney, James V. "The Natural, Terrestrial End of Man."
The Thomist 18 (1955) 273-95.

2238. Murphy, Laurence T. The Role of Nature and Connaturality in Moral
Philosophy According to Saint Thomas Aquinas. Notre Dame: University
of Notre Dame Dissertation, 1964. 134 pp.

2239. Murray, Michael V. Problems in Ethics. New York: Holt,
Rinehart, and Winston, 1960.

2240. _____. Problems in Conduct. New York: Holt, Rinehart, and
Winston, 1963.

2241. Muzio, Giuseppe. "Il fondamento ontologico e psicologico della
moralità secondo S. Tommaso," in Thomistica Morum (Symp) 135-43.

2242. Nelson, Ralph C. Jacques Maritain's Conception of Moral Philosophy Adequately Considered. Notre Dame: University of Notre Dame
Dissertation, 1961.

2243. Nicolosi, Salvatore. "Morale tomista tra antico e moderno."
Aquinas 17 (1974) 107-38.

2244. Noi, P. De la. La prudencia en la formación moral a la luz
de Santo Tomás. Santiago: Pont. Univ. Gregorianae, 1963.

2245. Noonan, John T. Jr. "Masked Man: Person and Persona in the
Giving of Justice." Proceedings of the American Catholic Philosophical
Association (Symp) 1974. 228-37.

2246. _____. "Maxima amicitia," in Tommaso d'Aquino (Symp Roma)
5, 344-51.

2247. _____. "Tokos and Atokion: An Examination of Natural Law
Reasoning Against Usury and Against Contraception." Natural Law Forum
10 (1965) 215-35.

2248. Novak, David. Suicide and Morality in Plato, Aquinas, and Kant.
Washington, D.C.: Georgetown University Dissertation, 1971. 302 pp.

2249. _____. Suicide and Morality: The Theories of Plato, Aquinas,
and Kant. New York: Scholars' Studies Press, 1975. 136 pp.

2250. O'Connor, William R. The Eternal Quest: The Teaching of St.
Thomas Aquinas on the Natural Desire for God. New York: Longmans,
Green, 1947.

ETHICS   2251 - 2266

2251. _____. "The Natural Desire for God in St. Thomas." The New Scholasticism 14 (1940) 213-67.

2252. _____. The Natural Desire for God. Milwaukee: Marquette University Press, 1948.

2253. Oesterle, John A. "Conscience and Contingency," in XIII Congreso Internacional de Filosofia. Mexico. 1964. 7, 369-75.

2254. _____. Ethics: The Introduction to Moral Science. Englewood Cliffs, N.J.: Prentice-Hall, 1957. 269 pp.

2255. _____. "How Good is the Pleasurable Good?" The Thomist 28 (1964) 391-408.

2256. _____. "St. Thomas, Moral Evil, and the Devil," in Tommaso d'Aquino (Symp Roma) 5, 510-5.

2257. O'Hara, M. Kevin. The Connotations of Wisdom According to St. Thomas Aquinas. Washington, D.C.: Catholic University of America Press, 1956. v-40 pp.

2258. O'Neil, Charles J. "Is Prudence Love?" The Monist 58 (1974) 119-39.

2259. _____. "The Notion of Beauty in the Ethics of St. Thomas." The New Scholasticism 14 (1940) 340-78.

2260. _____. Imprudence in St. Thomas Aquinas. Milwaukee: Marquette University Press, 1955. 176 pp.

2261. _____. "Prudence, the Incommunicable Wisdom," Essays in Thomism. R. E. Brennan, ed. New York: Sheed and Ward, 1942. 187-204.

2262. Peal, M. Janet. Contemplation in the Natural Ethics of Thomas Aquinas. Brooklyn, N.Y.: St. John's University Dissertation, 1968. 156 pp.

2263. Pegis, Anton C. "Creation and Beatitude in the 'Summa contra Gentiles' of St. Thomas Aquinas." Proceedings of the American Catholic Philosophical Association 29 (1955) 52-62.

2264. _____. "Matter, Beatitude and Liberty, " in Maritain Volumne of The Thomist (Symp) 265-80.

2265. _____. "Nature and Spirit: Some Reflections on the Problem of the End of Man." Proceedings of the American Catholic Philosophical Association 23 (1949-1950) 3-20.

2266. _____. "St. Thomas and the Nicomachean Ethics: Some Reflections on Summa contra Gentiles III, 44, 5." Mediaeval Studies 25 (1963) 1-25.

2267. Pérez Alcocer, Antonio. "El acto moral según S. Tomás y las distintas corrientes en etica." Revista Filosofica. Mexico. 10 (1977) 223-32.

2268. Perez Delgado, Esteban. "La epiqueya a su relación con otras virtudes confluyentes o conflictivas." Escritos del Vedat 4 (1974) 571-610

2269. Perotto, Alberto. "Il sentimentalismo critico come valore etico contemporaneo." Divus Thomas. Piacenza. 61 (1958) 253-66.

2270. Pétrin, J. "L'Habitus des principles spéculatifs et la synderèse." Revue de l'Université d'Ottawa 18 (1948) 208-16.

2271. Petritz, Margaret M. The Philosophy of Anger in Relation to the Virtues in the Philosophy of St Thomas Aquinas. Washington: Catholic University of America Press, 1953.

2272. Petzall, A. "La syndérèse." Theoria 20 (1954) 64-77.

2273. Pincakaers, S. "Le désir naturel de voir Dieu." Nova et Vetera. Geneva. 51 (1976) 255-73.

2274. Pizzorni, Reginaldo M. "Il contenuto del diritto naturale secondo S. Tommaso d'Aquino," in Studi Tomistici (Symp) 4, 191-221.

2275. _____. "Diritto e morale." Aquinas 10 (1967) 20-39.

2276. _____. "Il diritto naturale nella scolastica del sec. XIII prima di S. Tommaso d'Aquino." Apollinaris. Roma. 49 (1976) 363-417.

2277. _____. "La lex aeterna come foundamento ultimo del diritto secondo S. Tommaso." Aquinas 4 (1961) 57-109.

2278. _____. "Naturalità e storicità del diritto naturale secondo S. Tommaso d'Aquino." Aquinas 17 (1974) 139-87.

2279. Ponferrada, Gustavo E. "Reflexiones sobre los fundamentos ontologicos de la ética tomista." Sapientia 3 (1976) 223-8.

2280. Poppi, Antonino. "The Background of Situation Ethics." Philosophy Today 1 (1957) 266-77.

2281. _____. La morale di situaqione, esposizione e critica. Roma: Miscellanea Francescana, 1957.

2282. Raeymaeker, Louis de. "Le sens et le fondement de l'obligation morale," in Thomistica Morum (Symp) 8-23.

2283. Redding, James F. The Virtue of Prudence in the Writings of St. Thomas Aquinas. New York: Fordham University Dissertation, 1950. 176 pp.

ETHICS   2284 - 2299

2284. Reiner, Hans. "Obligatio bei Thomas von Aquin," in Sein und
Ethos. P. Engelhardt, ed. Mainz: Brunewald, 1963.

2285. _____. Die Philosophische Ethik. Heidelberg: Quelle and
Meyers, 1964. 224 pp.

2286. _____. "Thomistische und phänomenologische Ethik." Zeitschrift für Philosophische Forschung. Postfach, W. Germany. 16 (1960)
247-63.

2287. _____. "Wesen und Grund der sittlichen Verbindlichkeit
(obligatio) bei Thomas von Aquin," in Sein und Ethos. Mainz:
Gunewald, 1963. 236-66.

2288. _____. "An Introduction to the Philosophy of the Existential
Moral Act." The New Scholasticism 28 (1954) 145-69.

2289. _____. The Philosophy of Morality. Milwaukee: Bruce, 1953.
248 pp.

2290. Rintelen, Fritz Joachim von. Values in European Thought.
Pamplona, Spain: Ediciones Naiversidad de Navarra, 1972. ix-565 pp.

       Aquinas on 317-413 pp.

2291. Rommen, Heinrich. The Natural Law. T. R. Hanley, tr. St.
Louis: B. Herder, 1948. xii-290 pp.

2292. Ross, James F. "Justice is Reasonableness: Aquinas on Human
Law and Morality." The Monist 58 (1974) 86-103.

2293. Rouleau, Mary Celeste. The Place of Love and Knowledge in Human
Activity According to Selected Texts of St. Thomas Aquinas. St. Louis:
Saint Louis University Dissertation, 1961. 370 pp.

2294. Rousseau, Félicien. "Aux sources de la loi naturelle," in
Laval Thomas d'Aquin (Symp) 279-313.

2295. Ryan, John A. Distributive Justice. New York: Macmillan, 1942.

2296. _____. "Quodlibetal Questions VII, Thought and Conduct."
American Ecclesiastical Review 132 (1955) 84-9.

2297. Sainte-Marcelle d'Auvergne, Soeur. "De la matière du droit
naturel." Laval Théologique et Philosophique 23 (1967) 116-45.

2298. Sanchis, Antonio. "La anticoncepción: interpretacion etica de
un conflicto matrimonial. Reflexión desde los principios tomistas."
Escritos del Vedat 4 (1974) 337-74.

2299. _____. "La estructura moral de la persona en la pensamiento
de santo Tomás." Angelicum 51 (1974) 212-34.

2300. Santiago, Jaime Ruiz de. "El Problema de la diversificacion de las especies morales in el pensamiento de sto Tomas de Aquino." Revista Filosofica. Mexico. 6 (1973) 85-119.

2301. Savagnone, Giuseppe. "La vocazione intellettuale secondo San Tommaso d'Aquino." Aquinas 19 (1976) 287-305.

2302. Schall, James V. "Human Destiny and World Population. The Individual as Horizon and Frontier." The Thomist 41 (1977) 92-104.

2303. Schultz, Janice L. Thomas Aquinas and R. M. Hare: The Good and Moral Principles. Buffalo: State University of New York dissertation, 1978. 493 pp.

2304. Sciacca, Michele Federico. "El principio de finalidad en Santo Tomás," in Mikael (Symp) 4-57.

2305. Selvaggi, Joao Batista. "O processo ético em Santo Tomás de Aquino," in Presenca Filosofica (Symp) 114-24.

2306. Sertillanges, A. D. La Philosophie morale de s. Thomas d'Aquin Paris: Aubier, 1942, 1946. 433 pp.

2307. Sheehan, Robert J. The Philosophy of Happiness According to St. Thomas Aquinas. Washington, D.C.: Catholic University of America Press, 1956.

2308. Simon, Yves. "Introduction to the Study of Practical Wisdom." The New Scholasticism 35 (1961) 1-40.

2309. Slattery, Kenneth F. The Thomistic Concept of the Virtue of Temperance and Its Relation to the Emotions. Washington: Catholic University of America Press, 1952.

2310. Smith, Gerard. "The Natural End of Man." Proceedings of the American Catholic Philosophical Association 23 (1949) 47-61.

2311. _____. "Philosophy and the Unity of Man's Ultimate End." Proceedings of the American Catholic Pholosophical Association 27 (1953) 60-83.

2312. _____. The Truth That Frees. Milwaukee: Marquette University Press, 1956.

2313. Smith, Vincent E. "Natural Philosophy and Natural Ethics." Thomistica morum (Symp) 78-86.

2314. Smyth, Anastasia M. M. The Nature and Role of Prudence According to the Philosophy of St. Thomas Aquinas. Toronto: University of Toronto Dissertation, 1944.

2315. Steger, E. Ecker. "Verbum cordis: Mediation Between I and Thou." Divus Thomas. Piacenza. 81 (1978) 40-53.

ETHICS   2316 - 2331

2316. Stevens, Gregory. "Moral Obligation in St. Thomas." The
Modern Schoolman 40 (1962) 1-21.

2317. Sullivan, Robert P. Man's Thirst for God. Westminster MD:
Newman, 1952. 120 pp.

2318. Toccafondi, E. T. Philosophia moralis generalis. Roma:
Angelicum, 1943. 318 pp.

2319. Tokarcyzk, Roman. "Tomasz y Akwinu o prawie naturalnym."
Przeglad Religioznawczy. Lublin. (1974) 31-9.

2320. Tonneau, J. Alsolu et obligation en morale. Paris: Vrin,
1965.

2321. _____. "Devoir et morale." Revue des Sciences Philosophiques
et Théologiques. Le Saulchoir/Paris. 38 (1954) 233-52.

2322. Tranøy, K. E. Thomas av Aquino som Moral Filosof. Oslo:
Universitetsforlget, 1957. 144 pp.

       Norwegian with English summary.

2323. Utz, Arthur F. "L'etica di S. Tommaso. Coincidenze e differenze
tra l'etica aristotelica e tomistica." Sacra Doctrina 19 (1974)
391-400.

2324. Valentino-Ferrari, M. "La disputa su virtù e felicità e
l'eudemonismo estetico di Tommaso d'Aquino." Rivista di Teologia
Morale 8 (1976) 627-53.

2325. Vann, Gerald. Man and Morality. New York: Sheed and Ward,
1960.

2326. Vanni Rovighi, Sofia. "C'è un etica filosofica in San Tommaso?"
in Tommaso d'Aquino (Symp Roma-Napoli) 5, 194-210.

2327. _____. "Ce' Un'etica Filosofica in San Tommaso d'Aquino?"
Rivista di Filosofia Neo-Scolastica. Milano. 66 (1974) 653-
70.

2328. _____. "Filosofia morale." Studium 55 (1959) 847-53.

2329. _____. "Il fondamento dell'etica di S. Tommaso." Cultura
e Scuola 13 (1974) 185-92.

2330. Veatch, Henry B. "Are There Non-Moral Goods?" The New
Scholasticism 52 (1978) 471-99.

2331. _____. "The Defense of Natural Law in the Context of
Contemporary Analytic Philosophy." American Journal of Jurisprudence
14 (1969) 54-68.

2332. _____. "Kant and Aquinas: A Confrontation on the Contemporary Meta-Ethical Field of Honor." The New Scholasticism. Aquinas Septicent. 1974   73-99.

2333. _____. Rational Man. Bloomington, IN: University of Indiana Press, 1964. 226 pp.

2334. Voellmecke, Frank W. Moral Reasoning: Aquinas and Hare. Notre Dame: University of Notre Dame Dissertation, 1976.

2335. Vogel, Cornelia J. de. "L'éthique d'Aristote offre-t-elle une base appropriée à une éthique chrétienne?" in Tommaso d'Aquino (Symp) 5, 135-43.

2336. Volkomener, Mary T. Thomistic Ethics and Anthropological data: Some Possible Contributions of Empirical Materials to Moral Science. St. Louis: Saint Louis University Dissertation, 1960. 178 pp.

2337. Vries, Joseph de. "Gedanken zur ethischen Erkenntnis." Scholastik 39 (1964) 46-66.

2338. Wallace, William. "Existential Ethics. A Thomistic Appraisal." The Thomist 27 (1963) 493-515.

2339. Ward, Leo R., ed. Ethics and the Social Sciences. Notre Dame, IN: University of Notre Dame Press, 1959.

2340. _____. Christian Ethics. St. Louis: B. Herder, 1952.

2341. Wild, John. Plato's Modern Enemies and the Theory of Natural Law. Chicago: University of Chicago Press, 1953.

2342. Wilhelmsen, Frederick D. The Metaphysics of Love. New York: Sheed and Ward, 1962.

2343. William, Mary. "The Relationships of the Intellectual Virtue of Science and Moral Virtue." The New Scholasticism 36 (1962) 475-505.

2344. Williams, Cornelius. "The Hedonism of Aquinas." The Thomist 38 (1974) 257-90.

2345. Wingell, A. B. The Relationship of Intellect and Will in the Human Act According to St. Thomas Aquinas. Toronto: University of Toronto Dissertation, 1966.

2346. Wojtyla, Karol (Pope John Paul II). "O kierowniczej lub sluzebnej roli rozumu w etyce, Na tle pogladów Tomasza z Akwinu, Hume a i Kanta." Roczniki Filozoficzne 6 (1958) 13-31.

2347. Wylleman, André Louis. "Le fondement de l'éthique," in XIII Congreso Internacional de Filosofia. Mexico City, 1964. , 435-41.

ETHICS   2348 - 2363

2348. Yarz, Francis J. Order and Moral Perfection in the Philosophy
of St. Thomas Aquinas. St. Louis: Saint Louis University Dissertation, 1968. 183 pp.

2349.   . "Order and Right Reason in Aquinas' Ethics."
Mediaeval Studies 37 (1975) 407-18.

2350.   . "Virtue as Ordo in Aquinas." The Modern Schoolman
47 (1970) 305-20.

2351. Yedlicka, J. "Synderesis as Remorse of Conscience." The
New Scholasticism 37 (1963) 204-12.

2352. Young, James A. Knowledge of Good in Moore and Aqninas.
Austin, TX: University of Texas Dissertation, 1961. 312 pp.

SOCIO-POLITICAL-LEGAL PHILOSOPHY

2353. Adler, Mortimer J. How to Think About War and Peace. New York:
Simon and Schuster, 1944.

2354. Agócs, Sándor. "The Road to Charity Leads to the Picket lines:
the Neo-Thomist Revival and the Italian Catholic Labor Movement."
International Review of Social History 18 (1973) 28-50.

2355. Ambrosetti, Giovanni. Diritto naturale Cristiano. Roma:
Editrice Studium, 1970.

2356. Amoroso Lima, Alecu. "Alguns principios sociais tomistas."
A Ordem. Rio de Janeiro. I (1974) 32-46.

2357. Anan, Seichi. "Some Trends of Legal Thought and Natural Law
Study in Japan." Natural Law Forum 7 (1962) 109-19.

2358. Aubert, Jean-Marie. Le Droit romain dans l'oeuvre de s. Thomas.
Bibliothèque Thomiste, xxx. Paris: Vrin. 1954. 168 pp.

2359. Babin, E. "S. Thomas d'Aquin et le droit de propriété."
Revue de l'Université Laval 7 (1952-1953) 706-18.

2360. Bagen, John J. The Brotherhood of Man in the Philosophy of
St. Thomas Aquinas. Washington: Catholic University of America
Press, 1951.

2361. Barath, Desiré. "The Just Price and the Costs of Production
According to St. Thomas." The New Scholasticism 34 (1960) 413-30.

2362. Bartell, Ernest. "Value, Price, and St. Thomas." The Thomist
25 (1962) 325-81.

2363. Battifol, Henri. "Analyse ratiónelle et téléologie dans la
conception thomiste du droit," in Studi Tomistici (Symp) 4, 21-39.

2364 - 2378 SOCIO-POLITICAL-LEGAL PHILOSOPHY

2364. Beis, Richard H. "Contraception and the Logical Structure of the Thomist Natural Law Theory." Ethics 75 (1965) 277-84.

2365. Bellofiore, Luigi. "La filosofia del diritto nella problematica tomistica e Vichiana." Aquinas 18 (1975) 182-208.

2366. Benkert, Gerald F. The Thomistic Conception of an International Society. Washington, D.C.: Catholic University of America Press, 1942.

2367. Børresen, Kari Elizabeth. Subordination et équivalence. Nature et role de la femme d'après Augustin et Thomas d'Aquin. Oslo: Universitetsforlaget, 1968. 306 pp.

2368. Bourke, Veroon, J. "Material Possessions and Thomistic Ethics," in Philosophic Thought in France and the United States. Marvin Farber, ed. Buffalo: University of Buffalo Publications in Philosophy, 1950 613-27.

2369. _____. L activité philosophique contemporaine en France et aux Etats-Unis, 2 vols. Presses Universitaires de France, 1950. Vol. I, 302-20.

2370. _____. Filozofia Amerykanska. Boston University Press, 1958. 146-62.

2371. _____. "Two Approaches to Natural Law." Natural Law Forum 1 (1956) 92-6.

     Reprinted in Commonweal 64 (1956) 562-3.

2372. Bradley, Raymond J. Selected Problems Concerning the Natural Law in Thomas Aquinas and in Some of his Modern Commentators. Pittsburgh: Duquesne University Dissertation, 1973.

2373. Breen, Joseph S. Religion and Secularism in the Light of Thomistic Thought. Washington: Catholic University of America Press, 1952.

2374. Brennan, Robert E. "The Thomistic Concept of Culture," in Maritain ... Thomist (Symp) 111-36.

2375. Brezik, Victor B. Friendship and Society: A Study in Thomistic Social Philosophy. Toronto: University of Toronto Dissertation, 1944.

2376. Briancesco, Eduardo. "Tomás de Aquino, maestro de vida social." Teologia. Buenos Aires. 11 (1974) 7-23.

2377. Brown, Oscar J. P. Natural Rectitude and Divine Law in Aquinas: An Approach to an Integral Interpretation of the Thomistic Doctrine of Law. Toronto: University of Toronto Dissertation, 1977.

2378. Bruch, R. "Intuition und Überlegung beim sittlichen Naturgesetz

SOCIO-POLITICAL-LEGAL PHILOSOPHY 2379 - 2394

nach Thomas von Aquin." Theologie und Glaube 67 (1977) 29-54.

2379. Buchanan, Scott. Rediscovering Natural Law. Santa Barbara,
CA: Center for Study of Democratic Institutions, 1960.

2380. Buckley, Michael J. "A Thomistic Philosophy of History." The
New Scholasticism 35 (1961) 342-62.

2381. Cairns, Huntington. Legal Philosophy from Plato to Hegel.
Baltimore: John Hopkins University Press, 1949.

2382. Camus, Pierre. "Le my the de la femme chez Saint Thomas
d'Aquin." Revue Thomiste 76 (1976) 243-65.

2383. Capitani, Ovidio, ed. L'etica economica medievale. Bologna:
Mulino, 1974. 218 pp.

        See contributions on St. Thomas by A. Sapori and J.J. Noonan.

2384. Carstens, Ronald Wayne. The Notion of Obligation in the Political
Philosophy of St. Thomas Aquinas. Oxford, Ohio: Miami University
Dissertation, 1974. 282 pp.

2385. Catto, Jeremy. "Ideas and Experience in the Political Thought
of Aquinas." Past and Present. Oxford. 71 (1976) 3-21.

2386. _____. "The Social Ideas of St. Thomas and his Contemporaries."
Scientia. Malta. 37 (1974) 6-16.

2387. Cenacchi, Giuseppe. Il lavoro nel pensiero di Tommaso d'Aquin.
Roma: Coletti Editore, 1977. 196 pp.

2388. Charette, Léon. "Philosophie politique et méthode chez s.
Thomas d'Aquin." Revue de l'Université d'Ottawa 42 (1972) 83-96.

2389. Chenu, M.-D. "Creation et histoire," in St. Thomas Aquinas
1274-1974 (Symp) 2, 391-9.

2390. Choza, Jacinto. "Hábito y espiritu objectivo. Estudio sobre la
historicidad en S. Tomás y en Dilthey." Anuario Filosofico 9 (1976)
9-71.

2391. Christensen, William N. and John King-Farlow. "Aquinas and
the Justification of War: Establishmentarian Misconstructions."
The Thomist 35 (1971) 94-112.

2392. Chroust, Anton-Hermann. "The ius gentium in the Philosophy of
Law of St. Thomas Aquinas." Notre Dame Lawyer 17 (1941) 25ff.

2393. _____. "The Philosophy of Law from St. Augustine to St.
Thomas." The New Scholasticism 20 (1946) 26-71.

2394. _____. "The Philosophy of Law of St. Thomas Aquinas: His

Fundamental Ideas and Some of His Historical Predecessors." American Journal of Jurisprudence 19 (1974) 1-38.

2395. Collins, Joseph P. "God's Eternal Law." The Thomist 23 (1960) 497-532.

2396. Coniglio, G. "Le concept d'esclavage dans s. Thomas d'Aquin." R. Herval, tr. Bulletin Cercle Thomiste. Caen. 15 (1953) 40-4.

2397. Conover, Milton. "St. Thomas Aquinas in Some Recent Non-Scholastic Writers on Political Philosophy." The New Scholasticism 30 (1956) 1-16.

2398. Cooke, Terence J. Thomistic Philosophy in the Principles of Social Group Work. Washington, D.C.: 1951.

2399. Cotta, Sergio. Il concetto di legge nella Summa Theologiae di S. Tommaso d'Aquino. Turin: Giappichelli, 1955.

2400. Cox, John F. A Thomistic Analysis of the Social Order. Washington: Catholic University Press, 1943.

2401. Crofts, Richard A. "The Common Good in the Political Theory of Thomas Aquinas." The Thomist 37 (1973) 155-73.

2402. Croteau, Jacques. Les fondemento thomistes du personnalisme de Maritain. Ottawa: Ed. de l'Université, 1955. 262 pp.

2403. Crowe, Michael B. "St. Thomas and Ulpian's Natural Law: A Puzzling Preference," in St. Thomas Aquinas Comm. Studies. Toronto: PIMS, 1974. vol. I, 261-82.

2404. Crowe, Michael B. "Synderesis and the Notion of Law in St. Thomas," Actes du Premier Congrès International de philosophie médiévale. Louvain: 1958. 601-9.

2405. D'Agostino, F. "Lex indita e lex scripta: La dottrina della legge divina positiva (lex nova) secondo S. Tommaso d'Aquino," in Atti del congresso Internazionale di diritto canonico (Roma-Milano) 1972. 2, 401-15.

2406. Darbellay, Jean. "Les prolongements thomistes de la notion aristotélicienne de nature et de droit naturel," in Studi Tomistici (Symp) 4, 54-72.

2407. Davitt, Thomas. The Nature of Law." St. Louis: B. Herder, 1951.

2408. De la Vega, Francis J. Social Progress and Happiness in the Philosophy of St. Thomas Aquinas and Contemporary American Sociology. Washington, D.C.: Catholic University of America Press, 1949.

SOCIO-POLITICAL-LEGAL PHILOSOPHY   2409 - 2422

2409. Delhaye, Philippe. "La 'loi naturelle' dans l'enseignement de
s. Thomas." in Studi Tomistici (Symp) 4, 73-103.

2410. Della Penta, C. J. Hope and Society: A Thomistic Study of
Social Optimism and Pessimism. Washington, D.C.: Catholic University
of America Press, 1942. xi-196 pp.

     The Catholic University of America Philosophical Series,
     Vol. 71.

2411. Delos, J.-T. "La sociologie de s. Thomas et le fondement du
droit international." Angelicum 22 (1945).

2412. D'Entrèves, A. Passerin. Natural Law. London: Hutchinson,
1951.

2413. _____. "The Case for Natural Law Re-examined." Natural Law
Forum. Notre Dame. I (1956) 5-52.

2414. DeRoover, Raymond A. La pensée économique des scolastiques:
doctrines et méthodes. Montréal: University of Montréal, 1971.

2415. Di Carlo, E. La filosofia giuridica e politica di S. Tommaso
d'Aquino. Palermo: Palumbo, 1945. 174 pp.

2416. Doherty, R. T. The Relation of the Individual to Society in
the Light of Christian Principles as Expounded by the Angelic Doctor.
Rome: Gregorianum, 1957.

2417. Dolan, J. V. "Natural Law and Modern Jurisprudence." Laval
Théologique et Philosophique 16 (1960) 49-59.

2418. Dougherty, George V. The Moral Basis of Social Order According to St. Thomas. Washington,D.C.: Catholic University of America
Press, 1941. xv-81 pp.

2419. Downing, Paul M. A Comparison of the Doctrines of St. Thomas
Aquinas and John Locke on the Right of Political Authority. New York:
Columbia University Dissertation, 1960. 156 pp.

2420. Eberenz, James H. The Concept of Sovereignty in the Medieval
Political Philosophers: John of Salisbury, St. Thomas Aquinas, Egidius
Colonna, and Marsilius of Padua. Washington, D.C.: Catholic University
of America Dissertation, 1968. 313 pp.

2421. Eschmann, Ignatius T. "Studies in the Notion of Society in St.
Thomas Aquinas." Medieval Studies. Toronto. 18 (1946) 1-42; 19
(1947) 19-55.

2422. _____. "A Thomistic Glossary on the Principle of the Pre-
eminence of a Common Good." Mediaeval Studies. Toronto. 5 (1943)
123-65.

2423. Evans, Joseph W. Developments of Thomistic Principles in Jacques
Maritain's Notion of Society. Notre Dame: University of Notre Dame
Dissertation, 1951. 235 pp.

2424. _____ and Leo R. Ward, eds. The Social and Political Philosophy of Jacques Maritain. Reprint. Garden City, N.Y.: Doubleday.
1965. 354 pp.

2425. Faller, F. Die rechtsphilosophische Begründung der gesellschaftlichen und staatlichen Autorität bei Thomas von Aquin. Heidelberg:
Kerle, 1954. 86 pp.

2426. Farrell, Patrick M. "Sources of St. Thomas' Concept of Natural
Law." The Thomist 20 (1957) 237-94.

2427. Farrell, Walter. "Law in Aristotle and St. Thomas." The New
Scholasticism 24 (1950) 439-44.

2428. _____. "Person and the Common Good in a Democracy."
Proceedings of the American Catholic Philosophical Association 20
(1945) 38-47.

2429. _____ and Mortimer J. Adler. "The Theory of Democracy."
The Thomist 3 (1941) 588-652.

2430. Fasso, Guido. La legge della ragione. Bologna: Il Mulino,
1964.

2431. _____. "Natural Law in Italy in the Past Ten Years."
Natural Law Forum I (1956) 122-34.

2432. _____. Storia della filosofia del diritto. 2 vols. Bologna:
Li Mulino, 1966-1968.

   On Aquinas, 255-70 pp.

2433. Ferree, William. The Act of Social Justice in the Philosophy
of St. Thomas Aquinas and in the Encyclicals of Pope Pius XI. Washington,
D.C.: Catholic University of America Press, 1942. vii-221 pp.

2434. Finance, Joseph De. "Droit naturel et histoire chez s. Thomas,"
in Studi Tomistici (Symp) 4, 104-28.

2435. Fisher, Luke. Social Leadership According to Thomistic Principles.
Washington, D.C.: Catholic University of America Press, 1943.

2436. Foster, P. Two Cities, A Study of Church-State Conflict.
London: Blackfriars, 1955. xii-110 pp.

2437. Friedberger, Walter. Der Reichtumserwerb im Urteil des hl.
Thomas von Aquin und der Theologen im Zeitalter des Frühkapitalismus.
Passau: Verlag Passavia, 1967. 240 pp.

SOCIO-POLITICAL-LEGAL PHILOSOPHY   2438 - 2455

2438. Galimberti, Andrea. "La realtà della storia e San Tommaso."
Sapienza 30 (1977) 24-42.

2439. Gelinas, Elmer T. "I us and Lex in Thomas Aquinas." American
Journal of Jurisprudence 15 (1970) 154-70.

2440. _____. "Right and Law in Thomas Aquinas." Proceedings of
the American Catholic Philosophical Association 45 (1971) 130-8.

2441. Genicot, Léopold. "Le De regno: spéculation ou réalisme?" in
Aquinas and Problems (Symp) 1976. 3-17.

2442. Giguere, Robert J. The Social Value of Public Worship According
to Thomistic Principles. Washington, D.C.: Catholic University of
America Dissertation, 1950. 176 pp.

2443. Gilby, Thomas. Between Community and Society: A Philosophy
and Theology of the State. London: Longmans, 1953. xiv-344 pp.

2444. _____. The Political Thought of Thomas Aquinas. Chicago:
University of Chicago Press, 1958. 383 pp.

     Published in England under the title, Principality and Polity.

2445. _____. Principality and Polity. Aquinas and the Rise of
State Theory in the West. Longon: Longmans, 1958. xxvi-357 pp.

2450. Giuliani, Ubaldo. "Il problema della monarchia oggi alla luce
del pensiero di S. Tommaso." Revista di Letteratura e di Storia
Ecclesiastica. Napoli. 6 (1974) 55-64.

2451. Gmür, Harry. Thomas von Aquino und der Krieg. Nachdr. d. Ausg.
Leipzig, Berlin: Teubner, 1933; Hildesheim: Gerstenberg, 1971. viii-
78 pp.

2452. Goertz, Hans J. "Staat und Widerstandsrecht dei Thomas von
Aquin." Frieburger Zeitschrift fuer Philosophie und Theologie 17
(1970) 308-43.

2453. Golding, Martin P. "Aquinas and Some Contemporary Natural Law
Theories." Proceedings of the American Catholic Philosophical Association 48 (1974) 238-47.

2454. Gonzalez Uribe, Hector. "Algunos puntos capitales de la doctrina
social y politica de Santo Tomas de Aquino a la luz de las exigencias
de la conciencia contemporanea." Revista Filosofica. Mexico. 6 (1974)
17-34.

2455. Gordon, Barry. Economic Analysis Before Adam Smith. New York:
Barnes and Noble, 1975. xiii-282 pp.

     Chapter 5 is on Thomas Aquinas.

2456. Graneris, Giuseppe. "L'amoralità della legge giuridica di fronte alla dottrina di s. Tommaso." Rivista di Filosofia Neoscolastica 38 (1946) 1-25.

2457. Graney, Maurice R. Natural Law as a Ground for the Common Good in Jacques Maritain. St. Louis: Saint Louis University Dissertation, 1976.

2458. Grassi, Joseph G. "International Unity and Religion According to St. Thomas Aquinas." Sapienza 27 (1974) 452-7.

2459. Greenleaf, W. H. "The Thomasian Tradition and the Theory of Absolute Monarchy." English Historical Review 79 (1964) 747-60.

2460. Grenier, H. "L'équité selon s. Thomas." Studia Canonica. Ottawa. 9 (1975) 305-8.

2461. Grijs, F. J. A. De. "Mensenmacht. Enige aantekeningen bij 'De Rengo' van Thomas van Aquino." Bijdragen 35 (1974) 250-97.

2462. Gullo, Giuseppe. Prudenza e politica. Lettura critica del pensiero di Tommaso d'Aquino sul problema di fondo della filosofia politica. Napoli-Acireale: Ed. Domenicane, 1974. 215 pp.

2463. Guzikowski, Maximilian E. A Philosophy of Liberalism According to Thomistic Principles. Washington, D.C.: Catholic University of America Dissertation, 1949. 311 pp.

2464. Harding, Alan. "The Reflection of 13th Century Legal Growth in St. Thomas' Writings," in Aquinas and Problems (Symp) 18-37.

2465. Henrich, Franz, ed. Naturgesetz und christliche Ethik. München Kösel, 1970.

2466. Heydte, Freiherr von der. "Politicità nella Summa Theologica di San Tommaso," in Studi Tomistici (Symp) 4, 129-40.

2467. Hogan, Joseph E. The Virtue of Prudence in the Social Philosophy of St. Thomas. Washington, D.C.: Catholic University of America Press, 1951.

2468. Hughes, Walter D. Law in Quintessence: According to St. Thomas and Suarez. Brooklyn, N.Y.: St. John's University Dissertation, 1972. 235 pp.

2469. Hutchins, Robert M. St. Thomas and the World State. Milwaukee: Marquette University Press, 1949.

2470. Inagaki, Bernard. The Constitution of Japan and the Natural Law. Washington, D.C.: Catholic University of America Press, 1955.

2471. Indigoras, José L. "El tomismo, come instrumento de reaccion."

SOCIO-POLITICAL-LEGAL PHILOSOPHY 2472 - 2486

Revista Teologica Limense. Lima, Peru. 8 (1974) 183-99.

2472. Jacklin, Edward G. The Problem of Individualism in St. Thomas Aquinas. New York: Fordham University Dissertation, 1950. 176 pp.

2473. James, Theodore. "Some Historical Aspects of St. Thomas' Treatment of the Natural Law." Proceedings of the American Catholic Philosophical Association 24 (1950) 147-55.

2474. Joubert, Gerard R. The Qualities of Citizenship in St. Thomas. Washington,D.C.: Catholic University of America Press, 1941.

2475. Jung, Hwa Yol. The Foundation of Jacques Maritain's Political Philosophy. Gainesville, Fla.: University of Florida Press, 1960.

     University of Florida Monographs: Social Sciences. No. 7.

2476. Kalinouski, Georges (Jerzy). "Fondement objectif du droit d'après la Somme théologique de s. Thomas d'Aquin." Archives de Philosophie du Droit 18 (1973) 59-75.

2477. _____. "Sur l'emploi métonymique de terme ius par Thomas d'Aquin et sur la mutabilité du droit naturel selon Aristote." Archives de Philosophie du Droit 19 (1973) 331-9.

2478. Kane, Anne Virginia. Truth and Political Freedom According to Thomistic Principles. Washington, D.C.: Catholic University of America Press, 1950.

2479. Kaufmann, Arthur. "The Ontological Structure of Law." Natural Law Forum 8 (1963) 79-96.

2480. Kelly, J. Vincent. "Thomistic Principles Concerning the Human Person in Political Philosophy." Proceedings of the American Catholic Philosophical Association 21 (1946) 111-3.

2481. Keraly, Hugues. "La seience politique selon s. Thomas." Itineraires 180 (1974) 98-111.

2482. Kilzer, Ernest. "Natural Law and Natural Rights. Proceedings of the American Catholic Philosophical Association 24 (1950) 156-60.

2483. Klubertanz, George P. and Philip S. Land. "Practical Reason, Social Fact, and the Vocational Order." The Modern Schoolman 28 (1951) 239-66.

2484. Krempel, Antoine. "Hiérarchie des fins d'use société d'après s. Thomas," in L'Homme et son destin (Symp) 611-8.

2485. La Centra, Walter J. Freedom and Society in Jacques Maritain. Brooklyn, N.Y.: St. John's University Dissertation, 1964.

2486. Lachance, Louis. Le Concept de Droit Selon Aristote et S. Thomas.

Ottawa: Editions du Levrier, 1948.   336 pp.

2487. _____. Le Droit et les droits de l'homme. Paris: Sirey, 1959.

2488. _____. L'Humanisme politique de s. Thomas d'Aquin: Individu et Etat. Ottawa: Ed. du Lévrier, 1939. 746 pp. 2 me éd. Paris: Sirey, 1965. 398 pp.

2489. _____. "Peace and the Family." The Thomist 9 (1946) 129-71.

2490. Lagor, Jean Louis. La philosophie politique de s. Thomas d'Aquin. Paris: Editions nouvelles, 1948. 187 pp.

2491. Laje, Enrique. "La propiedad en la Suma Teologica." Ethos. Buenos Aires. I (1973) 81-90.

2492. Langlois, Jean. "La Categorie Moderne de L'Histori et le Thomisme." Dialogue. Montréal. 7 (1968) 66-77.

2493. Lantz, Göran. Eigentumsrecht-ein Rechi oder ein Unricht? Eine kristische Beurteilung der ethischen Argumente für das Privateigentum bei Aristoteles, Thomas v. Aquin. Stockholm: Liber Tryck, 1977. 154 pp.

Uppsal Studies in Social Ethics, no. 4.

2494. Lawler, Justus. Nuclear War, the Ethic, the Rhetoric, the Reality. Westminster, MD: Newman, 1965.

2495. Le Claire, M. St. Ida. Utopias and the Philosophy of St. Thomas Aquinas. Washington, D.C.: Catholic University of America Press, 1941.

2496. Leclercq, Jacques. Du Droit naturel à la sociologie. 2 vols. Paris: Editions Spec, 1960.

2497. _____. Lecons de droit naturel. IV, Les droits et devoirs individuels I. Vie, disposition de soi. 2. Travail, propriété. 3 me éd. 2 vols. Namur: Wesmael-Charlier, 1955. 195 and 391 pp.

2498. _____. "Natural Law the Unknown." Natural Law Forum 7 (1962) 1-15.

2499. _____. "Suggestions for Clarifying Natural Law." Natural Law Forum 2 (1957) 64-87.

2500. Legaz y Lacambra, Luis. "La función politica del derecho y la noción del derecho en santo Tomas de Aquino," in Studi Tomistici (Symp) 4, 155-68.

2501. Lewis, Ewart. "Natural Law and Expediency in Medieval Political Theory." Ethics 50 (1940) 144-63.

SOCIO-POLITICAL-LEGAL PHILOSOPHY 2502 - 2516

2502. Lewis, John U. "Aquinas and Professor Kelsen: Their Differing Conceptions of Legal Science." Proceedings of the American Catholic Philosophical Association 48 (1974) 248-58.

2503. _____. "Kelsen and Aquinas: A Conflct Over the Nature of Law and Legal Obligation." The Jurist 34 (1974) 94-106.

2504. Lottin, Odon. "Natural Law, Natural Right and Natural Reason." Philosophy Today 3 (1959) 10-8.

2505. Luijpen, W. A. Phenomenology of Natural Law. Pittsburg: Duquesne University Press, 1967.

2506. Lynam, Gerald J. The Good Political Ruler According to St. Thomas Aquinas. Washington, D.C.: Catholic University of America Press, 1953. 49 pp.

2507. McCool, Gerald A. "Social Authority in Transcendental Thomism." Proceedings of the American Catholic Philosophical Association 49 (1975) 13-23.

2508. McCormick, Mary J. Diagnostic Casework in the Thomistic Pattern. New York: Columbia Univeristy Press, 1954. 237 pp.

2509. _____. Thomistic Philosophy in Social Casework. New York: Columbia University Press, 1948. 158 pp.

2510. MacGuigan, Mark R. The Best Form of Government in the Philosophy of St. Thomas Aquinas. Toronto: University of Toronto Dissertation, 1957. 137 pp.

2511. _____. "St. Thomas and Legal Obligation." The New Scholasticism 25 (1961) 281-310.

2512. McNabb, Vincent. St. Thomas Aquinas and Law. London: Blackfriars 1955. 19 pp.

       Aquinas Papers, 24.

2513. McSweeney, Alan J. The Social Role of Truth According to St. Thomas Aquinas. Washington: Catholic University of America Press, 1943. xii-157 pp.

2514. _____. Truth and Society According to St. Thomas Aquinas. Washington, D.C.: Catholic University of America Dissertation, 1943.

2515. Manser, Gallus. Das Naturrecht in Thomistischer Beleuchtung. Freiburg i. Sch: Paulusverlag, 1944. viii-149 pp.

2516. Marchesi, Angelo. "Il pensiero di S. Tommaso d'Aquino e delle encicliche sociali dei papi sul tema della proprietà privata." Rivista di Filosofia Neo-Scolastica. Milano. 62 (1970) 334-44.

2517. Maritain, Jacques. Man and the State. Chicago: University of Chicago Press, 1951, 1963.

2518. _____. The Person and the Common Good. New York: Scribners, 1947.

2519. _____. On the Philosophy of History. New York: Scribners, 1959.

2520. _____. The Rights of Man and the Natural Law. New York: Scribners, 1943.

2521. _____. Scholasticism and Politics. New York: Macmillan, 1941.

2522. May, William E. "The Meaning and Nature of the Natural Law in Thomas Aquinas." American Journal of Jurisprudence 22 (1977) 168-89.

2523. Messner, Johannes. "The Postwar Natural Law Revival and Its Outcome." Natural Law Forum 4 (1959) 101-5.

2524. _____. Sociologia moderna y derecho natural. Barcelona: Herder, 1964.

2525. Michels, T. Der Wandel im politischen Weltbild des Mittelalters bei Thomas von Aquin. Münster: Aschendorff, 1972.

2526. Midgley, E. B. F. "Natural Law and Fundamental Rights." American Journal of Jurisprudence 21 (1976) 144-55.

2527. _____. The Natural Law Tradition and the Theory of International Relations. London: Elek Books, 1975; New York: Harper and Row, 1975. xx-588 pp.

2528. Miller, Clyde L. "Rule by One Man and Its Rewards: Aquinas' De Regno 1, 2 and 1, 8-11 in The Thirteenth Century. Acta 3 (1976) 53-64.

2529. Mohan, Robert P. A Thomistic Philosophy of Civilization and Culture. Washington, D.C.: Catholic University of America Dissertation, 1949. 311 pp.

2530. Mueller, Robert Matthias M. Thomistic Social Science. River Forest, IL: Aquinas Library, 1961. 77 pp.

2531. Mulvaney, Robert J. "Political Wisdom. An Interpretation of Summa Theol II-II, 50." Mediaeval Studies. Toronto. 35 (1973) 294-305.

2532. Murdoch, John Emery and Edith Dudley Sylla, eds. The Cultural Context of Medieval Learning. Boston: Reidel, 1975.

SOCIO-POLITICAL-LEGAL PHILOSOPHY   2533 - 2549

2533. Myers, Joseph R. Social Distance According to St. Thomas Aquinas.
Washington, D.C.: Catholic University of America Press, 1955.

2534. Narciso, Enrico. "Autoritarismo e dissenso nel pensiero di S.
Tommaso d'Aquino," in La Voce della Coltura (Symp) 1974. 25-32.

2535. Newman, Jeremiah H. Foundations of Justice. A Historico-
Critical Study in Thomism. Cork: Cork University Press, 1954.
148 pp.

2536. Nielsen, Kai. "An Examination of the Thomistic Theory of Natural
Moral Law." Natural Law Forum 4 (1959) 44-71.

2537. Niemeyer, Mary F. The One and the Many in the Social Order
According to St. Thomas Aquinas. Washington, D.C.: Catholic University
of America Dissertation, 1951.

2538. Noonan, John T., Jr. Banking and the Scholastic Analysis of
Usury. Washington: Catholic University of America Press, 1951.

2539. _____. The Scholastic Analysis of Usury. Cambridge, Mass:
Harvard University Press, 1957.

2540. O'Brien, William V. Nuclear War, Deterrence and Morality.
Westminster, MD: Newman, 1967.

2541. O'Connor, D. J. Aquinas and Natural Law. London: Macmillan;
New York: St. Martin's Press, 1968. 93 pp.

2542. O'Donoghue, Noel Dermot. "The Law Beyond the Law." American
Journal of Jurisprudence 18 (1973) 150-64.

2543. _____. "The Thomist Conception of Natural Law." Irish
Theological Quarterly 22 (1955) 101ff.

2544. Olgiati, Francesco. Il concetto di giuridicità in San Tommaso
d'Aquino, ed 2a. Milano: Vita e pensiero, 1944. xi-251 pp.

2545. Onclin, W. "Le Droit naturel selon les romanistes des XII et XIII
siècles," in Miscellanea Moralia A. Jansen. Louvain: Nauwelaerts, 1948.
2, 329-37.

2546. Overbeke, Paul M. van. "Saint Thomas et le droit, commentaire
de II-II, 57." Revue Thomiste 55 (1955) 519-64.

2547. _____. "La loi naturelle et le droit naturel selon s. Thomas."
Revue Thomiste 57 (1957) 53-78, 450-98.

2548. _____. "Droit et morale, essai de synthèse thomiste." Revue
Thomiste 58 (1958) 285-324, 674-96.

2549. Paparella, Benedict A. Sociality and Sociability. A Philosophy of
Sociability According to St. Thomas Aquinas. Washington, D.C.: Catholic

University of America Press, 1955.

2550. Parsons, Wilfrid. "Democracy-Stalin and St. Thomas." The Modern Schoolman 23 (1946) 131-4.

2551. _____. "Saint Thomas Aquinas and Popular Sovereignty." Thought 16 (1941) 473-92.

2552. Phelan, Gerald B. "Justice and Friendship," in Maritain... Thomist (Symp) 153-70.

2553. _____. "Law and Morality," in Progress in Philosophy (Symp) 177-97.

        J.A. McWilliams, ed. Milwaukee: Bruce, 1955.

2554. Pieper, Josef. Leizure, the Basis of Culture. A. Dru, tr. New York: Pantheon Books, 1952.

2555. Piolanti, Antonio, ed. San Tommaso e la filosofia del diritto oggi. Roma: Pontificia Accademia di S. Tommaso, 1975. 297 pp.

2556. Pizzorni, Reginaldo M. "Il diritto naturale come naturalis conceptio e naturalis inclinatio." Angelicum 39 (1962) 150-72.

2557. _____. Il fondamento etico-religioso del diritto secondo S. Tommaso d'Aquino. Roma: Università Lateranense, 1968. 232 pp.

2558. _____. "Secolarizzazione o Desacralizzazione del diritto naturale." Angelicum 51 (1974) 349-82.

2559. Raffo Magnasco, Benito R. "Bien común y politica en la concepción filosofica de Santo Tomas de Aquino," in Actas del Primer Congreso Nacional de Filosofia. Mendoza, Argentina: Universidad Nacional, 1949. 2022-32.

2560. Ramirez, Santiago M. El derecho de gentes. Madrid: Studium, 1955. 230 pp.

2561. Recasens Siches, Luis. "Axiologia juridica y derecho natural," in Symposium sobre derecho natural y axiologia. Mexico: Universidad Autonoma, 1963. 119-43.

2562. Riedl, John O. "Thomas Aquinas on Citizenship." Proceedings of the American Catholic Philosophical Association 37 (1963) 159-66.

2563. Riga, Peter J. "Prudence and Jurisprudence: Authority as the Basis of Law in Thomas Aquinas." The Jurist 37 (1977) 287, 294-306.

2564. Rommen, Heinrich. The State in Catholic Thought. St. Louis: Be Herder, 1945.

SOCIO-POLITICAL-LEGAL PHILOSOPHY   2565 - 2580

2565. Roos, Leon J. Natural Law and Natural Right in Thomas Aquinas and Aristotle. Chicago: University of Chicago Dissertation, 1972.

2566. Rowan, John P. St. Thomas' Doctrine of Peace. Toronto: University of Toronto Dissertation, 1947.

2567. Ryan, John K. Modern War and Basic Ethics. Milwaukee: Bruce, 1940.

2568. Sacheri, Carlos A. "Santo Tomás y el orden social." Mikael (Symp) 85-97.

2569. St. Hilaire, Mary G. Precepts of Natural Law in the Text of St. Thomas. St. Louis: Saint Louis University Dissertation, 1962.

2570. Sattler, Henry V. Philosophy of Submission: A Thomistic Study in Social Philosophy. Washington, D.C.: Catholic University of America Dissertation, 1948.

2571. Schall, James V. "The Totality of Society: From Justice to Friendship." The Thomist 20 (1957) 1-26.

2572. Schmölz, Franz-Martin. "Die Demokratie und die Gleichheit aller Menschen, eine Überlegung zur Politik des Aristoteles von Thomas von Aquin," in Gedenkband...Thomas von Aquin (Symp) 1974. 315-20.

2573. _____. "Das Glück in der Politik? Bemerkungen zur ersten Lektio des Kommentars von Thomas von Aquin zur Politik des Aristoteles," in Thomas...Interpretation (Symp) 196-201.

2574. Schumacher, Leo S. The Philosophy of the Equitable Distribution of Wealth. Washington, D.C.: Catholic University of America Press, 1949.

2575. Sheppard, Vincent F. Religion and the Concept of Democracy: A Thomistic Study in Social Philosophy. Washington, D.C.: Catholic University of America Dissertation, 1949.

2576. Sigmund, P. E. Natural Law in Political Thought. Cambridge: Cambridge University Press, 1971. 214 pp.

2577. Simec, M. Sophie. Philosophical Bases for Human Dignity and Change in Thomistic and American Non-Thomistic Philosophy. Washington, D.C.: Catholic University of America Press, 1953. 240 pp.

2578. Simon, Yves R. Freedom and Community. Charles P. O'Donnell, ed. New York: Fordham University Press, 1968.

2579. _____. The Nature and Functions of Authority. Milwaukee: Marquette University Press, 1940.

2580. _____. Philosophy of Democratic Government. Chicago: University of Chicago Press, 1952. ix-324 pp.

2581 - 2595 SOCIO-POLITICAL-LEGAL PHILOSOPHY

2581. _____. The Tradition of Natural Law. A Philosopher's
Reflections. Vukan Kuic, ed. New York: Fordham University Press,
1965.

2582. Smetana, Alexander. The Best Form of Government According to
Aristotle, Cicero, St. Thomas, and Locke. Washington, D.C.: Catholic
University of America Press, 1950.

2583. Smith, Ignatius. "St. Thomas Aquinas and Human Social Life."
The New Scholasticism 19 (1945) 285-321.

2584. _____. "Thomistic Thoughts on Government and Rulers," in
Progress in Philosophy (Symp) 1955. 199-216.

2585. Speltz, George H. The Importance of Rural Life According to
the Philosophy of St. Thomas Aquinas. Washington, D.C.: Catholic
University of America Press, 1945. xvi-184 pp.

2586. _____. The Importance of Rural Life According to the
Philosophy of St. Thomas Aquinas. Washington, D.C.: Catholic University
of America Dissertation, 1944.

2587. Stevens, Gregory. "The Relations of Law and Obligation."
Proceedings of the American Catholic Philosophical Association 29
(1955) 195-205.

2588. Stupp, Herbert. Mos geometricus oder Prudentia als Denkform der
Jurisprudenz. Eine Untersuchung an Hand der methodologischen Lenren des
Chr. Wolff und des Thomas von Aquin. Koln: Dissert. Jurisp., 1970.
xii-127 pp.

2589. Szaszkiewicz, Jerzy. Filosofia della cultura. Roma: Università
Gregoriana, 1974. 206 pp.

2590. Tabbah, Bichara. Droit politique et humanisme. Univ. Saint-
Joseph de Beyrouth, Annales de Droit. Paris: Librairie gèn. de droit
et de jurisprudence, 1955. xix-329.

2591. Thibault, Pierre. Savoir et Pouvoir. Philosophie thomiste et
politique cléricale au xxe siècle. Québec: Les Pressed de l'Université
Laval, 1972.

2592. Tonneau, J. "The Teaching of the Thomist Tract on Law." The
Thomist 34 (1970) 13-83.

2593. Tooke, Joan D. The Just War in Aquinas and Grotius. London:
Society for Promotion of Christian Knowledge, 1965. 337 pp.

2594. Tozzi, Glauco. I fondamenti dell' economia in Tommaso d'Aquino.
Melano: U. Mursia, 1970. 333 pp.

2595. Troxler, Ferdinand. Die Lehre vom Eigentum bei Thomas von Aquin
und Kare Marx. Freiburg, Schw: Imba Verlag, 1973. 171 pp.

SOCIO-POLITICAL-LEGAL PHILOSOPHY 2596 - 2610

2596. Velez, James S. The Doctrine of the Common Good in the Works
of St. Thomas Aquinas. Notre Dame: University of Notre Dame Dissertation, 1950. 176 pp.

2597. Verdross, Alfred. "Begriff und Bedeutung des 'Bonum commune',"
in Studi Tomistici (Symp) 4, 239-57.

2598. Verpaalen, A. P. Der Begfiff des Gemeinwohls bei Thomas von
Aquin. Heidelberg: Kerle, 1954. 84 pp.

2599. Versfeld, Martin. "Law and the Idea of the Contemporary."
Natural Law Forum 10 (1965) 146-7.

2600. _____. On Justice and Human Rights. Acta Juridica I.
Capetown: University of Capetown Law School, 1960.

2601. Villey, Michel. "De l'enseignement de la politique selon s.
Thomas," in Studi Tomistici (Symp) 4, 258-68.

2602. Villoro Toranzo, Miguel. "Una explicacion moderna del concepto
Tomista del derecho." Revista Filosofica. Mexico. 6 (1974) 49-60.

2603. Wagstaffe, M. Joseph. The Thomistic Philosophy of Culture and
the Virtue of Art. Washington, D.C.: Catholic University of America
Press, 1951.

2604. Walters, LeRoy B. Five Classic Just-War Theories: A Study in
the Thought of Thomas Aquinas, Vitoria, Suarez, Gentili and Grotiuis.
New Haven: Yale University Dissertation, 1971. 451 pp.

2605. Wetter, Gustav A. Dialectical Materialism. New York: Praeger,
1958.

2606. Wistuba, Halina. "Intelektualne podstawy tworow kultury wedlug
filozofii sw Tomasza z Akwinu." Studia Philosophiae Christianae 7
(1971) 243-75.

2607. Zappone, Giuseppe. "Considerazioni sul progetto sociale di
Tommaso d'Aquino." Sapienza. Napoli. 27 (1974) 379-414.

2608. Zimmermann, R. "Das jus utendi bei Thomas von Aquin und in den
papstlichen Sociallehren." Freiburger Zeitschrift für Philosophie und
Theologie I (1954) 302-13.

ESTHETICS

2609. Beck, Heinrich (hrsq.). "Ereignismacht im Schönen. Vorbemerkung-
en zu einer Ontologie und Theologie des Asthetischen," in Salzburger
Jahrbuch...Gedenkband (Symp) 283-314.

2610. Callahan, John L. A Theory of Esthetic According to the Principles
of St. Thomas Aquinas. 2nd ed. Washington, D.C.: Catholic University
of American Press, 1947.

2611. Cranero, Jose M. J. "Des fenomeno estetico a la naturaleza de lo bello en el pensamiento de Santo Tomas." Sapientia 26 (1971) 443-7.

2612. Duffy, John. A Philosophy of Poetry: Based on Thomistic Principles. Washington, D.C.: Catholic University of America Press, 1945. 258 pp.

2613. Eckert, Willehad Paul. "Der Glanz des Schönen und seine Unerfüllbarkeit im Bilde. Gedanken zu einer Theologie der Kunst des hl. Thomas von Aquino," in Thomas...Interpretation (Symp) 229-44.

2614. Eco, Umberto. Il problema estetico in San Tommaso. Turino: Edizioni di 'Filosofia,' 1956; ed. za, 1970.

2615. Fearon, John. "The Lure of Beauty." The Thomist 8 (1945) 149-84.

2616. Greif, Gary F. "The Relation Between Transcendental and Aesthetical Beauty According to St. Thomas." The Modern Schoolman 40 (1963) 163-82.

2617. Grisez, Germain. "References to Beauty in St. Thomas." The Modern Schoolman 29 (1951) 43-4.

2618. Hamm, Victor M. Language, Truth and Poetry. Milwaukee: Marquette University Press, 1960.

        An Aquinas Lecture.

2619. Hunter, A. Richard. Analogy and Beauty: Thomistic Reflections on the Transcendentals. Bryn Mawr, PA: Bryn Mawr College Dissertation, 1978.

2620. Ishikawa, Takeshi. "Die hylemorphologische Begrunendung der Schoenheitstheorie Thomas Von Aquina." Bigaku 23 (1972) 33-43.

        The Japanese Journal of Aesthetics.

2621. _____. "The Causality of Beauty in the Summa Theologiae of St. Thomas Aquinas." Bigaku 25 (1974) 1-10.

2622. Kovach, Francis J. Die Ästhetik des Thomas von Aquin. Berlin: De Gruyter, 1961. 279 pp.

2623. _____. "Beauty as a Transcendental," in New Catholic Encyclopedia. New York, 1967. 2, 205-7.

2624. _____. "The Empirical Foundation of St. Thomas' Philosophy of Beauty." Southwestern Journal of Philosophy 2 (1971) 93-102.

2625. _____. "Esthetic Disinterestedness in Thomas Aquinas," in Proceedings of the Fifth International Congress of Aesthetics. Amsterdam, 1964. 769-70.

ESTHETICS   2626 - 2642

2626. _____. Philosophy of Beauty. Norman, Okl: University of Oklahoma Press, 1974.

2627. _____. "The Transcendentality of Beauty Revisited." The New Scholasticism 52 (1978) 404-12.

2628. Kunkel, Frank L. "Beauty in Aquinas and Joyce." The Thomist 12 (1949) 261-71.

2629. Maritain, Jacques. Art and Scholasticism, and The Frontiers of Poetry. Jos. Evans, tr. New York: Scribners, 1962.

2630. Nemetz, Anthony A. Art in Thomas Aquinas. Chicago: University of Chicago Dissertation, 1953.

2631. _____. "Art in St. Thomas." The New Scholasticism 25 (1951) 282-9.

2632. O'Malley, Judith Marie. Justice in Shakespeare: Three English Kings in the Light of Thomistic Thought. New York: Pageant Press, 1964. 57 pp.

2633. Philippe, M.-D. "Détermination philosophique de la notion du Beau." Studia Patavina. Padova. 15 (1955) 133-52.

2634. Pike, Alfred. "The Phenomenology of Music and the Thomistic Aesthetic." The Thomist 29 (1965) 281-94.

2635. Pöltner, Günther. Schönheit: ein Untersuchung zum Ursprung d. Denkens bei Thomas von Aquin. Wien/Freiburg i. Br./Basel: Herder, 1978. 214 pp.

2636. _____. "Zum Gedanken des Schönen bei Thomas von Aquin," in Gedenkband...Thomas von Aquin (Symp) 1974. 239-81.

2637. Putnam, Caroline C. "The Mode of Existence of Beauty: A Thomistic or a Kantian Interpretation?" Studies in Philosophy and in the History of Philosophy 5 (1970) 223-41.

2638. Roblin, Ronald E. "Is Beauty a Transcendental?" The New Scholasticism 51 (1977) 220-33.

2639. Rover, Thomas Dominic. The Poetics of Maritain: A Thomistic Critique. Washington, D.C.: Thomist Press, 1965. 228 pp.

2640. Sanabria, José R. "Trascendentalidad de la belleza en el pensamiento de S. Tomás." Sapienza 29 (1974) 185-206.

2641. Soria, Fernando. "Los temas esteticos en Santo Tomás. Estudios Filosoficos 23 (1974) 287-307.

2642. Steinberg, Charles S. "The Aesthetic Theory of St. Thomas Aquinas." Philosophical Review 50 (1941) 483-97.

2643. Steiss, J. A. "Outline of a Philosophy of Art." The Thomist 2 (1940) 14-57.

2644. Tamme, Anne Mary. A Critique of John Dewey's Theory of Fine Art in the light of the Principles of Thomism. Washington, D.C.: Catholic University of America Press, 1956. 139 pp.

2645. Zenteno, Manuel Ivan. "Tomás de Aquino y el arte." Logos. Mexico. 2 (1974) 53-63.

EDUCATIONAL THEORY

2646. Adler, Mortimer J. "Controversy in the Life and Teaching of Philosophy." Proceedings of the American Catholic Philosophical Association 30 (1956) 16-35.

2647. Ashley, Benedict M. Constructing the Philosophy Curriculum. River Forest, IL: Albertus Magnus Lyceum, 1961.

2648. _____. "The Role of the Philosophy of Nature in Catholic Liberal Education." Proceedings of the American Catholic Philosophical Association 30 (1956) 62-85.

2649. Bauer, Theodore, and others. Thomistic Principles in a Catholic School. St. Louis: Herder, 1943.

2650. Benito Alzaga, José Ramón. "El pensamiento de S. Tomás sobre la relaciones entre el maestro y el alumno..." Revista Filosofica. Mexico. 6 (1974) 215-26.

2651. Bolzan, J. E. Qué es la educación. Buenos Aires: Ed. Guadalupe, 1974. 91 pp.

2652. Buehler, Walter E. The Role of Prudence in Education. Washington, D.C.: Catholic University of America Press, 1950.

2653. Carcuro, Vito. "Il pensiero pedagogico in S. Tommaso d'Aquino." Rassegna di Scienze Filosofiche. Napoli. 27 (1974) 269-303.

2654. Caturelli, Alberto. La doctrina agustiniana sobre el maestro y su desarrollo en S. Tomás de Aquino. Cordoba, Arg.: Instituto de Metafisica, Univ. de Cord., 1954. 70 pp.

2655. Conway, Pierre H. Principles of Education: A Thomistic Approach. Washington, D.C.: The Thomist Press, 1960. 217 pp.

2656. _____, Benedict Ashley. "The Liberal Arts in St. Thomas Aquinas." The Thomist 22 (1959) 460-532.

2657. _____. The Liberal Arts in St. Thomas Aquinas. A Thomist Reprint. Washington, D.C.: Thomist Press, 1959. 74 pp.

2658. Crowell, Alice Marie. The Concept of Fortitude According to St.

EDUCATIONAL THEORY   2659 - 2674

Thomas Aquinas and Its Implications for Education. Washington, D.C.:
Catholic University of America Dissertation, 1963. 159 pp.

2659. Deferrari, Roy. "The Seminar on the Integrating of the Philosophic
Studies," in Integration in Catholic Colleges and Universities. Washington,
D.C.: Catholic University of America, 1950. 396-407.

2660. Derisi, Octavio N. "El Maestro según santo Tomás." Sapientia
32 (1977) 321-4.

2661. Donohue, J. W. Thomas Aquinas and Education. New York: Random
House, 1968.

2662. Ducci, Edda. Essere e comunicare. Bari: Adriatica, 1974.
283 pp.

2663. Dufault, Lucien. "The Aristotelian-Thomistic Concept of Education."
The New Scholasticism 20 (1946) 239-56.

2664. Flores d'Arcais, G. La pedagogia di S. Tommaso. Milano:
Marzorati, 1954. xiv-1329 pp.

2665. Formentin, Justo. "Elementos educativos de la angelologia de
Tomás de Aquino," in Escritos del Vedat (Symp) 1974. 687-97.

2666. Gallagher, Donald A, ed. Some Philosophers on Education.
Milwaukee: Marquette University Press, 1956. 95 pp.

2667. Garcia Martinez, F. "The Place of St. Thomas in Catholic
Philosophy." Cross Currents 8 (1958) 43-66.

2668. Gulley, Anthony D. The Educational Philosophy of Saint Thomas
Aquinas. New York: Pageant Press, 1964. 153 pp.

2669. _____. A Philosophical Study of the Efficient Causes of
Learning According to St. Thomas Aquinas. Washington, D.C.: Catholic
University of America Dissertation, 1961. 141 pp.

2670. Guzie, Tad. The Analogy of Learning: An Essay Toward a Thomistic
Psychology of Learning. New York: Sheed and Ward, 1960. 253 pp.

2671. Hampsch, John H. "Integrative Determinants in the Philosophy of
Education of St. Thomas Aquinas." Educational Theory 9 (1959) 31-40.

2672. Henle, Robert J. "The Modern Liberal University: Reflective
Intelligence versus Tradition." Confluence 6 (1957) 184-95.

2673. Hopkins, John Orville. The Social Ethics of Jacques Maritain and
Justification of Afro-American Education." New York: Columbia University
Dissertation, 1976.

2674. Horrigan, Alfred F. Metaphysics as a Principle of Order in the
University Curriculum. Washington, D.C.: Catholic University of America

Press, 1944.

2675. Jackson, Arthur F. Can One Man Teach Another: A Comparative Analysis of Treatments in Plato, Aristotle, Augustine, Aquinas, Buber and Lonergan. Boston: Boston College Dissertation, 1973. 254 pp.

2676. Jafella, Sara A. "Notas sobre la filosofia y su aplicacion a la educacion en el Tomismo y el pragmatismo." Revista de Filosofia 20 (1968) 72-80.

2677. Johnston, Herbert. "College Education - For What Habits?" The Catholic Educational Review 53 (1955) 505-13.

2678. _____. "The Social and the Moral Sciences." The Catholic Educational Review 55 (1957) 1-37.

2679. Joly, R. P. The Human Person in a Philosophy of Education. New York: Humanities Press, 1965.

2680. Joseph, Ellis A. Jacques Maritain on Humanism and Education. Fresno, CA: Academy Guild Press, 1966.

2681. Koninck, Charles De. "Philosophy in University Education." Laval Théologique et Philosophique. Québec. 8 (1952) 123-9.

2682. Kuničič, J. "Principia didactica S. Thomae." Divus Thomas. Piacenza. 58 (1955) 398-411.

2683. Linnenborn, M. Das Problem des Lehrens und Lernens bei Thomas von Aquin. Freiburg i. Br.: Lambertus Verlag, 1956. 304 pp.

2684. McCauley, H. C. "The Teaching-Learning Relationship. A Thomist Perspective on the Standard Thesis," in Philosophy and Totality (Symp) 1977. J. McEvoy, ed. Belfast: The Queen's University. 63-89.

2685. McInerny, Ralph. "The Prime Mover and the Order of Learning." Proceedings of the American Catholic Philosophical Association 30 (1956) 129-37.

2686. Mangieri, G. "Presupposti di un'educazione nel pensiero di S. Tommaso." Sapienza 4 (1951) 309-24.

2687. Margiotta, Umberto. "La pedagogia di Tommaso d'Aquino." Aquinas 17 (1974) 322-39.

2688. Maritain, Jacques. "Thomist Views on Education," in Modern Philosophies and Education Chicago: University of Chicago Press, 1955.

2689. Masterson, Reginald, ed.   Theology in the Catholic College Dubuque: Priory Press, 1961.

2690. Mullaney, James V. "The Liberal Arts in the Aristotelian-Thomist

EDUCATIONAL THEORY   2691 - 2705

Scheme of Knowledge." The Thomist 19 (1956) 481-505.

2691. Naughton, E. Russell. Freedom in Education According to Thomistic Principles. Washington, D.C.: Catholic University of America Dissertation, 1950.

2692. Pegis, Anton C. "St. Thomas Aquinas," in Encyclopedia of Education New York: Macmillan, 1971. I, 250-7.

2693. _____. "Teaching and the Freedom to Learn," in the McAuley Lectures 1953. West Hartford, CT: St. Joseph College, 1954. 17-28.

2694. Petersen, Thomas R. The Albertus Magnus Lyceum: A Thomistic Approach to Science Education. Urbana, IL: University of Illinois at Urbana Dissertation, 1977. 180 pp.

2695. Pousson, Leon Bernard. The Totalitarian Philosophy of Education. Washington, D.C.: Catholic University of America Press, 1944. xi-164.

2696. Salman, D.-H. La place de la philosophie dans l'université idéale. Montréal: Inst. d'Etudes Méd., 1954. 67 pp.

2697. Smith, Gerard. "The Position of Philosophy in a Catholic College." Proceedings of the American Catholic Philosophical Association 29 (1955) 20-40.

2698. Smith, Sixtus Robert. A Thomistic Theory of the Liberal Arts. Quebec: Universite Laval Dissertation, 1947. 104 pp.

2699. Sokolowski, Robert S. "De Magistro: The Concept of Teaching According to St. Thomas Aquinas." Studies in Philosophy and the History of Philosophy I (1963) 160-93.

2700. Spangler, Mary M. Aristotle on Teaching: An Analysis and Application of His Principles as Interpreted by St. Thomas Aquinas. Notre Dame: University of Notre Dame Dissertation, 1964. 563 pp.

2701. Steenberghen, Fernand van. Psychology, Morality, and Education. London: Burns Oates, 1958. ix-128 pp.

2702. Vargas, S. Alfonso. Psychology and Philosophy of Teaching According to Traditional Philosophy and Modern Trends. Washington, D.C.: Catholic University of American Dissertation, 1944.

2703. Wade, Francis C. The Catholic University and the Faith. Milwaukee: Marquette Univeristy Press, 1978.

2704. _____. "St. Thomas Aquinas and Teaching," in Some Philosophers on Education. Donald Gallagher, ed. Milwaukee, Marquette University Press, 1956. 67-85.

2705. Wolters, Jan. "Saint Thomas et la crise de l'université idiotique et idéologique," in Tommaso d'Aquino (Symp) 2, 123-38.

4
Theological Doctrines

GENERAL AND INTRODUCTORY

2706. Alfaro, Juan. "La dimensión trasendental en el con cimiento humano de Dios según S. Tomás." Gregorianum 55 (1974) 639-75.

2707. Arias Reyero, Maximino. Thomas von Aquin als Exeget. Einsiedeln: Johannes Verlag, 1971. 305 pp.

2708. Ashley, Benedict M. and Allan B. Wolter. "Thomism and Ecclesiastical Approbation," in Teaching Thomism Today (Symp) 97-124.

2709. Bandera, Armando. "Pio XII y Santo Tomás." Ciencia Tomista 78 (1951) 483-543.

2710. Barrois, George A. Presenting Aquinas to Reformed Theologians. Princeton, N.J.: Princeton Theological Seminary Dissertation, 1946. 325 pp.

2711. Bellemare, Rosaire. "La Somme de Théologie et la lecture de la Bible," in Colloque...Thomas d'Aquin, Eglise et Théologie. Ottawa. 5 (1974).

2712. Benard, Edmund D. The Problem of Belief in the Writings of J. H. Newman, William James and St. Thomas Aquinas. Washington, D.C.: Catholic University of America Press, 1950.

2713. Benoit, Pierre. "Saint Thomas et l'inspiration des Ecritures," in Tommaso d'Aquino. (Roma-Napoli Symp) 1974. I, 115-31.

2714. Benotti, Teofilo. "Ragione e fede in Tommaso d'Aquino," in Tommaso d'Aquino (Symp) 2, 15-21.

2715. Billot, L. De Deo uno et trino. Commentarius in primam partem S. Thomae. Romae: University Gregoriana, 1957. 665 pp.

2716. Blazquez, Pelegrin. "Bases tomistas para la teologia del Cristianismo anonimo." Studium 14 (1974) 319-39.

GENERAL AND INTRODUCTORY   2717 - 2732

2717. Bonnefoy, J. F. "La méthodologie théologique de s. Thomas."
Revista Espanola de Teologia. Madrid. 19 (1950) 41-81.

2718. Brady, Ignatius. "Schools Within the Church." in Theology in
Daily Life. Washington, D.C.: Franciscan Ed. Conference, 1953. 25-
39.

        Second National Meeting of Franciscan Teaching Sisterhoods.

2719. Bruening, William H. "Aqinas and Wittgenstein on God-Talk."
Sophia 16 (1977) 1-7.

2720. Camelot, Th. "Credere deo, credere Deum, credere in Deum. Pour
l'histoire d'une formule traditionelle." Les Sciences Philosophique et
Théologique I (1941-1942) 149-55.

2721. Casin, René. S. Thomas d'Aquin ou l'intelligence de la foi.
Quatre points chauds. Montsure (Mayenne): Résiac, 1973. 137 pp.

2722. Chenu, M.-D. "L'Evangélisme de s. Thomas d'Aquin." Revue des
Sciences Philosophiques et Théologiques. Le Saulchoir-Paris. 58 (1974)
391-403.

2723. _____. Faith and Theology. Denis Hickey, tr. New York:
Macmillan, 1968. 227 pp.

2724. _____. Is Theology a Science? New York: Hawthorn Books,
1959.

2725. _____. "Le naturalisme de s. Thomas," in Tomismo e Neotomismo
(Symp) 1, 142-50.

2726. _____. Saint Thomas d'Aquin et la Théologie. Paris: Editions
du Seuil, 1959.

2727. _____. La théologie comme science au XIIIe siècle. 2 me éd.
Paris: Vrin, 1943.

2728. _____. "La théologie de la loi ancienne selon s. Thomas."
Revue Thomiste 61 (1961) 485-97.

2729. Congar, Yves M. J. "Le sens de l'économie salutaire dans la
théologie de s. Thomas d'Aquin," in Festgabe Joseph Lortz (Symp) 2,
73-122.

2730. _____. Situation et taches présentes de la théologie. Paris:
Cerf, 1967.

2731. _____. "La théologie chez s. Thomas d'Aquin." Dict. Théol.
Cath. 15 (1946) Col. 378-92.

2732. _____. "Valeur et portée oecumeniques de quelques principes
hermeneutiques de saint Thomas d'Aquin." Revue des Science Philosophiques

et Théologique 57 (1973) 611-26.

2733. Conley, Kieran. A Theology of Wisdom: A Study in St. Thomas.
Dubuque, Iowa: Priory Press, 1963. 171 pp.

2734. Connolly, Thomas G. The Personal Structure of the Act of Faith
According to Jean Mouroux: Thomistic Metaphysics of the Human Spirit
Developed by Maréchal and Blondel and Applied to the Act of Faith. New
York: Fordham University Dissertation, 1978. 296 pp.

2735. Corbin, Michel. Le chemin de la théologie chez Thomas d'Aquin.
Paris: Beauchesne, 1974. 908 pp.

2736. Corvez, Maurice. "Le probleme de Dieu." Revue Thomiste 75
(1967) 65-104.

2737. Crowley, Theodore. "Humani Generis and Philosophy." Irish
Theological Quarterly 19 (1952) 25-32.

2738. DeLetter, P. "Reciprocal Causality: Some Applications in
Theology." The Thomist 25 (1962) 382-418.

2739. Dembowski, Bronislaw. "Encyklika Aeterni Patris w Polsce," in
Studia z Dziejow Mysli (Symp) 315-34.

2740. Dewart, Leslie. The Foundations of Belief. New York: Herder
and Herder, 1969.

        Deals with "Transcendental Thomism."

2741. Diekamp, F. Katholische Dogmatik nach dem Grundsätzen des hl.
Thomas, Band I, 12-13 Aufl. von K. Jüssen, Münster i. W: Aschendorff,
1957. xii-372 pp.

2742. Donlan, Th. C. Theology and Education. Dubuque, Iowa: Brown,
1952. viii-134 pp.

2743. Dubarle, Dominique. "L'ontologie du mystère chrétien chez s.
Thomas d'Aquin." Angelicum 53 (1976) 227-68.

2744. Ernst, Cornelius. "Metaphor and Ontology in Sacra Doctrina."
The Thomist 38 (1974) 403-25.

2745. Fanfani, L. Teologia per tutti secondo la dottrina di S. Tommaso.
4 vols. 2a ed. Proma: S.A.L.E.S., 1943.

2746. Fay, Thomas A. "The Problem of God-Language in Thomas Aquinas:
What Can and Cannot Be Said." Rivista di Filosofia Neo-Scolastica. 69
(1977) 385-91.

2747. Fontan, Pierre. "Critique et tradition chez Saint Thomas."
Revue Thomiste 77 (1977) 533-77.

GENERAL AND INTRODUCTORY   2748 - 2763

2748. Freeman, David H. A Comparative Study of the Relationship Between Philosophy and Theology as Exemplified by Representatives of Neo-Augustinianism, Neo-Thomism, and Neo-Existentialism. Philadelphia: University of Pennsylvania Dissertation, 1958. 186 pp.

2749. Gagnebet, R. "Dieu, sujet de la théologie selon s. Thomas d'Aquin," in Problemi scelti di teologia contemporanea. Roma: University Gregoriana, 1954. 41-55.

2750. Garrigou-Lagrange, Reginald. Reality: A Synthesis of Thomistic Thought. St. Louis: Herder, 1950. 432 pp.

2751. _____. La synthèse thomiste. Paris: Desclée, 1946. 739 pp.

2752. Geenan, G. "The Place of Tradition in the Theology of St. Thomas." The Thomist 15 (1952) 110-35.

2753. Geisler, Norman L. "Analogy: The Only Answer to the Problem of Religious Language." Journal of the Evangelical Theological Society 16 (1973) 167-80.

2754. _____. Philosophy of Religion. Grand Rapids, Mich.: Zondervan, 1974. 416 pp.

    Especially Part 2, 87-228.

2755. Gillet, Martin S. Thomas d'Aquin. Paris: Dunod, 1949. 282 pp.

2756. Gillon, L.-B. "Thomas d'Aquin. V. Signification historique de la théologie de s. Thomas." Dict. de Théol. Cath. 15 (1946) 651-93.

2757. Gonzalez Cordedal, O. Teologia y antropologia. El hombre 'imagen de Dios' en el pensamiento de S. Thomàs. Madrid, 1967.

2758. Grabmann, Martin. Mittelalterliches Geistesleben. Tome 3. Munchen: Max Hueber, 1956. xi-479 pp.

2759. Grijs, F. J. A. de. Goddelijk mensontwerp. 2 vols. Hilversum: Brand, 1967. 633 pp.

2760. Guzie, Tad W. "The Act of Faith According to St. Thomas: A Study in Theological Methodology." The Thomist 29 (1965) 239-80.

2761. Haggard, Frank Powell. An Interpretation of Thomas Aquinas as a Biblical Theologian with Special Reference to His Systematizing of the Economy of Salvation. Madison, N.J.: Drew University Dsssertation, 1972. 470 pp.

2762. Hennesey, James. "Leo XIII's Thomistic Revival: A Political and Philosophical Event," in Celebrating the Medieval Heritage (Symp) 1978.

2763. Horváth, Sandor. Studien zum Gottesbegriff, 2 stark erweiterte

Aufl. von Der thomistische Gottesbegriff. Frieburg, Sch: Paulusverlag, 1954. xii-316.

2764. Journet, Charles Cardinal. "Jacques Maritain: Theologian." The New Scholasticism 46 (1972) 32-50.

2765. Keefe, Donald J. Thomism and the Ontological Theology of Paul Tillich. A Comparison of Systems. Netherlands: E. J. Brill, 1971. 373 pp.

2766. Kelly, Anthony J. "To Know the Mystery: The Theologian in the Presence of the Revealed God." The Thomist 32 (1968) 1-66, 171-200.

2767. Kilgore, William J. Basic Concepts in Neo-Thomism. Louisville, KY: Southern Baptist Theological Seminary Dissertation, 1943. 292 pp.

2768. King-Farlow, John and W. N. Christensen. Faith and the Life of Reason. Dordrecht: Reidel, 1972.

2769. Kunicič, P. J. "S. Thomas et theologia 'kerygmatica'," Angelicum 32 (1955) 35-51.

2770. Labourdette, M. M. et M. J. Nicolas. "L'Analogie de la vérité et l'unité de la science théologique." Revue Thomiste 47 (1947) 425-8.

2771. Lang, A. "Die Gliederung und Reichweite Des Glaubens nach Thomas von Aquin und den Thomisten." Divus Thomas. Freiburg. 20 (1942) 207-36.

2772. Lonergan, Bernard. Method in Theology. New York: Herder and Herder, 1972.

2773. _____ . "Philosophy and Theology." Proceedings of the American Catholic Philosophical Association 44 (1970) 19-30.

2774. Lovejoy, Arthur O. "The Duality of the Thomistic Theology: A Reply to Mr. Veatch."   Philosophy and Phenomenological Research 7 (1947) 413-38.

2775. _____ . "Analogy and Contradiction: A Surrejoinder." Philosophy and Phenomenological Research 7 (1947) 626-34.

2776. _____ . "Necessity and Self-sufficiency in the Thomistic Theology: A Reply to President Pegis." Philosophy and Phenomenological Research 9 (1948) 71-88.

2777. _____ . "Comment on Mr. Pegis's Rejoinder, 'Principale Volitum'." Philosophy and Phenomenological Research 9 (1948) 284-90.

2778. McCool, Gerald A. "The Philosophy of the Human Person in Karl Rahner's Theology." Theological Studies 22 (1961) 537-62.

GENERAL AND INTRODUCTORY   2779 - 2793

2779. _____. "Scientific Theology: Bonaventure and Thomas Revisited."
Thought. New York. 49 (1974) 374-96.

2780. Mancini, Italo. "Tommaso d'Aquino e le forme attuali della
teologia." Asprenas 21 (1974) 347-88.

2781. Manteau-Bonamy, H. M. "Saint Thomas Théologien." Cahiers IPC
9 (1974) 79-83.

2782. Martinez Diez, Felicisimo. "El problema de Dios en la 'Suma
Teologica'. Perspectiva teológica o perspectiva antropológica?"
Studium 14 (1974) 341-70.

2783. Mascall, E. L. "Guide-Lines from St. Thomas for Theology Today,"
in St. Thomas Aquinas 1274-1974 (Symp) 2, 489-501.

2784. Michael, Chester P. A Comparison of the God-Talk of Thomas
Aquinas and Charles Hartshorne. Baltimore, Maryland: St. Mary's
University (S.T.D.) Dissertation, 1975. 333 pp.

2785. Morreall, John S. A Critical Examination of the Thomistic Theory
of Analogy as a Way of Talking About God. Toronto: University of
Toronto Dissertation, 1976.

2786. Mourant, John A. "Aquinas and Theology." Franciscan Studies
16 (1956) 202-12.

2787. Muniz, Francisco. "De diversis muneribus S. Theologiae secundum
doctrinam D. Thomae." Angelicum 24 (1947) 93-123.

2788. _____. The Work of Theology. Washington: Thomist Press,
1953. 47 pp.

2789. Nicolas, Jean-Hervé. "Liberté du théologien et authorité du
Magistère. La pratique et la théorie de s. Thomas d'Aquin." Freiburger
Zeitschrift für Philosophie und Theologie 21 (1974) 439-58.

2790. Nygren, Anders. Meaning and Method - Prolegomena to a Scientific
Philosophy of Religion and a Scientific Theology. Philadelphia:
Fortress Press, 1972.

2791. O'Brien, Thomas C. "Sacra Doctrina Revisited: The Context of
Medieval Education." The Thomist 41 (1977) 475-504.

2792. Palmer, H. Analogy: A Study of Qualification and Argument in
Theology. New York: St. Martin's Press, 1973. 186 pp.

New Studies in the Philosophy of Religion.

2793. Panella, G. E. "La 'lex nova' tra storia ed ermeneutica. Le
occasioni dell'esegesi di s. Tommaso d'Aquino," in Tomismo e Neotomismo
I, 11-106.

2794. Patfoort, A. "Théorie de la théologie ou réflexion sur le corpus des Ecritures? Le vrai sens, dans l'oeuvre de s. Thomas, des prologues du Super Libros Sententiarum et de la S.T." Angelicum 54 (1977) 459-88.

2795. Pelster, Franz. "The Authority of St. Thomas in Catholic Schools and Sacred Science." Franciscan Studies 13 (1953) 1-26.

2796. _____. "La autoridad de S. Thomás en las escuelas y ciencias eclesiásticas." Estudios Eclesiasticos 27 (1953) 143-66.

2797. Persson, Per Erik. Sacra Doctrina. Stockholm: Gleerup, 1957. 329 pp.

    Swedish text.

2798. _____. Sacra Doctrina: Reason and Revelation in Aquinas. Ross Mackenzie, tr. Philadelphia: Fortress Press, 1970. xii-317 pp.

2799. Pesch, Otto Hermann. "Paul as Professor of Theology. The Image of the Apostle in St. Thomas's Theology." The Thomist. Centenary Edition. 38 (1974) 584-605.

2800. _____. "Sittengebote, Kultvorschriften, Rechtssatzungen. Zur Theologiegeschichte von S.T., I-II, 99, 2-5," in Thomas...Interpretation (Symp. Mainz) 1974. 488-518.

2801. Peter, Carl J. "Metaphysical Finalism or Christian Eschatology?" The Thomist 38 (1974) 125-45.

2802. Phillppe, M. D. "Reverentissime Exponens Frater Thomas." The Thomist 32 (1968) 84-105.

2803. Piemontese, F. "San Tommaso apologista." Studium. Roma. 70 (1974) 795-801.

2804. Pieper, Josef. Hinführung zu Thomas von Aquin. München, 1958.

2805. _____. The Silence of St. Thomas. J Murray and D. O'Connor, trs. New York: Pantheon Books, 1957. 122 pp.

2806. Preller, Victor S. Scientia Dei and Scientia Divina,A Reformulation of Thomas Aquinas. Princeton, N.J.: Princeton University Dissertation, 1965. 400 pp.

2807. _____. Divine Science and the Science of God, A Reformation of Thomas Aquinas. Princeton, N.J.: Princeton University Press, 1967. 281 pp.

2808. Rahner, Karl. Foundations of Christian Faith: An Introduction to Christianity. New York: Seabury, 1978. xv-470.

2809. _____. Hearers of the Word. New York: Herder and Herder, 1969.

GENERAL AND INTRODUCTORY   2810 - 2825

2810. _____. Inquires. New York: Herder and Herder, 1964.

2811. _____. A Rahner Reader. Gerald McCool, ed. New York: Seabury, 1975.

2812. _____. Theological Investigations. 5 vols. Baltimore, MD: Helicon, 1964-1967.

2813. Ramirez, Jacobus (Santiago) M. Obras Completas. 7 tomos. Madrid: Instituto de Filosofia 'Luis Vives', 1970-1974.

    Some edited by Victorino Rodriguez.

2814. _____. De Auctoritate Doctrinali S. Thomae Aquinatis. Salamanca: S. Stephanus, 1952.

2814A. _____. "The Authority of St. Thomas Aquinas." The Thomist 15 (1952) 1-109.

2815. _____. De ordine placita quaedam Thomistica. Salmantical: San Esteban, 1963. 369 pp.

2816. Ramm, Bernard. Types of Apologetic Systems, An Introductory Study to the Christian Philosophy of Religion. Wheaton, IL: Van Kampen Press, 1953.

2817. Rodriguez Rosado, J. J. Veritas et sapientia en el VII Centenario de S. Tomás de Aquino. Ed. Rodriguez Garcia, P. Pamplona: Ed. Universidad de Navarra, 1975. 392 pp.

2818. Scheeben, M. J. Handbuch der katholischen Dogmatik. 2 vol. 3 Aufl., Freiburg: Herder and Herder, 1948.

2819. Schillebeeckx, Edward. Revelation and Theology. N. D. Smith, tr. 2 vols. New York: Sheed and Ward, 1967-1968. I, xvi-266; II, x-212 pp.

2820. Seckler, Max. "Thomas von Aquin und die Theologie." Theologische Quartalschrift 156 (1976) 3-14.

2821. Sineux, Raphaël. Initiation à la théologie de s. Thomas d'Aquin. Tournai: Desclée, 1953. 852 pp.

2822. Smalley, Beryl. "William of Auvergne, John of La Rochelle and St. Thomas Aquinas on the Old Law," in St. Thomas Aquinas (Symp) 1974. 2, 11-71.

2823. Sweeney, Leo. "Preller and Aquinas." The Modern Schoolman 48 (1971) 267-73.

2824. Swierzawski, Waclaw. "L'exégèse biblique et la théologie spécula- tive de s. Thomas d'Aquin." Divinitas 18 (1974) 138-53.

2825. Toner, Jules J. The Notion of Spiritual Nature According to St.

2826 - 2839   GENERAL AND INTRODUCTORY

Thomas Aquinas. Toronto: University of Toronto Dissertation, 1953.

2826. Van Ackeren, Gerald F. "Reflections on the Relation Between Philosophy and Theology." Theological Studies 14 (1953) 527-50.

2827. _____. Sacra Doctrina: The Subject of the First Question of the Summa Theologica. Rome: Catholic Book Agency, 1952.

2828. Van Der Ploeg, J. "The Place of Holy Scripture in the Theology of St. Thomas." The Thomist 10 (1947) 398-422.

2829. Vella, Andrew P. "The 'subject-matter of holy teaching' as Discussed by Aquinas and other Medieval Writers." Scientia. Malta. 37 (1974) 17-29.

2830. Veres, Tomo. "Sto je teologija u Tome Akvinskog?" Obnovljeni Zivot. Zagreb. 29 (1974) 338-63.

What is Theology for Thomas Aquinas?

2831. Vesely, Jiri M. "La 'sacra doctrina' di Tommaso d'Aquino e la 'sancta praedicatis' di Domenico de Guzman, Riflessioni sulla S.T., I, q. I," in Thommaso d'Aquino (Symp) 2, 116-22.

2832. Walgrave, Jan Hendrik. Unfolding Revelation. The Nature of Doctrinal Development. London: Hutchinson; Philadelphia: Westminster, 1972. xii-418 pp.

St. Thomas on 98-102 pp.

2833. _____. "The Use of Philosophy in the Theology of Thomas Aquinas," in Aquinas and Problems (Symp) 181-93.

2834. Weisheipl, James A. "The Meaning of Sacra Doctrina in Summa Theologiae, I. q. I. The Thomist. Centenary of St. Thomas Aquinas, 1274-1974. 38 (1974) 49-81.

2835. White, Victor. Holy Teaching. The Idea of Theology According to St. Thomas Aquinas. London: Aquin Press, 1958.

2836. _____. "St. Thomas's Conception of Revelation." Dominican Studies. Osford. 1 (1948) 3-34.

2837. Winance, Eleuthàre. "Logical Note on the Co-existence of Faith and Reason." The Thomist 35 (1971) 276-92.

GOD AS ONE

2838. Barry, Lawrence E. "Eternity and Critical Insight." The New Scholasticism 47 (1974) 351-9.

2839. Bauer, Johannes. "Können die Namen Gottes synonyme Sein? Mit besonderer Bezugnahme suf Thomas von Aquin," in Gedenkband...Thomas von

GOD AS ONE   2840 - 2855

Aquin (Symp) 1974. 83-91.

2840. Branick, Vincent P. "The Unity of the Divine Ideas." The New Scholasticism 42 (1968) 171-201.

2841. Carrington, William T. Jr. Divine Immutability Revisited: The Doctrine of St. Thomas in the Face of Some Contemporary Challenges. New York: Fordham University Dissertation, 1973.

2842. Cooper, Burton. The Idea of God: A Whiteheadian Critique of Thomas Aquinas' Concept of God. New York: Union Theological Seminary Dissertation, 1968. 226 pp.

2843. Donlan, Thomas C. "The Beauty of God." The Thomist 10 (1947) 158-225.

2844. Fontan, Pierre. "Dieu, premier ou dernier connu. De Spinoza à saint Thomas d'Aquin." Revue Thomiste 74 (1974) 244-78.

2845. Guillou, M.-J. le. "Le Dieu de saint Thomas," in Tommaso d'Aquino.. problemi fondamentali (Symp) 1974. 161-71.

2846. Hill, William J. "Does the World Make a Difference to God?" The Thomist. Centenary of St. Thomas Aquinas, 1274-1974. 38 (1974) 146-64.

2847. _____. "In What Sense Is God Infinite? A Thomistic View." The Thomist 42 (1978) 14-27.

2848. Horwath, A. "Der thomistische Gottesbegriff." Divus Thomas. Fribourg. 18 (1940) 141-210.

2829. Kelly, Charles J. "The Intelligibility of the Thomistic God." Religious Studies 12 (1976) 347-64.

2850. Knuuttila, Simo. "The Increase of 'God's Possibilities' in the Middle Ages. A Statistical Interpretation of the Possibilities According to Averroes and St. Thomas Aquinas." Teologinen Aikauskirja 79 (1974) 105-21.

2851. Lacy, W. L. "Aquinas and God's Knowledge of the Creatures." Southern Journal of Philosophy 2 (1964) 43-8.

2852. Martin, J. A. Jr. "St. Thomas and Tillich on the Names of God." Journal of Religion 37 (1957) 256ff.

2853. Mascall, Eric L. He Who Is. London: Longmans, Green, 1943.

2854. Maurer, Armand. "St. Thomas on the Sacred Name Tetragrammaton." Mediaeval Studies 34 (1972) 275-86.

2855. Monette, A. La beauté de Dieu. Montréal: Fides, 1950. 126 pp.

2856. Moonan, Lawrence. "St. Thomas on Divine Power," in Tommaso d'
Aquino (Symp. Roma-Napoli) 3, 366-407.

2857. Neidl, Walter M. The archia. Die Frage nach dem Sinn von Gott bei
Pseudo-Dionipius Areopagitica und Thomas von Aquin... Regensburg: Josef
Habbel, 1976. 509 pp.

2858. Nicolas, Jean Hervé. "L'acte pur de s. Thomas et le Dieu vivant
de l'Evangile." Angelicum 51 (174) 511-32.

2859. Ochagavia, J. "Dios en Santo Tomás." Teologia y Vida. Santiago
de Chile. 17 (1976) 3-18.

2860. Pernoud, Mary Anne. "The Theory of the Potentia Dei According to
Aquinas, Scotus and Ockham." Antonianum. Roma. 47 (1972) 69-95.

2861. Pousset, Edouard. "Une Relecture du traité de Dieu dans la
'Somme Théologique' de saint Thomas." Archives de Philosophie. Paris.
38 (1975) 559-93; 39 (1976) 61-89.

2862. Rahner, Karl. "Über die Unbegreiflichkeit Gottes bei Thomas von
Aquin," in Thomas von Aquin 1274-1974(Symp) 33-45.

    Also in Tommaso d'Aquino...problemi fondamentali (Symp) 1974.
    101-13.

2863. _____. "Thomas Aquinas on the Incomprehensibility of God,"
in Celebrating the Med. Heritage (Symp) 1978.

2864. Rossner, William L. "Toward an Analysis of 'God is Love'."
The Thomist 38 (1973) 633-67.

2865. Spiazzi, Raymond. "Toward a Theology of Beauty." The Thomist
17 (1954) 350-66.

THE TRINITY

2866. Aranda Lomena, A. "Santo Tomás, teologo trinitario," in
Universidad de Navarra (Symp) 273-97.

2867. Cabasilas, Nilus (14th century). Nilus Cabasilas et theologia S.
Thomae de processione Spiritus Sancti. Città del Vaticano: Biblioteca
Apostolica Vaticana, 1945. xv-427 pp.

2868. Chambat, Lucien. Présence et union: les missions des personnes
de la Sainte-Trinite, selon s. Thomas d'Aquin. Abbaye S. Wandrille:
Editions de Fontenelle, 1945. 202 pp.

2869. Chatillon, Jean. "Unitas, Aequalitas, Concordia vel Connexio.
Recherches sur les Origines de la Théorie Thomiste des Appropriations
S.T. I, 39,7-8," in St. Thomas Aquinas 1274-1974 (Symp) I, 337-80.

2870. Cunningham, Francis L. The Indwelling of the Trinity: A Historico-

THE TRINITY   2871 - 2884

doctrinal study of the theory of St. Thomas Aquinas. Dubuque: Priory
Press, 1955. 414 pp.

2871. Dondaine, H.-F. "Qualifications dogmatiques de la théorie de
l'Assumptus-homo dans les oeuvres de s. Thomas," in Les Sciences philosophiques et théologiques. Paris: Vrin, 1941-1942. 163-8.

2872. Donnelly, Malechi J. "The Inhabitation of the Holy Spirit. A
Solution According to De la Taille." Theological Studies 8 (1947)
445-70.

2873. Egan, J. M. "Naming in St. Thomas' Theology of the Trinity,"
in From an Abundant Spring (Symp) 152-71.

2874. Faricy, Robert L. "The Trinitarian Indwelling." The Thomist
35 (1971) 369-404.

2875. Fitzgerald, Thomas J. De inhabitatione Spiritus Sancti doctrina
S. Thomae Aquinatis. Mundelein, IL: Seminarium S. Mariae ad Lacum,
1949. 141 pp.

2876. Froget, Barthélemy. The Indwelling of the Holy Spirit in the
Souls of the Just According to St. Thomas. Sydney A. Raemers, tr.
Baltimore: Carroll Press, 1950. xv-240 pp.

2877. Garrigou-Lagrange, Reginald. The Trinity and God the Creator.
Frederic C. Eckhoff, tr. St. Louis: Herder, 1952.

2878. Goichon, A.-M. Le mystère de la Sainte Trinité d'après S. Thomas
d'Aquin. Paris: Desclée, 1944. 121 pp.

2879. Hawkins, Benis J. B. "On Nature and Person in Speculative Theology."
Downside Review 80 (1962) 4ff.

2880. Hill, William J. Proper Relations to the Indwelling Divine Persons.
Washington, D.C.: Thomist Press. 1955, xvii-120 pp.

2880A. Krapiec, M. A. "Inquisitio circa doctrinam divi Thomae de Spiritu
Sancto prout amore." Divus Thomas. Piacenza. 53 (1950) 474-95.

2881. Lonergan, Bernard J. De Deo Trino, I et II. 2 vols. Romae:
Gregorianum, 1964. 326 pp.

2882. _____. Divinarum Personarum conceptio analogica. Roma:
Libreria Gregoriana, 1959. 303 pp.

2883. Malet, A. Personne et amour dans la théologie trinitaire de S.
Thomas d'Aquin. Paris: Vrin, 1956. 200 pp.

2884. Marinelli, Francesco. Personalismo trinitario nella storia della
salvezza...nello Scriptum super Sententiis de S. Tommaso. Roma:
Università Lateranense. 437 pp.

2885. Morency, R. L'Union de grace selon s. Thomas. Montréal: Ed.
de l'Immaculée Conception, 1950. 287 pp.

2886. _____. "L'union du juste à Dieu par voie de connaissance et
d'amour." Sciences Esslés 2 (1949) 27-79.

2887. Paissac, H. Théologie du Verbe. S. Augustin et S. Thomas. Paris:
Cerf, 1951.

2888. Pagé, Jean-Guy. "Le mystère trinitaire: quelques notations
théologiques," in Laval Thomas d'Aquin (Symp) 1974. 227-36.

2889. Pelikan, Jaroslav. "The Doctrine of Filioque in Thomas Aquinas
and Its Patristic Antecedents. An Analysis of S.T., I, q. 36," in
St. Thomas Aquinas 1274-1974 (Symp) I, 315-36.

2890. Richard, Robert L. The Problem of an Apologetical Perspective in
the Trinitarian Theology of St. Thomas Aquinas. Rome: Gregorian University Press, 1963. 336 pp.

2891. Ruello, Francis. "Saint Thomas et Pierre Lombard. Les relations
trinitaires..." in Studi Tomistici (Symp. Roma) 1974. I, 176-209.

2892. Strater, C. "Het Begrip 'appropriatie' bei S. Thomas." Bijdragen.
Tyds. Philos. Theol. Nijmegen. 9 (1948) 1-41, 144-86.

2893. Vagaggini, C. "La hantise des rationes necessariae de s. Anselme
dans la théologie des processions trinitaire de s. Thomas." Spicilegium
Beccense I (1959) 118ff.

2894. Vanier, Paul. "La relation trinitaire dans la Somme théologique
de s. Thomas d'Aquin." Sciences Ecclésiastiques. Montréal. I (1948)
143-60.

2895. _____. Théologie trinitaire chez saint Thomas d'Aquin.
Montréal: Institut d'etudes médiévales, 1953. 156 pp.

CREATION, ANGELOLOGY, PROVIDENCE

2896. Arfeuil, Jean-Pierre. "Le dessein sauveur de Dieu. La doctrine
de la predestination selon S. Thomas d'Aquin." Revue Thomiste 74 (1974)
591-641.

2897. Baget-Bozzo, Gianni. "La teologia delle idee divine in San
Tommaso." Rivista Filosofia Neo-Scolastica 66 (1974) 295-311.

2898. Boyer, Charles. "De l'accord de S. Thomas et de S. Augustin sur
la prédestination," in Tommaso d'Aquino (Symp) I, 217-22.

2899. Caturelli, Alberto. "La idea de creación en santo Tomàs y el
sentido de su negación en el pensamiento moderno," in Studi Tomistici
(Symp) 3, 57-77.

CREATION, ANGELOLOGY, PROVIDENCE 2900 - 2915

2900. Congar, Yves. La pneumatologie dans la théologie catholique."
Revue des Sciences Philosophiques et Théologiques 51 (1967) 250-9.

2901. Donnelly, P. T. "St. Thomas and the Ultimate Purpose of Creation."
Theological Studies 2 (1941) 53-83.

2902. Du Bruck, Edelgard. "Thomas Aquinas and Medieval Demonology."
The Michigan Academician 7 (1974) 167-83.

2903. Garrigou-Lagrange, Reginald. La Predestinación de los Santos y
la Grazia. Doctrina de S. Tomás... Buenos Aires: Desclée, 1947.
457 pp.

2904. Geach, Henry. "The Future." New Flackfriars (1973).

       St. Thomas Day Lecture, Blackfriars, Oxford.

2905. Geiger, Louis B. "Les idées divines dans l'oeuvre de s. Thomas,"
in St. Thomas Aquinas (Symp Toronto) I, 175-209.

2906. Hengstenberg, H. E. Von der göttlichen Vorsehung. Münster:
Regensberg, 1940. 216 pp.

2907. Hill, W. J. "Does God Know the Future? Aquinas and Some Moderns."
Theological Studies 36 (1975) 3-18.

2908. Holböck, Ferdinand. "Thomas von Aquin als 'Doctor Angelicus' und
'Doctor Angelorum'," in Studi Tomistici (Symp) 2, 199-217.

2909. Iglesias, Eduardo. De Deo in operatione naturae vel voluntatis
operante. Mexico, D.F.: Buena Prensa, 1946. 405 pp.

2910. Iseminger, Gary. "Foreknowledge and Necessity. Summa Theologiae
Ia 14, 13, Ad 2." Midwest Studies in Philosophy. Morris, Minnesota.
I (1976) 5-11.

2911. Kainz, Howard P. "Active and Passive Potency" in Thomistic
Angelology. Hague: Nijhoff, 1972. 111 pp.

2912. McGinn, Bernard. "Development of the Thought of Aquinas on the
Reconciliation of Divine Providence and Contingent Action." The Thomist
39 (1975) 741-52.

2913. McKian, John D. "What Man May Know of the Angels: Some Suggestions
of the Angelic Doctor." The New Scholasticism 29 (1955) 259-77; 441-
40; 30 (1956) 49-63.

2914. Marieb, Raymond E. "The Impeccability of the Angels Regarding
Their Natural End." The Thomist 28 (1964) 409-74.

2915. Martinez del Campo, Rafael. Doctrina s. Thomae de Actu et potentia
et de concursu. Mexico, D.F.: Buena Prensa, 1944. xii-235.

2916 - 2930 CREATION, ANGELOLOGY, PROVIDENCE

2916. Montano, Edward J. The Sin of the Angels: Some Aspects of the
Teaching of St. Thomas. Washington, D.C.: Catholic University of
America Press, 1955. xvi-359 pp.

2917. Mulligan, Robert W. "Divine Foreknowledge and Freedom: A Note
on a Problem of Language." The Thomist 36 (1972) 293-9.

2918. Murphy, W., T. Donlan, J. Reidy and F. Cunningham. God and His
Creation. A Basic Synthesis for the College. Dubuque, Iowa: Priory
Press, 1958. xviii-516 pp.

2919. Padoin, Giacinto. Il fine della creazione nel pensiero di S.
Tommaso. Rome: Editrice Laterano, Pontifica Universita Lateranense,
1959. 129 pp.

2920. Philippe de la Trinité, O. C. D. "Du péché de Satan et de la
destinée de l'esprit d'après s. Thomas d'Aquin." Etudes Carmélitaines.
Paris. 27 (1948) 44-85.

2921. Pieper, Josef. "The Concept of 'Createdness' and Its Implications,"
in Tommaso d'Aquino...Problemi fondamentali (Symp) 1974. 189-98.

2922. _____. "Kreatürlichkeit. Bemerkungen über die Elemente eines
Grundbegriffs," in Thomas von Aquin 1274-1974 (Symp) 47-71.

2923. Redlon, Reginald A. "St. Thomas and the Freedom of Creative Act."
Franciscan Studies 20 (1960) 1-18.

2924. Rock, John P. "Divine Providence in St. Thomas Aquinas." Boston
College Studies in Philosophy 1 (1966) 67-103.

2925. Rousseau, Edward L. The Distinction Between Essence and Supposit
in the Angel According to St. Thomas Aquinas. New York: Fordham
University Dissertation, 1954.

2926. Rousseau, Edward L. "Essence and Support in the Angels According to St. Thomas." The Modern Schoolman 33 (1956) 241-56.

2927. Saranyana, José I. "La creación ab aeterna. Controversia de
S. Tomás y Raimundo Marti con S. Buenaventura." Scripta Theologica 5
(1973) 127-74.

2928. _____. "Sobre el fin de los dias La escatologia del mundo
según S. Tomás." Anuario Filosofico 10 (1977) 219-41.

2929. Seckler, Max. Das Heil in der Geschichte. Geschichtstheologisches
Denken bei Thomas von Aquin. München: Kösel, 1964. 267 pp.

2930. _____. Le salut et l'histoire: la pensée de s. Thomas d'Aquin
sur la théologie de l'histoire. Paris: Cerf, 1967. 256 pp.

     Anon. trans. from German.

CREATION, ANGELOLOGY, PROVIDENCE   2931 - 2946

2931. Sertillanges, A.-D. Dieu gouverne. Paris: Spes, 1942. 135 pp.

2932. _____. L'idée de création et ses rétentissements en philosophie. Paris: Aubier, 1945. 229 pp.

2933. _____. Le problème du mal II. La solution. Paris: Aubier, 1951. 152 pp.

2934. Wallace, William A. "Aquinas on Creation: Science, Theology, and Matters of Fact." The Thomist. Centenary Edition. 38 (1974) 485-523.

2935. Ysaac, Walter L. "The Certitude of Providence in St. Thomas." The Modern Schoolman 38 (1961) 305-23.

SUPERNATURAL, GRACE, GIFTS

2936. Battló, Ricardo Marimón. "Orden natural y orden sobre natural en Santo Tomás de Aquino." Sapientia 33 (1978) 17-38.

2937. Bizzarri, Paolo. "Il 'De Gratia' della S.T. di S. Tommaso d' Aquino secondo le interpretazioni di alcuni studiosi recenti." Doctor Communis 30 (1977) 339-77.

2938. Boublik, Vladimiro. L'azione divina 'praeter ordinem naturae' secondo S. Tommaso d'Aquino. Roma: Università Lateranense, 1968. 143 pp.

2939. Bouillard, Henri. Conversion et grace chez S. Thomas d'Aquin. Etude historique. Paris: Aubier, 1944. xv-246 pp.

2940. Crosignani, Giacomo. La Teoria del naturale e del soprannaturale secondo S. Tommaso d'Aquino. Paicenza: Collegio Alberoni, 1974. 104 pp.

2941. Crowley, Charles B. "The Role of Sacramental Grace in Christian Life." The Thomist 2 (1940) 519-45.

2942. Daley, Mary C. The Notion of Justification in the Commentary of St. Thomas Aquinas on the Epistle to the Romans. Milwaukee: Marquette University Dissertation, 1971. 238 pp.

2943. Fairweather, A. W., ed. Aquinas on Nature and Grace. Philadelphia: Westminster Press, 1954. 386 pp.

2944. Flick, M. L'attimo della giustificazione secondo S. Tommaso. Romae: University Gregoriana, 1947. 206 pp.

2945. Gervais, Michel. "Nature et grace chez s. Thomas d'Aquin, I" in Laval Thomas d'Aquin (Symp) 333-48.

2946. _____. "Nature et grace chez s. Thomas d'Aquin, II." Laval Théologique et Philosophique 31 (1975) 293-321.

2947 - 2961 SUPERNATURAL, GRACE, GIFTS

2947. Greenstock, David L. "Exemplar Causality and the Supernatural Order." The Thomist 16 (1953) 1-31.

2948. Heinrichs, Johannes. "Ideologie oder Freiheitslehre. zur Rezipierbarkeit der thomanischen Gandenlehre von einem tranzendentaldialogischen Standpunkt." Theologie und Philosophie 49 (1974) 395-436.

2949. Hoffmann, A. M. "Die Gnade der Gerechten des Alten Bundes nach Thomas von Aquin." Divus Thomas. Fribourg. 29 (1951) 167-87.

    Title changed in 1954 to Freibruger Zeitschrift für Philosophie und Theologie.

2950. Janssen, Friedrich. Dynamische Heilsexistenz. Die Wachstumbedingungen der Rechtfertigungsgnade nach Thomas von Aquin... Kevelaer: Butzon and Bercher, 1974. 261 pp.

2951. Kelly, Anthony J. "The Gifts of the Spirit: Aquinas and the Modern Context." The Thomist 38 (197) 193-231.

2952. Lachance, C.-M. Le sujet de la grace et sa guérison selon s. Thomas. Ottawa-Montréal: Ed. du Lévrier, 1944. ix-178 pp.

2953. Ladrille, G. "Grace et motion divine chez s. Thomas d'Aquin." Salesianum. Torino. 12 (1950) 37-84.

2954. Lais, Hermann. Die Gnadenlehre des hl. Thomas. München: Zink, 1951. xvi-244 pp.

2955. Laporte, Jean Marc. "The Dynamics of Grace in Aquinas: A Structural Approach." Theological Studies 34 (1973) 203-26.

2956. _____. Les structures dynamiques de la grace. Grace medicinale et grace elevante selon Thomas d'Aquin. Montréal: Bellarmin; Tournae: Desclée, 1973. 244 pp.

2957. Lawler, Michael G. "Grace and Free Will in Justification: A Textual Study in Aquinas." The Thomist 35 (1971) 601-30.

2958. Lonergan, Bernard J. F. Grace and Freedom: Operative Grace in the Thought of St. Thomas Aquinas. J. Patout Burns, ed. New York: Herder and Herder, 1971. 187 pp.

2959. _____. "St. Thomas' Thought on Gratia Operans." Theological Studies 3 (1942) 573ff.

2960. Lubac, Henri de. Surnaturel. Etudes historiques. Paris: Aubier, 1946. 498 pp.

2961. _____. The Mystery of the Supernatural. New York: Herder and Herder, 1967.

SUPERNATURAL, GRACE, GIFTS   2962 - 2977

2962. McCarthy, B. "El modo del conocimiento profético y escriturístico según Santo Tomas de Aquino." Scripta Theologica 9 (1977) 425-84.

2963. McGuinness, Joseph Ignatius. "The Distinctive Nature of the Gift of Understanding." The Thomist 3 (1941) 217-78.

2964. Marimón Battló, Ricardo. "Orden natural y orden sobrenatural en S. Tomás de Aquino. Un reajuste del llamado 'humanismo integral' cristiano." Sapientia 33 (1978) 17-38.

2965. Meijer, B. De eerste levensvraag in het intellectualisme van St. Thomas van aquino en het integraal-realisme van M. Blondel. Roermund-Maaseik: Romen en Zonen, 1940. 342 pp.

2966. Mitchell, J. "Nature and Surnature. I. St. Thomas' Doctrine." Downside Review. Bath. 70 (1952) 23-36.

2967. Morency, Robert. L'Union de grace selon s. Thomas. Montréal: Editions de l'Immaculée-Conception, 1950. 287 pp.

2968. Moretti, Roberto. "Trinità e vita soprannaturale nella sintesi di San Tommaso," in Studi Tomistici (Symp) II, 248-60.

2969. Munoz Cuenca, José Maria "Doctrina de Santo Tomás sobre los dones del Espiritu Santo en la Suma teologica." Ephemerides Carmeliticae 25 (1974) 157-243.

2970. Ocariz Brana, Fernando. "La santisima Trinidad y el misterio de nuestra deificacion," in Universidad de Navarra (Symp) 363-90.

2971. O'Neill, C. E. "L'homme ouvert à Dieu. cupax Dei," in L'Anthropologie (Symp) Fribourg. 54-74.

2972. Przywara, Erich. "Der Grundsatz: 'Gratia non destriut sed supponit et perficit naturam.' Eine ideengeschichtliche Interpretation." Scholastik 17 (1942) 178-86.

2973. Ruini, Camillo. La trascendenza della grazia nella teologia di s. Tommaso d'Aquino. Roma: University Gregoriana, 1971. 363 pp.

2974. Ryan, John K. "Cognoscere Coniecturaliter per Signa: A Gloss on S.T., I-II, Q. 112, art. 2." The Modern Schoolman 49 (1971) 51-4.

2975. Schillebeeckx, Edward. "Arabisch-neoplatoonse achtergrond van Thomas' opvatting over de ontvankelijkheid van de mens voor de genade." Bijdragen. Nijmegen. 35 (1974) 298-308.

2976. _____. "Salut, rédemption et émancipation," in Tommaso d'Aquino (Roma-Napoli Symp) I, 529-34.

2977. Schleck, Charles A. "St. Thomas on the Nature of Sacramental Grace." The Thomist 18 (1955) 1-30; 242-78.

2978. Spiazzi, R.-M. "Il carattere perfettivo del soprannaturale secondo S. Tommaso." Scuola Cattolica. Venegono. 76 (1948) 131-42.

2979. Teselle, Eugene A. Jr. Thomas and the Thomists on Nature and Grace: An Interpretation of the Theological Anthropology of Thomas Aquinas in the Light of Recent Scholarship. New Haven: Yale University Dissertation, 1963. 178 pp.

2980. Tonneau, J. "Où commence dans la Somme le traité de la grace?" Bulletin du Cercle Thomiste. Caen. 67 (1974) 3-11.

2981. Van Roo, William. Grace and Original Justice According to St. Thomas. Rome: University Gregoriana, 1955. 211 pp.

2982. Wheeler, M. Cecelia. "Actual Grace According to St. Thomas." The Thomist 16 (1953) 334-60.

2983. Yearley, Lee H. Natural and Supernatural Activity in the Tradition Represented by St. Thomas and Cardinal Newman. Chicago: University of Chicago Dissertation, 1969. 280 pp.

2984. _____. "The Nature-Grace Question in the Context of Fortitude." The Thomist 35 (1971) 557-80.

MORAL THEOLOGY, VIRTUES, SINS

2985. Alvarez, Jesus. "Sexualidad y libertad en la doctrina Tomista." Libro Anual I.S.E.E. Mexico. I (1974) 131-49.

2986. Aubert, Jean-Marie. "La liberté du chrétien face aux normes éthiques," in Tommaso d'Aquino (Symp Roma-Napoli) I, 199-226.

2987. _____. "La spécificité de la morale chrétienne selon s. Thomas," in Vivre et croire, chemins de sérénité. Paris: Cerf. 1974. 61-84.

2988. Bain, Homer A. A Compatibility of Rational and Irrational Action in the Theology of Saint Thomas Aquinas and the Ego Psychology of Heinz Hartmann. Chicago: University of Chicago Dissertation, 1971. 343 pp.

2989. Basso, Domingo M. "La ley eterna en la teologia de santo Tomás." Teologia. Buenos Aires. II (1974) 33-63.

2990. _____. "Un pilar de la moral tomista. La doctrina del apetito recto," in Tommaso d'Aquino (Symp Roma) 5, 375-402.

2991. Berg, L. Die Gottebenbildlichkeit im Moralsubjekt mach Thomas von Aquin. Mainz: Kirchheim, 1948. 120 pp.

2992. Bernard, Ch. A. Théologie de l'espérance selon s. Thomas d'Aquin. Paris: Vrin. 1961. 174 pp.

2993. Bezic, Zivan. "Vitalnost u Tominoj Boncepciji kiscanske nade."

MORAL THEOLOGY, VIRTUES, SINS 2994 - 3006

Zbornik (Symp) 107-17.

    Thomistic view of hope.

2994. Bezzina, E. De valore sociali caritatis secundum principia s. Thomae Aquinatis. Neapoli: d'Auria, 1952. 220 pp.

2995. Bogliolo, Luigi. "Sulla fondazione tomista della morale," in Tommaso d'Aquino (Symp) 5, 107-121.

2996. Bonnin Aguiló, Francisco. "Santo Tomás de Aquino y la felicidad imperfecta." Estudios Filosoficos. Las Caldas de Besaya. 27 (1978) 111-25.

2997. Bourgeois, Daniel. "'Inchoatio vitae aeternae.' La dimension eschatologique de la vertu théologale de foi chez s. Thomas d'Aquin." Sapienza. Napoli. 27 (1974) 272-314.

2998. Boyle, John P. "Lonergan's Method in Theology and Objectivity in Moral Theology." The Thomist 37 (1973) 589-94.

2999. Broglie, Guy de. "La doctrine de s. Thomas sur le fondement communautaire de la chasteté," in Tommaso d'Aquino (Symp Roma) 5, 297-307.

3000. Budrovic, Dominik. "O savjesti. Prema II Vatikanskom Koncilu i sv. Tomi," in Zbornik (Symp) 85-105.

    On Conscience.

3001. Bullet, Gabriel. Vertus morales infuses et vertus morales acquises selon s. Thomas d'Aquin. Freiburg, Schio ed. Universitaires, 1958. xiv-180 pp.

3002. Bussoni, Anselmo. "Leggi e strutture: fissità o combiamento? Che ne pensa S. Tommaso?" Revue d'Asčtique et de Mystique 66 (1974) 511-32.

3003. Bustinza, Román. "La religión y el actuar humano en la 'Suma Teologica' de santo Tomás de Aquino." Teologia. Buenos Aires. 11 (1974) 118-32.

3004. Cacciabue, Luigi. La carità soprannaturale come amicizia con Dio Studio storico sui Commentatori di S. Tommaso dal Gaetano ai Salmanticesi. Roma: Universita Gregoriane, 1972. 207 pp.

3005. Cambareri, Reginaldo G. Alle radici de male morale. Fondamenti metafisici e genesi psicologica in S. Tommaso. Napoli-Acireale: Ed. Domenicane Italiane, 1974. 151 pp.

3006. Capone, Domenico. "S. Tommaso e S. Alfonso in teologia morale." Asprenas. Napoli. 21 (1974) 439-93.

3007. Cardona, Carlos. "Introducción a la Quaest. Disp. De Malo,
contribución al diagnóstico de una parte de la situación contemporánea,"
in Universidad de Navarra (Symp) 111-43.

3008. Carlson, Sebastian. "The Virtue of Humility." The Thomist 7
(1944) 135-78; 8 (1944) 363-414.

3009. Chenu, M.-D. "L'Originalité de la morale de s. Thomas-Morale et
Evangile," in Initiation théologique, tome III, théologie Morale.
Paris: 1955. 7-12.

3010. _____. The Theology of Work. Chicago: Regnery, 1963.

3011. Chereso, C. The Virtue of Honor and Beauty According to St.
Thomas Aquinas. River Forest, IL: Aquinas Library, 1960.

3012. Colavechio, Xavier G. Erroneous Conscience and Obligations: A
Study of the Teaching from the Summa Halesiana, Saint Bonaventure, Saint
Albert the Great, and Saint Thomas Aquinas. Washington, D.C.: Catholic
University of America Dissertation, 1961. 174 pp.

3013. Compagnoni, F. La specificità della morale cristiana. Bologna:
Edizioni Dehoniane, 1972. 182 pp.

    Capter 2 on S. Tommaso.

3014. Composta, Dario. "Lineamenti di una teologia del diritto naturale."
Divinitas 14 (1970) 465-96.

3015. Condit, Ann. "The Increase of Charity." The Thomist 17 (1954)
367-86.

3016. Congar, Yves M. J. "Le Saint Esprit dans la thé logie thomiste de
l'agir moral," in Tommaso d'Aquino (Roma-Napoli Symp) I, 175-87.

3017. _____. "Le traité de la force dans la 'Somme théologique' de
s. Thomas d'Aquin." Angelicum. Roma. 51 (1974) 331-48.

3018. Connell, F. J. Outlines of Moral Theology. Milwaukee: Bruce,
1953. 247 pp.

3019. Couesenongle, Vincent de. "Le 'Dieu de l'espérance' de s. Thomas
d'Aquin." Studia Theologica Varsaviensis. Warsaw. 12 (1974) 103-
20.

3020. Crowe, Frederick. "Complacency and Concern in the Thought of
Thomas Aquinas." Theological Studies. Baltimore, Maryland. 20 (1959)
1-39, 193-230, 343-81.

3021. Crowe, Michael B. "The Term Synderesis and the Scholastics."
Irish Theological Quarterly 23 (1956) 151-64, 228-45.

3022. Curran, Charles E., ed. Absolutes in Moral Theology? Washington,

MORAL THEOLOGY, VIRTUES, SINS   3023 - 3037

D.C.:   Corpus Books, 1968.   320 pp.

    Articles by R.H. Springer, D.C. Maguire, Curran, J.C. Hilhaven, C.J. Van der Poel, D. Doherty, M. Nolan and K. Nolan.

3023. _____. Themes in Fundamental Moral Theology. Notre Dame-London: University of Notre Dame Press, 1977. 241 pp.

3024. De Ferrari, Teresa Mary. The Problem of Charity for Self: A Study of Thomistic and Modern Theological Discussion. Washington, D.C.: Catholic Univeristy of America Press, 1963. 211 pp.

3025. De Letter, P. "Hope and Charity in St. Thomas." The Thomist 13 (1950) 204-48; 325-52.

3026. _____. "Original Sin, Privation of Original Justice." The Thomist 17 (1954) 469-509.

3027. _____. "The Reparation of Our Fallen Nature." The Thomist 23 (1960) 564-83.

3028. _____, "Theology of Satisfaction." The Thomist 21 (1958) 1-28.

3029. _____. "Venial Sin and Its Final Goal." The Thomist 16 (1953) 32-70.

3030. Delhaye, Philippe. "Pourquoi une morale révélée?" in Tommaso d'Aquino (Symp) 5, 128-34.

3031. De Lima Vaz, Henrique. "Teocentrismo e beatitude: sobre a actualidade do pensamento de s Tomas de Aquino." Revista Portuguesa de Filosofia. Braga. 30 (1974) 39-79.

3032. Deman, Thomas H. Aux origines de la théologie morale. Montréal: Inst. d'études médiévales, 1951. 115 pp.

3033. _____. "Le 'précepte' de la prudence chez s. Thomas d'Aquin." Recherches de Théologie Ancienne et Médiévale. Louvain. 20 (1953) 40-59.

3034. Derisi, Octavio N. "El sentido de la nada en la filosofia moderna contemporanea y en la filosofia de S. Tomás." Filosofar Cristiano. Córdoba, Arg. I (1977) 25-37.

3035. Dianich, Deverino. L'opzione fondamentale nel pensiero di S. Tommaso. Brescia: Morcelliana, 1968. 300 pp.

3036. Diaz-Alegria, I. M. "De libertate conscientiarum in civitate servanda juxta principia S. Thomae Aquinatis," in Thomistica Morum (Symp) 114-9.

3037. Di Marino, Antonio. "Antropologia Tomista e morale cristiana."

Rivista di Teologia Morale. Bologna. 6 (1974) 697-713.

3038. Fairweather, Eugene R. The Nature and Function of Faith According to St. Thomas Aquinas and the Classical Thomist Commentators. New York: Union Theological Seminary Dissertation, 1949. 248 pp.

3039. Falanga, Anthony J. Charity the Form of the Virtues According to St. Thomas. Washington, D.C.: Catholic University of America Dissertation, 1949. 342 pp.

3040. Fanfani, L. J. Manuale theorico-practicum theologiae moralis ad mentem D. Thomae. 4 vols. Romae: Ferrari, 1949-1951. xix-648; xx-716; xvi-552; xxv-1038 pp.

3041. Farley, Margaret A. "Fragments for an Ethic of Commitment in Thomas Aquinas." in Celebrating the Medieval Heritage (Symp) 1978.

3042. Fearon, John. "States of Life." The Thomist 12 (1949) 1-16.

3043. Fernandez, Aurelio. "La liberdad en el pensamiento cristiano." Theologica. Braga. 9 (1974) 280-313.

3044. Ferrara, Ricardo. "'Fidei infusio' y revelación en santo Tomas de Aquino. Summa Theol. I-II, 100, 4, ad primum." Teologia. Buenos Aires. II (1974) 24-32.

3045. Ferrari, Mario V. "'Et non faciamus mala ut veniant bona' (Rom. 3,8). Uno studio...alla luce di S. Tommaso d'Aquino," in Studi Tomistici (Symp) 3, 152-84.

3046. _____. "Il fine giustifica i mezzi? Riflessioni sul detto, seguendo Tommaso d'Aquino." Rivista di Teologia Morale. Bologna. 6 (1974) 321-58.

3047. Finance, Joseph De. "Sentido y limites del objetivismo moral en S. Tomás en relación con el problema de la conciencia erronea." Revista Filosofica. Mexico. 6 (1974) 75-98.

3048. _____. "Sens et limites de l'objectivisme moral chez s. Thomas A propos des problèmes de la conscience erronée." Revista Portuguesa de Filosofia 30 (1974) 107-26.

3049. Fitzpatrick, Edmund J. The Sin of Adam in the Writings of St. Thomas Aquinas. Mundelein, IL: St. Mary of the Lake Semianry, 1950. 179 pp.

3050. Flanagan, Francis J. The Image of God in Man as the Foundation of Charity According to the Doctrine of St. Thomas Aquinas. Washington, D.C.: Catholic University of America Dissertation, 1943.

3051. Flick, Maurizio. L'Attimo della giustificazione secondo S. Tommaso. Romae: Gregorianum, 1947.

MORAL THEOLOGY, VIRTUES, SINS   3052 - 3068

3052. Francini, Innocenzo. "'Vivere insieme? Un aspetto della 'koinonia' aristotelica nella teologia della carità, secondo S. Tommaso." Ephemerides Carmeliticae. Roma. 25 (1974) 267-317.

3053. Fuchs, Josef. "The Absoluteness of Moral Terms. Gregorianum 52 (1971) 415-58.

3054. _____. Lex Naturae. Zur Theologie des Naturrechts. Dusseldorf: Patmos, 1955. 192 pp.

3055. _____. Natural Law: A Theological Investigation. H. Reckter, and J. A. Dowling, trs. Dublin: Gill and Son, 1965.

3056. Gallagher, Conan. "Concupiscence." The Thomist 30 (1966) 228-59.

3057. Garrigou-Lagrange, Reginald. The Theological Virtues. St. Louis: B. Herder, 1965.

3058. Geiger, Louis B. "L'homme, image de Dieu. A propos de Summa Theol. I, 93, 4." Rivista di Filosofia Neo-Scolastica. Milano. 66 (1974) 511-32.

3059. _____. "Morality According to St. Thomas and Depth Psychology." Philosophy Today 6 (1962) 227-38.

3060. _____. Le Probleme de l'amour chez s. Thomas d'Aquin. Montréal: Inst. d'Etudes Médiévales, 1952. 132 pp.

3061. Ghoos, J. "L'Acte à double effet-Etude de theologie positive." Ephemerides Theologicae Lovaniesses 27 (1951) 30-52.

3062. Gilleman, G. The Primacy of Charity in Moral Theology. Trans. W. F. Ryan and André Vachon. Westminster, MD: Newman, 1959.

3063. Gillon, L.-B. "A propos de la théorie thomiste de l'amitié." Angelicum 25 (1948) 3-17.

3064. Glenn, Mary Michael. "A Comparison of the Thomstic and Scotistic Concepts of Hope. The Thomist. 20 (1957) 27-74.

3065. Goulet, Denis A. "Kierkegaard, Aquinas, and the Dilemma of Abraham." Thought 32 (1957) 165-88.

3066. Guindon, André. "La 'crainte honteuse' selon Thomas d'Aquin." Revue Thomiste 69 (1969) 589-623.

3067. _____. "L'influence de la crainte sur la qualité humaine de l'action selon Thomas d'Aquin." Revue Thomiste 72 (1972) 33-57.

3068. _____. La pédagogie de la crainte dans l'histoire du salut selon Thomas d'Aquin. Tournai: Desclée, 1975. 424 pp. Montréal: Bellarmin.

3069 - 3083 MORAL THEOLOGY, VIRTUES, SINS.

3069. Guindon, Roger. Béatitude et théologie morale chez s. Thomas d'
Aquin. Ottawa: Université d'Ottawa, 1956.

3070. Guttierez, Juan. "Realización del ser humano por el amor, según
el pensamiento de S. Tomas." Revista Teologica Limense. Lima, Peru.
8 (1974) 131-52.

3071. Häring, Bernard. La Loi du Christ. Théologie morale à l'intention
des pretres et des laics. 3 vols. Tournai-Paris: Desclée, 1957-1959.
450, 388, 773 pp.

3072. _____. "La théologie morale de s. Thomas d'Aquin à s. Alphonse
de Liguori." Nouvelle Revue Théologique. Tournai-Louvain. 77 (1955)
683-5.

3073. Hall, Theodore. Paul Tillich's Appraisal of St. Thomas' Teaching
on the Act of Faith. Rome: Catholic Book Agency, 1967. 104 pp.

3074. Hamain, L. "Morale chrétienne et réalités terrestres--une
réponse de s. Thomas d'Aquin. la béatitude imparfaite." Recherches de
théologie ancienne et médiévale 35 (1968) 134-76, 260-90.

3075. Hanley, Katherine Rose. "Freedom and Fault." The New Scholasticism
51 (1977) 494-512.

3076. Heck, Erich. Der Begriff religio bei Thomas von Aquin. Seine
Bedeutung für unser heutiges Verständnis von Religion. Paderborn,
Wien: Schöningh, 1971. xxviii-307 pp.

3077. Helema, Giovanni. "La 'legge vecchia' e la 'legge nuvva' secondo
S. Tommaso d'Aquino." Ephemerides Carmeliticae. Roma. 25 (1974) 28-
139.

3078. Henry, A.-M. Morale et vie conjugale. Paris: Cerf. 1957.
240 pp.

3079. Hoogen, T. Van den. "'Pastorale theologie': het theologisch
procède' volgens Chenu." Tijdschrift voor Theologie. Nijmegen. 12
(1972) 396-416.

3080. Horvath, T. Caritas est in Ratione. Die Lehre des hl. Thomas
uber die Einheit der Intellektiven und Affectiven Begnadung des Menschen.
Munster: Aschendorff, 1966. xi-293 pp.

3081. Ibertis, Enrico. S. Tommaso d'Auino e le beatitudini. Turino:
Centro Libr. Domenicano, 1974. 148 pp.

3082. Ilien, Albert. Wesen und Funktion der Liebe bei Thomas von Aquin.
Freiburg i. Br. Basel Wien: Herder, 1975. 231 pp.

3083. Javorka, Josepho. Amor a Dios sobre todas las cosas y amor a si
mismo, segun santo Tomás. Buenos Aires, 1964. 94 pp.

MORAL THEOLOGY, VIRTUES, SINS   3084 - 3097

3084. Joseph, N. Benedict. The Virtue of Observance According to
St. Thomas Aquinas. Washington, D.C.: The Thomist Press, 1954. 94 pp.

3085. Jossa, F. "Attualità di S. Tommaso nel problema del rapporto
tra scienze e fede." Asprenas. Napoli. 22 (1975) 376-95.

3086. Kaczynski, Edward. La legge nuova. L'elemento esterno della
legge nuova secondo San Tommaso. Roma-Vicenza: Libreria Francesane,
1974. 181 pp.

3087. Kalter, Richard B. The Relation of Conscience to Providence in
the Thought of St. Thomas Aquinas: A Critical Evaluation of the Methodology of Catholic Moral Theology. Cambridge, Mass: Harvard University
Dissertation, 1962. 199 pp.

3088. Keating, Charles J. The Effects of Original Sin in the Scholastic
Tradition from St. Thomas Aquinas to William Ockham. Washington, D.C.:
Catholic University of America Dissertation, 1960. 166 pp.

3089. Kelly, Kevin T. A Thomistic Appraisal of the Concept of Conscience
and Its Place in Moral Theology in the Writings of Bp. Robert Sanderson
and other Early English Protestant Moralists. London: 1967.

3090. Kenny, John P. Moral Aspects of Nuremberg. Washington:
Dominican House of Studies, 1949. xii-168 pp.

3091. Klubertanz, George P. "Une théorie sur les vertus morales
'naturelles' et 'surnaturelles'," Revue Thomiste 42 (1959) 565-75.

3092. Knauer, Peter. "Das rechtverstandene Prinzip von der Doppelwirkung
als Grundnorm jeder Gewissensentscheidung." Theologie und Glaube.
Paderborn. 57 (1967) 107-33.

3093. _____. "The Hermeneutic Function of the Principle of Double
Effect." Natural Law Forum. Notre Dame, Indiana. 12 (1967) 132-
62.

          Changed to American Journal of Jurisprudence in 1969.

3094. Kühn, Ulrich. "Evangelische Anmerkungen zum Problem der Begründung
der moralischen Autonomie des Menschen im Neuen Gesetz nach Thomas."
Angelicum 51 (1974) 235-45.

3095. _____. Via caritatis: Theologie des Gesetzes bei Thomas von
Aquin. Göttingen: Vandernhoeck-Ruprecht, 1965. 279 pp.

3096. Kuniċić, Jordan. "Preorijentacija moralke. U svjetlu Tomine
teoloske sinteze." in Zbornik (Symp) 65-83.

          Renovation of morals, in the light of Thomistic Theology.

3097. Labourdette, M.-M. Le péché originel et les origines de l'homme.
Paris: Alsatia, 1953. xx-210 pp.

3098 - 3113   MORAL THEOLOGY, VIRTUES, SINS

3098. Laguna, Justo. "La doctrina de santo Tomás sobre el pecado y su vigencia ante las concepciones modernas..." in Tommaso d'Aquino (Symp) 405-19.

3099. Langevin, Gilles. "Capax Dei": La créature intellectuelle et l'intimité de Dieu. Paris: Desclée de Brouwer, 1966. 138 pp.

3100. Lanza, A. Theologia moralis. I. Theologia moralis fundamentalis. Taurini: Marietti, 1949. xxiv-570. pp.

3101. Laporta, Jorge. La destinée de la nature humaine selon s. Thomas d'Aquin. Paris: Vrin, 1965   168 pp.

3102. Larrabe, José Luis. "La virtudes de iniciativa cristiana según S. Tomás." Studium 14 (1974) 567-92.

3103. Lécuyer, Joseph. "Prolégoménes thomistes à la théologie de la satisfaction," in Studi Tomistici (Symp) 2, 82-103.

3104. Llamera, Marceliano. "El concepto de moral teologica y sus caracteres teocentrico y antropologico según santo Tomás," in Tommaso d'Aquino (Symp Roma-Napoli) 1, 227-52.

3105. _____. "Teocentrismo de la vida y de la ciencia moral cristiana segun S. Tomás." Theological Studies. Baltimore. 18 (1974) 279-97.

3106. Lopez, Teodoro. "La existencia de una moral cristiana especifica. Su fundamentación en Santo Tomás," in Universidad de Navarra. (Symp) 239-71.

3107. Lottin, Odon. Morale fondamentale. Tournai: Desclée. 1954.

3108. _____. "Le péché originel chez Albert le Grand, Bonaventure et Thomas d'Aquin." Recherches de théologie ancienne et médiévale 12 (1940) 275-328.

3109. _____. "Pour une réorganisation du traité thomiste de la moralité," in Acta Congressus scholastici intern. Romae. Romae: Antonianum, 1951. 307-51.

3110. _____. Principes de morale. 2 vols. Louvain: Mont César, 1947. 341 et 277 pp.

3111. _____. Psychologie et morale aux XIIe et XIIIe siècles, 6 tomes. Gembloux: Duculot, 1942-1960.

3112. Lumbreras, P. "Notes on the Connections of the Virtues." The Thomist 8 (1945) 218-40.

3113. McCormick, Richard A. Ambiguity in Moral Choice. Milwaukee: Marquette University Press, 1973. 112 pp.

MORAL THEOLOGY, VIRTUES, SINS   3114 - 3127

3114. _____ and Paul Ramsey, eds. Doing Evil to Achieve Good. Moral Choice in Conflict Situations. Chicago: Loyola University Press, 1978. 267 pp.

   Articles by B.A. Brody, W.K. Frankena, B. Schüller and the Editors.

3115. _____. "Notes on Moral Theology." Theological Studies.

   Washington, D.C. annual since 1965.

3116. McHugh, J. A. and C. J. Callan. Moral Theology: A Complete Course Based on St. Thomas Aquinas and the Best Modern Authorities. 2 vols. New York: J. Wagner, 1959.

   Revised by E.P. Farrell.

3117. McNicholl, Ambrose J. "The Ultimate End of Venial Sin." The Thomist 2 (1940) 373-409.

3118. Magrath, Oswin. "St. Thomas' Theory of Original Sin. The Thomist 16 (1953) 161-89.

3119. Mahoney, John. "The Spirit and Moral Discernment in Aquinas." Heythrop Journal 13 (1972) 282-97.

3120. Majdanski, C. Le role des biens extérieurs dans la vie morale d'après s. Thomas d'Aquin. Vanues, Seine: Imprim. Franciscaine Missionaire, 1951. xii-136 pp.

3121. Mangan, J. T. "An Historical Analysis of the Principle of Double Effect. Theological Studies. Baltimore. 10 (1949) 41-61.

3122. Margerie, Bertrand de. "La securité temporelle du juste Relation intrinsèque entre biens temporels et verties théologales d'après la doctrine de s. Thomas d'Aquin," in Studi Tomistici (Symp) 2, 283-306.

3123. Mateo-Seco, Lucas-Francisco. "El concepto de verdad en S. Tomás de Aquino y en la teologia de la liberación." Scripta Theologica. Pamplona. 9 (1977) 1043-62.

3124. _____. "El concepto de muerte en la doctrina de santo Tomás de Aquino," in Universidad de Navarra (Symp) 173-208.

3125. Mausbach, Joseph. Teologia moral católica. 3 vols. Baranain: Eunsa, 1974.

3126. Mersch, E. Morale et Corps mystique. 3 me éd. Paris: Desclée, 1949. 278, 152 pp.

3127. Miano, Vincenzo. "La religione e le religioni nel pensiero tomistico," in Tommaso d'Aquino (Symp) 4, 331-47.

3128 - 3142   MORAL THEOLOGY, VIRTUES, SINS

3128. Milhaven, John G. "Moral Absolutes and Thomas Aquinas." in
Absolutes in Moral Theology? Charles E. Curran, ed. Washington, D.C.:
1968. 154-85.

3129. Mohler, James A. The Beginning of Eternal Life: The Dynamic
Faith of Thomas Aquinas. Origins and Interpretation. New York:
Philosophical Library, 1968. 144 pp.

3130. Monahan, William B. The Moral Theology of St. Thomas Aquinas.
3 vols. Worcester and London: Trinity Press (ca. 1942).

3131. Monda, Antonio M. di. La legge nuova della libertà secondo
S. Tommaso. Napoli: D'Auria, 1954.

3132. _____. "La povertà evangelica in S. Tommaso d'Aquino e in
S. Bonaventura di Bagnoreggio." Recherches de Théologie Ancienne et
Médiévale. Louvain. 25 (1974) 48-72.

3133. Mangillo, Dalmazio. "La foundazione dell'agire nel prologo della
I-II." Sapienza. Napoli. 27 (1974) 261-71.

3134. _____. "Potere normativo della 'ratio' nella Legge Nuova."
Angelicum 51 (1974) 169-85.

3135. Montagnes, Benoit. "Les activités Seculières et le mépris du
monde chez Saint Thomas d'Aquin." Revue des sciences Philosophiques et
Théologiques 50 (1971) 231-349.

3136. _____. "Autonomie et dignité de l'homme." Angelicum 51
(1974) 186-211.

3137. Noonan, John T. Jr. "Abortion and the Catholic Church: A
Summary History." Natural Law Forum 12 (1967) 85-131.

        Aquinas on 101-4 pp.

3138. _____. Contraception: A History of Its Treatment by the
Catholic Theologians and Canonists. Cambridge: Harvard University
Press, 1965.

3139. _____, ed. The Morality of Abortion: Legal and Historical
Perspectives. Cambridge, Mass: Harvard University Press, 1970.

3140. Osbourn, James C. "The Morality of Imperfections." The Thomist
4 (1942) 388-430; 4 (1942) 649-91.

3141. _____. The Morality of Imperfections. Thomistic Studies: no.
1. Washington: Pontifical Faculty of Theology. Dominican House of
Studies, 1943. xiii-247 pp.

3142. _____. "The Theological Ingredients of Peace," in Maritain
Volume of The Thomist (Symp) 1943. 23-54.

MORAL THEOLOGY, VIRTUES, SINS   3143 - 3158

3143. Ouwerkerk, C. A. J. van. Caritas et Ratio: Etude sur le double principe de la vie morale chrétienne d'après s. Thomas d'Aquin. Niymegen: 1956.

3144. Padellaro de Angelis, Rosa. I temi della colpa e della pena nella riflessione di S. Thomasso d'Aquino. Roma: Libreria de Santis, 1969. 168 pp.

3145. Paulo vera Urbano, F. De. "Aportación de S. Tomás a la doctrina de la liberdad religiosa." Revista Espanola de Derecho Canonico. Madrid. 31 (1975) 29-48.

3146. Peinador, A. Cursus brevior theologiae moralis ex D. Thomae principiis inconcussis. Madrid: Coculsa, 1950. xxiv-562 pp.

3147. Penelhum, Terence. "The Analysis of Faith in St. Thomas Aquinas." Religious Studies. London. 13 (1977) 133-54.

3148. Pesch, Otto H. "Die bleibende Bedeutung der thomanischen Tagend-lehre." Freiburger Zeitschrift fur Philosophie und Theologie. 21 (1974) 359-91.

     Before 1954, Divus Thomas. Freiburg.

3149. Pfürtner, S. Triebleben und sittliche Vollendung. Eine moral-psychologische Untersuchung nach Thomas von Aquin. Freiburg, Schw. Universitätsverlag, 1958. xxvi-366 pp.

3150. Pieper, Josef. Sull'amore. Brescia: Morcelliana, 1974. 216 pp.

3151. _____. Belief and Faith. New York: Pantheon, 1963.

3152. _____. Glück und Kontemplation. München: Kösel, 1957. 136 pp.

3153. _____. Happiness and Contemplation. Richard and Clara Winston, trs. New York: Pantheon, 1958.

3154. _____. The Four Cardinal Virtues. Notre Dame: University of Notre Dame Press, 1967.

3155. _____. Ueber die Gerechtigkeit. München: Kösel, 1953. 143 pp.

3156. _____. Justice. Lawrence Lynch, tr. New York: Pantheon, 1955.

3157. _____. Ueber die Klugheit. Olten: Summa-Verlag, 1947. 109 pp.

3158. _____. Prudence. Richard and Clara Winston, trs. New York: 1956.

3159 - 3173   MORAL THEOLOGY, VIRTUES, SINS

3159. _____. Zucht und Mass. Ueber die vierte Kardinaltugend.
München: Kösel, 1949. 125 pp.

3160. _____. Fortitude and Temperance. D. F. Coogan, tr. New
York: Pantheon Books, 1954.

3161. _____. Die Wirklichkeit und das Gute. Münster: Aschendorff,
1949.

3162. _____. Reality and the Good. Stella Lange, tr. Chicago:
Regnery, 1967. 94 pp.

3163. Pinckaers, S. "La structure de l'acte humain suivant s. Thomas."
Revue Thomistic 55 (1955) 393-412.

3164. Pinon, Antonio T. "Thomas Aquinas on Human and Christian
Liberty." Unitas. Manila. 47 (1974) 325-94.

3165. Pohier, Jacques-Marie. "Le moraliste chrétien d'aujorird' hui
doit-il lire s. Thomas?" Revue des Sciences Philosophiques et
Théologiques 58 (1974) 405-26.

3166. Prummer, D. M. Vademecum theologiae moralis in usum examinandorum
et confessariorum. E. M. Münch, ed. Ed. 6a. Friburgi Brisg: Herder,
1947. xxiii-586 pp.

3167. Pupi, Angelo. "La carità seondo Tommaso d'Aquin." Rivista di
Filosofia Neo-Scolastica. Milano. 68 (1976) 301-439, 585-609.

3168. Quelquejeu, Bernard. "De l'attention aux questions d'épistémologie
Trois questions sur l'article précédent de J.-M. Pohier." Revue des
Sciences Philosophiques et Théologiques. Le Saulchoir-Paris. 58
(1974) 427-43.

3169. Queralt, Antonio. "Todo acto de amor al projimo incluye necesari-
amente el amor de Dios? Investigación critica del pensamiento de S.
Tomás sobre la caridad." Gregorianum. Roma. 55 (1974) 273-317.

3170. Reilly, Richard. "Weakness of Will: The Thomistic Advance,"
in Thomas and Bonaventure (Symp) Proceedings of the American Catholic
Philosophical Association 198-207.

3171. Riley, L. J. The History, Nature and Use of Epikeia in Moral
Theology. Washington, D.C.: Catholic University of America Press,
1948.

3172. Ruiz De Santiago, Jaime. "Naturaleza e implicaciones del juicio
de conciencia errónea en las perspectivas de la reflexion moral."
Revista Filosofica. Mexico. 6 (1974) 187-213.

3173. Ryan, Louis A. "Charity and the Social Order." The Thomist
3 (1941) 539-63; 4 (1942) 70-120, 247-65.

MORAL THEOLOGY, VIRTUES, SINS   3174 - 3189

3174.   Santagada, Osvaldo D.   "Ley antigua y culto.   Los preceptos ceremoniales de la ley antigua en la Suma Theologica de s. Tomás de Aquino."   Teologia.   Buenos Aires.   11 (1974) 64-117.

3175.   Santamaria, A.   Quaenam sit solemnitas votorum iuxta s. Thomam. Manila: Univ. S. Thomae, 1949. 228 pp.

3176.   Saranyana, José Ignacio.   "Entre la tristeza y la esperanza. S. Tomás comenta el libro de Job," in Universidad de Navarra   (Symp) 329-61.

3177.   Schilling, O.   Grundriss der Moraltheologie.   2 Aufl.   Freiburgi: Herder, 1949.   xii-453 pp.

3178.   Schmaus, Michael.   "Das natürliche Sittengesetz und das Gesetz des Evangeliums," in Studi Tomistici   (Symp) 4, 222-38.

3179.   Scholz, Franz.   "Durch ethische Grenzsituation aufgeworfene Normenprobleme."   Theologisch-praktische Quartalschrift.   Stuttgart. 123 (1975) 341-55.

3180.   Sherman, J. E.   The Nature of Martyrdom.   A Dogmatic and Moral Analysis According to the Principles of St. Thomas Aquinas.   Paterson, N.J.: Paulist Press, 1942.

3181.   Simon, René.   Fonder la morale.   Dialectique de la foi et de la raison pratique.   Paris: Seuil, 1974.   224 pp.

3182.   Slipko, Tadeusz.   Etos chrześcijanski.   Zarys etyki ogolny. Krakow: Wyd. Apostolstwa Modlitwy, 1974.   390 pp.

3183.   Smith, Ignatius.   The Militant Christian Virtues."   The Thomist 4 (1942) 193-220.

3184.   Smith, Raymond.   "The Virtue of Docility."   The Thomist 15 (1952) 572-623.

3185.   Smurl, James F.   The Development of Saint Thomas' Thought in the Measure of Moral Rectitude: The Genesis of a Thomistic Formula. Washington, D.C.:   Catholic University of America (STD) Dissertation, 1963.   202 pp.

3186.   Solages, Bruno de.   La Théologie de la Guerre Juste.   Paris: Desclée de Brouwer, 1946.

3187.   Stevens, Gregory.   "The Disinterested Love of God: According to St. Thomas and Some of His Modern Interpreters."   The Thomist   16 (1953)   307-33; 497-542.

3188.   _____.   "Thomistic Morality and Openness to Being."   The Thomist   26 (1963) 67-99.

3189.   Sullivan, John J.   Commandment of Love: The First and Greatest

3190 - 3205 MORAL THEOLOGY, VIRTUES, SINS

of the Commandments Explained According to the Teachings of St. Thomas
Aquinas. New York: Vantage Press, 1956.

3190. Tanguerey, Adolphe. Theologia Moralis Fundamentalis. 2 vol.
reprint. Parisiis-Tornaci-Romae: Desclée, 1955.

3191. Tonneau, J. "Au seuil de la 'Secunda Pars? Morale et théologie,"
in Initiation théologique. tome 3: Théologie Morale, Paris: 1955.
13-36 pp.

3192. Tracy, David. "St. Thomas Aquinas and the Religious Dimension of
Experience: the Doctrine of Sin," in Thomas and Bonaventure (Sym)
Proceedings of the American Catholic Philosophical Association. 166-76.

3193. Vallery, Jacques. L'identité de la morale chrétienne. Louvain-
la-Neuve: Centre Cerfaux-Lefort, 1976. 195 pp.

3195. VanDer March, William H. M. "Ethics as a Key to Aquinas's
Theology." The Thomist 40 (1976) 535-54.

3196. _____. Toward a Christian Ethic. A Renewal in Moral Theology.
Westminster, MD: Newman Press, 1967. 176 pp.

3197. _____. "Toward a Renewal of the Theology of Marriage." The
Thomist 30 (1966) 307-42.

3198. Vella, Arthur G. Love Is Acceptance: A Psychological and
Theological Investigation of the Mind of St. Thomas Aquinas. Malta:
Malta University Press, 1959. xxii-200 pp.

3199. Völkl, R. Die Selbstliebe in der Heiligen Schrift und bei Thomas
von Aquin. München: Zink, 1956. xix-354 pp.

3200. Walgrave, Jan H. "'Geloven' bij Sint-Thomas van Aquino."
Tijdschrift voor Geestelijk Leven. Leuven. 30 (1974) 145-62.

3201. Wallace, William A. The Role of Demonstration in Moral Theology:
A Study of Methodology in St. Thomas Aquinas. Vol. II. Washington,
D.C.: Thomist Press, 1962.

3202. Watte, Pierre. Structures philosophiques du péché originel. S.
Augustin, S. Thomas, Kant. Gembloux: Duculot, 1974. 239 pp.

3203. Williams, C. De multiplici virtutum forma juxta doctrinam s.
Thomas Aquinatis, expositio synthetico-speculativa. Romae: Desclée,
1954. xv-159 pp.

3204. Wolf, José De. La justification de la foi chez s. Thomas d'Aquin
et le P. Rousselot. Bruxelles: Ed. Universelle; Paris: Desclée,
1946. 127 pp.

3205. Woroniecki, J. Katolicka Etyka Wychowawcza. 3 vols. Krakow:
Wydawnictwo Mariackie, (ca. 1946).

MORAL THEOLOGY, VIRTUES, SINS   3206 - 3222

3206. Wright, John H. The Order of the Universe in the Theology of St. Thomas Aquinas. Rome: Gregorianum, 1957. 233 pp.

3207. Xiberta, Bartholomaeus M. "Ontologica Dei Omnidominatio radix et causa ordinis moralis," in Thomitica Morum (Symp) 222-30 pp.

3208. Zagar, Janko. "Aquinas and the Social Teaching of the Church." The Thomist. Centenary Edition. 38 (1974) 826-55.

3209. Zalba, Marcelino. "Moralitas abortus in doctrina Sti. Thomae. Doctor Communis 25 (1972) 105-27.

3210. _____. "Nihil prolibet unius actus esse dous effectus. S.T. II-II, 64, 7. Namquid applicari potest principium in Abortu therapeutico?" in Tommaso d'Aquino (Symp Roma) 5, 557-68.

3211. _____. "Santo Tomás a favor del aborto terapeutico? Opinión de algunos moralistas del s. XIX." Doctor Communis. Roma. 27 (1974) 42-69.

3212. _____. Theologiae Moralis, Summa I: Theologia Moralis Fundamentalis. Madrid: Biblioteca de Autores Cristianos, 1952.

SPIRITUAL LIFE

3213. Aumann, Jordan. "Spiritual Theology in the Thomistic Tradition." Angelicum 51 (1974) 571-98.

3214. Boyle, Leonard E. "The Quodlibets of St. Thomas and Pastoral Care." The Thomist 38 (1974) 232-56.

3215. Chenu, M.-D. "Body and Body Politics in the Creation Spirituality of Thomas Aquinas." Listening 13 (1978) 214-32.

3216. Ciappi, Luigi. "S. Tommaso maestro di vita spirituale," in Voce della Coltura (Symp) 50-4.

3217. Curran, John W. "The Thomistic Concept of Devotion." The Thomist 2 (1940) 410-43, 546-80.

3218. DeLetter, P. "Merit and Prayer in the Life of Grace." The Thomist 19 (1956) 446-80.

3219. Dewan, Lawrence. "St. Thomas and the Ontology of Prayer." Divus Thomas. Piacenza. 77 (1974) 392-402.

3220. Gonzalez Alvarez, Angel. "Tomás de Aquino y las tres esferas del espiritu." Sapientia 33 (1978) 87-98.

3221. Greenstock, David L. "St. Thomas and Christian Perfection." The Thomist 13 (1950) 1-15.

3222. Hödl, Ludwig. "Das totale christliche leben im Zeugnis und

3223 - 3236   SPIRITUAL LIFE

Verstandnis des Thomas von Aquin." Rivista di Filosofia Neo-Scolastica.
Milano. 66 (1974) 552-70.

3223. Hoye, William J. Actualitas Omnium Entium. Man's Beatific Vision
of God as Apprehended by Thomas Aquinas. Meisenheim: Verlag Anton
Heim, 1975. 363 pp.

3224. Huerga, Alvaro. "La espiritualidad Tomista." Divinitas 18
(1974) 115-37.

3225. _____. Santo Tomás de Aquino, teologo de la vida cristiana.
Madrid: fundación Universitaria Espanola, 1974. 132 pp.

3226. Kinzel, Margaret M. The Metaphysical Basis of Certain Principles
of the Religious Life According to the Philosophy of St. Thomas Aquinas.
Washington, D.C.: Catholic University of America Dissertation, 1960.
135 pp.

3227. Kishi, Augustin Hideshi. Spiritual Consciousness in Zen from a
Thomistic Theological Point of View. Theologica Montis Regii, 46.
Nishinomiya-shi, Japan: Catholic Bishop's House of Osaka, 1966.
123 pp.

3228. Lecca, Jesus M. "La union a Cristo. Una interpretación del
pensamiento Paulino a traves...S. Tomas." Salesianum (Roma-Torino)
21 (1974) 7-26.

3229. Leclercq, Jean. "Tradition patristique et monastique dans
l'enseignement de la S.T. sur la vic concemplative," in Studi Tomistici.
I, 129-53.

3230. Lepargneur, Hubert. "Sao Tomás de Aquino e a mistica." A Ordem
1 (1974) 47-67.

3231. Lippini, Pietro. "La spiritualità di S. Tommaso." Bollettino
di S. Domenico (1974) 67-72.

3232. McCann, Leonard. The Doctrine of the Void as Propounded by Saint
John of the Cross Viewed in the Light of Thomistic Principled. Quebec:
Universite Laval Dissertation, 1974. 164 pp.

3233. Mahoney, John. "The Spirit and Community Discernment in Aquinas."
Heythrop Journal 14 (1973) 147-61.

3234. Mailhiot, M.-Bernard. "The Place of Religious Sentiment in
Saint Thomas." The Thomist 9 (1946) 22-65, 222-65.

3235. Pavlovic, Augustin. "Tomina misao o redovnickom zivotu," in
Zbornik (Symp) 155-74.

    Thomas' principles of the religious life.

3236. Pepler, C. The Basis of the Mysticism of St. Thomas. London:

SPIRITUAL LIFE   3237 - 3250

Blackfriars, 1953.

3237. Peter, Carl J. Participated Eternity in the Vision of God: A
Study of the Opinion of Thomas Aquinas and his Commentators on the
Duration of the Acts of Glory. Rome: Gregorian University Press, 1964.
308 pp.

3238. Petry, R. C. "The Social Character of Heavenly Beatitude."
The Thomist 7 (1944) 65-79.

3239. Pigna, Arnaldo. "Consigli, precetti e saatità secondo S. Tommaso."
Ephemerides Carmeliticae. Roma. 25 (1974) 318-76.

3240. Plé, Albert. Chastity and the Affective Life. New York: Herder
and Herder, 1966.

3241. Roberge, R.-Michel. "'Interius spirituale sacrificium' selon s.
Thomas d'Aquin." Laval Théologique et Philosophique. Québec. 27
(1972) 129-48.

3242. Robles, Laureano. "En torno a una vieja polemica: el 'Pugio
Fidei y Tomás de Aquino." Revista Espanola de Teologia. Madrid.
35 (1975) 21-42.

3243. Roy, L. Lumière et sagesse. La grace mystique dans la théologie
de s. Thomas d'Aquin. Montréal: Loyola, 1948. 299 pp.

3244. Schillebeeckx, Edouard. "Salut, redemption et emancipation,"
Tommaso d'Aquino...problemi fondamentali (Symp) 1974. 529-34.

3245. Scott, David A. Egocentrism and the Christian Life: A Study
of Thomas Aquinas and Martin Luther and an Attempted Reformation.
Princeton, N.J.: Princeton University Dissertation, 1968. 279 pp.

3246. Wainwright, William J. "Two Theories of Mysticism: Gilson and
Maritain." The Modern Schoolman 52 (1975) 405-26.

CHRISTOLOGY

3247. Bertetto, Domenico. "San Tommaso e la questione circa il fine
prossimo primario dell'Incarnazione," in Studi Tomistici (Symp)
2, 70-81.

3248. Biffi, Inos. "I 'misteri' di Cristo nel 'compendium Theologiae'
di S. Tomm so." Divinitas 18 (1974) 287-302.

3249. _____. I misteri della vita di Cristo in S. Tommaso d'Aquino.
Varese: Pont. Fac. Teol. di Milano, 1972. 77 pp.

3250. _____. "Misteri di Cristo, sacramenti, escatologia nello
'Scriptum super Sententiis' di S. Tommaso d'Aquino." Scuola Catholica.
Milano. 102 (1974) 569-623.

3251 - 3264   CHRISTOLOGY

3251. _____. "La teologia dei misteri di Cristo in S. Tommaso: dal
'De veritate' alle 'Collationes'," Studia Patavina.   Pavia.   21
(1974) 298-353.

3252. Bonnefoy, J. F. "La place du Christ dans le plan divin de la
création." Mélanges de Science Religieuse. Lille. 4 (1947) 258-84;
5 (1948) 40-62.

3253. Bouëssé, H. Le Sauveur du monde. Chambéry-Leysse: Collège
Théol. Domin; Paris: Office General du Livre, 1951-1953. 317, 838 pp.

        I. La place du Christ dans le plan de Dieu; II. Le mystère de
        l'Incarnation.

3254. Bracken, W. Jerome. Why Suffering in Redemption? A New Interpretation of the Theology of the Passion in the Summa Theologica, 3. 46-
49, by Thomas Aquinas. New York: Fordham University Dissertation,
1978. 440 pp.

3255. Carré, A. M. Le Christ de s. Thomas d'Aquin. Paris: Revue
des Jeunes, 1944. 30 pp.

3256. Catäo, Bernard. Salut et redemption chez s. Thomas d'Aquin:
l'acte sauveur du Christ. Paris: Aubier, 1965. 215 pp.

3257. Ciappi, Luigi. "Reconciliation and Renewal in the Mind of St.
Thomas." Boletin Eclesiastico de Filipinas. Manila. 48 (1974)
742-50.

3258. Corbin, Michel. "La parole devenue chair: Lecture de la premiere
question de la Tertia Pars de la Somme Théologique." Revue des Sciences
Philosophiques et Théologiques. Le Saulchoir-Paris. 62 (1978) 5-40.

3259. Crotty, Nicholas. "The Redemptive Role of Christ's Resurrection."
The Thomist 25 (1962) 54-106.

3260. Cuesta, Rogelio. "Valor sacramental de la humanidad de Cristo...
segun Tomás de Aquino." Escritos Del Vedat 2 (1972) 53-85.

3261. Degl'Innocenti, W. Cristo nella teologia di S. Tommaso. Rovigo:
Ist. Padano di Arti Grafiche, 1958. 160 pp.

3262. Diepen, H. "La psychologie humaine du Christ selon S. Thomas
d'Aquin." Revue Thomiste 50 (1950) 82-118.

3263. Febrer, Mateo. El concepto de persona y la unión hipostatica
revisión tomista del problema. Valenica: Editorcal F.E.D.A., 1951.
380 pp.

3264. Ferraro, Giuse pe. "L'ora di Cristo e della Chiesa nel Commento
di San Tommaso al quarto Vangelo," in Studi Tomistici (Symp) 2, 125-
55.

CHRISTOLOGY   3265 - 3281

3265. Galtier, P. De Incarnatione ac Redemptione. Ed. nova. Paris:
Beauchesne, 1947. viii-506 pp.

3266. Gier, G. De. La science infuse du Christ d'après s. Thomas
d'Aquin. Tilbourg: Bergmans, 1941. 152 pp.

3267. Gillon, Louis B. Christ and Moral Theology. Staten Island.
New York: Alba House, 1967. 144 pp.

3268. _____. "L'imitation du Christ et la morale de s. Thomas."
Angelicum 36 (1959) 263-86.

3269. Glorieux, Palémon. "La christologie du Compendium theologiae."
Sciences Ecclésiastiques. Montréal. 13 (1961) 7-34.

3270. Hoffmann, Adolf. "Die Proexistenz Christi nach Thomas," in
Thomas...Interpretation (Symp) 158-69.

3271. Innocenti, Umberto degl'. Cristo nella teologia de s. Tommaso.
Rovigo: Istituto Padano di arti grafiche, 1958. 159 pp.

3272. _____. Il problema della persona nel pensiero di San Tommaso.
Roma: Universita Lateranense, 1967. 249 pp.

3273. Kol, A. van. Christus' plaats in S. Thomas' moraalsysteem.
Roermond-Maaseik: Romen en Zonen, 1947. 143 pp.

3274. Langer, Hans-Dieter. "Zur hermeneutik theozentrischer und christ-
ologischer Aussagen bei Thomas von Aquin," in Thomas...Interpretation
(Symp) 16-47.

3275. LeClerc, Giovanni. La notion de personne dans l'incarnation selon
Saint Thomas. Quebec: Universite Laval Dissertation, 1943. 127 pp.

3276. Le Guillou, M. J. Christ and Chruch: A Theology of the Mystery.
Charles E. Schaldenbrand, tr. New York: Desclée, 1967. 375 pp.

3277. Leroy, Marie-Vincent. "Incarnation du Verbe et 'efficience divine,"
in Studi Tomistici (Symp) 2, 45-60.

3278. _____. "L'union selon l'hypostase d'après s. Thomas d'Aquin."
Revue Thomiste. Toulouse. 74 (1974) 205-43.

3279. Lonergan, Bernard J. De constitutione Christi ontologica et
psychologica. Romae: Gregorianum, 1964. 150 pp.

3280. _____. De verbo incarnato. Romae: Gregorianum, 1964.
598 pp.

3281. Loosen, J. "Unsere Verbindung mit Christus. Eine Prüfung ihrer
scholastischen Begrifflichkeit bei Thomas und Scotus." Scholastik 16
(1941) 53-78, 193-213.

3282. McMorrow, Kevin F. A Reevaluation of Christ's Special Religious Knowledge (Beata): An Historical Investigation of Thomas Aquinas and His Commentators. Washington, D.C.: Catholic University of America Dissertation (STD), 1969. 238 pp.

3283. Maritain, Jacques. De la grace et de l'humanité de Jésus. Bruges: Desclée, 1967.

   Translation by Joseph Evans, On the Grace and Humanity of Jesus. New York: Herder and Herder, 1969.

3284. Meegiren, Van. De causalitate instrumentali humanitates Christi juxta D. Thomae doctrinam expositio exegetica. Nijmegen: Dekker Van de Vegt, 1940. 189 pp.

3285. Mitterer, Alois. Geheimnisvoller, Leib. Christi nach St. Thomas von Aquin und nach Papst Pius XII. Wien: Herder, 1950.

3286. Mostert, Wilhelm. Menschwerdung. Eine historische und dogmatische Untersuchung über das Motiv der Inkarnation des Gottessohnes bei Thomas von Aquin. Tubingen: Mohr, 1978. vi-189 pp.

3287. Mullaney, Thomas U. "De la Taille and the Incarnation." The Thomist 22 (1959) 255-77.

3288. _____. "The Incarnation: de la Taille vs. Thomistic Tradition." The Thomist 17 (1954) 1-42.

3289. Nicolas, Jean-Hervé. "l'humanité perdue et retrouvée dans le Christ," in L'Anthropologie (Symp Fribourg) 1974. 161-80.

3290. _____. "Chronique de christologie." Revue Thomiste 51 (1951) 663-70.

3291. O'Connor, W. R. "Chalcedon, St. Thomas Aquinas, and the Concept of Person." American Ecclesiastical Review. Washington, D.C. 127 (1952) 194-99.

3292. O'Leary, Joseph M. The Development of the Doctrine of Saint Thomas Aquinas on the Passion and Death of Our Lord. Chicago: J. S. Paluch, 1952. 143 pp.

3293. Parente, P. L'Io di Cristo. 2a ed. Brescia: Morcelliana, 1955. 394 pp.

3294. Patfoort, A. L'Unité d'etre dans le Christ d'apres saint Thomas. Paris: Desclée, 1964. 326 pp.

3295. Philippe de la Trinité, O. C. D. "Un problème theologique: la conscience du Christ et sa divinité," in Studi Tomistici (Symp) 2, 61-9.

3296. Potvin, Thomas R. "Authority in the Church as Participation in the Authority of Christ According to St. Thomas," in Colloque (Ottawa

CHRISTOLOGY   3297 - 3311

Symp) 1974. 227-51.

3297. _____. The Theology of the Primacy of Christ According to
St. Thomas and Its Scriptural Foundations. Fribourg, Schw: University
Press, 1973. xxviii-327 pp.

3298. Prete, Benedetto. "Le apparizioni di Cristo risorto nell'ermeneutica di S. Tommaso (S.T. III, 55, 1-6)." Studia Patavina 21
(1974) 354-76.

3299. _____. "La tentazione di Geuś nella ermeneutica della Summa
Theologiae (III, q. 41)," in Sacra Doctrina (Symp) 429-55.

3300. Principe, Walter H. "St. Thomas on the Habitus-theory of the
Incarnation," in St. Thomas Aquinas (Symp Toronto) 1, 381-418.

3301. Re, Germano. Il Cristocentrismo della vita cristiana. Brescia:
Morcelliana, 1968. 462 pp.

3302. Rohoff, J. La sainteté substantielle du christ dans da théologie
seclastique. Fribourg (Suisse): Ed. Saint-Paul, 1952. xv-129 pp.

3303. Rossi, Bonifacio. "Severità e Bontà nella passione di Cristo
(S.T. III, 47, 3)." Ephemerides Carmeliticae. Roma. 25 (1974)
140-56.

3304. Sauras, Emilio. "Thomistic Soteriology and the Mystical Body."
The Thomist 15 (1952) 543-71.

3305. _____. "El valor salvador del misterio de la encarnación,"
in Tommas d'Aquino (Roma-Napoli Symp) 133-60.

3306. Schillebeeckx, Eduard. Jezus. Het verhaal van een levende.
Brugge: Emmaïis; Bloemendaal: Nelissen, 1974. 622 pp.

     Translated as Jezus: An Experiment in Christology. New York:
     Seabury, 1978. Generally critical of St. Thomas.

3307. Schontz, Jean. "La manifestation de la résurrection chez S.
Thomas (S.T. III, q. 55)," in Studi Tomistici (Symp) 2, 104-24.

3308. Schoof, T. M. "Jesus, Gods werktuig voor ons heil. Peiling
naar de theologische procedure van Thomas van Aquino." Tijdscrift voor
Theologie. Nijmegen. 14 (1974) 217-44.

3309. Schweizer, O. Person und hypostatische union bei Thomas von
Aquin. Freiburg (Schw): Universitäts verlag, 1957. xiv-124 pp.

3310. Seckler, Max. "Das Haupt aller Menschen. Zur Auslegung eines
Thomastextes," in Virtus Politica (Symp) 107-25.

3311. _____. "Das Haupt aller Menschen. Zur Auslegung eines
Thomastextes, (S.T. III, 8, 3)." Rivista di Filosofia Neo-Scolastica

66 (1974) 636-52.

3312. Speekenbrink, B. W. M. "De heilsbetekenis van Christus' ver-
rijzenis: formulering en betekenis van een verrijzenis-adagium vanaf
St. Augustinus tot St. Thomas," Studia Catholica 30 (1955) 1-24,
81-98, 161-84.

3313. Tschipke, Th. Die Menschheit Christi als Heilsorgan der Gottheit,
unter besonderer Berücksichtigung der Lehre de hl. Thomas. Freiburg:
Herder, 1940. xv-198 pp.

3314. Wiederkehr, Dietrich. "Spannungen in der Christologie des Thomas
von Aquin." Freiburger Zeitschrift für Philosophie und Theologie 21
(1974) 392-419.

    Before 1954, Divus Thomas, Freiburg.

3315. Wolfer, Stanley J. The Prayer of Christ According to the Teaching of St. Thomas Aquinas. Washington, D.C.: Catholic University of
America Dissertation, 1942.

3316. Wolfer, M. Vianney. The Prayer of Christ According to the Teaching of St. Thomas Aquinas. Washington, D.C.: Catholic University of
Ameirca Press, 1958. x-64 pp.

3317. Zimolag, Eduardus. Valor soteriologicus resurrectionis Christi
secundeem sanctum Thomam Aq. Romae: Dissertation Università a S.
Thoma in Urbe, 1972. 141 pp.

MARIOLOGY

3318. Anonymous. Thomistische Literaturschau. Die Lehre von der
Gottesmutter. Divus Thomas. Freiburg. 28 (1950) 37-9.

3319. _____. Virgo Immaculata. Acta Congressus mariologici-mariani
6 vols. Romae: Academia Mariana Internationalis, 1955.

3320. Bernard, R. Le mystère de Marie. 4 me éd. Paris: Desclée,
1954. 344 pp.

3321. Besutti, G. Bibliografia mariana (1950); Bibliografia mariana
(1950-1951). Roma: Marianum, 1950 et 1952. 96 et 164 pp.

3322. Eupizi, S. Il pensiero di Tommaso d'Aquino riguardo al dogma
della Immacolata Concezione. Varallo Sesia: Aldina, 1941. 168 pp.

3323. Fabro, Cornel o. "La partecipazione di Maria alla grazia di
Cristo secondo san Tommaso." Eclesia Mater (1974) 170-88.

3324. Feckes, C., ed. Die heilsgeschichthiche Stellvertretung der
Menschheit durch Maria. Paderborn: Schöningh, 1954. xi-395 pp.

3325. Giuliani, Samuele. "Prospetto tomistico di vita cristiana in

MARIOLOGY   3326 -3339

consonanza con la maternità divina di Maria." Revue d'Ascétique et de Mystique. Toulouse. 25 (1974) 33-47.

3326. Koninck, Charles de. Ego Sapientia...La Sagesse qui est Marie. Québec: Université Laval, 1943.

    English translation, "The Wisdom that Is Mary." The Thomist 6 (1943) 1-81.

3327. Kunicić, J. "De B. M. Mariae conceptione apud D. Thomam." Estudios Marianos. Madrid. 7 (1958) 105-24.

3328. Manteau-Bonamy, H.-M. Maternité divine et Incarnation. Etude historique et doctrinale de s. Thomas à nos jours. Paris: Vrin, 1949. xiii-253 pp.

3329. Mullaney, Thomas U. "Mary Immacualte in the Writings of St. Thomas." The Thomist 17 (1954) 433-68.

3330. _____. "The Mariology of St. Thomas." American Ecclesiastical Review 123 (1950) 188-201.

3331. O'Connor, E. D, ed. The Dogma of the Immaculate Conception. History and Significance. Notre Dame, IN: University of Notre Da e Press, 1958. xx-648 pp.

3332. Roschini, Gabriele M. "Cio che è stato scritto sulla Mariologia di S. Tommaso," in Studi Tomistici (Symp) 2, 159-95.

3333. _____. La mariologia di San Tommaso. Roma: Belardetti, 1950. 311 pp.

3334. Soria, Fernando. "San José en Mt 1-2 segùn los commentarios de S. Tomàs." Estudios Josefinos. Valladolid. 28 (1974) 177-97.

ECCLESIOLOGY AND LITURGY

3335. Carretero, M. Useros. 'Statuta Ecclesiae' y 'Sacramenta Ecclesiae' en la eclesiologia di S. Tomàs. Rome, 1962.

3336. Ciappi, Luigi. "Libertà di pensero e Magistero dell Chiesa in S. Tommaso d'Aquino." Doctor Communis. Roma. 28 (1975) 64-73.

3337. Congar, Yves M. J. "Aspects écclésiologiques de la quérelle entre mendicants et séculiers dans la seconde moitié du XIII siècle et le debut du XIV." Archives d'Histoire Doctrinale et Littéraire du Moyen Age. Paris. 28 (1961) 23-40.

3338. _____. "'Ecclesia' et 'populus (fidelis)' dnas l'ecclésiologie de s. Thomas," in St. Thomas Aquinas 1274-1974 (Symp) 159-74.

3339. _____. Esquisses du mystere de l'église. Paris: Cerf, 1941. 168 pp.

3340 - 3355   ECCLESIOLOGY AND LITURGY

3340. _____. "L'Idée de l'église chez s. Thomas d'Aquin." Revue des Sciences Philosophiques et Théologiques. Le Saulchoir-Paris. 29 (1940) 31-58.

3341. _____. "La noción de Iglesia según Santo Tomás," in Ensayos sobre el misterio de la ' Iglesia. Barcelona: Ed. Estela, 1961.

3342. _____. "St. Thomas and the Infallibility of the Papal Magisterium. Summa Theologiae, II-II, q. I, a. 10." The Thomist. Centenary of St. Thomas 1274-1974. 38 (1974) 81-105.

3343. _____. "Saint Thomas d'Aquin et l'esprit oecuménique." Freiburger Zeitschrift für Philosophie und Theologie 21 (1974) 331-46.

3344. _____. "Aquinoi Szent Tamás és az ökumenizmus szelleme." Mérleg 10 (1974) 347-64.

3345. _____. "St. Thomas Aquinas and the Spirit of Ecumenism." New Blackfriars. Oxford. 55 (1974) 196-209.

3346. _____. "Thomas von Aquin als. Vorläufer ökumenischen Geistes," Internationale Katholische Zeitschrift. Frankfurt, Germany. 3 (1974) 248-61.

3347. Darquennes, Achilles. De Juridische Structuur van de Kerk volgens Sint Thomas van Aquino. Leuven: N. V. de Vlaamse, 1949. 225 pp.

3348. Dolan, George E. The Distinction Between the Episcopate and the Presbyterate According to the Thomistic Opinion. Washington, D.C.: Catholic University of America Press, 1950. vii-173 pp.

3349. Fernandez, Pedro. "Liturgia y Teologia en la 'Summa' de sento Tomás." Angelicum 51 (1974) 383-418.

3350. _____. "Teologia de la liturgia en la Summa de S. Tomás." Ciencia Tomista, La. Salamenca. 101 (1974) 253-305.

3351. Fries, Albert. "Einfluss des Thomas auf liturgisches und homiletisches Schrifttum des 13, Jahrhunderts," in Thomas...Interpretation (Symp) 309-454.

3352. Gilson, Etienne, ed. The Church Speaks to the Modern World: The Social Teachings of Leo XIII. Garden City, N. Y.: Doubleday, 1954.

3353. Hayen, André. Saint Thomas d'Aquin et la vie de l'Eglise. Louvain: Publications Universitaieres, 1952. 109 pp.

3354. _____. Saint Thomas d'Aquin et la vie de l'Eglise. Louvain-Paris: Desclée, 1952. 105 pp.

3355. _____. San Tammaso d'Aquino e la vita della chiesa oggi.

ECCLESIOLOGY AND LITURGY   3356 - 3368

Milano: Ente Editoriale Dell'Universita, 1967. 151 pp.

3356. Horst, Ulrich. "Papst-Uafehlbarkeit-Konzil. Der papstliche
Primate nach Thomas von Aquin und der spanischen Dominikanertheologie
des 16 Jahrhunderts," in Thomas...Interpretation (Symp) 779-822.

3357. Journet. Ch. L'Eglise du Verbe Incarné. Essai de théologie
speculative. Sa structure interne et son unité catholigue. Paris:
Desclée, 1951. xlviii-1393 pp.

3358. Kuhn, Ulrich. "Thomas von Aquin-ökumenisches Erbe." Freiburger
Zeitschrift für Philosophie und Theologie 21 (1974) 347-58.

3359. Mahoney, John. "The Church and the Holy Spirit in Aquinas."
Heythrop Journal 15 (1974) 18-36.

3360. Malone, Edward F. Apostolic Zeal According to the Principle of
Saint Thomas Aquinas. Mary Knoll, New York: 1957. 179 pp.

3361. Manna, Salvatore. "S. Tommaso e gli Orientali," in La Voce
della Coltura (Symp) 44-9.

3362. Maritain, Jacques. De l'Eglise du Christ. Paris: Desclée,
1970.

        Translated by Jos. Evans, On the Church of Christ. Notre Dame:
        Notre Dame University Press, 1973.

3363. Mattia Spirito, Silvana di. "Il problema della povertà e della
perfezione religiose nell' ambito delle polemiche tra clero secolare e
ordini mendicanti," in Tommaso d'Aquino (Symp) 2, 49-58.

3364. Ménard, Etienne. La Tradition: révélation, écriture, Eglise,
selon s. Thomas d'Aquin. Bruges: Decclée, 1964. 272 pp.

3364A. Molley, Noel. "Hierarchy and Holiness: Aquinas on the Holiness
of the Episcopal State." The Thomist 39 (1975) 198-252.

3365. Nalpathamkalam, Caesarius. "Teaching and Preaching Orders
According to St. Thomas Aquinas." Laval Théologique et Philosophique
23 (1967) 269-305.

3366. _____. Religious Institutes Ordered to the Works of Preaching
and Teaching are Active and Not Mixed According to St. Thomas Aquinas.
Quebec: Universite Laval Dissertation, 1967. 242 pp.

3367. Nau, Paul. Le mystère du Corps et du Sang du Seigneur. La messe
d'après s. Thomas d'Aquin; son rite d'après l'histoire. Solesmes:
Editions de Solesmes, 1976. 215 pp.

3368. O'Neill, Colman. "St. Thomas on Membership of the Church."
The Thomist 27 (1963) 88-140.

3369 - 3382   ECCLESIOLOGY AND LITURGY

3369. Paris, G. M. Ad mentem S. Thomae Aq. Tractatus de Ecclesia
Christi... 2a ed. Melitae: J. Muscat, 1949. 224 pp.

3370. Roberge, Michel. La notion commune de sacrifice chez s. Thomas
d'Aquin exégèse analytique et discursive de la pensée de s. Thomas.
Québec: Universite Laval Dissertation, 1972. 353 pp.

3371. Saladino, Cayetano. La dignidad sacerdotal del nuevo pueblo de
Dois según la doctrina de Santo Tomás de Aquino. Buenos Aires, 1967.
57 pp.

3372. Sartori, Luigi. "S. Tommaso d'Aquino e l'ecumenismo." Studia
Patavina 21 (1974) 261-73.

3373. Stenger, Robert P. The Development of a Theology of the Episcopacy
from the Decretum of Gratian to the Writings of Saint Thomas Aquinas.
Washington, D.C.: Catholic University of America Dissertation, 1963.
221 pp.

3374. Stickler, Alfons M. "Papal Infallibility - A 13th c. Invention?
Reflections on a Recent Book (Cf. Tierney)." Catholic Historical
Review 60 (1974) 427-41.

3375. Stiegman, Emero. "Charism and Institution in Aquinas." The
Thomist 38 (1974) 723-33.

3376. Stolz, Wilhelm. Theologisch-dialektischer Personalismus und
kirkliche Einheit: apologetisch-kritische Studie zu Emil Brunners
Lehre von der Kireche im Lichte der thomistischen Theologie. Freiburg,
Schw: Universitatsverlag, 1953.

3377. Tierney, Brian. "On the History of Papal Infallibility. A
Discussion with Remigius Bäumer." Theologische Revue. Münster.
70 (1974) 185-94.

3378. Travers, Jean C. Valeur sociale de la liturgie d'apres s. Thomas
d'Aquin. Paris: Editions du Cerf, 1946. 331 pp.

3379. Ullmann, Walter. The Medieval Papacy, St. Thomas and Beyond.
London, W.C.I.: The Aquin Press, 1960. 31 pp.

     The Aquin Society of London, Aquinas Paper No. 35.

3380. Useros Carretero, Manuel. "Statuta ecclesiae" y "Sacramenta
Ecclesiae" en la eclesiologia de St. Thomás de Aquino. Roma: Univ.
Gregoriana, 1962. 359 pp.

3381. Walsh, Liam G. "Liturgy in the Theology of St. Thomas." The
Thomist 38 (1974) 557-83.

3382. Zuckerman, Charles. "Aquinas' Conception of the Papal Primacy in
Ecclesiastical Government." Archives d'Histoire Doctrinale et Litteraire du Moyen Age 48 (1973) 97-134.

SACRAMENTS

3383. Adam, A. Das Sakrament der Firumng nach Thomas von Aquin.
Freiburg I. Br: Herder, 1958. xii-132 pp.

3384. Blazquez, Pelegrin. De la causalidad dispositiva de los
sacramentos segun Sto. Tomás. Roma: Dissertation Universitá a S.
Thoma in Urbe, 1972. 90 pp.

3385. Brazzarola, B. La natura della grazia sacramentale nella
dottrina di S. Tommaso. Grottaferrata: Scuola Tip. Italo-Orientale
S. Nilo, 1941. 252 pp.

3386. Bro, B. "Notion métaphysique de tout et union Hypostatique."
Revue Thomiste 67 (1967) 29-62.

3387. Broglie, G. De. "La conception thomiste des deux finalités du
mariage." Doctor Communis 27 (1974) 3-41.

3388. Burr, David D. Ockham's Relation to Thomas Aquinas and John
Duns Scotus in His Formulation of the Doctrine of Real Presence.
Durham, N.C.: Duke University Dissertation, 1967. 248 pp.

3389. Ciappi, Luigi. "Il primato dell'Eucaristia in S. Tommaso e nel
magisterio della Chiesa." Revue d'Ascétique et de Mystique. Toulouse.
25 (1974) 19-32.

3390. Dittoe, John T. "Sacramental Incorporation into the Mystical
Body." The Thomist 9 (1946) 469-514.

3391. Frenay, Adolf D. The Spirituality of the Mass in the Light of
Thomistic Theology. St. Louis: B. Herder, 1953. x-296 pp.

3392. Frendo, George A. "St. Thomas Aquinas on the Sacrament of Faith."
Scientia. Malta. 37 (1974) 30-8.

3393. Garland, P. B. The Definition of Sacrament According to St.
Thomas. Ottawa: University of Ottawa Press, 1959. 116 pp.

3394. Gillis, James R. "The Case for Confirmation." The Thomist 10
(1947) 159-84.

3395. Heaney, Seamus Phelim, The Development of the Sacrament of Marriage From Anslem of Laon to Thomas Aquinas. Washington, D.C.: Catholic
University of America Dissertation, 1963. 175 pp.

3396. Joseph de Sainte-Marie, O. C. D. "L'Eucharistie, sacrement et
sacrifice du Christ et de l'Eglise. Developpements des perspectives
thomistes." Divinitas 18 (1974) 234-86, 396-436.

3397. Journet, Charles Cardinal. "Transubstatiation." The Thomist
Centenery Edition of St. Thomas Aquinas 1274-1974. 38 (1974) 735-
46.

3398. Kasten, Horst. Taufe und Rechtfertigung bei Thomas von Aquin
und Martin Luther. München: Kaiser, 1970. 298 pp.

3399. Larrabe, J. L. La Iglesia y el sacramento de la unción de los
enfermos. Salamanca: Sigueme, 1974. 216 pp.

3400. Lécuyer, J. "Les étapes de l'enseignement thomiste sur l'episcopat."
Revue Thomiste 57 (1957) 29-52.

3401. Lorca Navarrete, José F. "Il divorzio nella dottrina tomista."
Rivista di Letteratura e di Storia Ecclesiastica. Napoli. 6 (1974)
46-54.

3402. Loughery, Ann Francis A. The Eucharist. The End of All Sacraments
According to St. Thomas and His Contemporaries. Fribourg: Dissertation
University of Fribourg, 1972. xxii-421, xiv-201.

3403. McCormack, Stephen. "The Configuration of the Sacramental Character." The Thomist 7 (1944) 458-91.

3404. Marinelli, Francesco. Segno e Realtà. Studi di sacramentaria
tomista. Roma: Lateranum, 1977. 303 pp.

3405. Mascall, E. L. Corpus Christi. London: Longmans, 1953.
xii-188 pp.

3406. Meyer, Charles R. The Thomistic Concept of Justifying Contrition.
Mundelein, IL: Seminary of St. Mary of the Lake, 1949. 236 pp.

3407. Miralles, Antonio. "Gracia, fe y sacramentos," in Universidad de
Navarra (Symp) 299-328.

3408. Nicolas, Marie Joseph. "La doctrine de s. Thomas sur le sacerdoce,"
in Studi Tomistici (Symp) 2, 309-29.

3409. O'Neill, Colman. "The Role of the Recipient and Sacramental
Signification." The Thomist 21 (1958) 257-301, 508-40.

3410. Salado Martinez, Domingo M. "Sobre el valor antropologico del
tratado eucaristico de S. Tomás." Ciencia Tomista 101 (1974) 215-
51.

3411. Sauras, Emilio. "Ministerio y culto en el sacerdocio ministerial,"
in Universidad de Navarra (Symp) 145-72.

3412. _____. "El sacerdocio ministerial ev la doctrina de s. Tomás,"
in Studi Tomistici (Symp) 2, 329-43.

3413. Schillebeeckx, Eduard. De sacramentele heilseconomie; theologische
bezinning op S. Thomas' sacramentenleer... Antwerpen: H. Nelissen,
1952. x-689.

SACRAMENTS   3414 - 3415

3414. Strle, Anton. "Sv. Tomaz Akvinski, 'Doctor eucheristicus',"
Bogoslovni Vestnik. Lublin. 34 (1974) 33-50.

3415. Swierzawsky, Waclaw. "Faith Professed in the Eucharist. An
Interpration of St. Thomas Aquinas." Divus Thomas. Piacenza. 77
(1974) 373-91.

5

Relations:
Historical and Doctrinal

GENERAL RELATIONS

3416. Anderson, James F. "Is Scholastic Philosophy Philosophical?" Philosophy and Phenomenological Research 10 (1949-1950) 251-9.

3417. Anscombe, G. E. M. and Peter T. Geach. Three Philosophers: Aristotle, Aquinas, Frege. Oxford: Blackwell, 1961.

3418. Aranda Perez, Gonzalo. "Una norma del magisterio de la Iglesia para el estudio de la Sagrada Escritura: Santo Tomás de Aquino, maestro y guia." Scripta Theologica 6 (1974) 399-438.

3419. Bartolomei, Mario. "S. Tommaso espressione del rinnovamento evangelico ed ecclesiastico degli Ordini mendicanti," in Tommaso d' Aquino (Symp) 2, 9-15.

3420. Bastable, James D. "Thomism and Modern European Philosophy." Philosophical Studies I (1951) 3-16.

3421. Bernacer, José Luis. "Influence of St. Thomas Aquinas in the Salesian Society." Philippiniana Sacra. Manila. 9 (1974) 115-31.

3422. Blazquez, Niceto. "Santo Tomás de Aquino y la frustración intelectual," in Tommaso d'Aquino (Symp) 2, 21-7.

3423. Bogliolo, Luigi. Il problema della filosofia cristiana. Brescia: Morcelliana, 1959.

3424. _____. "Realismo moderno e realismo tomista," in Studi Tomistici (Symp Roma) 1974. 3, 33-66.

3425. Bourke, Vernon J. "Thomas Aquinas and Early British Ethics." Rivista di Filosofia neo-scolastica. Milano. 66 (1974) 818-40.

3426. _____ and Daniel O'Grady. "The Value of Modern Non-Thomistic Philosophy." Proceedings of the American Catholic Philosophical Assoc-

GENERAL RELATIONS   3427 - 3442

iation   17 (1941) 150-6.

3427. Brauer, Theodore. "Thomism and Modern Philosophy," in Thomistic Principles in a Catholic School. St. Louis: Herder, 1943. 69-108.

3428. Callus, Daniel A. "Les sources de s. Thomas. Etat de la question," in Aristote et s. Thomas d'Aquin (Symp) 93-174.

3429. Calvo, Salvador C. "Herejes e infieles en la obra de Santo Tomàs," in Tommaso d'Aquino (Symp) 2, 27-34.

3430. Cardone, Elsa. "S. Tommaso d'Aquino: oltre i limiti del pensiero medioevale," in Tommaso d'Aquino (Symp) 2, 438-441.

3431. Cenacchi, Giuseppe. Tomismo e Neotomismo a Ferrara. Roma: Pontifica Accademia Teologica Romana, 1975. 216 pp.

3432. Colish, Marcia L. "St. Thomas Aquinas in Historical Perspective: The Modern Period." Church History. Oreland, Pennsylvania. 34 (1975) 1-17.

3433. Crombie, A. C. Augustine to Galileo. The History of Science, A.D. 400-1650. Cambridge, Mass.: Harvard University Press, 1953.

3434. Danièlou, Jean. "Le pluralisme de la pensée." Sapienza 19 (1966) 11-23.

3435. Derisi, Octavio N. Filosofia moderna y filosofia tomista. Buenos Aires: Cultura Catolica, 1945.

3436. Dezza, Paolo. Alle origini del neotomismo. Milano: Bocca, 1940.

3437. Doriga, Enrique L., Mario A. Valdez, and José Leon Barandiaran. La aventura intelectual de Santo Tomàs. Lima: Universidad del Pacifico, 1975. 148 pp.

3438. Fabro, Cornelio. L'avventura della teologia progressista. Problemi Attuali. Milano: Rusconi, 1974. 324 pp.

3439. _____. "Le grandi correnti della scolastica e S. Tommaso d'Aquino." Rivista di Filosofia Neo-Scolastica. Milano. 31 (1940) 329-40.

3440. _____. Introduzione all'ateismo moderno. Roma: Studium, 1964.

3441. _____. Tomismo e pensiero moderno. Cathedra Sancti Thomae, 12. Roma: Università Lateranese, 1969.

3442. Froidurf, M. "La théologie protestante peut-elle se reclamer de Saint Thomas?" Revue des Sciences Philosophiques et Théologiques. 51 (1967) 53-61.

3443. Galimberti, Andrea. "Il realismo tomista e la filosofia moderna." in Tommaso d'Aquino (Symp) 2, 485-513.

3444. Giannini, Giorgio. Aspetti del tomismo. Roma: Città Nuova Editore, 1975. 265 pp.

3445. Gilson, Etienne. History of Christian Philosophy in the Middle Ages. New York: Random, 1955.

    Thomas Aquinas: 361-83 pp. Bibliography, 709-17 pp.

3446. _____. "On the Art of Misunderstanding Thomism." West Hartford, CT: St. Joseph College, 1966. 33-44.

    The McAuley Lectures, 1966.

3447. _____. "Science, Philosophy and Religious Wisdom." Proceedings of the American Catholic Philosophical Assoication 26 (1952) 5-13.

3448. Gonzalez, Marcos R. "Santo Tomás de Aquino, desde ayer y para siempre." Mikael (Symp) 18-41.

3449. Harvanek, Robert F. "The Church and Scholasticism," in Proceedings of the American Catholic Philosophical Association 32 (1958) 215-25.

3450. _____. "Philosophical Pluralism and Catholic Orthodoxy." Thought 25 (1950) 21-52.

3451. Hawkins, Denis J. B. A Sketch of Mediaeval Philosophy. New York: Sheed and Ward, 1947.

3452. Hayen, André. Thomas von Aquin Gestern und Heute. Frankfurt am Main: Verlag Josef Knecht-Carolus-d'rackerei, 1954. 144 pp.

3453. Kadowaki, Johannes K. "Ways of Knowing: A Buddhist-Thomist Dialogue." International Philosophical Quarterly. New York. 6 (1966) 574-95.

3454. Keynolen, Michael. "Le thomisme et la Chine," in Tommaso d'Aquino (Symp) 2, 360-6.

3455. Klocker, Harry R. Thomism and Modern Thought. New York: Appleton-Century-Crofts, 1962. 320 pp.

3456. Klubertanz, George P. "The Doctrine of St. Thomas and Modern Science." Sapientia Aquinatis. Romae: Officium Libri Catholici, 1955. 89-104.

3457. Korolec, Jerzy B. "Itinerarium S. Thomae Jana Sartoris," in Studia Sw. Tomasza (Symp Lublin) 185-94.

GENERAL RELATIONS   3458 - 3473

3458. Koudelka, Vladimir J. "S. Tommaso d'Aquino e la Boemia," in
in Tommaso d'Aquino (Symp) 2, 348-53.

3459. Kühn, Ulrich. "Thomas von Aquin und die evangelische Theologie, "
in Thomas von Aquin 1274-1974 (Symp München) 13-31.

3460. Lacombe, Olivier. "S. Thomas et les sagesses de l'Asie." in
Tommaso d'Aquino (Symp) 4, 357-63.

3461. Lepargneur, Hubert. "Sao Tomás e o futuro da teologia latino-
americana," in Presenca Filosofica (Symp) 161-73.

3462. Long, T. K. "Sankaracharya and Aquinas." Indian Eccesiastical
Studies. Bangalore. 13 (1974) 163-70.

3463. Lu, Matthias. "La diffusione delle opere di Tommaso d'Aquino
in Cina." in Tommaso d'Aquino (Symp) 2, 367-74.

3464. McLean, George F. "Philosophic Continuity and Thomism," in
Teaching Thomism Today (Symp) 3-38.

3465. Malevez, L. "Le croyant et le philosophe." Nouvelle Revue
Théologique. 82 (1960) 897-917.

3466. Marimón, Ricardo. "Santo Tomás, integrador de la futura filosofia
y teologia cristianas segun el magisterio de la Iglesia," in Tommaso
d'Aquino (Symp) 2, 540-51.

3467. Maurer, Armand A. "Revived Aristoteliansim and Thomistic Philosophy," in A History of Philosophical Systems. Vergilius Ferm, ed.
New York: Philosophical Library, 1950. 197-211.

3468. Mullaney, James V. "The Authority of St. Thomas in Philosophy."
Proceedings of the American Catholic Philosophical Association 25
(1951) 141-7.

3469. _____. "On Being Thomistic." Proceedings of the American
Catholic Philosophical Association 25 (151).

3470. Naud, André. Le Problème de la philosophie chrétienne: éléments
d'use solution thomiste. Montréal: Faculté de Theologie, 1960.

3471. Nédoncelle, Maurice. Is There a Christian Philosophy? I.
Trethowan, tr. Englewood Cliffs, N.J.: Hauthorn Books, 1960.

       Twentieth Century Ency. of Catholicism.

3472. Orlando, Pasquale. "L'accademia tomista a Napoli. Storia e
filosofia," in Saggi (Symp) 141-219.

3473. Paulo VI, (Pope). "S. Tomás de Aquino luminar da Igreja e do
mundo inteiro." Theologica. Braga. 9 (1974) 507-24.

3474 - 3489   GENERAL RELATIONS

3474. Pegis, Anton C. "The Middle Ages and Philosophy." Proceedings of the American Catholic Philosophical Association 21 (1946) 16-24.

3475. _____. "St. Thomas and the Origin of Creation," in Philosophy and the Modern Mind. Detroit, Mich: Sacred Heart Seminary, 1961. 49-65.

The Cardinal Mooney Lectures, 1960.

3476. Petruzzellis, Nicola. "Tommaso d'Aquino e le istanze del pensiero moderno." Rassegna di Scienze Filosofiche Napoli. 27 (1974) 173-93.

3477. Phelan, Gerald B. "St. Thomas and the Modern Mind." The Modern Schoolman 20 (1942) 37-47.

3478. Pires, Celestino. "Tomás de Aquino no diálogo das filosofias." Revista Portuguesa de Filosofia. Braga. 31 (1975) 169-78.

3479. Racette, Jean. Thomisme on pluralisme? Bruges: Desclée de Brouwer; Montréal: Editions Bellarmin, 1967. 127 pp.

3480. Rodriguez Cruz, Agueda Maria. "Presencia de S. Tomás de Aquino en las universidades hispano-americanas: periodo hispanico," in Tommaso d'Aquino (Symp) 2, 387-407.

3481. Salerno, Luigi. "Relazione, opposizione e dialettica nel pensiero moderno ed in Tommaso d'Aquino," in Tommaso d'Aquino (Symp) 2, 621-36.

3482. Sermoneta, Giuseppe. "Per una storia del tomismo ebraico," in Tommaso d'Aquino (Symp) 2, 354-9.

3483. Sertillanges, A.-D. Le christianisme et les philosophes. 2 vols. Paris: Aubier, 1941. 383, 591 pp.

3484. Shaughnessy, Thomas O. "La Theorie thomiste de la contingence chez Plotin et les penseurs arabes." Revue Philosophique de Louvain 65 (1967) 36-52.

3485. Siri, Giuseppe. "La via di San Tommaso d'Aquino." Divinitas (1974) 197-208.

3486. Smith, Ignatius. "Aquinas and Some American Freedoms." The New Scholasticism 21 (1947) 105-53.

3487. Staffa, Dino. "The Revival of Thomism." The Thomist 26 (1963) 129-37.

3488. Steelman, Edmund H. The Aristotelian Influence in Neo-Thomism. Philadelphia, PA: Temple University Dissertation, 1946.

3489. Steenberghen, Fernand van. "L'avenir du thomisme." Revue Philosophique de Louvain 54 (1956) 201-18.

GENERAL RELATIONS   3490 - 3502

3490. Swiezawski, Stefan. "Histoire de la pensée de s. Thomas.
Recherches polonaises," in Tommaso d'Aquino (Symp Roma-Napoli) 2,
335-47. 1976.

3491. _____. Zagadnienia historii filosofi. Warsaw, 1966.

   The Problematics of the History of Philosophy.

3492. _____. "Quelques déformations de la pensée de s. Thomas
dans la tradition thomiste," in Aquinas and Problems (Symp) 38-
54.

3493. Vanni Rovighi, Sofia. Studi di filosofia medioveale. Milano:
Vita e Pensiero, 1978. lxx-285; 311 pp.

   Vol. I: Da sant'Agostino al XII secolo. Vol. II: Secoli XIII
   e XIV.

3494. Wallace, William A. "Thomism and Modern Science: Relationships
Past, Present, and Future." The Thomist 32 (1968) 67-88.

3495. Wosiek, Barbara Rut. "Sw. Tomasz w srodowiskach mlodziezy
akademickiej i mlodij intelligencji polskiej okresu miedzywojennego,"
in Studia z Dziejow Mysli (Symp) 351-66.

GREEKS AND ROMANS

3496. Antoniotti, L. M.   "Boèce et s. Thomas d'Aquin: le miroir
ou le mitador de l'eternité: in speculo vel in specula?" in Tommaso
d'Aquino (Symp) I, 361-8.

3497. Arcoleo, S. "S. Tommaso e la 'Politica' di Aristotele," in
Tommaso d'Aquino (Symp) I, 149-55.

3498. Armstrong, A. Hilary. Aristotle, Plotinus and St. Thomas.
London: Blackgriars, 1946.

   Aquinas Papers, 4.

3499. Atherton, P. "The Validity of Thomas' interpretation of 'noesis
noeseos'," in Tommaso d'Aquino (Symp) I, 156-62.

3500. Beeretz, F. L. "Begriff und Aufgabe der 'Metaphysik' der Aristoteles," in Tommaso d'Aquino (Symp) I, 163-8.

3501. Bourke, Vernon J. "The Nicomachean Ethics and Thomas Aquinas."
St. Thomas Aquinas 1274-1974 (Symp) Toronto: Pontifical Institute of
Mediaveal Studies, 1974. I, 239-59.

   Commemorative Studies with foreword by Etienne Gilson, edited by
   Armand A. Maurer et al., 2 vols.

3502. Bourke, Vernon J. St. Thomas and the Greek Moralists. Milwaukee:

3503 - 3516   GREEKS AND ROMANS

Marquette Univeristy Press, 1947. 63 pp.

3503. Carmody, Michael F. References to Plato and the Platonici in the
"Summa Theologiae" of St. Thomas Aquinas. Pittsburgh: University of
Pittsburgh Dissertation, 1949. 108 pp.

3504. Cavarnos, Constantine. The Classical Theory of Relations. A
Study in the Metaphysics of Plato, Aristotle and Thomism. Belmont, MA:
Institute for Byzantine and Modern Greek Studies, 1975. 223 pp.

3505. Clarke, W. Norris. "Feature Review: St. Thomas and Platonism."
Thought 32 (1957) 437-44.

       Cf. R. J. Henle.

3506. _____. "The Platonic Heritage of Thomism." Review of Metaphysics 8 (1954) 105-24.

3507. Corvino, F. "I commenti al 'De anima' aristotelico di Alberto
Magno e di Tommaso d'Aquino," in Tommaso d'Aquino (Symp) I, 168-80.

3508. Deman, Thomas. "Remarques critiques de s. Thomas sur Aristote
interprète de Platon." Les Sciences philosophiques et théologiques
I (1941-1942) 133-48.

3509. _____. "Socrate dans l'oeuvre de s. Thomas d'Aquin." Revue
des Sciences Philosophiques et Théologiques. Le Saulchoir-Paris. 29
(1940) 177-205.

3510. Dobler, E. Nemesius von Emesa und die Psychologie des menschlichen
Aktes bei Thomas von Aquin. Dissertation, Werthenstein. Luzern. 1950.

3511. Doherty, Kevin F. "St. Thomas and the Pseudo-Dionysian Symbol
of Light." The New Scholasticism. Washington, D.C. 34 (1960) 170-
89.

3512. Dragona-Monachou, Myrto. "St. Thomas Aquinas' Prejudiced Silence
on Stoicism in 'Summa Theologica'," in Tommaso d'Aquino (Symp) 2,
43-8.

3513. Ducoin, Georges. "Saint Thomas, commentateur d'Aristote."
Archives de Philosophie. Paris. 20 (1957) 240-71, 392-445.

3514. _____. "Saint Thomas: Commentator of Aristotle." Philosophy
Today. I (1957) 53-5.

3515. Fabro, Cornelio. "Platonism, Neo-Platonism and Thomism: Conver-
gencies and Divergencies." The New Scholasticism 44 (1970) 69-100.

3516. Farre, Luis. Tomas de Aquino y el Neoplatonism. Esayo histórico
y doctrinal. La Plata: Universidad Nacional de la Plata Instituto de
Filosofia, 1966. 127 pp.

GREEKS AND ROMANS   3517 - 3532

3517. Faucon, Pierre. Aspects néo-platoniciens de la doctrine de s. Thomas d'Aquin. Lille: Université Lille; Paris: Champion, 1975. 714 pp.

3518. Flood, Patrick. Thomas Aquinas and Denis the Areopagiet on the Being of Creatures. Ottawa: Univeristy of Ottawa Dissertation, 1970.

3519. Garrigou-Lagrange, Reginald. "Thomas d'Aquin. IV. Saint Thomas commentateur d'Aristote." Dictionnaire de Théologie Catholique 15 (1946) 641-51.

3520. Geiger, L. B. Aristote et s. Thomas d'Aquin. Paris: Vrin, 1957.

3521. _____. "Saint Thomas et la métaphysique d'Aristote," in Aristote et saint Thomas d'Aquin. (Symp Louvain) 1957. 177-9.

3522. Gerstein, Louis C. On the Conception of God in the Philosophy of Maimodides and St. Thomas Aquinas. New York: New York University Dissertation, 1943.

3523. Giacon, Carlo. "S. Tommaso filosofo, continuatore critico de Aristotele." Doctor Communis 30 (1977) 303-15.

3524. Grosser, Elmer J. St. Thomas and the Politics of Aristotle. Toronto: University of Toronto Dissertation, 1954.

3525. Guzzo, Augusto. "San Tommaso e Bisanzio." Filosofia 28 (1977) 137-8.

3526. Heath, Thomas R. Aristotelian Influence in Thomistic Wisdom. A Comparative Study. Washington, D.C.: Catholic University of America Dissertation, 1957. 135 pp.

3527. _____. "More on St. Thomas' Exposition of Aristotle." The New Scholasticism 35 (1961) 525-6.

3528. _____. "St. Thomas and the Aristotelian Metaphysics." The New Scholasticism 34 (1960) 438-60.

3529. Henle, Robert J. Saint Thomas and Platonism. A Study of the Plato and Platonici Texts in the Writings of Saint Thomas. Hague: Nijhoff, 1956. xxiii-487 pp.

3530. Isaac, Jean. "Saint Thomas interprète des oeuvres d'Aristote." Scholastica. Roma. 9151. 353-64.

3531. Ivanka, A. von. "S. Thomas platonisant," in Tommaso d'Aquino (Symp) I, 236-58.

3532. Jaworski, Marian. Arystotelesowska i Tomistyczna. Teoria Przyczyny sprawczej na tle Pojecia Bytu. Lublin: Katolickeigo Uniw. Lubelskiego, 1958. 135 pp.

3533 - 3548   GREEKS AND ROMANS

3533. Knight, Samuel R. A Thomistic Interpretation of Aristotle's Theory of Universals. Charlottesville: University of Virginia Dissertation, 1954. 145 pp.

3534. Little, Arthur. The Platonic Heritage of Thomism. Dublin: Golden Eagle Books, 1950. 305 pp.

3535. Mansion, Auguste. Introduction à la physique aristotélicienne. 2me éd. Louvain: Institut Sup. de Philosophie, 1946.

3536. Minio-Paluello, Lorenzo. "Note sull' Aristotele medievale." Rivista di Filosofia Neoscolastica. Milano. 42 (1951) 222ff.

3537. Moreau, Joseph. "Le platonisme dans la 'Somme Théologique'," in Tommaso d'Aquino...problemi fondamentali (Symp) 1974. 45-59.

3538. Moutsopoulos, Evanghelos. "l'Hellénisation du thomisme au XIVe siécle," in Tommaso d'Aquino (Symp) 2, 324-8.

3539. Owens, Joseph. "Aquinas as Aristotelian Commentator," in St. Thomas Aquinas Comm. Studies. Toronto: PIMS, 1974. I, 213-38.

3540. Pegis, Anton C. "Cosmogony and Knowledge, I. St. Thomas and Plato." Thought 18 (143) 643-64.

3541. _____. "Cosmogony and Knowledge, II. The Dilemma of composite Essences." Thought 19 (1944) 269-90.

3542. _____. "Cosmogony and Knowledge. III. Between Thought and Being." Thought 20 (1945) 473-98.

3543. Pelster, Franz, "Neuere Forschungen über die Aristotelesiiber- setzungen des 12. und 13. Jahrhunderts." Gregorianum. Roma. 30 (1949) 46-77.

3544. Powers, William E. Plato's Philosophy of Participation with a Critical Evaluation According to the Basic Principles of Thomism. Chicago: Loyola University Dissertation, 1950. 176 pp.

3545. Rand, E. K. Cicero in the Courtroom of St. Thomas. Milwaukee: Marquette University Press, 1945. 115 pp.

3546. Rosso, Luciano. "Aspetti della problematica di Dionigi il mistico in S. Tommaso nel pensiero di Ceslao Pera. Aquinas 18 (1974) 403- 11.

3547. Steenberghen, Fernand van. Aristote en Occident. Les origines de l'aristotélisme parisien. Louvain: Publications Universitaires, 1946. 200 pp.

3548. _____. Aristotle in the West. L. Johnston, tr. Louvain: Nauwelaerts, 1955.

GREEKS AND ROMANS   3549 - 3562

3549. Strasser, Michael William. Saint Thomas' Critique of Platonism in the Liber de Causis. Toronto: University of Toronto Dissertation, 1963.

3550. Thiry, A. Saint Thomas et la morale d'Aristote. Louvain: Nauwelaerts, 1957.

3551. Turner, Walter H. "St. Thomas's Exposition of Aristotle: A Rejoinder." The New Scholasticism. Washington, D.C. 35 (1961) 210-24.

3552. Tyn, Thomas. "Prochoros und Demetrios Kydones. Der byzantinische Thomismus des 14 Jahrhunderts," in Thomas...Interpretation (Symp) 837-912.

3553. Vansteenkiste, Clemente. "Cicerone nell'opera di s. Tommaso." Angelicum 36 (1959) 343-82.

3554. Verbeke, Gérard. "Saint Thomas et le stoicisme," in Antike und Orient im Mittelalter. Berlin: Miscellanea Mediaevalia, 1962. 48-68.

3555. _____., ed. Thémistius. Commentaire sur le traité de l'ame d'Aristote. Traduction de Guillaume de Moerbeke. Louvain: Publications Universitaires; Paris: Béatrice-Nauwelaerts, 1957. xcvii-320 pp.

With a study on the use of the Commentary in the work of St. Thomas.

3556. Villey, Michel. "Bible et philosophie gréco-romaine de s. Thomas au droit moderne." Archives de Philosophie du Droit. Paris. 18 (1973) 27-57.

3557. Weisheipl, James. "Thomas' Evaluation of Plato and Aristotle." The New Scholasticism. Aquinas Septicent. (Symp) 1974. 100-24.

3558. Yardan, John. "Aristotelianism, Pegis, and the Summa contra Gentiles." The New Scholasticism. Washington, D.C.: 35 (1961) 369-72.

ISLAMIC THOUGHT

3559. Anawati, G. C. et Beaurecueil, P. de. "Une preuve de l'existence de Dieu chez Ghazali et s. Thomas d'Aquin," in MIDEO (1956) 207-14.

3560. Answati, Georges C. "S. Thomas d'Aquin dans le monde arabe moderne et contemporain," in Tommaso d'Aquino (Symp) I, 268-83.

3561. _____. "Saint Thomas d'Aquin et la métaphysique d'Avicenne," in St. Thomas Aq. (Toronto) 1974. I, 449-65.

3562. Asin Palacios, M. Huellas del Islam, Santo Tomas de Aquino, Pascal, san Juan de la Cruz. Madrid: Espasa-Calpe, 1941. 310 pp.

3563 - 3578   ISLAMIC THOUGHT

3563. Casciaro, José Maria. El dialogo teológico de santo Tomás con musulmanes y judios. El tema de la profecia y la revelacion. Madrid: Inst. "Francisco Suarez," 1969. 259 pp.

3564. Chisaka, Y. "S. Thomas d'Aquin et Avicenne (sur les interprétations de l'etre et de l'essence), in Tommaso d'Aquino (Symp) I, 284-95.

3565. Colish, M. L. "Avicenna's Theory of Efficient Causation and Its Influence on St. Thomas Aquinas," in Tommaso d'Aquin (Symp) I, 296-306.

3566. Contenson, P. M. de. "S. Thomas et l'avicennisme latin." Revue des Sciences Philosophiques et Théologiques. Le Saulchoir-Paris. 43 (1958) 3-31.

3567. Cruz-Hernandez, M. "Santo Tomás y la primera recensión de Averroes por los latinos," in Tommaso d'Aquino (Symp) I, 307-24.

3568. Dondaine, H.-F. "A propos d'Avicenne et de s. Thomas: de la causalité dispositive à la causalité instrumentale." Revue Thomiste 59 (1951) 441-53.

3569. Fakhry, Majid. Islamic Occasionalism and Its Critique by Averroes and Aquinas. London: Allen and Unwin, 1958. 220 pp.

3570. Flynn, J. G. "St. Thomas Aquinas' Use of the Arab Philosophers on the Nature of God." Al -Mushir. Rawalpindi. 16 (1974) 278-86.

    Also in Tommaso d'Aquino (Symp) I, 325-33.

3571. Gardet, Louis. "La connaissance que Thomas d'Aquin put avoir du monde islamique," in Aquinas and Problems (Symp) 139-49.

3572. _____. "St. Thomas et ses prédécesseurs arabes," in St. Thomas Aquinas (Symp Toronto) 1974. I, 419-48.

3573. Giacon, Carlo. "In tema di dipendenze di S. Tommaso da Avicenna," in L'Homme et son destin (Symp) 535-44.

3574. Gomez Nogales, Salvador. "Los arabes en la vida y en la doctrina de S. Thomás," in Tommaso d'Aquino (Symp) I, 334-40.

3575. _____. "Saint Thomas. Averroès et l'averroisme," in Aquinas and Problems (Symp) 161-77.

3576. _____. "Filosofia musulmana y humanismo integral de santo Tomás." Miscelanea Comillas. Santander. 47-48 (1967) 229-57.

3577. _____. "Santo Tomás y los arabes. Bibliografia." Miscelanea Comillas 63 (1975) 205-50.

3578. Hana, G. C. "Reviser l'abord thomiste d'Averroes?" in Tommaso d'Aquino (Symp) I, 341-6.

ISLAMIC THOUGHT   3579 - 3593

3579. Judy, A. G. The Use of Avicenna's Metaphysics VIII, 4 in the
'Summa contra Gentiles.' Toronto: Pontifical Institute of Medieval
Studies Dissertation, 1969.

3580. Kainz, Howard P. "The Multiplicity and Individuality of Intellects:
St. Thomas' Reaction to Averroes." Divus Thomas. Piacenza. 74 (1971)
155-79.

3581. Lobato, Abelardo. Avicena y Santo Tomás en la teoria del cono-
cimento. Granada: 1957.

3582. Lohmann, Johannes. "Saint Thomas et les Arabes (Structures
linguistiques et formes de pensée). Revue Philosophique de Louvain.
Louvain, Belg. 74 (1976) 30-44.

3583. Mazzarella, Pasquale. "La critica di S. Tommaso all'Averroismo
gnoseologico." Rivista di Filosofia Neoscolastica. Milano. 66 (1974)
246-83.

3584. Nader, Albert N. "L'influence de la pensée musulmane sur la
philosophie de s. Thomas d'Aquin," in Tommaso d'Aquino (Symp) I,
346-51.

3585. _____. "L'Influence de la pensée musulmane sur la philosophie
de s. Thomas d'Aquin," in Tommaso d'Aquino...problemi fondamentali
(Symp) 1974. 61-8.

3586. O'Shaughnessy, Thomas. "St. Thomas and Avicenna on the Nature of
the One." Gregorianum 41 (1960) 665-79.

3587. _____. "St. Thomas' Changing Estimate of Avicenna's Teaching
on Existence as an Accident." The Modern Schoolman. St. Louis. 36
(1958-1959) 245-60.

3588. Raeymaeker, Louis De. "La esencia avicenista y la esencia tomista."
Sapientia 11 (1956) 154-65.

3589. _____. "L'Etre selon Avicenne et selon s. Thomas d'Aquin,"
in Avicenna Commemoration Volume ed. V. Courtois. Calcutta: 1956.
119-31.

3590. Renzi, Stanislao "Una fonte della tertia via: Avicenna."
Freiburger Zeitschrift für Philosophie und Theologie 13-14 (1966-
1967) 283-93.

3591. Riet, Simone Van. "La Somme contre les Gentils et la polémique
islamo-chrétienne," in Aquinas and Problems (Symp) 150-60.

3592. Rousseau, Mary F. "Avicenna and Aquinas on Incorruptibility."
The New Scholasticism 51 (1977) 524-36.

3593. Saadé, I. "El pensamiento arabe en el siglo de Santo Tomás
de Aquino," in Tommaso d'Aquino (Symp) I, 352-60.

3594. Shanab, Robert E. Abu. "Ghazali and Aquinas on Causation." The Monist. Los Gatos, California. 58 (1974) 140-50.

3595. _____ . "Points of Encounter Between Al-Ghazali and St. Thomas Aquinas," in Tommaso d'Aquino (Symp) I, 261-8.

3596. Vansteenkiste, C. M. J. "Autori Arabi e Giudei nell'opera di San Tommaso." Angelicum 37 (1960) 336-401.

3597. _____ . "Avicennacitaten bij S. Thomas." Tijdschrift voor Philosophie 15 (1953) 457-507.

3598. Waltz, J. "Muhammad and the Muslims in St. Thomas Aquinas." The Muslim World. Hartford, CT. 66 (1976) 81-95.

3599. Weisheipl, James A. "Motion in a Void: Aquinas and Averroes," in St. Thomas Aquinas 1274-1974 (Symp) I, 467-88.

3600. Wrobel, J. "Wplyw Metafizyki Awicenny i Ksiegi o przyczynach na filosofie Tomasza z Akwinu." Studia Philosophiae Christianae 10 (1974) 225-30.

    Influence of Avicenna on the philosophy of St. Thomas.

3601. Zedler, Beatrice H. "Saint Thomas and Avicenna in the 'De potentia Dei'," Traditio. New York. 6 (1948) 105-59.

3602. _____ . St. Thomas Critique of Avicennism in the 'De Potentia Dei.' New York: Fordham University Dissertation, 1947.

3603. _____ . "St. Thomas, Interpreter of Avicenna." The Modern Schoolman 33 (1955) 1-18.

JUDAIC THOUGHT

3604. Bertola, Ermenegildo. "Mosè Maimonide e Tommaso d'Aquino di fronte alla prova razionale della esistenza di Dio," in Aquinas and Problems (Symp) 92-100

3605. Brunner, F. Platonisme et aristotélisme. La critique d'Ibn Gabirol par s. Thomas d'Aquin. Louvain: Publications Universitaires, 1965.

3606. Catao, Francesco. "Thomas d'Aquin lit Maimonide." Sidic. Revue du service international de documentation judéo-chrétienne. Roma. 7 (1974) 4-17.

3607. Dienstag, Jacob I. "St. Thomas Aquinas in Maimonidian Scholarship." The Monist 58 (1974) 104-18.

3608. Elders, Léon "Les rapports entre la doctrine de la prophétie en s. Thomas et le 'Guide des 'egarès' de Maimonide." Divus Thomas. Piacenza. 78 (1975) 449-56.

JUDAIC THOUGHT   3609 - 3622

3609. Fox, M. "Maimonides and Aquinas on Natural Law." Dine' Israel
3 (1972) 5-27.

3610. Greive, Hermann. "Thomas von Aquin in der philosophisch-theol-
ogischen Diskussion des Judentums," in Thomas...Interpretation (Symp
Mainz) 913-32.

3611. Pinès, Shlomo. "Saint Thomas et la pensée juive médiévale:
quelques notations," in Aquinas and Problems (Symp) 118-29.

3612. _____. Scholasticism After Thomas Aquinas and the Teaching
of Hasdai Crescas and His Predecessors. Jerusalem: Central Press,
The Israel Academy of Sciencws and Humanities. 101 pp.

CHURCH FATHERS, GREEK AND LATIN

3613. Boyer, Charles. "S. Thomas et s. Augustin," in Studi Tomistici
(Symp Roma) 1974. I, 72-82.

3614. Burunat, Julio. Thomas Aquinas' Use of Augustine's Work: A
Study in Development. New York: Fordham University Dissertation, 1973.
380 pp.

3615. Chroust, Anton-Hermann. "The Meaning of Some Quotations from
St. Augustine in the Summa Theologica of St. Thomas." The Modern
Schoolman 27 (1950) 280-96.

3616. Dobler, E. Nemesius von Emesa und Die Psychologie des menschlichen
Aktes bei Thomas von Aquin. Werthenstein: Sendbote der hlg. Familie,
1950. 144 pp.

3617. Dondaine, Antoine. "La Documentation patristique de s. Thomas."
Revue des Sciences Philosophiques et Théologiques. Le Saulchoir-Paris.
29 (1940) 326-7.

3618. Dondaine, H.-F. "Note sur la documentation patristique de s.
Thomas à Paris en 1270." Revue des Sciences Philosophique et Théologiques
47 (1963) 403ff.

3619. Faucon de Boylesve, P. "Aspects augustiniens de la noétique
thomiste," in Tommaso d'Aquino (Symp) I, 222-31.

3620. Gates, John F. The Attempted Reconciliation of Augustine and
Aquinas in Gilson. Philadelphia: Temple University Dissertation,
1951.

3621. Geenen, G. "Thomas d'Aquin. VII. Saint Thomas et les Pères."
Dict. de Théol. Cath. 15 (1946) 738-61.

3622. Gherardini, Brunero. "La tradizione Agostiniana nella sintesi
Tomista," in Studi Tomistici (Symp Roma) 1974. I, 83-108.

3623 - 3636   CHURCH FATHERS, GREEK & LATIN

3623. Giannini, Giorgio. "Riflessi della concordanza tra S. Agostino
e S. Tommaso nel pensiero moderno," in Tommaso d'Aquino (Symp)
I, 231-8.

3624. Guzzo, Augusto. Agostino e Tommaso. Torino: Ed. di Filosofia,
1958. viii-276 pp.

3625. Halligan, Nicholas. "Partistic Schools in the Summa." The
Thomist. Washington, D.C. 7 (1944) 271-323, 505-43.

3626. Hulsboch, A. "Cyrillus von Alexandrie en Thomas van Aquino over
de hypostatische vereniging." Werkgenootschap van katholieke theologen
in Nederland. Hilversum. (1951) 156-78.

3627. Linage, A. "Santo Tomàs y la vida y la regla de San Benito,"
in Tommaso d'Aquino (Symp) I, 384-92.

3628. Masnovo, Amato. S. Agostino e S. Tommaso: concordanze e sviluppi.
2 ed. riv. Milano: Vita e pensiero, 1950. 200 pp.

3629. Mitterer, Alois. Die Entwicklungslehre Augustins im Vergleich mit
dem Weltbild des hl. Thomas von Aquin und dem der Gegenwart. Wien-
Freiburg: Herder, 1956. 348 pp.

3630. Pegis, Anton C. At the Origins of the Thomistic Notion of Man.
New York: Macmillan, 1963. 82 pp.

     St. Augustine Lecture, 1962.

3631. Phelan, Gerald B. Some Illustrations of St. Thomas' Development
of the Wisdom of St. Augustine. Chicago: The Argus Press, 1946.
57 pp.

     The Mu Nu Sigma Lecture in 1946 at Mundelein College.

3632. Pouliot, V.-M. "Identification du 'per se potestativum' de
Thomas d'Aquin avec le 'to autexousion' de Nemesius d'Emesa." Studies
of Medieval Thought. Tokyo. 2 (1959) 139-56.

3633. Principe, Walter H. "Thomas Aquinas' Principles for Interpretation
of Patristic Texts," in Studies in Medieval Culture, 7-8. Western
Michigan University, Kalamazoo. 1976. 111-22.

3634. Riga, Peter J. "The Act of Faith in Augustine and Aquinas."
The Thomist 35 (1971) 143-74.

3635. Siglari, A. "Una fonte di Tommaso d'Aquino: Goivanni di Damasco,"
in Tommaso d'Aquino (Symp) I, 384-92.

3636. Toner, N. "La sapienza nel pensiero agostiniano e tomistico,"
in Tommaso d'Aquino (Symp) I, 248-56.

CHURCH FATHERS, GREEK AND LATIN   3637 - 3650

3637. Vansteenkiste, Clement. (S. Bernard, citations par S. Thomas), in Rassegna di Letterature Tomistica (Supplemento 1974), 10 (1978) 35-47.

3638. _____. "S. Tommaso e S. Ilario di Poitiers," in Studi Tomistici (Symp Roma) 1974. I, 65-71.

3639. Verbeke, Gérard. "Fatalism and Freedom According to Nemesius and Thomas Aquinas," in St. Thomas Aquinas 1274-1974 (Symp) I, 283-314.

FIFTH TO TWELFTH CENTURIES

3640. Brecher, Bob. "Aquinas On Anselm." Philosophical Studies. Dublin, Ireland. 23 (1975) 63-6.

3641. Chenu, M.-D. La théologie au douzième siècle. Paris: Vrin, 1957.

3642. _____. Nature, Man, and Society in the Twelfth Century. Essays on New Theological Perspectives in the Latin West. Selected, ed. and trans. by Jerome Taylor and Lester K. Little. Chicago: University of Chicago Press, 1968. xxii-362 pp.

3643. Cosgrove, Matthew R. "Thomas Aquinas on Anselm's Argument." Review of Metaphysics. Commem. Issue, Thomas Aquinas. 27 (1974) 513-30.

3644. Gingjan, Fr. Discretio. Les origines patristiques et monastiques de la doctrine sur la prudence chez s. Thomas d'Aquin. Assen: Van Gorcum, 1967. 272 pp.

3645. Gélinas, Y. D. "La critique de Thomas d'Aquin sur l'éxégese de Joachim de Flore," in Tommaso d'Aquino (Symp) I, 368-76.

3646. Gomez Nogales, Salvador. "Audacia de S. Tomás en la asimilación de pensamiento heterodoxo de su epoca." Revista Portuguesa de Filosofia 30 (1974) 185-204.

3647. Landgraf, A.-M. Einführung in die Geschichte der theologischen Literatur der Frühscholastik... Regensburg: Gregorius Verlag, 1948. 143 pp.

3648. McInerny, Ralph. "Boethius and St. Thomas Aquinas." Rivista di Filosofia Neoscolastica 66 (1974) 219-45.

3649. Masiello, Ralph J. "Reason and Faith in Richard of St. Victor and St. Thomas. The New Scholasticism 48 (1974) 233-42.

3650. O'Grady, Daniel. "The Value of the Historical Study of Some Types of Pre-Thomistic Christian Philosophy." Proceedings of the American Catholic Philosophical Association. Washington, D.C. 17 (1941) 156-9.

3651 - 3665   FIFTY TO TWELFTH CENTURIES

3651. Palazzini, Pietro. "Una citazione errata di S. Tommaso, il 'Privilegium Romanae Ecclesiae' e la missione milanese di S. Pier Damiani," in Studi Tomistici (Symp Roma) 1974. I, 154-75.

3652. Thomas, R. "Die Präfiguration thomistischen Denkens bei Petrus Lombardus," in Tomaso d'Aquino (Symp) I, 393-98.

3653. Vogel, Cornelia J. De. "Some Reflections on the Liber de Causis." Vivarium 4 (1966) 67-82.

3654. Weigand, Rudolf. "Die Vorläufer der thomistischen Naturrechtslehre bei den Legisten und Dekretisten des 12 a. 13 Jahrhunderts," in Studi Tomistici (Symp Roma) 1974. 4, 269-97.

THIRTEENTH CENTURY

3655. Alverny, Marie-Thérèse d'. "Un adversaire de Saint Thomas: Petrus Iohannis Olivi," in St. Th mas Aquinas 1274-1974 (Symp) 2, 179-218.

3656. Arrighi, Gino. "Le matematiche nel secolo di Tommaso d'Aquino." in Tommaso d'Aquino (Symp Roma) 9, 87-91.

3657. Baget-Bozzo, Gianni. "Modello trinitario e modello cristologico nella teologia della storia: Gioacchino da Fiore e Tommaso d'Aquino." Renovatio 9 (1974) 39-50.

3658. Balič, Carlo. "Il decreto del 7 marzo 1277 del vescovo di Parigi e l'origine dello scotismo," in Tommaso d'Aquino (Symp) 2, 279-85.

3659. Bazàn, Bernardo Carlos. "Le dialogue philosophique entre Siger de Brabant et Thomas d'Aquin. A propos de...E.H. Wéber." Revue Philosophique de Louvain 72 (1974) 53-155.

3660. Benz, E. "Joachim-Studien III. Thomas von Aquin und Joachim de Fiore," in Joachim of Fiore (Symp) 1975. 387-451.

3661. Bolzan, J. E. "Santo Tomàs y los capitulos de la orden de los hermanos predicadores, 1278-1370." Sapienza. Napoli. 29 (1974) 263-78.

3662. Bougerol, J. G. et alü. "Confronti tra S. Tommaso e S. Bonaventura." Sapienza 27 (1974) 458-80.

3663. Boyle, Leonard E. "The Summa Confessorum of John of Freiburg and the Popularization of the Moral Teaching of St. Thomas and of Some of His Contemporaries," in St. Thomas Aquinas 1274-1974 (Symp) 2, 245-68.

3664. Brady, Ignatius. "Background to the Condemnation of 1270: Master William of Baglione, O.F.M." Franciscan Studies. St. Bonaventure, New York. 30 (1970) 5-48.

3665. Bukowski, Thomas P. et Bertrand Dumoulin. "L'influence de Thomas

THIRTEENTH CENTURY   3666 - 3678

d'Aquin sur Boèce de Dacie." Classica et Mediaevalia. Copenhagen. 30 (1969) 482-7.

Also in Revue des Sciences Philosophiques et Théologiques. Le Saulchoir-Paris. 57 (1973) 627-31.

3666. Buonaiuti, E. "Gioacchimo de Fiore, San Bonaventura, San Tommaso," in Joachim of Fiore (Symp) 1975. 377-85.

3667. Burbach, Maur. "Early Dominican and Franciscan Legislation Regarding St. Thomas." Mediaeval Studies. Toronto. 4 (1942) 141ff.

3668. Callus, Daniel A. The Condemnation of St. Thomas At Oxford. Oxford: Blackfriars, 1946; Westminster, MD: Newman, 1946. 38 pp.

Aquinas Papers, 5.

3669. _____. "The Philosophy of St. Bonaventure and of St. Thomas." Blackfriars 21 (1940) 151-64, 249-67.

3670. _____. "The Problem of the Unity of Form and Richard Knapwell, O.P." in Mélanges offerts à Etienne Gilson (Symp) 150ff.

3671. Cappelluti, G. "Fra Pietro di Andria e i segretari di s. Tommaso," in Tomismo e Neotomismo (Symp) I, 151-66.

3672. Cousins, Ewert H. "St. Bonaventure, St. Thomas, and the Movement of Thought in the 13th Century." International Philosophical Quarterly 14 (1974) 393-409.

3673. Crisciani, Chiara. "I Domenicani e la tradizione alchemica nel duecento," in Tommaso d'Aquino (Symp) 2, 35-42.

3674. Crowley, Theodore. "John Peckham, O.F.M., Archbiship of Canterbury, versus the New Aristotelianism." Bulletin of the John Rylands Library Manchester, England. 33 (1950) 242-55.

3675. Dowd, J. "Matthew of Aquasparta's De Productione Rerum and its Relation to St. Thomas Aquinas and Bonaventure." Franciscan Studies 34 (1974) 34-73.

3676. Fortin, Ernest L. and Peter D. O'Neill, trs. "Condemnation of 219 Propositions," (Paris A.D. 1277) Translated in Medieval Political Philosophy: A Sourcebook, ed. Ralph Lerner and Muhsin Mahdi. New York: Free Press, 1963. 335-54.

3677. Glorieux, Palémon. Les premières polémiques thomistes: II. Le Correctorium Corruptorii 'Sciendum.' Paris: Vrin, 1956. 356 pp.

3678. _____. "Pro et contra Thomam. Un survol de cenquante années," in Sapientiae Procerum Amore (Symp) 1974. 255-87.

3679 - 3692   THIRTEENTH CENTURY

3679. Gorce, Matthieu-Maxime. L'Essor de la pensée au moyen-age. Albert le Grand, Thomas d'Aquin. Genève: Slatkine; Paris: Champien, 1978. xviii-422 pp.

3680. Grabmann, Martin. "Adenulf von Anagni, Propst von Saint-Omer (1290): ein Freund und Schüler des hl Thomas von Aquinas." Traditio 5 (1947) 269-84.

3681. _____. "Guglielmo di Moerbeke, O.P., il tradultore delle opere di Aristotile." Miscellanea Historiae Pontificae. Roma, Univ. Gregoriana. II, 20 1946.

3682. _____. Mittelalterliches Geistesleben. 3 vols. München: Max Hueber, 1926, 1939, 1956.

3683. Hissette, Roland. Enquete sur les 219 articles condamnés à Paris le 7 mars 1277. Louvain: Publications Universitaires, 1977. 340 pp.

3684. Hödl, Ludwig. "Die theologische Diskussion des Heinrich von Gent (+ 1293) über die thomasische Lehre vom vollkommenen christlichen Leben (Quodl. XII, 28-9)," in Thomas...Interpretation (Symp) 470-87.

3685. Knowles, David. The Historical Context of the Philosophical Works of St. Thomas Aquinas. London: Aquin Press, 1958.

3686. Lefevre, Charles. "Siger de Brabant a-t-il influencé s. Thomas? Propos sur la cohérence de l'anthropoligie thomsite." Mélanges de Science Religieuse 31 (1974) 203-15.

3687. Livi, Francesco. "Lullo e san Tommaso: qualche osservazione sulla 'Declaratio Raimundi per modum dialogi edita." Sapienza 29 (1976) 82-91.

3688. Lopez Medel, Jesus. "Condicionamientos historico-sociales del Tomismo," in Tommaso d'Aquino (Symp) 2, 79-83.

3689. Lottin, Odon. "Saint Thomas à la faculté des arts de Paris aux approches de 1277." Recherches de Théologie Ancienne et Médiévale. 16 (1949) 292-313.

3690. Lubac, Henri de. "Joachim de Flore jugé par S. Bonaventure et S. Thomas," in Pluralisme et Oecuménisme en Recherches Théologiques. Gembloux: Duculot, 1976. 37-50.

3691. McKeon, Richard P. "Philosophy and Theology. History and Science in the Thought of Bonaventura and Thomas Aquinas," in Celebrating the Medieval (Symp) 387-412.

3692. Mahoney, Edward P. "St. Thomas and Siger of Brabant Revisited." Review of Metaphysics 17 (1974) 531-53.

THIRTEENTH CENTURY   3693 - 3707

3693. Marlasca Lopez, Antonio. "De nuevo, Tomás de Aquino y Siger de Brabante." Estudios Filosoficos. Las Caldas de Besaya. 23 (1974) 431-9.

    Also in Tommaso d'Aquino (Symp) 2, 92-101.

3694. Masnovo, Amato. Da Guglielmo d'Auvergne a S. Tommaso d'Aquino. 2 ed. 3 vols. Milano: Società Editrice, 1945-1946. 547 pp.

3695. Mathes, Richard. "Thomas von Aquin und Albertus Magnus," in Tommaso d'Aquino (Symp) 2, 102-8.

3696. Minio-Paluello, Lorenzo. "Moerbeke, William of," in Dictionary of Scientific Biography. New York: Scribners, 1974. 9, 434-40.

3697. Montane, Pedro Ribes. "Algunos precedentes Albertinos del Tomismo." Espiritu 24 (1975) 5-26.

3698. _____. "Conoció Santo Tomás la 'Explanatio Symboli' de Ramón Martt?" Espiritu 26 (1977) 93-7.

3699. Napoli, G. Di. "San Bonaventura da Bagnoregio e San Tommaso d'Aquino." Revista Portuguesa de Filosofia. Braga. 30 (1974) 205-36.

3700. Nardone, Henry F. St. Thomas Aquinas and the Condemnation of 1277. Washington, D.C.: Catholic University of America Dissertation, 1963. 132 pp.

3701. Nash, Peter W. "Giles of Rome: Auditor and Critic of St. Thomas." The Modern Schoolman 28 (1950) 1-20.

3702. Nédoncelle, Maurice. "Remarques sur la réfutation des Averroistes par s. Thomas." Rivista di Filosofia Neo-Scolastica. Milano. 66 (1974) 284-92.

3703. Pelster, Franz. Declarationes Magistri Guilelmi de la Mare, O.F.M., de variis sententiis S. Thomae Aquinatis. Münster (W.): Aschendorff, 1956.

3704. Pelzer, Auguste. Etudes d'histoire littéraire sur la scolastique médiévale. Louvain: Publications Universitaires, 1964. 596 pp.

3705. Steenberghen, Fernand van. The Philosophical Movement in the Thirteenth Century. Edinburgh: Nelson, 1955. x-116 pp.

3706. _____. La philosophie au XIIIe siècle. Louvain-Paris: Béatrice-Nauwelaerts, 1966. 594 pp.

3707. _____. "Thomas d'Aquin devant la crise du XIIIe siècle," in Tommaso d'Aquino...problemi fondamentali (Symp) 1974. 35-44.

    Also in Tommaso d'Aquino (Symp) I, 97-104.

3708. Sweeney, Leo. "Some Mediaeval Opponents of Divine Infinity."
Mediaeval Studies 19 (1957) 233-45.

3709. Synan, Edward A. "Brother Thomas, the Master, and the Masters,"
in St. Thomas Aquinas 1274-1974 (Symp) 2, 219-42.

3710. Torrell, Jean-Pierre. "Hugues de Saint-Cher et Thomas d'Aquin.
Contribution à l'histoire du traité de la propétie." Revue Thomiste
74 (1974) 5-22.

3711. Trapé, Dario. "I problemi filosofici di Egidio Romano e lo
sviluppo del pensiero tomistico," in Tommaso d'Aquino (Symp) 2,
109-15

3712. Vella, Andrew P. Les premières polémiques thomistes: Robert
d'Orford. Paris: Vrin, 1968. 192 pp.

3713. Wéber, Edouard-Henri. Dialogue et discussions entre s. Bonaventure
et s. Thomas à Paris (1252-1273). Préface de Yves Congar. Paris:
Vrin, 1974. 519 pp.

3714. _____. L'Homme en discussion à l'Université de Paris en 1270.
La controverse de 1270...et la pensée de s. Thomas d'Aquin. Paris:
Vrin, 1970. 328 pp.

3715. West, Delno C., ed. Joachim of Fiore in Christian Thought.
Essays on the Influence of the Calabrian Prophet. 2 vols. New York:
Burt Franklin, 1975. xxiv-227, 228-631.

3716. Wicki, N. Die Lehre von der himmlischen Seligkeit in der mittelal-
terlichen Scholastik von Petrus Lombardus bis Thomas von Aquin. Freiburg
(Schw.) Universitäts-Verlag, 1954. xvi-334 pp.

3717. Wilshire, Leland E. "Were the Oxford Condemnations of 1277
Directed Against Aquinas?" The New Scholasticism. Washington, D.C.
Aquinas Septicent. 1974. 125-32.

3718. Wippel, John F. "The Condemnations of 1270 and 1277 at Paris."
Journal of Medieval and Renaissance Studies. Burham. 7 (1977)
169-201.

3719. Zimmermann, Albert. "Die Kritik an Thomas von Aquin im Meta-
physikkommentar des Ferrandus de Hispania," in Tommaso d'Aquino
(Symp) 2, 259-67.

FOURTEENTH AND FIFTEENTH CENTURIES

3720. Beckmann, Jean P. "Der ideentheoretische Grundansatz bei Thomas
von Aquin, Duns Scotus und Wilhelm von Ockham," in Tommaso d'Aquino
(Symp) 2, 286-96.

3721. Bolzan, J. E. "Navaja de Ockham o navaja de Santo Tomas?"
Sapientia 29 (1974) 207-16.

FOURTEENTH AND FIFTEENTH CENTURIES   3722 - 3734

3722. Buda, C. "Influsso del tomismo a Bisanzio nel secolo XIV."
Byzantinische Zeitschrift. München, Germany. 49 (1956) 318-
31.

3723. Callistos Angelicudes (14th century). Callistos A. contre
Thomas d'Aquin. Introducion-texte critique par s. Papadopoulos (in
Greek) Athênes: Kas. Grigoris, 1970. 321 pp.

3724. Cappello, G. "Umanesimo e scolastica: II Valla, gli umanisti
e Tommaso d'Aquino." Rivista di Filosofia Neo-Scolastica. Milano.
69 (1977) 423-42.

3725. Collins, Ardis Bea. The Doctrine of Being in the 'Theologia
Platonica' of Marsilio Ficino, with Special Reference to the Influence
of Thomas Aquinas. Toronto: University of Toronto Dissertation,
1968.

3726. _____. The Secular Is Sacred. Platonism and Thomism in
Marsilio Ficino's Platonic Theology. Hague: Nijhoff, 1974. x-
233 pp.

3727. DeRosa, Giuseppe. "La figura dell'Angelico nel pensiero e nell'
insegnamento teologico dell'Oriente cristiano slavo-bisantino."
Divus Thomas 52 (1949) 249-75.   (Piacenza)

3728. Fischer, Heribert. "Thomas von Aquin und Meister Eckhart."
Theologie und Philosophie. Frankfurt a. M.-Pullach-Freiburg i. B.
49 (1974) 213-35.

3729. Foster, Kenelm. St. Thomas, Petrarch and the Renascence.
London: Blackfriars, 1949.

        Aquinas Papers, 12.

3730. _____. "St. Thomas and Dante." New Blackfriars 55 (1974)
148-55.

3731. Gallego Salvadores, Jordan. "Santo Tomás y los Dominicos en la
tradición teológica de Valencia durante los siglos XIII, XIV y XV."
Escritos del Vedat. Valencia, Espana. 4 (1974) 479-569.

3732. Grabmann, Martin. "Johannes Capreolus O.P....in der Geschichte
der Thomistenschule." Divus Thomas. Freiburg. 22 (1944) 85-109,
145-70.

3733. Gray, Hanna H. "Valla's Encomium of St. Thomas Aquinas and
the Humanist Conception of Christian Antiquity," in Essays in History
and Literature...Stanley Pargellis, ed. H. Bluhm. Chicago: University
of Chicago Press, 1965. 37-43.

3734. Griesbach, Marc F. The Relationship Between Temporal and Spiritual
Powers in John of Paris and James of Viterbo. A Study of Early Fourteenth Century Thomistic Political Philosophy. Toronto: University of

3735 - 3747 FOURTEENTH & FIFTEENTH CENTURIES

Toronto Dissertation, 1956.

3735. Hödl, Ludwig. "Die philosophische Gotteslehre des Thomas von Aquin in der Diskussion der Schulen um die Wende des 13. zum 14. Jahrhundert." Rivista di Filosofia Neo-Scolastica. Milano. 70 (1978) 113-34.

3736. Hoffmann, Fritz. "Thomas-Rezeption bei Robert Holcot?" Theologie und Philosophie. Frankfurt a. M.-Pullach-Freiburg i. B. 49 (1974) 236-51.

3737. Kennedy, Leonard A. "A Fifteenth Century Authentic Thomist." The Modern Schoolman 42 (1965) 193-7.

3738. Kristeller, Paul Oskar. Le thomisme et la pensée de la renaissance. Montréal: Institut d'Etudes Médiévales, 1967. 287 pp.

3739. _____. "Thomism and the Italian Thought of the Renaissance," in Medieval Aspects of Renaissance Learning. Durham, N.C.: Duke University Press, 1974. 29-91.

3740. _____. "Il tomismo e il pensiero italiano del Rinascimento." Rivista di Filosofia Neo-Scolastica. Milano. 66 (1974) 841-96.

3741. Kuc, Leszek. "Z badań nad pojeciem 'theoria' w szkole tomistycznej xv wieku," in Studia Sw. Tomasza (Symp Lublin) 47-90.

Notion of 'Theory' in 15th Century Thomistic School.

3742. Kuksewicz, Zdzislaw. Albertyzm i tomizm w XV weiku w krakowie i Koloni, Doctrina pychologiczna. Wroclaw: Polska Akademia Nauk, Instytut Filozofi i Socjologü, 1973.

3743. Marchesi, Angelo. "Analogia ed univocità dell'essere in Tommaso d'Aquino e Duns Scoto," in Tommaso d'Aquino (Symp) 2, 268-78.

3744. Markowski, Mieczystaw. "Tomizm w logice, teorii poznania, filozofii przyrody i psychologii w Polsce w latach 1400-1525," in Studia Sw. Tomasza (Symp Lublin) 195-262.

Thomism in Logic, Theory of Knowledge, Philosophy of Nature and Psychology in Poland from 1400 to 1525.

3745. Mesnard, Pierre. "Une application curieuse de l'humanisme critique à la théologie: l'Eloge de s. Thomas par Laurent Valla." Revue Thomiste 55 (1955) 159-76.

3746. Oddasso Cartotti, Adriana. "La dottrina di S. Tommaso d'Aquino insegnata e vissuta da S. Caterina da Siena." Recherches de Théologie Ancienne et Médiévale. Louvain. 25 (1974) 321-32.

3747. Ott, Ludwig. "Die Auseinandersetzung des Durandees de S. Porciano

FOURTEENTH AND FIFTEENTH CENTURIES   3748 - 3760

mit Thomas von Aquin in der lehre vom Weihesakramente," in Thomas...
Interpretation (Symp) 519-58.

3748. Palacz, Ryszard. "Le thomisme dans la philosphie Polonaise en
seconde moiteé du XVe siécle," in Tommaso d'Aquino (Symp) 2, 329-
34.

3739. Papadopoulos, Stylianos G. "Thomas in Byzanz. Thomas-Rezeption
und Thomae-Kritik in Byzanz zwischen 1354 und 1435," Theologie und
Philosophie 49 (1974) 274-304.

3750. Podskalsky, Gerhard. "Die Rezeption der thomistischen Theologie
bei Gennadios II Scholariso," Theologie und Philosophié. Frankfurt a.
M.-Pullach-Freiburg i. B. 49 (1974) 305-23.

3751. Prezioso, Faustino A. "Cristica di alcune teorie filosofiche di
S. Bonaventura e di S. Tommaso nell'Ordinatio di Duns Scoto."
Sapienza. Napoli. 27 (1974) 472-80.

3752. Rosa, R. "San Tommaso e Marsilio Ficino: Contributo per lo
studia della 'Theologia Platonica de Immortalitate Animarum."
Sapienza 25 (1972) 335-45.

3753. Scaltriti, Giacento Arturo. "Il tomismo di Savonarola." Aquinas
3 (1964) 345-85.

3754. Scaltriti, Giacinto M. "S. Tommaso d'Aquino nel Savonarola."
Palestra del Clero. Rovigo. 53 (1974) 854-67, 932-55, 1034-49,
1085-97, 1149-63.

3755. Scapin, Pietro. Il prologo della 'Summa Theologiae' di S.
Tommaso e dell' Ordinatio di Duns Scoto, " in Tommaso d'Aquino
(Symp) 2, 297-305.

3756. Stroick, Clemens. "Eine Pariser Disputation vom Jahre 1305. Die
Verteidigung des thomistischen Individuations-prinzips gegen J. Duns
Scotus durch Guillelmus Petri de Godino, O.P." in Tommaso d'Aquino
(Symp) 2, 306-15.

3757. Swiezawski, Stefan. "Le thomisme á la fin du moyen age," in
Studi Tomistici (Symp) I, 225-48.

3758. Thomas of Sutton. Contra Quodlibet Johannis Duns Scoti. Ed.
Johannes Schneider. Munchen: C. H. Beck, 1978. xiii-112 pp.

     Defence of Aquinas.

3759. Thro, Linus J. The Critique of St. Thomas in the 'Reportata
Parisiensia' and the Orientation of the Scotistic Metaphysics. Toronto:
University of Toronto Dissertation, 1948.

3760. Walz, Angelus. "Thomas-Stellen in Heinrich Seuses Schriften,"
in Thomas...Interpretation (Symp) 656-62.

3761 - 3772 SIXTEENTH TO EIGHTEENTH CENT.

3761. Wtodek, Zofia. "Tomasza Suttona filosoficzna interpretacja
powstawania bytów materialnych," in Studia Sw. Tomasza (Symp Lublin)
31-46.

       Thomas of Sutton's Interpretation of the Origin of Material Being.

SIXTEENTH TO EIGHTEENTH CENTURIES

3762. Adler, Mortimer J. "Little Errors in the Beginning," (Thomas
and Modern Philosophers.) The Thomist. Washington, D.C. Centenary of
St. Thomas Aquinas 1274-1974. 38 (1974) 27-48.

3763. Agresti, Guglielmo Di. "Affinità dottrinali tra Tommaso d'Aquino
e S. Caterina de' Ricci," in Studi Tomistici (Symp) I, 291-304.

3764. Almeida Rolo, Raul de. "Duas linhas de restauracao tomista na
segunda escolastica do século XVI," in Tommaso d'Aquino (Symp) 2,
230-41.

3765. Balz, Albert G. A. "Concerning the Thomistic and Cartesian
Dualisms: A Rejoinder to Professor Mourant." Journal of Philosophy
54 (1957) 383-89.

       See Mourant infra.

3766. Barth, Hilarius. "Die Dominikaner im Augsburger Probabilismus-
streit 1759-62...Thomismus in der Moraltheologie," in Thomas...
Interpretation (Symp) 663-727.

3767. Baur, Jörg. "Fragen eines evangelischen Theologen an Thomas von
Aquin," in Thomas von Aquin 1274-1974 (Symp München) 160-74.

3768. Borraccini, Antonio. "Il tomismo nell'800 Italiano: Pasquale
Galluppi," in Tommaso d'Aquino (Symp) 2, 169-80.

3769. Brantschen, Johannes. "De servo oder de Libero Arbitrio, Luther
und Thomas im Gesprach." Freiburger Zeitschrift für Philosophie und
Theologie 13-14 (1966-1967) 239-58.

3770. Bushinski, Edward A. An Introduction to the Natural Theology of
John of St. Thomas. New York: Fordham University Dissertation, 1953.
172 pp.

3771. Carvin, Walter P. The Concept of Creation in Leibniz in Relation
to Early Modern Science and in Comparison to Thomas Aquinas. Princeton,
N.J.: Princeton Theological Seminary Dissertation (Th.D.) 1969.
193 pp.

3772. Colosio, Innocenzo. "Giovanni Maria di Lauro O.P. (+ dopo 1753).
Uno sconosciuto tomista del settecento e la sua 'Teologia mistica',"
Recherches de Théologie Ancienne et Médiévale. Louvain. 25 (1974)
131-49.

SIXTEENTH TO EIGHTEENTH CENTURIES   3773 - 3786

3773. Colosio, Innocenzo. "Un testo 'tipico' di Lutero contro S.
Tommaso e la Scolastica." Palestra del Clero. Rovighi. 53 (1974)
333-49.

3774. _____. "S. Tommaso d'Aquino visto da Lutero." Recherches
de Théologie Ancienne et Médiévale. Louvain. 25 (1974) 103-23.

3775. Connell, Desmond. "The Thomistic Origin of Malebranche's
Ontologism." Irish Theological Quarterly. Maynooth. 34 (1967)
207-19.

3776. Crow, Michael Bertram. "An Eccentric Seventeenth-Century Witness
to the Natural Law: John Selden (1584-1654)." Natural Law Forum
12 (1967) 184-95.

3777. Crowley, Patricia J. "Burke and Scholasticism." The New
Scholasticism 28 (154) 170-85.

3778. Czerkawski, Jan. "Filozofia tomistyczna w Polsce w XVII wieku,"
in Studia Sw. Tomasza (Symp Lublin) 263-314.

      Thomistic Philosophy in Poland in the 17th Century.

3779. Derisi, Octavio N. "La doctrina del concepto en Kant y en S.
Tomás." Revista Filosofica. Mexico. 6 (1974) 151-85.

3780. Domanski, Juliusz. "Sw. Tomasz, Erasm z Rotterdam i humanizm
biblijny," in Studia Sw. Tomasza (Symp Lublin) 91-166.

      St. Thomas, Erasmus and Biblical Humanism.

3781. Finnis, J. M. "Blackstone's Theoretical Intentions." Natural
Law Forum 12 (1967) 163-83.

3782. Frank, Isnard W. "Der Wiener Dominikaner Johannes Werd (+ 1510)
als Verfasser von Thomaskommentaren," Thomas...Interpretation (Symp)
609-40.

3783. Gründler, Otto. "The Influence of Thomas Aquinas upon the Theology
of Girolamo Zanchi," in Studies in Medieval Culture, ed. J. R. Sommer-
feldt. Dalamazoo: University of Western Michigan, 1964.

3784. _____. Thomism and Calvinism in the Theology of Girolamo
Zanchi (1516-1590). Princeton: Princeton Theological Seminary Dissertation (Th.D.) 1961. 175 pp.

3785. Henrici, Peter. "Saint Thomas Après Kant?" Gregorianum 56
(1975) 163-8.

3786. Hopkin, Charles E. The Share of Thomas Aquinas in the Growth of
the Witchcraft Delusions. Philadelphia: University of Pennsylvania
Dissertation, 1940. 126 pp.

3787 - 3800   SIXTEENTH TO EIGHTEENTH CENT.

3787. Kennedy, Leonard A. "Thomism at the University of Salamanca in the Sixteenth Century: The Doctrine of Existence," in Tommaso d'Aquino (Symp) 2, 254-58.

3788. Lakebrink, Bernhard. "Analektik und Dialektik. Zur Methode des thomistischen und Hegelschen Denkens," in St. Thomas Aquinas 1274-1974 (Symp) 2, 459-87.

3789. Laky, John J. A Study of George Berkeley's Philosophy in the Light of the Philosophy of St. Thomas. Washington, D.C.: Catholic University of America Press, 1951.

3790. _____. A Study of George Berkeley's Philosophy in the Light of the Philosophy of St. Thomas. Washington, D.C.: Catholic University of America Dissertation, 1951.

3791. Lamacchia, Ada. "Tommaso d'Aquino e Kant. Strutturazione dei fantasmi e schematismo trascendentale," in Tommaso d'Aquino (Symp Roma) 6, 239-51.

3792. Markowski, Mieczyslaw. "Tomizm w logice, teorii poznania, filozofii przyrody i psychologii w Polsce w latach 1400-1525," in Studi z Dziejow Mysli (Symp) 195-262.

3793. Melquiades, Andrès Martin. "La escuela teologia de Salamanca," in Tommaso d'Aquino (Symp) 2, 242-53.

3794. Miranda, Maria do Carmo Tavaresde. O ser da meteria (estudo em Kant e Sap Tomàs). Recife: Imprense Universitaria, 1976. 114 pp.

3795. Morales, Josè. "La formacion espiritual e intelectual de Tomàs Moro y sus contactos con la doctrina y obras de santo Tomàs de Aquino." Scripta Theologica 6 (1974) 439-89.

3796. Mournant, John A. "Cartesian Man and Thomistic Man." Journal of Philosophy 54 (1957) 373-82.

        See Balz supra.

3797. Munoz Delgado, Vicente. "Logica y filosofia en el Curso tomista (1754) de Celestino del Santissimo Sacramento." Estudios Tomista. Quito, Ecuador. 30 (1974) 331-70.

3798. Marciso, Encrico I. La Summa Philosophica di Salvatore Roselli e la rinascità del Tomismo. Roma: Ed. Università Lateranense, 1966.

3799. Pesch, Otto H. Die Theologie der Rechtfertigung bei M. Luther und Thomas von Aquin. Mainz: Matthias-Grunewald, 1967. 1010 pp.

3800. Peyrous, B. "Un grand centre de thomisme au XVIIe siècle. Le couvent des Frères Precheurs de Bordeaux et l'enseignement de Jean-Baptiste Gonet." Divus Thomas. Piacenza. 77 (1974) 452-73.

SIXTEENTH TO EIGHTEENTH CENTURIES   3801 - 3814A

3801. Pfürtner, Stephanus. Angoisse et certitude de notre salut. Luther et s. Thomas au-delà des oppositions traditioneles. Paris: Centurion, 1967. 125 pp.

3802. _____. Luther and Aquinas on Salvation. Translated by Edward Quinn. New York: Sheed and Ward, 1965. 160 pp.

3803. _____. Luther und Thomas im Gespräch. Heidelberg: F. H. Kerles, 1961. 183 pp.

3804. Piolanti, Antonio. "L'oratoriano Cesare Becilli (+ 1649) e lo studio della Summa Theologica di S. Tommaso." Divinitas 18 (1974) 180-9.

3805. Piolanti, Antonio. Il 'Trattadello della disposizione che si ricerca a recever la gratia del Spirito Santo' di Fra Lorenzo da Dergamo, O.P. Ed., Introd., e Note. Città del Vaticano: Libreria Ed. Vaticana, 1974. 57, 44 pp.

3806. Powell, Francis D. A Thomistic Evaluation of James Wilson and Thomas Reid. Washington, D.C.: Georgetown University Dissertation, 1951.

3807. Reilly, John P. "Cajetan, Essentialist or Existentialist." The New Scholasticism. Washington, D.C. 41 (1967) 191-222.

3808. Roensch, Frederick J. The Early Thomistic School. Chicago: Priory Press, 1954. 351 pp.

3809. Rosa, R. "Tomismo e antitomismo in Battista Spagnoli Mantovano (1447-1516)," in Tomismo e Antitomismo (Symp) 2, 227-64.

3810. Rossi, Giovanni F. Il movimento neotomista piacentino iniziato al Collegio Alberoni... Città del Vatican: Ed. Vaticana, 1974.

3811. Ruiz Maldonado, Enrique. "Tomás de Aquino, Bartolomé de las Cusas y la controversia de Indias." Studium. Avila-Madrid. 14 (1974) 519-42.

3812. Ryan, John K. "The Reputation of St. Thomas Among English Protestant Thinkers of the Seventeenth Century." The New Scholasticism 22 (1948) 1-33, 126-208.

3813. _____. The Reputation of St. Thomas Among English Protestant Thinkers of the 17th Century. Washington, D.C.: Catholic University of America Press, 1948. 135 pp.

3814. Scharlemann, Robert P. Thomas Aquinas and John Gerhard. New Haven: Yale University Press, 1964. 282 pp.

3814A. Ulloa Herrero, Daniel. "El Tomismo en el Mexico del siglo XVI." Logos. Mexico. 2 (1974) 149-69.

3815 - 3828   NINETEENTH & TWENTIETH CENT.

3815. Wallace, William A. "Galileo and the Thomists," in St. Thomas Aquinas 1274-1974 (Symp) 2, 293-330.

3816. Zammit, P. N. and P. H. Hering, eds. Thomas De Vio Cardinalis Caietanus: De Nominum Analogia. De Conceptu Entis. Rome: Angelicum, 1952. 123 pp.

3817. Agazzi, Evrando. "Il messaggio di S. Tommaso e la cultura contemporanea," in Presenca Filosofica (Symp) 149-60.

NINETEENTH AND TWENTIETH CENTURIES

3818. Ales Bella, A. "Edith Stein: da Edmund Husserl a Tommaso d'Aquino," in Tomismo e Antitomismo (Symp) 2, 265-76.

3819. Amato, Joseph. Mounier and Maritain: A French Catholic Understanding of the Modern World. University, Ala." University of Alabama Press, 1975. 238 pp.

3820. Anderson, James F. "In Defense of Etienne Gilson: Concerning a Recent Book About Thomistic Metaphysics." The Thomist 28 (1964) 373-80.

        A review article; See John M. Quinn infra.

3821. Anzenbacher, Arno. "Thomism and the I-Thou Philosophy." Philosophy Today. Celina, Ohio. 11 (1967) 238-56.

3822. Arruda Campos, Francisco. "A reelaboracao do tomismo no mundo de hoje: a pensamento de Jono Baptista Lotz. Revista Portuguesa de Filosofia. Braga. 33 (1977) 196-234.

3823. Azar, Larry. "Esse in the Philosophy of Whitehead." The New Scholasticism 37 (1963) 462-71.

3824. Balzer, Carmen. "El Pensamiento de Tomás de Aquino y los problemas de nuestro tiempo." Sapientia. Argentina. 30 (1975) 199-206.

3825. Bars, Henry. Maritain en notre temps. Paris: Grasset, 1959. 397 pp.

3926. Baseheart, Mary Catherine. The Encounter of Husserl's Phenomenology and the Philosophy of St. Thomas in Selected Writings of Edith Stein. Notre Dame: University of Notre Dame Dissertation, 1961. 210 pp.

3827. Beach, John D. "Another Look at the Thomism of Etienne Gilson." The New Scholasticism 40 (1976) 522-8.

3828. Belgenio, Maria Teresa. "Due Accademie Tomistiche e Mons. Bonaventura Gargiulo." Studi e Ricerche Francescane. Napoli. 3 (1974) 5-44.

NINETEENTH AND TWENTIETH CENTURIES   3829 - 3843

3829. Bello, Angela Ales. "A proposito della 'philosophia perennis' Tommaso d'Aquino e E. Husserl nell'interpretazione di E. Stein." Sapienza 27 (1974) 441-51.

3830. Belti, R. Bessero. "Antonio Rosmini per l. studio di San Tommaso." Rivista di Filosofia Neo-Scolastica. Milano. 66 (1974) 761-75.

3832. Berg, I. J. M. Van Den. Er was meer te doen in de wereld van Thomas van Aquino dan in onze tijd. Haarlem: Gottmer, 1974. 82 pp.

3833. Blanchette, Oliva. "Philosophy and Theology in Aquinas: On Being a Disciple in Our Day." Science et Esprit. Montréal. 28 (1976) 23-53.

   Also in Tommaso d'Aquino (Symp) 2, 427-32.

3834. Boas, George. "The Misuse of Scholasticism," in St. Louis Studies in Honor of St. Thomas Aquinas I (1943) 43-4.

3835. Bochenski, Innocentius M. Contemporary European Philosophy. Berkeley and Los Angeles: University of California Press, 1956. 326 pp.

   Paperback edition in 1965.

3836. _____. "Thomism and Marxism-Leninsim." Studies in Soviet Thought. Dordrecht, Netherlands. 7 (1967) 154-68.

3837. Bogliolo, Luigi. "Rinovamento e Tomismo." Aquinas. Roma. 12 (1974) 3-40.

3838. Bourke, Vernon J. "Desenvolvimientos recientes de la filo- sofia tomista." Sapientia: Revista Tomista de Fifosofia. 11 (1956) 39-40.

3839. _____. "Esse, Transcendence, and Law: Three Phases of Re- cnet Thomism." The Modern Schoolman. St. Louis, MO. 52 (1974) 49-64.

3840. _____. "Natural Law and the Contemporary Mind," in Teaching Thomism Today. Edited by G. F. McLean. Washington, D.C.: Catholic University of America Press, 1963. 307-29.

3841. Boyle, Joseph M. "Aquinas and Prescriptive Ethics." Proceed- ings of the American Catholic Philosophical Association 49 (1975) 82-95.

3842. Bradley, Denis J. M. "Rahner's Spirit in the World: Aquinas or Hegel?" The Thomist 41 (1977) 167-99.

3843. Braza Diez, Mariano. "Tomàs de Aquino y el análisis linguistico." Studium. Avila-Madrid. 16 (1976) 463-93.

3844 - 3859 NINETEENTH & TWENTIETH CENT.

3844. Brazzola, Georges. Paul Chauchard, Jean Daujat, et Paul Grenet.
Actualité de Saint Thomas. Paris: Desclée, 1971. 152 pp.

3845. Caleo, Marcello. "Logica e metafisica come fondamenti del
pensiero filosofico in S. Tommmaso e in Hegel." Rassegna di Scienze
Filosofice. Napoli. 27 (1974) 305-34.

3846. Camara, Helder. "What Would St. Thomas Aquinas, the Aristotle
Commentator, Do if Faced with Karl Marx?" in Celebrating the Med.
Heritage (Symp) 1978.

3847. Caputo, John D. "The Problem of Being in Heidegger and Aquinas."
The Thomist 41 (1977) 62-91.

3848. Caroli, Arnaldo. "Profilo del tomista bolognese Card. Francesco
Battaglini (1892) sulla scorta di opere edite e di veri archivi,"
in Saggi (Symp) 260-302.

3849. Chapman, Emmanuel. "Living Thomism." The Thomist 4 (1942)
369-87.

3850. Charlesworth, Max J. Philosophy and Linguistic Analysis.
Pittsburgh: Duquesne University Press, 1959.

3851. _____. "St. Thomas Aquinas and the Decline of the Kantian-
Kierkegaardian Philosophy of Religion," in Tommaso d'Aquino (Symp)
I, 323-36; 5, 50-60.

3852. Chenu, M.-D. "L'Homme-dans-le-monde," (cf. Merleau-Ponty) in
S. Thomas Aujourd'hui (Symp) 171-5.

3853. Coathalem, Hervé. "Saint Thomas à Vatican II et à ses lendemains,"
in Tommaso d'Aquino (Symp) 2, 441-63.

3854. Coccia, Antonio. "Immanenza e trascendenza di Dio nel pensiero
di S. Tommaso e G. Gentile," in Tommaso d'Aquino (Symp) 2, 205-15.

3855. Conlan, F. Allan. A Critique of the Neo-Naturalistic Philosophy
of Religion of Henry Nelson Wieman in the Light of Thomistic Principles.
Washington, D.C.: Catholic University of America Dissertation, 1958.
110 pp.

3856. Copleston, Frederick. St. Thomas and Nietzsche. London:
Blackfriars, 1944.

3857. Corradi, Enrico. "Neoempirismo e metafisica tomistica." Aquinas
17 (1974) 283-92.

3858. Corvez, Maurice. "Principles thomistes et problématique contemporaine." Doctor Communis 29 (1976) 267-72.

3859. Cottier, Georges. "La doctrine thomiste des oppositions en rapport
avec la dialectique Hégélienne." Revue des Sciences Philosophiques et

NINETEENTH AND TWENTIETH CENTURIES   3860 - 3872

Théologiques. Le Saulchoir-Paris. 62 (1973) 354-82.

3860. Creaven, John A. "The Doctrine of God in Personalism."
The Thomist 14 (1951) 161-216.

3861. _____. "Personalism, Thomism and Epistemology." The
Thomist 8 (1945) 1-26.

3862. Cristaldi, Giuseppe. "Il De Magistro di S. Tommaso d'Aquino
oggi." Asprenas. Napoli. 21 (1974) 389-400.

3863. Croteau, Jacques. Les Fondements thomistes du personalisme
de Maritain. Ottawa: Editions de l'Université d'Ottawa, 1955.
259 pp.

3864. Crovini, Mario. "Mons. Giuseppe Buscarini vescovo di Fidenza
(+ 1872) pioniere del tomismo emiliano. Con documenti inediti."
in Saggi (Symp) ed Vatecana 1974. 48-98.

3865. Crowe, Frederick E. "The Exigent Mind: Bernard Lonergan's
Intellectualism." Continuum. Chicago, Illinois. 2 (1964) 316-33.

3866. Crowley, Theodore. "St. Thomas and Sir Edmund Whittaker:
Discussion of Whittaker's Space and Spirit." Irish Ecclesiastical
Record 69 (1947) 1066-82.

3867. Cunningham, G. Watts. "Must We All Be Thomists?" Philosophical
Review 57 (1948) 493-504.

        See Gerrity infra.

3867A. Czerkawski, Jan. "Tomizm a fenomenologia-X Tijdziėn Filo-
zoficzny." Zeszyty Naukowe KUL 9 (1966) 82-5.

3868. Da Cruz Pontes, J. M. "Martins Capela e o renascimento tomista
em Portugal no seculo XIX." Revista Portuguesa de Filosofia. Braga.
32 (1976) 63-90.

3869. Dall'Asta, Giuseppe. "La presenza di S. Tommaso nell'antropologia
filosofica e politica di Jacques Maritain." in Tommaso d'Aquino (Symp)
2, 464-74.

3870. Dandenault, Germain. "Le Congrès Internacional thomiste: souffle
du printemps ou vent d'automne?" Laval Théologique et Philosophique
30 (1974) 445-54.

3871. Darms, Gion. 700 Jahre Thomas von Aquin. Gedanken zu einem
Jubiläum. Freiburg i. Sch: Paulusverlag, 1974. 179 pp.

3872. Darnoi, Dennis N. Eduard von Hartmann's Metaphysics of the un-
conscious: A Historical Study and an Evaluation on the Basis of
Aristotelian and Thomistic Principles. Washington, D.C.: Catholic
University of America Dissertation, 1964. 270 pp.

3873 - 3888 NINETEENTH & TWENTIETH CENT.

3873. Deely, John N. "Classical Thomism, Modern Thought, and Maritain." Listening 9 (1974) 181-9.

3874. Delogu, Antonio. "La critica di Merleau-Ponty alla concezione tomista dell'uomo e della libertà" in Tommaso d'Aquino (Symp) 2, 475-9.

3875. Dembowski, Bronistaw. "Encyklika Aeterni Patris w Polsce," in Studia Sw. Tomasza (Symp Lublin) 315-34.

        Encyclical Aeterm Patris in Poland.

3876. Derisi, Octavio N. "Actualidad del intelectualismo tomista frente al inmanentismo irracionalista contemporaneo," in Tommaso d'Aquino (Symp) i, 105-18.

3877. _____. "Dos concepciones antagonicas del ser: Sartre y Santo Tomás," in Studi Tomistici (Symp) 3, 295-315.

3878. Dewan, Lawrence. "Leslie Dewart, St. Thomas and Knowledge." Downside Review. Bath. 91 (1973) 51-64.

3879. Dewart, Leslie. "The Relevance of Thomism Today." Proceedings of the American Catholic Philosophical Association. Washington, D.C. 48 (1974) 308-17.

3880. Dezza, Paolo, ed. I neotomisti italiani del XIX secolo. 2 vols. Milano: Bocca, 1942-1944.

3881. Donceel, Joseph, ed. & tr. A Maréchal Reader. New York: Herder and Herder, 1970. xiii-250 pp.

3882. _____. "A Thomistic Misapprehension?" Thought 32 (1957) 189-98.

3883. _____. "Transcendental Thomism." Listening. 9 (1974) 157-64.

3884. _____. "Transcendental Thomism." The Monist 58 (1974) 67-85.

3885. Doolan, Aegidius. Revival of Thomism. Dublin: Conmore and Reynolds, 1951. 54 pp.

3886. Doyle, John P. "Heidegger and Scholastic Metaphysics." The Modern Schoolman 49 (1972) 201-20.

3887. Dunn, Will Matthis. The Relevance of the Thomism of Jacques Maritain to the Present Philosophico Religious Crisis. Madison, N.J.: Drew University Dissertation, 1951.

3888. Esposito, Rosario F. "S. Tommaso nel pensiero di Giovanni Bovio," in Tommaso d'Aquino (Symp) 2, 217-29.

NINETEENTH AND TWENTIETH CENTURIES   3889 - 3904

3889. Evans, Joseph W. ed. Jacques Maritain, the Man and His Achievement. New York: Sheed and Ward, 1963. 270 pp.

3890. Fabro, Cornelio. "Attualità della contestazione tomistica."
Doctor Communis 27 (1974) 3-12.

3891. _____. "Freedom and Existence in Contemporary Philosophy
and in St. Thomas." The Thomist. Centenary Edition. 38 (1974)
524-56.

3892. _____. "L'interpretazione dell'atto in S. Tommaso e Heidegger,"
in Tommaso d'Aquino (Symp Roma-Napoli) 1, 505-17.

3893. _____. K. Rahner e l'ermeneutica tomistica. Ed 2s. Milano:
Rusconi, 1973.

3894. _____. "Il nouovo problema dell'essere e la fondazione della
metafisica," in St. Thomas Aquinas 1274-1974 (Symp) 2, 423-57.

3895. _____. "Nuove interpretazione del tomismo." Rassegna di
Filsoofia. Roma. 2 (1953) 239-51.

3896. _____. La svolta antropologica di Karl Rahner. Milano:
Rusconi, 1974. 252 pp.

3897. Fantini, Rodolfo. "La 'geografia tomista' di fine Ottocento nelle
indicazioni de 'La scienza Italiana'," in Saggi (Symp) 403-50.

3898. Fay, Thomas A. "Heidegger on the History of Western Metaphysics
as Forgetfulness of Being: A Thomistic Rejoinder," in Tommaso d'Aquino
(Symp) 2, 480-5.

3899. Fecher, Charles A. The Philosophy of Jacques Maritain. Westminister, MD: Newman Press, 1953. 375 pp.

3900. Fernandez, Aniceto. "Il pensiero di S. Tommaso nell'epoca post-
conciliare." Sapienza 19 (1956) 385-98.

3901. Ferraro, Joseph. "Marxism and Thomism: Basis for Dialgue."
International Philosophical Quarterly. New York. 10 (1970) 75-
101.

3902. Finance, Joseph De. "San Tommaso e noi," in Presence Filosofica
(Symp) 9-17.

3903. _____. "Valeur et taches actuelles du thomisme." Aquinas
3 (1960) 139ff.

3904. Fleckenstein, Norbert J. A Critique of John Dewey's Theory of
the Nature and the Knowledge of Reality in the Light of the Principles
of Thomism. Washington, D.C.: Catholic Univeristy of American Dissertation, 1954. 200 pp.

3905. Foley, Leo M. A Critique of the Philosophy of Being of Alfred
North Whitehead in the Light of Thomistic Philosophy. Washington,
D.C.: Catholic University of America Dissertation, 1946.

3906. Ford, Lewis S. "Tillich and Thomas: The Analogy of Being."
Journal of Religion 46 (1966) 229-45.

3907. Fox, Charles. "Tillich's Advice to Thomists." Listening 9
(1974) 144-52.

3908. Geisler, Norman L. "A New Look at the Relevance of Thomism for
Evangelical Apologetics." Christian Scholar's Review 4 (1975)
189-200.

3908A. _____. Christian Apologetics. Grand Rapids, Michigan:
Baker Book House, 1976. 393 pp.

3909. Gelinas, Jean Paul. La Restauration du Thomisme Sous Leon
XIII et les Philosophies Nouvelles. Washington, D.C.: Catholic
University of American Dissertation, 1960. 166 pp.

3910. Gerrity, Benignus. "Professor Cunningham and Thomism."
Philosophical Review 58 (1950) 585-98.

        See G. W. Cunningham.

3911. Gervais, Michel. "Note critique: L'Analogie selon s. Thomas
et Karl Barth." Laval Théologique et Philosophique. Québec. 29
(1973) 187-92.

        Cf. Henry Chavannes.

3912. Ghini, G. Giordano. "S. Tommaso a il Concilio Vaticano II,"
in Bollettino di S. Domenico (Symp) 1974. 101-25.

3913. _____. San Tommaso e Paolo VI. Bologna: Studio Teologico
Domenicano, 1974. 83 pp.

3914. Giacon, Carlo. "Un itinerario. Agostino, Rosmini, Tommaso."
Giornale di Metafisica. Genova-Bologna. 31 (1976) 531-43.

        Cf. F. Sciacca.

3915. Giannini, Giorgio. "A proposito del 'Thomas von Aquin und
wir' di J. Hessen." Aquinas 11 (1958) 40-74.

3916. _____. Il s. Tommaso di Sciacca." Giornale di Metafisica.
Genova-Bologna. 30 (1975) 155-62.

3917. _____. S. Tommaso e Rosmini. Considerazioni sulle rispettive
nozioni dell'essere." Aquinas 17 (1974) 188-203.

3918. Gillet, Martin S. Lettre encyclique sur l'enseignement de s.

NINETEENTH AND TWENTIETH CENTURIES   3919 - 3932

Thomas à d'heure présente. Civitas Vaticanna: Typis Polyglottis
Vaticanis, 1943. 102 pp.

3919. Gilson, Etiene. St. Thomas Aquinas and Our Colleagues. Princeton,
N.J.: Princeton University Press, 1953. 31 pp.

3919A. Gogacz, M. "Aktualne dyskusje wokół tomizmw." Zeszyty Naukowe
KUL 10 (1967) 59-70.

3920. _____. "Tomizm w polskich srodowiskach uniwersyteckich xx
wieku," in Studia Sw. Tomasza (Symp Lublin) 335-50.

     Thomism in 20th century Polish University Circles.

3921. Gonzalez, Antonio. "Musings on Structuralism by a Thomist."
Philippiniana Sacra 9 (1974) 187-230.

3922. Gongalez Alvarez, Angel. "Santo Tomàs de Aquino y el pensamiento
contemporaneo," in Tommaso d'Aquino...problemi fondamentali (Symp)
1974. 519-28.

     Also in Tommaso d'Aquino (Symp) I, 129-36.

3923. Greenstock, David L. "Thomism and the New Theology." The
Thomist 13 (1950) 567-96.

3924. Gregory, Thomas. "Gilsonian Thomism." Listening 9 (1974)
168-72.

3925. Griffin, John H. and Yves R. Simon. Jacques Maritain: Homage
in Words and Pictures. Albany, N.Y.: Magi Books, Inc. 1974.
96 pp.

3926. Guy, Alain. "Jacques Chevalier et le Thomisme." Sapientia
29 (1974) 279-90.

3927. Hartley, Thomas J. A. Thomistic Revival and the Modernist Era.
Toronto: University of St. Michael's College, 1970. 110 pp.

3928. Hayen, André. "Leggere san Tommaso oggi?" Scuola Cattolica
102 (1974) 539-45.

3929. Henle, Robert J. "Dorothy Emmelton Thomism." The Modern
Schoolman 26 (1948) 36-8.

3930. _____. "Professor Northrop's Idea of Thomsim." The Modern
Schoolman 24 (1947) 108-15.

3931. _____. "A Thomist on 'An Experimentalist on Being'."
The Modern Schoolman. St. Louis, Missouri. 35 (1958) 133-41.

3932. Henrici, Peter. "S. Thomas après Kant," in Tommaso d'Aquino
(Symp) 2, 514-19.

3933. Higgins, Edward Francis. A Critique of John Dewey's Theory of the Concrete Moral Good in the Light of the Philosophy of St. Thomas Aquinas. Brooklyn: St. John's University Dissertation, 1974. 491 pp.

3934. Hinrichs, Gerard. "Maritain: A Quixote or a Socrates?" Personalist 23 (1942) 387-95.

3935. _____. "Thomists-Black Cat-Dark Room." Personalist 21 (1940) 288-300.

3936. Hopkins, Martin. "St. Thomas and the Encyclical Mystici Corporis. The Thomist. Washington, D.C. 22 (1959) 1-24.

3937. Inagaki, Bernard R. "Thomism in Japan." Proceedings of the American Catholic Philosophical Assoication 37 (1963) 224-7.

3938. _____. and Joseph B. McAllister. "Japan, Philosophy, and Thomism." The Thomist 19 (1956) 250-61.

3939. Interdonato, Francisco. "Santo Tomás y el pensamiento contempor- aneo." Revista Teologica Limense. Lima, Peru. 8 (1974) 153- 82.

3940. Iturralde Colombres, Carlos A. "Necesidad de la directa con- frontación de textos." Sapienza 29 (1974) 135-50.

Critique of Joseph Maréchal.

3941. Jacquin, Robert. "Deux promoteurs inattendus de la philosophie de s. Thomas d'Aquin." Divinitas 18 (1974) 357-68.

On Domet de Vorges and Joseph Gardaié.

3942. _____. "La philosophie de s. Thomas d'Aquin en France au XIXe siécle avant l'encyclique Aeterni Patris," in Studi Tomistici (Symp) I, 325-37.

3943. Jette, C. R. The Philosophy of Nietzsche in the Light of Thomistic Principles. New York: 1967.

3944. John, Helen James. The Thomist Spectrum. New York: Fordham University Press, 1967. 208 pp.

3945. Journet, Charles. Actualité de saint Thomas. Paris-Bruxelles: Desclée, 1973.

3946. Jüssen, G. "Thomas von Aquin und die analytische Philosophie," in Thomas von Aquin im Philosophischen Gespräch (Symp) 1957. 132- 64.

3947. Kalinowski, Georges (Jerzy) "La philosophie de s. Thomas d'Aquin face á la critique de la métaphysique par Kant, Nietzsche et Heidegger,"

NINETEENTH AND TWENTIETH CENTURIES   3948 - 3961

in Studi Tomistici (Symp) 3, 257-83.

3948. _____. M. Jaworski, S. Kaminski, T. Styczen, and K. Klosak.
(Polish Discussions of the Approaches to Human Experience in K. Wojtyla,
Osoba i czyn, 1969, translated as The Acting Person, 1979.). in
Analecta Cracoviensia. Cracow, Poland. 5-6 (1973-1974)

3949. _____. and Stefan Swiezawski. La Philosophie à l'heure du
Concile. Paris: Société d'Editions Internationales, 1965.

3950. Kinney, Cyril Edwin. A Critique of the Philosophy of George
Santayana in the Light of Thomistic Principles. Washington, D.C.:
Catholic Univeristy of American Dissertation, 1942.

3951. Kirn, A. G. An Interpretation of Thomistic Freedom According to
Gustav Siewerth. Toronto: University of Toronot Dissertation, 1968.

3952. Klinch, David M. "Natural Law in French Catholicism During
the Late 18th and 19th Centuries." Revue de l'Université d'Ottawa
44 (1974) 497-506.

3953. Köster, Wilhelm. "Ueber die theologische Methodologie von Lund,"
in Tommaso d'Aquino (Symp) 2, 316-23.

3953A. Krapiec, M. A. "Neotomizm." Znak. Krakow. 10 (1958)
623-33.

3954. _____. "La problématique et le developpement de la philosophie de s. Thomas à l'Universita Cath. de Lublin," in Saint Thomas
(Symp Lublin) 5-14.

3955. Lacombe, Olivier. "Jacques Maritain Metaphysician." The New
Scholasticism 46 (1972) 18-31.

3956. Lakebrink, Bernhard. "Analektik und Dialektik. Zur Methode
des Thomistischen und Hegelschen Denkens," in Thomas Aquinas (Symp
Toronto) 2, 459-87.

3957. Langevin, Gilles. "De guel secours peut etre s. Thomas d'Aquin
pour le théologièn de notre temps?" in Colloque (Symp Ottawa)
213-26.

3958. Laverdière, Raymond. Le Principe de causalité: Recherches
thomistes récentes. Paris: Vrin, 1969. 273 pp.

3959. Lee, Anthony D. "Thomism and the Council." The Thomist
27 (1963) 451-92.

3960. Lefebvre, Marcus. "Wholeness in Wittenstein and Aquinas."
New Blackfriars 55 (1974) 100-11

3961. Lima Vaz, Henrique C., De. "Teocentrismo e beatitude. Sobre
a actualidade do pensamento de S. Tomàs de Aquino," Revista Portuguesa

3962 - 3975 NINETEENTH & TWENTIETH CENT.

de Filosofia 30 (1974) 39-78.

3962. Lobato, Abelardo. "Dialogo de nuestro tiempo con Tomás de Aquino," in Tommaso d'Aquino...problemi fondamentali (Symp) 1974. 9-23.

Also in Tommaso d'Aquino (Symp) 2, 529-39.

3963. Lonergan, Bernard J. "Aquinas Today. Tradition and Innovation," in Celebrating the Medieval Heritage (Symp) 1978.

3964. Lotz, Johannes B. "A atualidade do pensamento de S. Tomás. Um confronto entre o seu pensamento e o de Heidegger quanto ao problema do ser." Presence Filosofica (Sao Paolo Symp) 81-90.

3965. _____. "Das Sein nach Heidegger und Thomas von Aquin," in Tommaso d'Aquino (Symp Roma) 6, 35-49.

3966. _____. "Mensch-Zeit-Sein. Nachvollziehen einer thematik von Heidegger bei Thomas von Aquin." Gregorianum 55 (1974) 239-72, 495-540.

3967. _____. "Zur Thomas-Rezeption in der Maréchal-Schule." Theologie und Philosophie. Frankfurt a. M.-Pullach-Freiburg i. B. 49 (1974) 375-94.

3968. McBride, Joseph. "Christianity, ethics and alienation in contemporary atheistic humanism: F. Nietzsche and St. Thomas Aquinas," in Philosophy and Totality (Symp) 1977. 111-31.

3969. McCool, Gerald A. "Is St. Thomas' 'Science of God' Still Relevant Today?" International Philosophical Quarterly 14 (1974) 435-54.

3970. _____. "Social Authority in Transcendental Thomism." Proceedings of the American Catholic Philosophical Association 49 (1975) 13-23.

3971. _____. "Twentieth-Century Scholasticism," in Celebrating the Medieval Heritage (Symp) 1978.

3972. McInerny, Ralph M. "The Contemporary Significance of St. Bonaventure and St. Thomas." Southwestern Journal of Philosophy 5 (1974) 11-26.

3973. _____. Thomism in an Age of Renewal. Graden City, N.Y.: Doubleday, 1966.

3974. McLean, George F. Man's Knowledge of God According to Paul Tillich: A Thomistic Critique. Washington, D.C.: Catholic University of America Dissertation, 1958. 110 pp.

3975. McLuhan, Herbert Marshall. "The Medieval Environment, Yesterday

NINETEENTH AND TWENTIETH CENTURIES   3976 - 3989

or Today," Listening ((1974) 9-27.

3976. McQuade, Francis P. A Thomistic Interpretation of the Contemporary Crisis of Western Civilization. Washington, D.C.: Catholic University of American Dissertation, 1950.

3977. Macomber, William F. "De la Taille vs. Thomistic Tradtion: A Reply." The Thomist 22 (1959) 233-54.

       Cf. T. V. Mullaney.

3978. Margenau, Henry. St. Thomas and the Physics of 1958: A Confrontation. Milwaukee: Marquette University Press, 1958. 80 pp.

3979. Maritain, Jacques. Approches sans Entraves. Paris: Fayard, 1973.

3980. _____. Bergsonian Philosophy and Thomism. New York: Philosophical Library, 1955. 383 pp.

3981. _____. Journal de Raissa, publié par J.M. Paris: Desclée, 1963.

       Translated Raissa's Journal, presented by J. Maritain. Albany, New York: Magi Books, 1974.

3982. _____. Le Paysan de la Garonne. Paris: Desclée, 1966.

       Translated The Peasant of the Garonne, by Michael Cuddihy and Elizabeth Hughes. New York: Holt Rinehart and Winston, 1968.

3983. _____. Ransoming the Time. New York: Scribner's 1941.

3984. Marras, Ausonio. "The Thomistic Roots of Brentano's Conception of Intentionality," Rassegna di Scienze Filosofiche. Napoli. 27 (1974) 213-26.

3985. Marsh, James L. "Lonergan's Mediation of Subjectivity and Objectivity." The Modern Schoolman. St. Louis, Missouri. 52 (1975) 249-61.

3986. Martinelli, L. Thomas d'Aquin et l'analyse linguistique. Paris: Vrin; Montreal: Institut d'Etudes Médiévales, 1963. 78 pp.

3987. Mascall, E. L. "Thomism, Tradition or Transcendental?" Tijdschrift voor Philosophie. Leuven, Belgium. 36 (1974) 321-41.

3988. Maurer, Armand A. "A Thomist Looks at William Jame's Notion of Truth." The Thomist 57 (1973) 151-67.

3989. Meyer, Hans. Heidegger und Thomas von Aquin. München-Paderborn-Wien: Schöningh, 1964.

3990 - 4003   NINETEENTH & TWENTIETH CENT.

3990. Michalich, Joseph C. Existentialism and Thomism. New York: Philosophical Library, 1960. 91 pp.

3991. Micheletti, G. "Armando Carlini interprete di S. Tommaso." Sapienza 25 (1972) 346-9.

3992. Miele, M. "Due nuove serie di volumi per celebrare II centenario tomistico." Sapienza 27 (1974) 481-4.

3993. Miethe, Terry L. The Metaphysics of Leonard James Eslick: His Philosophy of God. St. Louis: Saint Louis University Dissertation, 1976. 280 pp.

3993A. _____. and Roy Emanual. "The Christian's Need to Know." Faith & Reason (1977) 6-17.

        Also published as a five part series with seperate titles for each part in Christian Standard May 8 through June 5, 1977.

3994. Milano, Andrea. "II 'divenire di Dio' in Hegel, Kierkegaard e S. Tommaso," in Studi Tomistici (Symp) 3, 284-94.

3995. Mohan, Robert P. "Philosophical Implications of Humani Generis." The American Ecclesiastical Review. Washington, D.C. 126 (1952) 425-31; 127 (1952) 58-66.

3996. Mullaney, James V. "Developmental Thomism." The Thomist 19 (1956) 1-21.

3997. Murphy, Cornelius. "Distributive Justice, Modern Significance." American Journal of Jurisprudence 17 (1972) 153-65.

3998. Muzio, Giuseppe. II Senso ortodosso e tomistico delle quaranta proposizioni Rosminiane. Rome: Sodalitas Thomistica, 1963. 99 pp.

3999. Nachbar, B. A. M. "Is It Thomism?" Continuum 6 (1968) 234ff.

        On Transcendental Thomism.

4000. Oeing-Hanhoff, Ludger. "Thomas von Aquin und die gegenwärtige katholische Theologie. Kritische Erwägungen eines Laien," in Thomas... Interpretation (Symp) 245-306.

4001. Olivier, Ann. Maritain's Creative Intuition and Its Relation to His Earlier and Later Epistemological Thought. Washington, D.C.: Catholic Univeristy of American Dissertation, 1971.

4002. O'Meara, William. "John Dewey and Modern Thomism," in Maritain... Thomist (Symp) 308-18.

4003. O'Neil, Charles J. "Discussion: A Thomist Textbook for Thomists." The New Scholasticism 27 (1953) 205-9.

NINETEENTH AND TWENTIETH CENTURIES   4004 - 4018

4004. Orlando, Pasquale. "Napoli nella storia del neotomismo del scolo XIX," in Tommaso d'Aquin (Symp) 2, 159-68.

4005. _____. Il Tomismo a Napoli nel secolo XIX. Roma: Angelicum, 1968.

4006. Owens, Joseph. "A Non-expendable Heritage." Proceedings of the American Catholic Philosophical Association 46 (1972) 212-8.

4007. Paolo VI (Papa) "Lumen Ecclesiae. Lettera al P. Vincenzo de Couesenongel...nel VII centenario...di S. Tommaso," in Tommaso d'Aquino (Symp Roma) 9, 499-533.

4008. Paul VI, Pope. "To the Participants in the Sixth International Congress of Thomism Held in Rome." The New Scholasticism 40 (1966) 80-3.

4009. Paulus VI, (Pope) "Allocutio in auditorio Pontificiae Studiorum Universitatis a S. Thoma Aquinato in Urbe..." Acta Apostolicae Sedis. Vaticana. 66 (1974) 265-68.

4010. Pegis, Anton C. "After Seven Hundred Years: St. Thomas in 1974," in Colloque (Symp Ottawa) 137-53.

4011. _____. "Autonomy and Necessity: A Rejoinder to Professor Lovejoy." Philosophy and Phenomenological Research 9 (1948) 89-97.

4012. _____. "Catholic Intellectualism at the Crossroad." (The McAuley Lectures, 1966, In Search of Saint Thomas Aquinas). West Hartford, CT: St. Joseph College, 1966. 3-17.

4013. _____. "Gilson and Thomism." Thought 21 (1946) 435-54.

4014. _____. "Medalists Address," (On the Philosophy of St. Thomas Today). Proceedings of the American Catholic Philosophical Association 49 (1975) 228-37.

4015. _____. "Thomism 1966." Proceedings of the American Catholic Philosophical Association. Washington, D.C. 40 (1966) 55-67.

4016. _____. "Who Reads Aquinas?" Thought. New York. 13 (1967) 488-504.

          Reprinted in Christian Witness in the Secular City, ed. E.J. Morgan. Chicago: Loyola University of Chicago Press, 1970. 60-75.

4017. Pennè, Maria Teresa. "Edith Stein, esempio di umiltà intellettuale e pratica nella linea di S. Tommaso," in Tommaso d'Aquin (Symp) 2, 552-8.

4018. Perini, Giuseppe. "Significato di un centenario." Divus Thomas.

Piacenza. 77 (1974) 317-72.

4019. Perrier, Joseph. The Revival of Scholastic Philosophy. New
York: Columbia University Press, 1948.

4020. Philippe de la Trinité. "De s. Thomas d'Aquin à Sainte Thérèse
de l'Enfant Jésus: Consonances doctrinales." Ephemerides Carmeliticae
25 (1974) 377-99.

4021. Piaia, Gregorio. "Alcune riflessioni sul tomismo e i problemi
del mondo attuale," in Tommaso d'Aquino (Symp) 2, 559-66.

4022. Pieper, Josef. "The Contemporary Aquinas." Philosophy Today
3 (1959) 73-5.

4023. _____. "The Contemporary Character of St. Thomas." Philosophy
Today 3 (1959).

4024. _____. "Semmiféle izmus sem lehetséges, amely tamást tekin-
thetne mesterének." Mérleg   10 (1974) 292-310.

4025. Piolanti, Antonio. "Pio IX e la rinascità del Tomismo," in
Study Tomistici (Symp) 1, 338-436.

       Reprinted: Roma: Libreria Ed. Vaticana, 1974. 115 pp.

4026. Pomian, Krzysztof. "Tomizm na tle przeobrażeń europejkiej
mysli filozoficznej na przetomie XIX i XX wieku," in Studia Sw.
Tomasza   (Symp Lublin) 167-84.

       Thomism Against the Changing Background of European Philosophy
       at the Turn of the 19th Century.

4027. Ponferrada, Gustavo Eloy. "Tomás de Aquino en su VII centerario."
Sapientia 29 (1974) 243-62.

4028. Prastaro, Anna Maria. "S. Tommaso oggi: fede e storia," in
Tommaso d'Aquino (Symp) 2, 567-82.

4029. Punten, L. Bruno "Die Seinsmetaphysik Thomas von Aquinas und
die dialektisch-spekulative Logik Hegels." Theologie und Philosophie
49 (1974) 343-74.

4030. Quinn, John M. The Thomism of Etienne Gilson. A Critical Study.
Villanova, Pa: Villanova University Press, 1971. xvi-188 pp.

4031. Raab, Heribert. "Die Wiederentdeckung der Staatslehre des Thomas
von Aquin in Deutschland im XIX Jht." Historisches Jahrbuch. München.
94 (1974) 191-221.

4032. Raeymaeker, Louis De. Le Cardinal Mercier et l'Institut
Supérieur de philosophie de Louvain. Louvain: Publications Universitaires, 1952.

NINETEENTH AND TWENTIETH CENTURIES   4033 - 4047

4033. Reese, William L. "Analogy, Symbolism, and Linguistic Analysis."
Review of Metaphysics 13 (1960) 447-68.

4034. Regnier, Marcel. "Le thomisme depius 1870," in Histoire de la
Philosophie, 3. Paris: Gallimard, 1974. 483-500.

4035. Renaud, Michel. "Le cercle herméneutique face à la rationalité
du discours philosophique chez s. Thomas et Hegel." Revue Philosophique
de Louvain 75 (1977) 276-91.

4036. Rioux, Bertrand. L'etre et la vérité chez Heidegger et s. Thomas
d'Aquin. Paris-Montréal: Vrin, 1963.

4037. _____. "La notion de vérité chez Heidegger et s. Thomas
d'Aquin," in S. Thomas Aeijourd'hui (Symp) 197-217.

4038. Rivera de Ventosa, Enrique. "De Kant a Santo Tomás," in
Tommaso d'Aquino (Symp) 2, 583-608.

4039. Riog Gironella, Juan. "Como debe ser hoy dia la investigación y
la ensenanza de la filosofia siguiendo las directrices de S. Tomás,
según...la Iglesia?" Espiritu 26 (1977) 40-7.

4040. Rolandetti, Vittorio. "Un messaggio essenziale di Tomismo:
Vincenzo Buzzetti (1777-1824) in Tommaso d'Aquino (Symp) 2,
191-9.

4041. Rossi, Amedeo. "Attualità di S. Tommaso in psicologia e
metafisica." Divus Thomas. Piacenza. 77 (1974) 425-51.

4042. Rotella, Oscar S. "Santo Tomás y Wittgenstein," in Tommaso
d'Aquino (Symp Roma) 6, 665-76.

       Also in Revista Filosofica. Mexico. 8 (1975) 301-17.

4043. Roy, Kuldip Kumar. "Togore and Thomistic Scholasticism." in
Tommaso d'Aquino (Symp) 2, 375-86.

4044. Ruda, Jorge. "Thomas d'Aquin et la problématique contemporaine."
Revue de l'Université d'Ottawa. Ottawa, Canada. 44 (1974) 487-96.

4045. Ruini, Camillo. Is rapporto natura-grazia in S. Tommaso d'Aquino
e la 'teologia politica' di J. B. Metz," in Studi Tomistici (Symp)
2, 261-82.

4046. Sacchi, Mario E. "Santo Tomás de Aquino interpretado por
Heidegger." Aquinas 19 (1976) 64-87.

4047. Salesses, William Edward, Jr. A Statement of the Ethical Theories
of Pragmatism and Thomism as expressed by John Dewey and Jacques Maritain
and a Critical Analysis of Pragmatic Theories as They Apply to the
Modern School, From the Thomistic Point of View. Claremont, CA: Claremont
Graduate School Dissertation, 1968. 155 pp.

4048 - 4063   NINETEENTH & TWENTIETH CENT.

4048. Santinello, Giovanni. "S. Tommaso nella fase spiritualistica di M. F. Sciacca." Giornale di Metafisica. Genova-Bologna. 31 (1976) 715-22.

4049. Schauf, Heribert. "Thomas als theologischer Kronzeuge auf dem Kölner Provinzialkonzil von 1860," in Studi Tomistici (Symp) I, 307-24.

4050. Sciacca, Michele F. Philosophical Trends in the Contemprary World. Notre Dame: University of Notre Dame Press, 1964.

4051. _____. "S. Tommaso, oggi," in San Tommaso...problemi fondamentali (Symp) 1974. 69-98.

4052. Shawel, S. S. ("Thomism and Transcendental Philosophy": in Ukrainian) Logos 25 (1974) 29-53.

4053. Sheehan, Thomas J. "Notes on a 'Lovers' Quarrel:' Heidegger and Aquinas." Listening 9 (1974) 137-43.

4054. Simon, Yves and John H. Griffin. Jacques Maritain: Homage in Words and Pictures. Albany, N.Y.: Magi Books, 1974.

4055. Slattery, Michael P. "Thomism and Positivism." The Thomist 20 (1957) 447-69.

4056. Sleeper, R. W. "Gilson's Saint Thomas." Listening 9 (1974) 119-36.

4057. Smith, Brooke W. Jacques Maritain: Antimodern or Ultramodern? An Historical Analysis. New York: Elsevier, 1976. 194 pp.

4058. Smith, Ferrer. "A Thomistic Appraisal of the Philosophy of John Dewey." The Thomist 18 (1955) 127-85.

4059. Sola, Francisco Bertaina de P. y Sebastián Roig Gironella, Juan. "Que importancia se ha de senalar hoy a Tomás de Aquino en la investigacion y en la ensenanza?" Espiritu. Barcelona. 26 (1977) 29-47.

4060. Spiazzi, Raimondo. "La Lettera del Papa Paolo VI nel Settimo Centenario, della morte di S. Tommaso d'Aquino." Divinitas. Attà del Vaticano. 19 (1975) 5-15.

4061. Staffa, Dino. Il Tomismo è vivo. Roma: Ed. Arti Grafiche A. Chicca, 1963.

4062. Steenberghen, Fernand van. Le Retour à s. Thomas a-t-il encore un sens aujourd'hui? Paris: Vrin; Montréal: Institute d'Etudes Médiévales, 1967. 60 pp.

4063. _____. "Thomism in a Changing World." The New Scholasticism 26 (1952) 37-48.

NINETEENTH AND TWENTIETH CENTURIES   4064 - 4077

4064. Stein, Edith. "La fenomenologia di Husserl e la filosofia di
S. Tommaso d'Aquino. Tentativo di confronto," in Tomismo e Antitomismo (Symp) 2, 277-303.

4065. Stengren, George L. "Connatural Knowledge in Aquinas and
Kierkegaardian Subjectivity," in Kierkegaardiana. København:
Reitzels, 1977. 182-9.

4065A. Stepień, Antoni B. "W zwiazku z teoria poznania tomizmu
egzystencjalnego." Roczniki Filosoficzne. Lublin. 8 (1960) 173-
83.

4066. Swiezawski, Stefan. "Apercu sur l'ouvrage: Histoire de la
pensée de saint Thomas," in Studia z Dziejow Mysli (Symp) 379-92.

4067. _____. Histoire de la pensée de s. Thomas, recherches
polonaises," in Tommaso d'Aquino (Symp) 2, 335-347.

4068. _____. La philosophie à l'heure du Concile. Lyon: Vitte,
1965.

4069. _____. "Polskie studia nad dziejami mysli sw. Tomasza."
Zycie i Mysl. Lublin. 11 (1974) 1455-70.

        Polish Studies on the History of St. Thomas' Thought.

4070. Tangheroni, Marco. "Deformazioni e travisamenti del pensiero
di San Tommaso." Rivista Letteratura e di Storia Ecclesiastica. Napoli.
6 (1974) 65-80.

        Criticism of R. Romano, W. Ullmann, M.-D. Chenu, K. Rahner,
        J. Maritain on the 'Order of the Universe'.

4071. Temple, William. "Thomism and Modern Needs." Blackfriars
25 (1944) 86-93.

4072. Tracy, David. The Achievement of Bernard Lonergan. New York:
Herder and Herder, 1970. xv-302 pp.

4073. _____. "Lonergan's Thomism." Listening 9 (1974) 173-
7.

4074. Traversi, Antonio. "Tommaso e Maritain," in Tommaso d'Aquino
(Symp) 2, 637-42.

4075. Trollope, Margaret E. Creativity in Thomas Aquinas and Berdyae.
Los Angeles: University of Southern California Dissertation.

4076. Valderama Andreade, Carlo. "Presencia del tomismo en la Colombia
del siglo XIX," in Tommaso d'Aquino (Symp) 2, 408-21.

4077. Vancourt, Raymond. "Anthropologie thomiste et anthropologie
marxiste." Mèlanges de Sciences Religieuse. Lille. 31 (1974) 145-75.

4078. Vancourt, Raymond. "Réalisme thomiste et materialisme marxiste."
Itinéraires 180 (1974) 112-39.

4079. Vansteenkiste, C. M. Joris. "Situation des 'etudes thomistes."
Bijdragen. Nijmegen. 35 (1974) 118-28.

In Italian in Sacra Doctrina (Symp) 357-75.

4080. Veatch, Henry B. "A Contemporary Modus Vivendi for St. Thomas."
Proceedings of the American Catholic Philosophical Association 45
(1971) 11-5.

4081. _____. For An Ontology of Morals: A Critique of Contemporary
Ethical Theory. Evanston, Illinois: Northwestern University Press,
1971. xi-172 pp.

4082. _____. "A Rejoinder to Professor Lovejoy's 'The Duality of
the Thomistic Theology'." Philosophy and Phenomenological Reserach
7 (1947) 622-25.

Supra # 2774.

4083. _____. Two Logics, The Conflict Between Classical and Neo-
Analytic Philosophy. Evanston, Illinois: Northwestern University
Press, 1969.

4084. Velecky, Lubor C. "Flew on Aquinas." Philosophy 18 (1968)
213-30.

4085. Walgrave, Jan H. "Kritik und Interpretation der Gottesbeweise
bei den Oxford-Thomisten," in Thomas...Interpretation (Symp) 144-
57.

On A. Farrer, E.L. Mascall, H.D. Lewis, and H.P. Owen.

4086. Walsh, Terence G. "Assimilation and the Problem of a Contemporary Thomism." The New Scholasticism. Washington, D.C. 44 (1970)
591-9.

4087. Walz, Angelus. "Il tomismo dal 1800 al 1879." Angelicum
20 (1943)

4088. Weeks, Louis, III. "Can Saint Thomas's Summa Theologiae Speak
to Moltmann's Theology of Hope?" The Thomist. Washington, D.C. 33
(1969) 215-28.

4089. Weisheipl, James A. "The Rivival of Thomism as a Christian
Philosophy," in New Themes in Christian Philosophy. Ed. R. M. McInerny
Notre Dame: University of Notre Dame Press, 1968. 164-85.

4090. Welte, Bernard. La foi philosophiaue chez Jaspers et s. Thomas
d'Aquin. Brieges: Desclée, 1958. 282 pp.

NINETEENTH AND TWENTIETH CENTURIES   4091 - 4097

4091. _____. "La Métaphysique de s. Thomas d'Aquin et la pensée de l'histoire de l'etre chez Heigegger." Revue des Sciences Philosophiques et Théologiques 50 (1966) 601-11.

4092. White, Victor. "Tasks for Thomists." Blackfrairs 25 (1944) 93-117.

4093. White, Willie. Faith and Existence: A Study in Aquinas and Kierkegaard. Chicago: University of Chicago Dissertation, 1966.

4094. Wilhelmsen, Frederick. "The Priority of Judgment over Question: Reflections on Transcendental Thomism." International Philosophical Quarterly 14 (1974) 475-93.

4095. William, Franz M. "Thomas von Aquin und Kardinal Newman." Theologie und Glaube. Paderborn. 64 (1974) 467-73.

4096. Woznicki, Andrew N. "Dialogistic Thomism and Dialectical Marxism." The New Scholasticism 52 (1978) 214-42.

4097. Zovatto, P. "Rosminianesimo e Tomismo." Aquinas 15 (1972) 98-126.

Appendix:
Titles of Periodicals Cited

Acta Apostolicae Sedis (Civitas Vaticana)

Acta Pontificae Academiae S. Thomas Aq. et Religionis Catholicae (Rome, Italy)

Aevum (Rome, Italy)

Aletheis (Dallas, Texas)

Al-Mushir (Rawalpindi, India)

American Ecclesiastical Review (Washington, D.C.)

American Journal of Jurisprudence (Notre Dame, Indiana)

American Philosophical Quarterly (Oxford, England)

Analecta Cracoviensia (Cracow, Poland)

Angelicum (Rome, Italy)

Antonianum (Rome, Italy)

Anuario Filosofico (Pamplona, Spain)

A Ordem (Rio de Janeiro, Brazil)

Apollinaris (Rome, Italy)

Aquinas (Rome, Italy)

Archiv für Geschichte der Philosophie (Bonn, W. Germany)

Archiv für Rechts- und Sozialphilosophie (Mainz-Wiesbaden)

Archives d'Histoire Doctrinale et Littéraire du Moyen Age (Paris, France)

Archives de Philosophie (Paris, France)

Archives de Philosophie du Droit (Paris, France)

Archivum Franciscanum Historicum (Rome, Italy)

Archivum Fratrum Praedicatorum (Rome, Italy)

Arzt und Christ (München, Germany)

Asprenas (Napoli, Italy)

Australasian Journal of Philosophy (Sydney, Australia)

Beiträge für Geschichte der Philosophie und Theologie des Mittelalters (Munster, Germany)

Biblica - English Historical Review

Biblica (Rome, Italy)

Bigaku, Japanese Journal of Aesthe-
    tics (Tokyo, Japan)

Bijdragen...der Nederlandschen
    Jezuiten (Nijmegen, Netherlands)

Bijdragen van de Philosophie en
    Theologie (Maastricht, Nether-
    lands)

Blackfriars (London, England)

Bogoslovni Vestnik (Lublin, Poland)

Boletin Eclesiastico de Filipinas
    (Manila, Philippines)

Bollettino di San Domenico
    (Bologna, Italy)

Boston College Studies in Phil-
    osophy (Boston, MA)

Bulletin de Littérature Ecclésiast-
    que (Toulouse, France)

Bulletin du Cercle Thomiste (Caen,
    France)

Bulletin of the John Rylands Libr-
    ary (Manchester, England)

Byzantinische Zeitschrift (München,
    Germany)

Cahiers I P C

Canadian Journal of Philosophy
    (Edmonton, Alberta)

The Catholic Educational Review
    (Washington, D.C.)

The Catholic Historical Review
    (Washington, D.C.)

Catholic Library World (Villanova,
    PA)

Church History (Oreland, PA)

La Ciencia Tomista (Salamanca,
    Spain)

Classica et Mediaevalia (Copenhagen,
    Denmark)

Commonweal (New York)

Confluence (Amsterdam, Netherlands)

Continuum (Chicago, IL)

Criterio (Buenos Aires, Argentina)

Crkva u Svijtu (Split, Yugoslavia)

Cuadernos de Filosofia (Buenos
    Aires, Argentina)

Cultura e Scuola (Rome, Italy)

Dialectics and Humanism (Firenze)

Dialogue (Montréal-Kingston, Ont.)

Didaskelia (Lisbon, Portugal)

Dine' Israel (Tel Aviv, Israel)

Divinitas (Rome, Italy)

Divus Thomas (Fribourg) Title
    changed in 1954 to Freiburger
    Zeitschrift fur Philosophie und
    Theologie

Divus Thomas (Piacenza, Italy)

Doctor Communis (Rome, Italy)

Dominican Studies (London, England)

Downside Review (Bath, England)

Eclesia Mater (Rome, Italy)

Educational Theory (Urbana, IL)

Eglise et Théologie (Ottawa, Canada)

English Historical Review (Edin-
    burgh, Scotland)

Ephemerides - Journal of the E...

Ephemerides Carmeliticae (Rome, Italy)

Ephemerides Theologicae Lovaniensir (Louvain, Belgium)

Escritos del Vedat (Valencia, Spain)

Espiritu (Barcelona, Spain)

Estudio Agustiniana (Valladolid, Spain)

Estudios Filosoficos (Las Caldas de Besaya, Spain)

Estudios Franciscanos (Barcelona, Spain)

Estudios Josefinos (Valladolid, Spain)

Estudios Teologicos y Filosoficos (Buenos Aires, Argentina)

Ethos (Buenos Aires, Argentina)

Filosofia (Torino, Italy)

Filosofar Cristiano (Cordoba, Argentina)

Franciscan Studies (St. Bonaventure, New York)

Franziskanische Studien (Munchen-Werl-Westfalen)

Freiburger Zeitschrift für Philosophie und Theologie (Freiburg, Germany) Before 1954, Divus Thomas, Freiburg.

Fuoco (Rome, Italy)

Giornale di Metafisica (Genova-Bologna)

Grazer Philosophische Studien (Amsterdam, Netherlands)

Gregorianum (Rome, Italy)

Heythrop Journal (Oxford, England)

Historisches Jahrbuch (München, Germany)

Humanitas (Tucumàn, Argentina)

Indian Ecclesiastical Studies (Bangelore, India)

Indian Philosophical Quarterly (Poona, India)

International Philosophical Quarterly (New York)

International Review of Social History (Assen, Netherlands)

Internationale Katholische Zietschrift (Frankfurt, Germany)

Irish Ecclesiastical Record (Dublin, Ireland)

Irish Theological Quarterly (Maynooth, Ireland)

Isis (Seattle, Washington)

Itinéraires (Paris, France)

Jahrubch des Stiftes Klosterneuburg (Klosterneuburg, Austria)

Journal of Indian and Buddhist Studies (Tokyo, Japan)

The Journal of Jewish Studies (London, England)

Journal of Medieval and Renaissance Studies (Durham, England)

Journal of Philosophy (New York)

Journal of Religion (Chicago, IL)

Journal of Religious Ethics (Waterloo, Ontario)

Journal of the Evangelical Theologoical Society (Wheaton, IL)

Journal of the H... - Past and Present

Journal of the History of Ideas
(Philadelphia, PA)

Journal of the History of Medicine
(New Haven, Yale)

The Jurist (Washington, D.C.)

Kant Studien (Berlin, Germany)

Kierkegaardiana (Copenhagen,
Denmark)

Laval Théologique et Philosophique
(Québec, Canada)

Les Sciences Philosophique et
Theólogique (See under Sciences)

Libro Anual I.S.E.E. (Mexico)

Listening. Journal of Religion and
Culture (River Forest, IL)

Logos (Mexico City, Mexico)

Louvain Studies (Louvain, Belgium)

Lumiére et Vie (Lyon, France)

Manuscripta (St. Louis, MO)

Mediaeval Studies (Toronto, Canada)

Medioevo. Rivista di Storia della
Filosofia Medievale (Padua,
Italy)

Mélanges de Sciences Religieuse
(Lille, France)

Memorie Domenicane (Rome, Italy)

Mérleg (Vienna, France)

Metaphilosophy (Oxford, England)

The Michigan Academician (Ann
Arbor, MI)

Midwest Studies in Philosophy
(Morris, MN)

Mikael (Parana, Argentina)

Mind: A Quarterly Review of
Psychology and Philosophy
(Oxford, England)

Miscelanea Comillas (Santander,
Spain)

Miscellanea Francescana (Rome,
Italy)

The Modern Schoolman (St. Louis,
MO)

The Monist (Los Gatos, CA)

Münchener Theologische Zeitschrift
(München, Germany)

The Muslim World (Hartford, CT)

Natural Law Forum (Notre Dame, IN)
Changed to American Journal of
Jurisprudence in 1969.

Naturaleza y Gracia (Salamanca,
Spain)

New Blackfriars (Oxford, England)

The New Scholasticism (Washington,
D.C.)

Notre Dame Journal of Formal Logic
(Notre Dame, IN)

Notre Dame Lawyer (Notre Dame, IN)

Nous (Bloomington, IN)

Nouvelle Revue Théologique
(Tournai-Louvain)

Nova et Verta (Geneva, Switzerland)

Obnovljeni Zivot (Zabreb, Ugo-
slavia)

Palestra del Clero (Rovigo)

Past and Present (Oxford, England)

Pensamiento - Revue Philosophique

Pensamiento (Madrid, Spain)

The Personalist (Los Angeles, CA)

Philippiniana Sacra (Manila,
    Philippines)

Philosogical Quarterly (Iowa City,
    IA)

Philosophia (Israel)

Philosophical Review (Ithaca, N.Y.)

Philosophical Studies (Dublin,
    Ireland)

Philosophisches Jahrbuch (Freiburg-
    München)

Philosophy and Phenomenological
    Research

Philosophy Today (Celina, Ohio)

Presenca Filosofica (Sao Paulo,
    Brazil)

The Priest (Huntingdon, IN)

Proceedings of the American Catholic
    Philosophical Association
    (Washington, D.C.)

Przeglad Religioznawczy (Lublin,
    Poland)

Rassegna di Letteratura Tomistica
    (Rome, Italy)

Rassegna di Scienze Filosofiche
    (Napoli, Italy)

Razón y Fé (Madrid, Spain)

Recherches de Science Religieuse
    (Paris, France)

Recherches de Théologie Ancienne et
    Médiévale (Louvain, Belgium

Religious Studies (London, England)

Renaissance Quarterly (New York)

Renascence (Milwaukee, WI)

Renovatio (Genova, Switzerland)

Review of Metaphysics (Washington,
    D.C.)

Revista Espanola de Derecho Canonico
    (Madrid, Spain)

Revista Espanola de Theologia
    (Madrid, Spain)

Revista de Estudios Politicos
    (Madrid, Spain)

Revista de Filosofia (Maracaibo,
    Venezuela)

Revista de Filosofia (Madrid,
    Spain)

Revista de Filosofia de la Univer-
    sidad de Costa Rica (San José)

Revista Filosofica (Mexico)

Revista Teologica Limense (Lima,
    Peru)

Revista Portuguesa de Filosofia
    (Braga, Portugal)

Revue Bénédictine (Bruxelles,
    Belgium)

Revue d'Ascétique et de Mystique
    (Toulouse, France)

Revue Internationale de Philosophie

Revue Néoscolastique de Philosophie
    (Louvain, Belgium) Name changed
    in 1946 to Revue Philosophique de
    Louvain

Revue Philosophique de Louvain
    (Louvain, Belgium)

Revue Philosophique de la France
    et de l'Etranger (Paris, France)

Revue de l'Univ... - Studia Philosophiae

Revue de l'Université Laval
      (Québec, Canada)

Revue de l'Université d'Ottawa
      (Ottawa, Canada)

Revue des Sciences Philosophiques
      et Théologiques   (Le Saulchoir-
      Paris)

Revue des Sciences Religieuses
      (Paris, France)

Revue Thomiste   (Toulouse, France)

Rivista di Filosofia Neo-Scolastica
      (Milano, Italy)

Rivista di Letteratura di Storia
      Ecclesiastica   (Napoli, Italy)

Rivista Rosminiana   (Domodossola,
      Milano)

Rivista di Storia della Medicina
      (Rome, Italy)

Rivista di Teologia Morale
      (Bologna,   Italy)

Rivista Rosminiana   (Domodosola-
      Milano)

Roczniki Filosoficzne   (Lublin,
      Poland)

Sacra Doctrina   (Bologna, Italy)

Saint Louis University Studies
      (St. Louis, MO)

Salesianum   (Rome-Torino)

Salmanticensis   (Salamanca, Spain)

Salzburger Jahrbuch für Philosophie
      (Salzburg-München)

Sapienza   (Napoli, Italy)

Scholastica   (Rome, Italy)

Scholastik   (Eupen, Belgium)

Science et Esprit   (Montréal,
      Canada)

Sciences Ecclésiastiques   (Montréal,
      Canada)

Les Sciences Philosophiques et
      Théologiques   (Paris, France)

Scientia   (Malta)

Scripta Theologica   (Pamplona,
      Spain)

Scriptorium   (Bruxelles, Belgium)

Scuola Cattolica   (Milano-Venegono)

Sidic.   Revue du service inter-
      national de documentation judéo-
      chrétienne   (Rome, Italy)

Sophia   (Padova, Italy)

Southern Journal of Philosophy
      (Memphis, TN)

Southwestern Journal of Philosophy
      (Norman, OK)

Speculum.   A Journal of Mediaeval
      Studies   (Cambridge, MA)

Spicilegium Beccesse   (Le Bec-
      Hellouin-Paris)

Studi e Ricerche Francescane
      (Napoli, Italy)

Studi Internazionale di Filosofia
      (Torino, Italy)

Studi Canonica   (Ottawa, Canada)

Studia Catholica   (Nijmegen,
      Netherlands)

Studia Mediewistyczne   (Warszawa,
      Poland)

Studia Patavina   (Pavia)

Studia Philosophiae Christianae
      (Warszawa, Poland)

Studia Theologica ... - Zycie i Mysl

Studia Theologica Varsaviensis
  (Warsaw, Poland)

Studies   (Dublin, Ireland)

Studies in Medieval Culture
  (Kalamazoo, MI)

Studies in Medieval Thought
  (Nagoya, Japan)

Studies in Philosophy and in the
  History of Philosophy   (Washington, D.C.)

Studies in Soviet Thought
  (Dordrecht, Netherlands)

Studium   (Avila-Madrid)

Teologia   (Buenos Aires, Argentina)

Teologia y Vida   (Santiago de Chile)

Teologinen Aikauskirja   (Helsinki,
  Finland)

Teorema   (Valencia, Spain)

Teoresi   (Catania, Sicily)

Theologica   (Braga, Portugal)

Theological Studies   (Baltimore,
  MD)

Theologie und Glaube   (Paderborn,
  Germany)

Theologie und Philosophie   (Frankfurt a. M.-Pullach-Freiburg i.
  B.)

Theologisch-praktische Quartalschrift   (Linz, Austria)

Theologische Quartalschrift
  (Stuttgart, Germany)

Theologische Revue   (Münster,
  Germany)

Theoria   (Lund, Sweden)

The Thomist   (Washington, D.C.)

Thought   (New York)

Tijdschrift voor Geestelijk Leven
  (Leuven, Belgium)

Tijdschrift voor Philosophie
  (Leuven, Belgium)

Tijdschrift voor Theologie
  (Nijmegen, Netherlands)

Traditio   (New York)

Triere Theologische Zeitschrift
  (Trier, Germany)

Unitas   (Manila, Philippine)

Universidad de Navarra: Scripta
  (Navarra, Spain)

Vivarium   (Assen)

Zeitschrift für Philosophische
  Forschung   (Postfach, W. Germany)

Zeszyty Naukowe Kat. Univ. Lubelskiego   (Lublin, Poland)

Znak   (Krakow, Poland)

Zycie i Mysl   (Lublin, Poland)

Personal Name Index

(The numbers given below are entry numbers, not page numbers. Underlined numbers indicate names within titles.)

Armstrong - Baur

Baxianus - Bougerol

Bouillard - Cajetan

Bouillard, H.   2939
Boulogne, C. D. 133
Bourgeois, D. 2997
Bourke, V. J.   5, 54, 56, 79, 93,
    112, 116, 134, 246, 295, 364,
    420, 436, 477-479, 646, 804,
    1182-1185, 1469, 2098-2111,
    2368-2371, 3425, 3426, 3501,
    3502, 3838-3840
Bovio, G. 3888
Boyer, C. 296, 480, 2898, 3613
Boyle, J. J. Jr. 2112, 3841
Boyle, J. P. 2998
Boyle, L. E. 52, 116, 3214, 3663
Bracken, W. J. 3254
Bradley, D. J. M. 1470, 3842
Bradley, R. J. 2372
Bradley, Ritamary. 805
Brady, Ignatius. 92, 481, 2718,
    3664
Brady, J. M. 1898
Brady, M. 1471
Branick, V. P. 2840
Brantschen, J. 3769
Brauer, T. 116, 3427
Braun, E. 1472
Braun, H. 1047
Braza Diez, M. 690, 1186, 3843
Brazzarola, B. 3385
Brazzola, G. 3844
Brecher, B. 3640
Bredin, H. 200
Breen, J. S. 2373
Brehier, E. 647
Brennan, A. J. 2113
Brennan, R. E. 54, 71, 1188-1191,
    2374
Brennan, M. A. 1187
Brenna, Rose E. 201, 273, 427B,
    1192, 2147
Brentano, F. 3984
Breton, S. 806, 1193, 1473
Brezik, V. B. 2375
Briancesco, E. 2376
Brie, G. A. de. 6
Bro, B. 3386
Braod, C. D. 691
Brody, B. A. 3114
Broglie, G. de. 2999, 3387
Brown, Barry F. 1474, 1475
Brown, Brendan. 81, 85
Brown, O. J. P. 2377
Brown, Patterson. 39, 1476, 1899

Bruch, R. 2378
Bruening, W. H. 2719
Brugger, W. 648, 1900
Brunner, E. 3376
Brunner, F. 3605
Bryar, W. J. 1901, 1902
Buber, M. 2657
Buchanan, S. 2379
Bucher, Zeno. 62, 1948
Bucley, G. M. 1477
Buckley, J. A. 1478
Buckley, M. J. 2380
Buda, C. 3722
Budrovic, D. 3000
Buchler, W. E. 2652
Bukowski, T. P. 482, 3665
Bullet, G. 3001
Buonaiuti, E. 3666
Burbach, M. 3667
Burch, G. B. 807
Buridan. 1150
Burke, C. 143
Burke, Edmund. 3777
Burns, J. P. 2958
Burns, J. V. 1049
Burr, D. D. 3388
Burrell, D. B. 808, 809, 901,
    1479-1481, 1535
Burroughs, J. A. 2114
Burunat, J. 3614
Busa, R. 483, 648, 649-652, 667,
    1482
Buscarini, G. 3864
Bushinski, E. A. 1485, 3770
Bushman, R. M. 2115
Bussoni, A. 3002
Bustinza, R. 3003
Buzzetti, V. 4040
Byles, W. E. 1483
Byrne, E. F. 2116
Burne, P. M. 254
Byrns, Ruth. 7

Cabasilas, Nilus. 2867
Cabral, R. 2117
Cacciabue, L. 3004
Cadden, J. 1050
Cahalan, J. C. 810
Cahill, M. C. 1484
Cairns, H. 2381
Cajetan, Thomas de Vio. 351, 430,
    678, 811, 904, 991, 1485, 1606,

Caldera - Ciliberto

Cunningham - Dolan

Dolan, G. E.   3348
Domanski, J.   50, 3780
Domet de Vorge, E.   3941
Dominic, St. 2831
Dominica, M.   702
Donagan, A. 39
Donceel, J. F.   79, 1507, 1926,
    3881-3884
Dondaine, A.   165, 268, 372, 376,
    497-500, 3617
Dondaine, H. F.   232, 501, 2871,
    3568, 3618
Dondeyne, A.   1529
Donlan, T. C.   2742, 2843, 2918
Donnelly, M. J. 2872
Donnelly, P. T.   2901
D'Onofrio, T.   204
Donohue, J. W. 2661
Donovan, M. Annice.   1927, 1928
Doolan, A.   3785
Dorigan, E. L.   3437
Dougherty, G. V. 2418
Dougherty, K. F.   1059, 1060
Dow, N. K. 839
Dowd, J. 3675
Downing, P. M.   2419
Doyle, A. I.   502
Doyle, John J.   503
Doyle, John P.   1929, 3886
Dragona-Monachou, M.   3512
Dubarle, D.   1961-1063, 2743
Dubay, T. 1221
Du Bruck, E.   2902
Du Cange, C.   659
Ducci, E. 2662
Duce, L. A.   1930
Ducharme, L. 1530
Ducoin, G. 3513, 3514
Dufault, L.   2663
Duin, J. J.   504
Dufault, L.   840
Duffy, J.   2612
Duggan, G. 1222
Dunn, W. M.   3887
Duggan, G. 1222
Dulles, A. R. 627
Dunn, W. M. 3887
Dumoulin, B.   3665
Dunphy, W. 1931
Duns Scotus. See John Duns
Duquesne, M.   703, 1932
Durandus de S. Porciano.   3747
Durbin, P. R. 841

Duska, R.   79, 505
Dwyer, W. J.   253

Eberenz, J. H.   2420
Echauri, R. 1531
Eckert, W. P.   113, 127, 128,
    166, 167, 2613
Eckhart, Meister. 3728
Eckhoff, F. C.   514, 742, 2877
Eco, W.   2614
Edwards, R. B.   1933, 1934
Edwards, S. 1532
Egan, J. M. 2873
Egidius Colonna. 2420
Egidius Romanus. See Giles of Rome
Ehrle, F.   704
Einstein, A.   1075, 1155
Elbert, E. J.   1223
Elders, L.   506-508,   1533, 2143
    3608
Eliot, T. S.   200
Emmett, D. M.   1534, 3939
Endres, J.   1224
Engelbert, P.   233
Erasmus. 3780
Erickson, Erik H.   1261
Ermatinger, C. J.   1225
Erni, R.   509
Ernst, C.   116
Ernst, C. 2744
Eschmann, I. T.   9, 278, 372, 376,
    395, 410, 660, 2144-2146, 2195
    2421, 2422
Eslick, L. J.   1535-1537, 3993
Esposito, R. G.   3888
Esser, G.   1538, 1936, 2147
Estebanez, E. G. 2148
Eupizzi, S.   3322
Evans, D. 1539
Evans, J. W.   10, 84, 1692, 2423,
    2424, 2629, 3283, 3362, 3889
Every, L.   266

Fabro, Cornelio.   11, 93, 112, 116,
    139, 168, 661, 662, 1226, 1540-
    1553, 1582, 1937, 2149, 3323,
    3438-3441, 3515, 3890-3896
Facchi, G.   1227
Fackenheim, E. L.   1554
Fäh, H. L.   285
Fagone, V.   2150

Gonzalez - Heidegger

Heinrich - Ivanka

Izzalini - Kelley

Kelly - Lakey

Lamacchia - Lottin

Lamacchia, A. 3791
Lamb, M. L. 307, 431
Lambert, R. T. 1274
Lambot, C. 553
LaMountain, G. F. L. 1661
Land, P. S. 2483
Landgraf, A. M. 3647
Landry, A. M. 227, 654
Lang, A. 2771
Lange, S. 3162
Langer, H. D. 3274
Langevin, G. 1662, 3099, 3957
Langlois, J. 2492
Lanigan, J. 1275
Lanna, D. 890
Lantz, G. 2493
Lanza, A. 3100
Laporta, J. 1276, 3101
Laporte, J. M. 1663, 2955, 2956
Larcher, R. F. 277, 308, 309, 328, 360, 431
Larkin, V. R. 336, 341
Larrabe, J. L. 3102, 3399
Las Casas, B. de. 3811
Laso, J. A. 891
La Spisa, M. 892, 1277, 1664
Lauer, J. Q. 1665
Lauer, R. Z. 116, 893, 1278, 1666
Lauro, Giovanni M. di. 3772
Lavatori, R. 1986
Laverdière, R. 3958
La Via, V. 1987
Lawler, J. 2494
Lawler, M. G. 2957
Lawler, R. D. 2199
Lazzaro, P. 1667
Leahy, L. 1279
Lebacqz, J. 1280
Leccisotti, T. 175
Lecea, J. M. 3228
Lechner, G. M. 210
Leckie, G. 302
Le Claire, M. St. Ida. 2495
Le Clerc. G. 3275
Leclercq, Jacques. 2199A, 2200, 2496-2499
Leclercq, Jean. 554, 3229
Lécuyer, J. 3103, 3400
Lee, A. D. 3959
Lefebvre, M. 3960
Lefevre, C. 1281, 3686
Legaz y Lacambra, L. 2500
Legrand, J. 1282

Le Guillou, M. J. 3276
Leibniz, G. W. 1685, 2124, 3771
Lemoine, M. 670
Lennon, J. L. 894, 1283
Leo XIII, Pope. 247, 250, 2762, 3352, 3909
Lepargneur, H. 3230, 3461
Lerner, R. 3676
Leroy, M. V. 1988, 3277, 3278
Lertora Mendoza, C. A. 1086
Lescoe, F. J. 408, 409, 555
Lewis, E. 2501
Lewis, H. D. 4085
Lewis, J. U. 112, 2502, 2503
Lima, A. A. 84
Lima Vaz, H. C. de. 3961
Linage, A. 3627
Lindbeck, G. A.
Lindon, L. J. 2201, 2202
Linnenborn, M. 2683
Lippini, P. 176, 3231
Lisska, A. J. 985, 986, 1284, 1285
Listfeldt, H. G. 1087
Litt, T. 1088
Little, A. 3534
Little, L. K. 3642
Litzinger, C. I. 313
Livi, F. 3687
Llamera, M. 3104, 3105
Llamzon, B. J. 1669
Lobato, A. 3581, 3962
Lobkowicz, N. 897, 1089, 1286
Lobo, J. A. 2203
Locke, John. 2419
Lofy, C. A. 898
Lohmann, J. 3582
Lonergan, B. 899-901, 965, 1670-1672, 1774, 1856, 1880, 2675, 2772, 2773, 2881, 2882, 2958, 2959, 2998, 3279, 3280, 3865, 3963, 3985, 4072, 4073
Long, T. K. 3462
Loosen, J. 3281
Lopez, J. G. 453, 902, 903, 1673
Lopez, T. 3106
Lopez Medel, J. 3688
Lorca Navarrete, J. F. 3401
Lorenzo da Dergamo, Fra. 3805
Lorite, J. 556
Lortz, Joseph. 59
Losada, C. R. 2204
Lottin, O. 2504, 3107-3111, 3689

Lotz - Manna

Messner, J. 2228-2231, 2523, 2524
Metz, J. B. 1305-1308, 4045
Meulen, H. Van der. 1998
Meurers, J. 1107, 1108
Meyer, C. R. 3406
Meyer, H. 742, 743, 3989
Miano, V. 3127
Michael, C. P. 2784
Michalich, J. C. 3990
Michaud-Quantin, P. 670, 671
Micheletti, G. 3991
Michels, T. 2525
Midgley, E. B. F. 2526, 2527
Miele, M. 3992
Miethe, T. L. 25, 26, 1999, 3993,
   3993A
Mignon, J. 2104
Migoya, F. 672
Milano, A. 3994
Milhaven, J. G. 2232, 3022, 3128
Miller, B. 930
Miller, C. L. 2000, 2528
Miller, Marianne. 1707 See also
   Childress
Miller, R. J. 1708
Minio-Paluedlo, L. 573, 574,
   3536, 3696
Miralles, A. 3407
Miranda, M. do Carmo Tavares de.
   3794
Mitchell, J. 2966
Mitterer, A. 3285, 3629
Miyakawa, T. 2001
Möller, J. 124
Mohan, R. P. 2529, 3995
Mohler, J. A. 3129
Mohr, W. 575
Milinaro, A. 931
Mollat, Michel. 37
Molloy, N. 3364A
Moltmann, J. 4088
Monagle, J. F. 2233
Monahan, W. B. 3130
Monan, J. D. 1599
Monda, A. M. di. 3131, 3132
Mondin, B. 93, 576-579, 932, 1309,
   1709
Monette, A. 2855
Mongillo, D. 3133, 3134
Montagnes, B. 1710, 1711, 3135,
   3136
Montague, M. 1310
Montane, P. R. 3697, 3698

Montano, E. J. 2916
Moody, E. A. 744
Moonan, L. 1012, 2856
Morales, J. 3795
Moran, L. 1109
More, St. Thomas. 3795
Moreau, J. 933, 1019, 1311, 3537
Morency, R. 2885, 2886, 2967
Moreno, A. 116, 1110, 1111, 1712
Moretti, R. 2968
Morgan, E. J. 4016
Morgan, J. D. 1713
Morin, E. 212
Morisset, B. 2234, 2235
Morkovsky, T. C. 2236
Morón Arroyo, C. 1714
Morreall, J. S. 2785
Morton, E. W. 1715, 1716
Mostert, W. 3286
Mounier, E. 3819
Mourant, J. A. 1717, 2786, 3765
   3796
Mouroux, J. 2734
Moutsopoulos, E. 3538
Muck, O. 1718
Müller, J. P. 105
Mueller, R. M. M. 2530
Muhammad (Prophet). 3598
Mullahy, B. I. 1112
Mullaly, J. 853
Mullaney, J. V. 745, 2237, 2690,
   3468, 3469, 3996
Mullaney, T. U. 1719, 3287, 3288,
   3329, 3330, 3977
Mullen, M. D. 1720
Muller-Thym, B. J. 1312, 1721,
   1722
Mulligan, R. W. 385, 1313, 1314,
   2917
Mulvaney, R. J. 2531
Munier, A. 1113
Muniz, F. 2787, 2788
Muniz, P. 2002
Munoz, J. 1315
Munoz-Alonso, A. 177
Munoz Cuenca, J. M. 2969
Munoz Delgado, V. 3797
Murdoch, J. E. 2532
Murnion, W. E. 934
Murphy, C. 3997
Murphy, L. T. 2238
Murphy, R. T. 1316
Murphy, T. 580

Murphy - Orlando

Murphy, W.   2918
Murray, J.   2805
Murray, M. V.   1317, 2239, 2240
Muzio, G.   1886, 2241, 3998
Myers, J. R.   2533

Nachbar, B. A. M.   3999
Nader, A. N.   3584, 3585
Nalpathamkalam, C.   3365, 3366
Napoli, G. di.   3699
Narciso, E. I.   2534, 3798
Nardone, H. F.   3700
Nash, H.   389
Nash, P. W.   2003, 3701
Nau, P.   3367
Naud, A.   3470
Naughton, E. R.   2691
Naus, J.   1318
Nėdoneelle, M.   93, 3471, 3702
Neidl, W. M.   2857
Nelson, R. C.   2242
Nemesius   3510, 3616, 3632, 3639
Nemetz, A. A.   935, 936, 2630,
   2631
Neumann, S.   937
Newman, J. H.   321, 2061, 2535,
   2712, 2983, 4095
Nicolas, J. H.   2789, 2858, 3289
Nicolas, M. J.   1114, 1115, 2770,
   3290, 3408
Nicholas of Cotrone.   499
Nielsen, K.   1911, 2004, 2109,
   2536
Niemeger, M. F.   2537
Nietzsche, F.   3856, 3943, 3947
   3968
Nink, C.   1723
Noi, P. De la.   2244
Nolan, K.   3022
Nolan, M.   3022
Nolan, P.   1319
Noon, W. T.   213
Noonan, J. P.   1724
Noonan, J. T. Jr.   85, 2245-2247,
   2383, 2538, 2539, 3137-3139
Northrop, F. S. C.   3930
Novack, D.   2248, 2249
Novalis.   1036
Nugent, F.   1725
Nugent, J. B.   2005
Nygren, Anders.   87, 2790

Oberarzbacher, F. P.   1726
Oberti, Sobrero, M.   581
O'Brien, A. M.   938
O'Brien, T. C.   2006, 2007, 2791
O'Brien, T. S.   1727
O'Brien, W. V.   2540
O'Callaghan, L. T.   1320
Ocariz, F.   1728
Ocariz Brana, F.   2970
Ochagavia, J.   2859
O'Connell, D. A.   582
O'Connell, M. J.   939
O'Connor, D.   2805
O'Connor, D. J.   2541
O'Connor, E. D.   3331
O'Connor, W. R.   1321-1323, 2250-
   2252, 3291
Oddasso Cartotti, A.   3746
O'Donnell, J. R.   27, 52
O'Donnell, R. A.   1729
O'Donoghue, N. D.   2008, 2542,
   2543
Oeing-Hanhoff, L.   114, 1324,
   1730, 4000
Osterle, Jean T.   351
Osterle, John A.   458, 746, 940,
   2253-2256
O'Flaherty, M. M.   747
O'Grady, Daniel.   3426, 3650
O'Grady, Donald.   1731
O'Hara, M. K.   2257
O'Leary, J. M.   3292
Olgiati, F.   2544
Olivier, A.   4001
Ols, Daniel 28, 142
O'Malley, J. W.   214
O'Malley, J. M.   2632
O'Meara, T. F.   116, 178
O'Meara, Wm.   71, 4002
Onclin, W.   2545
O'Neil, Campion.   1732
O'Neil, C. J.   54, 56, 79, 420,
   1325, 2107, 2258-2261, 4003
O'Neil, M. S.   2009
O'Neill, C. E.   2971, 3368, 3409
O'Neill, F.   459
O'Neill, P. D.   3676
Ong, W. J.   583
O'Rahilly, A.   295
O'Reilly, Peter.   270
Orlando, P.   748, 1326, 3472, 4004,

Peyrous - Ramm

Rouleau - Schüller

Schütz - Sousa Alves

Spangler - Tittley

Völkl - Wright

Wrobel - Zucherman

TERRY L. MIETHE has taught at several schools including Saint Louis University and Fuller Theological Seminary. He received his M.A. from Trinity Evangelical Divinity School, M.Div. from McCormick Theological Seminary, Ph.D. from Saint Louis University in philosophy, and is a Ph.D. candidate in social ethics at the University of Southern California. Dr. Miethe is a member of five national honor societies including Phi Beta Kappa and is listed in seventeen who's whos including the *Dictionary of International Biography, Who's Who in Religion,* and *The International Who's Who of Intellectuals*. He has published over thirty articles and chapters in books. Dr. Miethe is currently working on books on Saint Augustine and the Philosophy of God.

VERNON J. BOURKE is professor emeritus of philosophy at Saint Louis University. He received his B.A. from Saint Michael's College, M.A. from the University of Toronto, and Ph.D. from the Pontifical Institute of Mediaeval Studies at the University of Toronto where he worked under Etienne Gilson, and a Litt.D. from Bellarmine College. Dr. Bourke is listed in numerous who's whos including *Who's Who in America* and *Who's Who in the World*. He has published over one hundred articles and chapters of books as well as a contribution to the *Encyclopedia of Philosophy*. Dr. Bourke has authored fourteen books, among them: *Augustine's Quest for Wisdom, Aquinas' Search for Wisdom, The Essential Augustine, The Pocket Aquinas, History of Ethics,* 2 volumes, *Ethics in Crisis, Ethics: A Text Book in Moral Philosophy*, and *Joy in Augustine's Ethics*.